Phenomenologies of the Stranger

Series Board

James Bernauer

Drucilla Cornell

Thomas R. Flynn

Kevin Hart

Richard Kearney

Jean-Luc Marion

Adriaan Peperzak

Thomas Sheehan

Hent de Vries

Merold Westphal

Michael Zimmerman

John D. Caputo, *series editor*

Perspectives in
Continental
Philosophy

Edited by RICHARD KEARNEY
and KASCHA SEMONOVITCH

Phenomenologies of the Stranger
Between Hostility and Hospitality

FORDHAM UNIVERSITY PRESS
New York ■ *2011*

Copyright © 2011 Fordham University Press

All rights reserved. No part of this publication may be reproduced, stored in a retrieval system, or transmitted in any form or by any means—electronic, mechanical, photocopy, recording, or any other—except for brief quotations in printed reviews, without the prior permission of the publisher.

Fordham University Press has no responsibility for the persistence or accuracy of URLs for external or third-party Internet websites referred to in this publication and does not guarantee that any content on such websites is, or will remain, accurate or appropriate.

Fordham University Press also publishes its books in a variety of electronic formats. Some content that appears in print may not be available in electronic books.

Library of Congress Cataloging-in-Publication Data

Phenomenologies of the stranger : between hostility and hospitality / edited by Richard Kearney and Kascha Semonovitch.—1st ed.
    p. cm.— (Perspectives in Continental philosophy)
Chiefly proceedings of a conference held in 2009 at Boston College.
Includes bibliographical references (p.) and index.
ISBN 978-0-8232-3461-5 (cloth : alk. paper)
ISBN 978-0-8232-3462-2 (pbk. : alk. paper)
    1. Hospitality—Congresses. 2. Strangers—Congresses. I. Kearney, Richard.
II. Semonovitch, Kascha.
BJ2021.P48   2011
177′.1—dc22
                                    2011012127

14 5 4 3 2
First edition

Contents

Acknowledgments   ix

PRELUDE

At the Threshold: Foreigners, Strangers, Others
Richard Kearney and Kascha Semonovitch   *3*

Presentation of Texts
Richard Kearney and Kascha Semonovitch   *30*

PART I: AT THE EDGE OF THE WORLD

1   **Strangers at the Edge of Hospitality**
Edward S. Casey   *39*

2   **Putting Hospitality in Its Place**
Brian Treanor   *49*

3   **Things at the Edge of the World**
David Wood   *67*

PART II: SACRED STRANGENESS

4   **Hospitality and the Trouble with God**
John D. Caputo   *83*

5	The Hospitality of Listening: A Note on Sacramental Strangeness Karmen MacKendrick	98
6	Incarnate Experience Anthony J. Steinbock	109
7	The Time of Hospitality—Again Kalpana Rahita Seshadri	126

PART III: THE UNCANNY REVISITED

8	The Null Basis-Being of a Nullity, Or Between Two Nothings: Heidegger's Uncanniness Simon Critchley	145
9	Heidegger and the Strangeness of Being William J. Richardson	155
10	Progress in Spirit: Freud and Kristeva on the Uncanny Vanessa Rumble	168
11	The Uncanny Strangeness of Maternal Election: Levinas and Kristeva on Parental Passion Kelly Oliver	196

PART IV: HOSTS AND GUESTS

12	Being, the Other, the Stranger Jean Greisch	215
13	Words of Welcome: Hospitality in the Philosophy of Emmanuel Levinas Jeffrey Bloechl	232
14	Neither Close nor Strange: Levinas, Hospitality, and Genocide William H. Smith	242
15	Between Mourning and Magnetism: Derrida and Waldenfels on the Art of Hospitality Christopher Yates	258
16	The Stranger in the Polis: Hospitality in Greek Myth John Panteleimon Manoussakis	274

	Notes	285
	List of Contributors	333
	Index of Names	337

Acknowledgments

We wish to express our gratitude to those who so generously helped in the preparation of this volume, especially the assistants of the Guestbook seminar and conference held at Boston College in 2009 where most of the papers in this volume were first delivered. We also wish to thank Helen Tartar at Fordham University Press whose enthusiastic support and studious attention made work on this book a privilege and a pleasure. The editing staff at Fordham has patiently attended our many revisions and delays. We would like to thank Casey Renner for contributing his photo of the U.S.–Mexican border. We appreciate that Beacon Press, Farrar, Straus and Giroux, HarperCollins, and Passeggiata Press have permitted us to reproduce the poems that appear throughout our volume. Finally, we would like to pay tribute with this volume to one of our special contributors, William J. Richardson, whose ninetieth birthday was the occasion of the "Phenomenologies of the Stranger" conference at Boston College and whose teaching and writing has inspired several generations of phenomenological thinkers in the English-speaking world.

Phenomenologies of the Stranger

Prelude

Approaching you
in order to recoil from you
I discovered my senses
between approach and recoil
there is a stone the size of a dream
It does not approach
It does not recoil
You are my country
A stone is not what I am
therefore I do not like to face the sky
nor do I die level with the ground
but I am a stranger, always a stranger

—Mahmoud Darwish, "Psalm 9"

At the Threshold

Foreigners, Strangers, Others

RICHARD KEARNEY AND
KASCHA SEMONOVITCH

> What we desire, more than a season or weather, is the comfort
>   Of being strangers, at least to ourselves.
>
> —Mark Strand

This volume plays host to a number of texts that serve as "phenomenologies of the stranger." Who is the stranger? When and how does the stranger appear? And why does the question of the stranger matter so much, to philosophers and non-philosophers alike?

From the perspective of these authors situated in North America and Europe, responding to strangers matters a great deal. We belong to nations and cultures embroiled in debates about borders, immigration, and cultural assimilation. Our world calls on us to improve our capacity to respond responsibly: to learn to offer hospitality or to assess hostility.

So what exactly do we mean by "Stranger"? The Stranger, as we understand it, is not identical with the "Other" or with the "Foreigner." We shall use capitals to signal the three categories. These distinctions are facilitated somewhat in English by the fact that we have separate words for "stranger" and "foreigner," whereas in many other languages there is but one: *l'étranger, xenos, hostis, der Fremde*, and so on. The three terms Other, Foreigner, and Stranger are similar at times, but they are not the same. They command precise and prudent readings. But such readings are performed at dawn or dusk, in half-light. Our inquiries are in demitones. Careful descriptions are called for. Among the three, the Stranger will be the focus of our hermeneutic study.[1]

The place where we encounter the Stranger is a threshold. Quite literally, I might greet a stranger who comes to my door, and in that space and time discern something about this potential guest. Metaphorically, we can see "thresholds" defining the edges of human being in many ways: for example, I find a threshold at the limits of my physical body, a threshold of pain, of pleasure, a threshold at the limits of one culture and another, one political group and another.

At such thresholds of experience, we stand in an event: an opening onto hospitality. But doors can be opened or shut. Or stand ajar. It may be unclear who or what moves first. The event might lead to a welcome kiss or a violent struggle. In either case, a volatile ambiguity[2] awaits resolution into a particular meaning. Who can recall who spoke or reached out first? Did I receive the other, or did the other invite me to see, to speak, to engage her in battle or in friendship? Discerning the latent meaning requires *phronesis* on the part of both guest and host. Each must attend to the situation in which the encounter takes place.

When and where, then, do we encounter the Stranger? Sometimes we meet strangers when we are not at home: when we are in a foreign land or a foreign part of our own land. Other times we encounter strangers who arrive at our house. These entries and exits often provoke a sense of not-being-at-home, even at home. Both Heidegger and Freud called this crossing of the familiar and unfamiliar the "uncanny" (*das Unheimliche*). For Heidegger it was a matter of an ontological reckoning with our own nothingness—the void of not being ourselves now and no longer being at all in death. The anxiety that provokes this sense of not-being-at-home is a mood that comes neither from the inside, nor the outside;[3] a mood that arises in between—between self and other, guest and host, door and exterior. In short, at the threshold. For Freud the uncanny referred to the experience of something old and long-familiar returning as unfamiliar, a sense of fright before what ought to have remained secret but has come to light. These strange events often trigger a double response of fear and fascination when we confront someone concealed within ourselves. When we grasp ourselves as other, the familiar becomes utterly unfamiliar. We discover that we are "strangers to ourselves"—haunted by what Kristeva calls *"une étrangeté inquiétante."*[4] This shudder of the uncanny marks the limit of knowledge—knowledge of others, knowledge of ourselves.

Undergoing this mood of not-being-at-home at the edge of knowing has long marked the philosopher's experience. Western philosophy has understood itself as *"thaumazein,* a consciousness of strangeness," as Merleau-Ponty puts it.[5] And Heidegger quotes Novalis, who says, "philosophy is a homesickness."[6] Since Socrates asked to be considered "a stranger" to the language of the court in the *Apology*,[7] philosophy has practiced making strange the most ordinary aspects of our human condition. Plato asks the readers of the *Republic* to become Strangers to the terms "justice," "good," "imitation," "truth." He asks his readers, as Socrates asked his listeners, to consider the very human body and soul as if they were unknown. In the *Sophist* it is the Stranger (*Xenos*) who questions the traditional Parmenidean opposition between being and nonbeing, who challenges the power of the paternal Logos. From the beginning, the *Xenos* puts us in question and we respond with a word of welcome (*xenophilia*) or rejection (*xenophobia*). Faced with the *Xenos*, we are compelled to make a wager between hospitality and hostility. Western philosophy is the history of such wagers. Philosophers are "gamblers in the noble sense," suffering the exposure of wonder.[8]

It is not easy to read the Stranger. To cite Hamlet, the face of another is "like a book where men may read strange matters." The Stranger occupies the threshold between the Other and the Foreigner. It is a hinge that conceals and reveals, pointing outward and inward at the same time. Foreigner and Other are two faces of the Stranger, one turned toward us, the other turned away: the Foreigner is the Stranger we see; the Other is the Stranger we do not see. Two sides of the same visage—visible and invisible, inner and outer, immanent and transcendent. The stranger is doubled in that it is always similar and dissimilar in a play of unsettling ambivalence. It is because it is like us and yet not like us at all, hovering between the knowable and unknowable, that it strikes us as uncanny. The human being is, as Sophocles says in *Antigone*, "what is most strange on this earth."

Insofar as it comes toward us, the Stranger reveals its face as "Foreigner," someone with a name and identity, someone with papers and fingerprints, an accent and place of origin, however far away. The Stranger qua Foreigner (the French *étranger* covers both) is someone who is recognized by us in terms of different kinds of foreignness—as enemy, alien, visitor, invitee, or guest. Though we may love or hate foreigners, we can always place them as this or that *kind* of person, as here or there, as friend or foe. By contrast, what we term the Other as such, is precisely that which cannot appear according to any of our factical categories, political, psychological, or social.

The Stranger is the *mi-lieu* between the *non-lieu* of the nameless and the *lieu* of the named. It occupies the liminal in-between spanning the poles of Foreigner and Other. The Stranger may be radically Other at one point in a relationship and identifiably Foreign at another. As Other, it is so unexpected and transcendent that it eludes our knowledge. It becomes radically unseeable and unforeseeable. At this point, masks slip, the Foreigner loses face, absents itself without leave, absolves itself from habitation and name; it ceases to be recognizably foreign and becomes totally alien. Here we encounter what Levinas and Derrida call the "absolute Other": the Other as other rather than the other-for-me, alter rather than alter ego. Here we experience the Other as "incarnate absence"—there and not there at one and the same time, presenting as absenting through the face of the Stranger.

The Stranger renders us both capable and incapable of language. How? By changing names as it changes shirts, turning them inside out and back again. The Stranger qua *Other* has no name or face. Unnamable in its alterity, it becomes nameable as soon as it enters our lexicons, crosses our radar screens. The named Stranger is no longer fully strange but foreign. Once provided with passports or visas, defining one as resident or nonresident alien, legal or illegal immigrant, stowaway or refugee, the Stranger has become a Foreigner, someone who can be tracked, classified and computed, someone who is no longer uncanny, frightening, or surprising. Once the Stranger finds a home—even if it be a home away from home—it loses its otherness and becomes an ally or adversary. Foreigner and Other are, therefore, not different beings but two names we require to indicate—in Heidegger's sense of formal indication—the same being. Writing a phenomenology of the Stranger requires us to twist free of our ordinary assumptions and attend to the double nature of this phenomenon.[9]

A Brief History of the Phenomenology of the Stranger

What, then, of "phenomenology"? Phenomenology has a particular place in the history of philosophy as a practice of perceiving and attending to the strange in ordinary experience. The term itself can be used in either a broad or precise sense.

In the most general sense, phenomenology recounts the "manifestation" of the being or meaning of the "strange." Phenomenology has long understood consciousness as consciousness *of* something, of something *other* than itself. Consider, for example, Hegel's phenomenology of the struggle for recognition between slave and master, Mircea Eliade's comparative *Phenomenology of Religions* that examines the appearance of the divine Other, Norbert Schultz's pioneering investigations into the phenomenology of place as *genius loci*, or Bachelard's *Poetics of Space*, which explores an aesthetics of imaginary topology.

In the more precise sense used in this volume, phenomenology refers to a diverse range of practices defined by Edmund Husserl and his followers. The tradition of Husserlian phenomenology involved a turning toward the *manner* of appearance, in a concrete analysis of our existential life-world, not in some idealist dialectic as in Hegel. Husserl defined phenomenology as a return to the "things themselves." Such "things" include not just inanimate objects but also and most importantly animate others—human, animal, or divine. This puts a great demand on us as hosts to attempt radical hospitality in our all too human condition, in our historically and linguistically limited resources. Such efforts invariably involve a risk or wager. But the phenomenologist's "yes" does not mean that she forgoes *phronesis*—practical discernment—or ceases to pay attention to what has appeared. Phenomenology also entails a heightened attention to the ethical and political meaning of appearance. Each of the "others" who approach us provokes a special kind of phenomenological attention. This volume endeavors to inventory such acts of attention.

Like the Stranger itself, phenomenologies of the stranger do not come out of nowhere. They emerge from a particular place, history, and tradition. A full philosophical account would involve a genealogy of Western thought from Parmenides and Plato through classical and medieval metaphysics up to modern investigations of self and other. Such a tour de force is, of course, not possible here. Rather, we choose to concentrate on the phenomenological tradition inaugurated by Edmund Husserl at the outset of the twentieth century and extending through Heidegger, Levinas, and Merleau-Ponty to the hermeneutics of Ricoeur, the deconstruction of Derrida, and the psycho-semiotics of Kristeva. It is to this specific contemporary conversation about self and Stranger that the present volume endeavors to contribute.

Husserl: The Other Who Does Not Appear

So many phenomenological investigations grow from the root of Husserl's thought; phenomenologies of the Stranger are no exception. Husserl approaches the issue by retracing the Cartesian project in his *Cartesian Meditations*. These lectures delivered in Paris in 1929 were published the same year. Famously, in paragraphs 50 and 54 of the Fifth Meditation, Husserl reveals that phenomenology—purportedly an egology of the subject—must also take account of an intersubjective, shared world. Husserl's great innovation is to show that through phenomenological self-reflection, the other necessarily appears "within my primordial sphere"[10] but does so precisely by *not appearing as such*. Husserl answers the question "how do we experience someone else?" by claiming that the Other is never given as it is in itself, but only as presented through the ego's perspectives and projections.[11]

For Husserl, the transcendent other can only be apprehended by me as an "*immanent* transcendency."[12] Why? Because even at the most basic level of our corporeal relations with the other, my own animate organism is the only body that can be constituted originally. The other's body "over there" is grasped as an animate organism by an act of derivation from me to it. Husserl speaks accordingly of an "apperceptive transfer from my animate organism . . . done in a manner that excludes an actually direct, and hence primordial, showing (in perception proper)." Consequently, it might seem that a "similarity" connecting my body *over here* to that body *over there* can serve as a "motivational basis for the *'analogizing' apprehension* of that body as another animate organism."[13] As Ricoeur puts it in his reading of the passage, Husserl shows how "only a flesh (for me) that is a body (for others) can play the role of first *analogon* in the analogical transfer from flesh to flesh."[14] Thus, "the *illusion* of a solipsism is dissolved."[15] Husserl states clearly that "it by no means follows that there would be an inference from analogy. Apperception is not inference, not a thinking act."[16] A charitable reading of this passage in Husserl argues that it shows "I have an actual experience of the Other, and do not have to do with a mere inference."[17] Nonetheless, even this interpretation concludes that "the foreign subject eludes my direct experience."[18]

Herein lies both the success and limitation of the Husserlian account: he avoids solipsism (success) but nonetheless reduces understanding of the other to apperception (limitation). Husserl succeeds in changing our understanding of "mind" and "body" as *things* and transforms them into relations. As embodied, we are already extended—even distended—into the world by intentional consciousness, which is always consciousness of something that it is not; this distension occurs before the "I" or the "I can" at the site of active passive synthesis.[19] As conscious corporeal beings, we appear to ourselves as both open to the world and other-to-the world. We must inscribe ourselves in the world or "*make* the flesh *part of the world*," as Ricoeur puts it.[20]

That said, Husserl's phenomenology of the Stranger ultimately falls short. We do not perceive the other directly, but only indirectly through apperception; we do not present the other immediately, but only through appresentation.[21] We are thus obliged, as Polonius put it, "by indirection to find direction out." The best I can do to conceive what it might be like for the other to experience its world from inside, from its own point of view, is to "make co-present" what the other experiences *as if* I were in the other's place—which I never am. So properly speaking, writes Husserl, "neither the other Ego himself, nor his subjective processes . . . nor anything else belonging to his own essence, becomes given in our (my) experience originally."[22] The other is invariably experienced from my experience.[23]

Husserl argues accordingly that the alter ego can only be apperceived by my ego in an act of "pairing" (*Paarung*), an act that works by association, similarity, and modification of my own subjective experience. Husserl sums up: "*An Other:* an Other Ego, 'Alter' signifies alter ego."[24] The other as alter ego is never actually Other as such. The Other as strange (*fremde*) is never given as such but as someone lacking, elsewhere, out of reach, beyond the grasp of my particular ownness. And so Husserl concludes that "the 'other' . . . is that primordially unfulfillable experience that does not give something itself originally but that consistently verifies something *indicated*."[25] In short, there is always an unbridgeable "gap" between the presentation of my experience and the appresentation of yours.[26]

Essentially, Husserl thought of the Other than me only as another me. He shows how we move out from the self toward the Other but never analyzes how the Other comes toward me from out of its own alterity.[27] In Husserl's phenomenology, interiority cannot be reconciled with exteriority. His transcendental idealism is unable to account for radical transcendence. The transcendental ego ultimately remains the foundation of the Other even as its otherness escapes me, slipping behind the intentional horizons by which I seek to capture it. In other words, for Husserl we can only guess at the Other in absentia, by default and omission, by apperception. Direct knowledge of the Other as such is impossible, an impossibility that cannot be gainsaid. In the final analysis, the Other refuses to be reduced to me, but the Other also refuses to appear directly at all. It explodes the limits of transcendental idealism that Husserl himself could never transcend.

Levinas: The Other Approaches and Disappears

Emmanuel Levinas starts where Husserl leaves off. He studied with Husserl in Freiburg in the years 1928–29 and was the French translator (along with Gabrielle Pfeiffer) of Husserl's *Cartesian Meditations* into French in 1931. The influence of this translation and his seminal article on Husserl's *Ideas* in 1929, provoked the first real discussion of Husserl in French. His doctoral thesis, *The Theory of Intuition in Husserl* (1930) offers a radical interpretation of his mentor's model of intersubjectivity and was to exert a formative influence on the development of phenomenology in France, being the first text to introduce thinkers such as Sartre and De Beauvoir to Husserl. In this early text, Levinas addressed only Husserl's work through *Ideas* and his critique is informed by Heidegger, remarking on the "deeply intellectualist character of Husserl's intuitionism."[28]

Later, Levinas agrees with Husserl in the Fifth Meditation that the Other surpasses all our attempts to mediate its otherness.[29] No intuition is ever adequate to our projections of the Other. The I, he confirms, does not have access to the contents of the other's mind or flesh: "The Other as Other is not only an alter ego: the Other is what I myself am not."[30] And here lies the difference: for Levinas, *pace* Husserl, this is a *good* thing. It is deeply ethical. Why so? Because it lets the other be *as Other*. It shows the incorrigible inadequacy of all my "presentations" and "presentifications" (by symbol, sign, image, analogy). We can admit the Other only as a limit of our own experience but decidedly cannot experience what the Other experiences in *its own* flesh in the mode of the "I." Husserl was entirely correct, therefore, to claim that we cannot see the Other directly from the inside (as flesh) but only from the outside (as body). For Levinas, however, our incapacity here is not a failure—as for Husserl—but an invitation to allow the Stranger to remain strange.[31] Far from being regrettable, this is a phenomenological truth that delimits the bounds of phenomenology itself (defined by Husserl, ideally, as the attempt to intuit the essence of persons and things in their totality without reminder or reserve). So Levinas argues that phenomenology's own self-interruption at this point is actually a signal for ethics: the openness of the host to the Other who comes from beyond, a visitor from on high, an alien whose most intimate proximity still bears traces of an elsewhere, the birthmarks of transcendence.

According to Levinas, therefore, Husserl's best phenomenological efforts still belong to the history of representation and totality.[32] Where Husserl's transcendental subject moves *out* to appropriate the Other in the world, the Levinasian Other moves *in* toward the subject, overtakes it, overwhelms it and even holds it "hostage."[33] Levinas presents a necessary corrective to Husserl's phenomenology; a countermovement of transcendence must complement the movement of immanence. Heidegger, it is worth noting, also saw the need to correct the isolation of the Husserlian subject through his notion of *Mitsein, Sorgen,* and *das Man*.[34] But in each case, the dispersion of the Heideggerian Dasein into social or ethical relations with others involves a loss of ontological selfhood, a falling or lapse into inauthenticity. What Levinas offers—that neither Husserl nor Heidegger do—is a view of the Other as first: as first and foremost demanding my care before my care for my own life. Levinas's ethical phenomenology heeds a Stranger prior to my self, both logically and temporally.

Levinas intervenes in the phenomenological venture, saving it from itself so it may serve the Other: namely, the widow, the orphan, and the stranger. Beyond the ontology of the same—ego, representation, adequation, totality—Levinas locates an ethics of radical alterity. But this ethics of service sometimes verges on obsession and possession by the Other. The Stranger is ultimately so irresistible in its commands that Levinas goes so far as to suggest that the subject who receives is ultimately, as noted, less "host" than "hostage." The self is not free to say no to the absolute Other, for it is already inhabited by the very otherness that precedes and exceeds it. The Other is, in the first and final analysis, always too much for me—a Stranger beyond me, in every sense.[35]

Thus Levinas brings Husserlian phenomenology to a point where it undoes itself, acknowledging its incapacity ever to grasp that Other who remains ineluctably alien and unknowable. The mortification of the "I can" is good. At the limit of my powers, I am compelled to confront a Stranger whose "face" refuses to be reduced to what is "similar" to me, to likeness or resemblance. In short, in Levinas's hands phenomenology implodes to reveal an alter beyond all alter egos. This turning toward the face of the Other who looks at me before I look at it, contests all phenomenologies of subjectivity which prevailed from Hegel and Husserl to Heidegger and Sartre. It opens the possibility of radical welcome.

Derrida: The Other Is Awaited, the Foreigner Arrives

Derrida's deconstructive phenomenology also begins with Husserl's Fifth Cartesian Meditation.[36] He agrees with Levinas that Husserl here undoes his own project, but where Levinas takes phenomenology to its external limit in the Other, Derrida begins by identifying the internal limits of the phenomenological method itself. Derrida disrupts phenomenology's pursuit of the Other by dismantling the transcendental ego, Cartesian, Kantian, or Husserlian. He deconstructs the traditional notion of the subject as a power capable of pure intentionality or sovereignty.[37] In his view, neither the subject nor the other can legitimately lay claim to autonomy. As a result, a meeting with the truly "Other" can never actually occur. The "Other," like the messiah, draws us forward, solicits the waiting that conditions hospitality, but the other as Other can never arrive.[38] The face that appears is always the face of the Foreigner-for-me. However, where Levinas critiques Husserl's pursuit of adequation between ego and Other,

Derrida, by contrast, commends Husserl for his discovery of the inexorable inadequation of consciousness. It is a difference of emphasis to be sure, but it is not insignificant. Levinas reproaches Husserl as a thinker of interiority whereas Derrida praises him as a thinker of exteriority—someone who refused to ignore the devastating implications of his own discovery.[39]

Derrida acknowledges that Levinas's ethics of absolute hospitality is "impossible." All hospitality is *in practice* conditional. Our welcome to actual foreigners, bound by law and finitude, is always limited. Pure unlimited hospitality—open to all comers, whoever they may be—must be subject to conventional demands of "the law*s* (in the plural), those rights and duties that are always conditioned and conditional."[40] Law—*nomos* and *le nom*, convention and name—situates and claims the Other as Foreigner, while the absolute Other transcends, vertically, its grasp. That is why Derrida claims that "pure hospitality" is never possible. If it were it would transgress the bounds of any practical ethics. It would be blind, mad, amoral. But at times Derrida seems to contradict his own critique of Levinas by espousing a position not radically different from Levinas's own. How, for example, can one not read the following passage by Derrida as a tacit preferential option for absolute hospitality? "Let us say yes *to who or what turns up*, before any determination, before any anticipation, before any *identification*, before any unexpected visitor, whether or not the new arrival is the citizen of another country, a human, animal, or divine creature, a living or dead thing, male or female."[41] Before the absolute Other the door is always open. In fact there is no door at all. And that, for Derrida no less than for Levinas, seems a "good" thing. Something we should strive to live by, no matter how impossible. In such passages, is Derrida's notion of hospitality to the Other not as hyperbolic as his mentor's?

Let us put this another way. It is difficult at times not to read Derrida as suggesting that absolute hospitality might well serve as a regulatory ideal, unachievable but desirable.[42] One senses a tacit "ought" whispering behind the deconstructive account. It is hard to keep the ethical out of it, in spite of Derrida's demurrals and deferrals. Yet if there is ethical persuasion here there is also cause for caution. If pure hospitality is so impossible is not one's everyday agency—bound by the laws of relativity—severely compromised? And, second, if one seeks to pursue pure hospitality to its hyperbolic limit, how avoid the perils of extremism? Derrida himself seems to hint at such dangers in his conclusion to *Of Hospitality* when he cites the perverse story of Lot, who offers his daughters as concubines rather than offend his guest.[43]

In sum, Derrida leaves phenomenology to puzzle with the aporetic relation between the Foreigner and the absolute Other—that is, between (1) *l'étranger* as identified by conditional rules of hospitality and (2) *l'étranger* who escapes such rules. So doing, he leaves us—readers—with these questions: if deconstruction is good for thought, is it good for life? What is the agency of host or guest? What is to be done?

Ricoeur: The Return from Hyperbole to Translation

Did the paradigm-shifting accounts of Levinas and Derrida go too far? Ricoeur suggests so. While Husserl places the Other at the frontier of experience, Levinas and Derrida rescind our right to hunt beyond that frontier. They do so for politically and ethically well-motivated reasons, attempting to check the colonizing subject from appropriating the Other. But in Ricoeur's view, both these thinkers have exaggerated the gulf dividing self and Stranger, overcompensating for the hyperbolic doubt and isolation of the Cartesian ego with an equally hyperbolic, epiphanic Other. In other words, if Husserl erred in his desire to capture the Other within the nets of the transcendental subject, Levinas and Derrida go to the opposite extreme of claiming that the Other deconstructs the subject altogether and holds the self "hostage."[44]

Ricoeur makes this clear in Study 10 of *Oneself as Another* where he critiques Husserl's Fifth Meditation in tandem with Levinas's hyperbolic ethics of the Other. For Ricoeur, neither Husserl's derivation of other from same nor Levinas's derivation of self from other suffices.[45] In hyperbolizing the Other to its absolute limit, Levinas—like Derrida after him—declares that our only pure relation to strangers is one of *non-relation*. There is no hermeneutic bridge between *le moi* and *l'Autrui*—only a trauma of rupture, irruption, catachresis, cut.[46]

To avoid hyperbole that risks effacing the difference between the hostile and hospitable Other, Ricoeur proposes that we enlist the human capacity for discernment—*phronesis*—and for dialogue.[47] With this in mind, he proposes a hermeneutic mediation of self and other via translation. Ricoeur terms the paradigmatic event of translation "linguistic hospitality."[48] Between the place of the self (*lieu*) and the no-place of the Other (*non-lieu*) there is the *mi-lieu* of translation.[49] In *On Translation*, Ricoeur salutes the task of the translator, who undergoes what he calls, citing Antoine Berman, "*l'épreuve de l'étranger*." This untranslatable word, *épreuve*, which denotes "experience," "trial," "test," "ordeal," or "difficult task," best describes translation. The *épreuve* of translating the Stranger is *difficile* but not *impossible*.[50] Here Ricoeur differs markedly from Derrida and Levinas, for whom translation seems to imply an act of hermeneutic violence.[51]

Far from a hermeneut trapped in a labyrinth of signs or signifiers, Ricoeur always has in mind the world beyond the text. He takes the textual translator as a model for human communication in general. Inter-linguistic translation symbolizes intra-linguistic translation. We might call this latter the "ontological paradigm" of translation, which describes the basic capacity to communicate between distinct human beings.[52] Estrangement, as this paradigm shows, happens not only when we travel, but also in the most familiar places. Even within one's own language, one can become "a foreigner in one's mother tongue."[53] Just as the child finds herself thrust from the womb of the mother, so the language speaker can estrange herself from her *langue maternelle*. Ultimately, Ricoeur claims, "there is something foreign in every other."[54] In love and friendship, we translate while always guarding an untranslatable "secret."[55]

Translation, whether between languages or between one human being and another, rewards the efforts of the translator. Ricoeur further points out that translation, though challenging, nonetheless grants pleasure and happiness, even as the translator mourns what is lost in translation.[56] The events at Babel, far from telling a tragic story of fallenness, should be recalled as a happy opportunity,[57] indicative of openness to a plurality of foreign tongues.[58] As Ricoeur says, in our concrete political and historical world, we find not a Platonic ideal of one Language but the pleasant multiplicity of *languages*.

Ricoeur's model of linguistic hospitality means that translation involves transition between host and guest languages. It is a way of hosting the speaker of a foreign tongue by serving two fidelities: the first to the possibility of receiving the Foreigner into one's home, the second to the impossibility of ever doing so completely. Thus we respect the "untranslatable kernel" that resists the lure of a "perfect translation," the temptation of a final account, the mirage of a total language (prelapsarian or utopian). To yield to such temptation is to run the risk of compelling otherness to suppress itself by becoming the same.[59]

Ricoeur's paradigm of translation thus serves as bridge between similar and dissimilar, same and other. Perhaps echoing Mallarmé's phrase "*Hypocrite lecteur, mon semblable, mon frère*" (which also serves as epigraph to Kristeva's *Strangers to Ourselves*), Ricoeur speaks of "*le semblable*," or "the similar." The similar is the paradox of the Stranger: the one who is recognizable enough to appear but who nonetheless retains a distance. Similarity allows a tentative and approximate "equivalence" of host and guest tongues. But such provisional equivalence is never consummated in exact or adequate correspondence: "the same thing can always be said in other ways."⁶⁰ And these ways are invariably strange, no matter how *semblable*. In a good translation, difference never effaces similarity any more than similarity effaces difference. *Traduttore, traditore*. While Ricoeur accepts the element of loss in every translation, he understands this as a loss *mourned* by the translator who, far from being a linguistic traitor, serves and suffers the differences between languages. In sum, the good translator is committed to the Other who promises to deliver even as she abstains and absents. Like Antigone in Heidegger's reading of *Der Ister*, the homely harbors the unhomely within itself, the Stranger who betrays herself to me withdraws into her strangeness.⁶¹ The guest is never totally assimilated to the home for she always remains, deep down, alternative to the native tongue. Translation remains a task, not a fait accompli.

Merleau-Ponty: The Other and the Wake of the Body

Merleau-Ponty restores the phenomenon of the Stranger to the condition of incarnation. His phenomenology fully acknowledges our multiple modes of situatedness—political, social, historical, geographical—but underlying all these sites of hospitality (or hostility) to Strangers, Merleau-Ponty identifies the "wild being" (*l'être sauvage*) of the living body. And to show this, he proffers two key supplements to the extant phenomenologies of the Stranger: namely, descriptions of the animal and of the flesh.

In the wake of Husserl, Merleau-Ponty wished to offer the flesh of the Stranger a "local habitation and a name."⁶² Unlike his predecessors and well before Derrida, Merleau-Ponty shows how the animal other erupts into the human order. In the French title of his earliest work, *La structure du comportement* (*The Structure of Behavior*), *comportement*, like its English equivalent "comportment," hints at the richly ambiguous intertwining of nature and culture, body and world that a phenomenology of embodiment portrays. In comportment, the physical and the cultural are inseparable⁶³—for example, one's comportment at a party includes both one's physical movements and the cultural appropriateness of those actions. Like other embodied, animal beings, humans engage in "prospective" action that is receptive but not passive per se.⁶⁴ For example, Merleau-Ponty describes how, "If I am in a dark room and a luminous spot appears on the wall and moves along, I would say that it has 'attracted' my attention."⁶⁵ When we admit that we are carnal, animate bodies, we fully understand the concrete implications of Husserl's (intellectual and abstract) passive-synthesis.⁶⁶ In the *Phenomenology of Perception*, he elaborates on Husserl's vision of flesh in the *Cartesian Meditations* and concludes, "The other can be evident to me because I am not transparent for myself, and because my subjectivity draws its body in its wake."[67]

In Merleau-Ponty's phenomenology of the flesh, we understand "The body as organ of the for-other."[68] Husserl's *Entflechtung* now has an organ: the body. Encountering the Stranger exercises this organ. Merleau-Ponty claims "there is a *natural* rooting of the for-other."[69] We identify others with similar schemas, "a relation to other corporal schemas" so that we find "among the things, there are living 'similars.'"[70] He shows us how we are animal and animate bodies, capable of recognizing conduct not only in our own species but in other life. He also suggests how we recognize our own species—our living "similar"—across difference by way of our corporeal being. To use Ricoeur's terms, this "identifying" occurs as the *ipse* rather that *idem* self: an identification not of identical beings, but *similar* beings despite an infinite multiplicity of variation in corporeal form and of conduct across time.

These living "similars," mentioned by both Merleau-Ponty and Ricoeur, are beings *like* ourselves, with whom we share the condition of both perceiving and being perceived. Yet these Others are no less *unlike* our self. As Arendt points out, were a plurality to contain only identical beings, "endlessly reproducible repetitions of the same model," there would be no need for communication at all.[71] The very fact that we are oriented to display for others affirms the otherness of others. When I am talking with someone else, "should the voice alter, should the unwonted appear in the score of the dialogue"—in short, if the person with whom I am speaking does anything that shows her to be alive and not a robot—then, "suddenly there breaks forth the evidence that yonder also, minute by minute, life is being lived."[72] When this happens, I cease to be confined by the apparent limits of my physical skin; when I face this speaking other, "another private world shows through . . . and for a moment I live in it."[73] In such instants of mutual traversal, my animal experience of the Other as "incarnate absence" (what Bernhard Waldenfels calls *der leibhaftige Abwesenheit*) becomes a word made flesh.[74] It is through this discussion of shared "flesh" that Merleau-Ponty develops his philosophy of embodiment into one of incarnation.[75] Linguistic hospitality arises from carnal hospitality, as perception gives birth to meaning. Or, as Merleau-Ponty himself puts it, an "original other from elsewhere" comes momentarily to life before me here and now, *en chair et en os*. Hospitality becomes a transubstantiation between self and Stranger where the two species cross without ever losing their difference. Hospitality to the Stranger becomes—to use another of Merleau-Ponty's favorite tropes—chiasmus.

Poetic Phenomenology: Aesthesis, Poiesis, Phronesis

Each of the phenomenologists discussed earlier offers rich perspectives and inflections on the experience of Strangers. It would efface our work if we here tried to bring these diverse accounts under one rubric; yet it is worth noting that each of these approaches remind us that Strangeness is not something added to selfhood from without but inhabits the very tenor of its lived experience.[76]

Incarnation and the Intertwining of Aesthesis-Poiesis

While the phenomenologies of the Stranger offered by Husserl, Levinas, and Derrida opened new ways of describing the Other, we suggest that they require further supplementation[77] by a poetic phenomenology informed by Heidegger, Ricoeur, and Merleau-Ponty. Simply put, where the Stranger appeared in the seminal Fifth Meditation as "alter ego," Husserl overemphasized the ego, while Derrida and Levinas overemphasized the "alter." By contrast, we noted how Ricoeur and Merleau-Ponty shift the focus to the hyphen in between. They concentrate on the middle space between the no-place of the absolute Other, quarantined by Levinas and Derrida, and the immanent place of Husserl's idealist Ego. To be incarnate in space and time, in flesh and blood, is to exist in a world of hostile as well as hospitable relations. Located and motivated by everyday social, moral, and political forces we must assess the Stranger, negotiating the terms of an all-too-conditioned hospitality.[78] It is with these fragile conditions in mind that a phenomenology of flesh calls for a triple hermeneutic of *aesthesis, poiesis,* and *phronesis*.[79] We must now ask: How do we sense, shape, and decipher the other in our midst? Fully acknowledging the fecund paradox of incarnation, Ricoeur and Merleau-Ponty offer a phenomenology of carnal and metaphorical beings, of hosts and strangers in all their linguistic and corporeal richness. Taking our cue from this analysis of the Other-in-between, we wish to sketch, in the second part of this essay, what we call a poetic phenomenology of the Stranger.

We suggest a critical development of the Husserlian tradition by placing it in dialogue not just with Ricoeur and Merleau-Ponty but also with Heidegger. In order to delve deeper into these extra layers of otherness we will espouse what we call a "poetic phenomenology" and present a "poetics of the Stranger." In this choice of terms, we show our debt to Heidegger and to a growing body of writing that takes "poetics" in "the broad sense of a productive act beholden to something beyond itself."[80] Like Heidegger, we imagine that "[p]oetry [*Dichten*] is thought of here in so broad a sense" that it takes us to the very limits of language and to the ground of ontology.[81]

In *Of Hospitality*, Derrida counsels us that "an act of hospitality can only be poetic."[82] Indeed, we agree with Derrida that the event at the threshold of experience is one of *poiesis*. But how can this be? Traditional accounts often oppose *poiesis* and *aesthesis*, and also tend to contrast their siblings *praxis* and *pathos*. *Aesthesis* connotes reception, while *poiesis* connotes a making, a putting into order, a creation of the beautiful, of the novel.[83] *Poiesis* and *aesthesis* thus apparently mark two modes of existence that dualistically contrast like making and judging, creating and receiving, speaking and listening, the poet and the reader, the artist and the witness. Traditionally, poetics marks the event of the possible rather than the actual: the new—the strange—erupting into the world. Aristotle's *Poetics* describes the tragedian's activity as an original putting-into-order or *mythos-mimesis*.[84] One of the poet's noted capacities is to introduce new terms or metaphors into conventional language.[85] If hospitality is poetic in that traditional sense, it would seem to be pure activity. But Heidegger reminds us that if hospitality is an action, it is a strange one: the host performs this action while remaining radically dependent on the contingent circumstances of the other. Properly understood, poetic hospitality must account for the fragile openness of a host entertaining a Stranger: action supplementing passion, production supplementing reception, force supplementing fragility.

Poiesis invokes as much the creative activity of the poet as her inspiration by the gods. This latter paradox was remarked on by Heidegger and Merleau-Ponty. Unlike the idealists and empiricists before them, these phenomenological thinkers refused to ignore the enigma that marks the limen of experience. On the threshold of the body, the world is welcomed in—is *here*—and existence goes out, goes *there*. Phenomenology shows that "one begins, but coming from elsewhere," as Waldenfels put it.[86] Phenomenology, in this sense, points the way between *aesthesis* and *poiesis*. Or, to put it Husserl's terms, it bears witness to the double movement of active and passive synthesis in our encounter with others.

Far from the idealist who shuts out the world like Descartes or the empiricist who must bear passively the visitation of the world, phenomenology lives in a house of being with doors and windows ajar. Phenomenologists demonstrate that consciousness participates in but does not nominally determine the world. We inhabit (Merleau-Ponty), we dwell (Heidegger) as guests as much as hosts in the house of being. We stand at the portal of interhuman relations, anticipating and anticipated by the very architecture of experience. Poetic inspiration and expression co-emerge like corporeal inspiration and expiration. The phenomenologist invigilates the revolving door of entrances and exits.

The poet paradigmatically *responds* to the call at the door, the call of being that precedes her. This is surely what Heidegger has in mind when he recalls Sophocles's description of the poetic soul as "something strange on the earth." He explains: "The German '*fremd* . . . really means—forward to somewhere else, underway toward . . . the site where it may stay in its wandering. Almost unknown to itself, the 'strange' is already following the call that calls it on the way into its own."[87] As Heidegger reminds us, the German Romantics—Schiller, Schelling, Hölderlin—point toward the poet as one who ushers the divine into being.

Welcoming the Stranger involves more than discourse: it also entails embodied comportment toward the other.[88] Heidegger points us toward the poetic disclosure of being, but he retreats from in-depth engagement with what he calls the "factical" details of bodies. Other phenomenologists, as noted, also fall short of a full account of incarnation. True, Levinas wrote of erotic desire for the Other—and especially the feminine Other—but the face of the Other so desired has no singular features or moods. The eyes of the face, qua trace of transcendence, have no color or complexion. For Levinas, embodiment is a lure, a carnal pretext for the ethical call of the Stranger. True, Derrida speaks of the situated identities of foreigners—in flesh and blood, here and now before us—but it is always as defined by us and in our terms (the absolute Other escapes us). These phenomenologists—and others like Sartre and De Beauvoir—have much to say about the situated "being there" of the Stranger, but they do not go far enough. Merleau-Ponty's phenomenological analysis of embodied being offers, we have been suggesting, a deeper analysis of the singular modalities of the Stranger incarnate in the "flesh of the world."

Merleau-Ponty saw that most traditional attempts to understand the role of the Other were limited to epistemological problems of other minds, metaphysical substances, body/soul dualisms, and related issues of consciousness and cognition. One of the key merits of the phenomenological method that Merleau-Ponty develops is the promise to bypass such dualist frameworks. Merleau-Ponty's phenomenology of the "between" (*l'entredeux*) points to the chiasmatic excess that is our status as flesh. Here the either/or alternatives of conditional and unconditional, interior and exterior, visible and invisible, are transcended. This has deep significance for a new understanding of the Stranger.

The real task is to take the question of hosting to the deeper level of incarnate imagination and the senses (in the Greek sense of *aesthesis*).

Such hospitable comportment includes, indecipherably, the cultural and natural, the physical and mental. The body of the host offers "the potentiality of a certain world," in this case, a world of welcome.[89] If the encounter with the Stranger takes place at the site of the body, then we must ask what experience that body makes possible (or impossible).

Dialogical Hermeneutics: Phronesis

So we find ourselves back at the threshold of risk: How are we to know the human from the inhuman, the divine from the undivine, the welcome Stranger from the violent aggressor? Poetic phenomenology must pay attention to the moment of *phronesis*—the assessment of the hostility or friendship of the one at the doorway or frontier. We touch here again on the double-edged root of the term *hostis*, connoting both ally and adversary.[90] The appeal to *phronesis* supplements poetic phenomenology with critical hermeneutics. In this we follow the phenomenological hermeneutic outlined by Ricoeur in *Oneself as Another* which calls for discernment between different kinds of others and different kinds of selves. The "self," Ricoeur shows, can be variously parsed as subject, ego, cogito, I, me, *ipse*, *idem*, oneself. The "self" is all of these and none of these. For example, Ricoeur claims that the "self is not the I." The self is not philosophy's clear point of departure, as for Descartes, but the mysterious and elusive aim of philosophical investigation. The "ego" (*moi*) we start with is not the self (*soi*) we end up with having traversed the world of multiple others. This requires a "long route," involving many hermeneutic detours (in contrast to the "short route" of the Cartesian cogito, which completely recovers itself after a brief albeit radical doubt). This is what Ricoeur means when he says the "shortest route from self to self is through the other." Only by journeying through the worlds of others can one become oneself-as-another.

This dialogue with the self via the other and vice versa, we prefer to call "diacritical hermeneutics."[91] By diacritical we refer to a process of careful and vigilant discernment. The prefix "dia" here is crucial in that it adds a note of scrupulous attention to the act of critical discrimination. "Dia" is the prefix of *between*, as in dialogue, dialectic, diaphony, diaphora. As such, it interprets the face of the other according to inflections of speech, tone, color, shade, and light. As a linguistic term, diacritical refers more specifically to signs that mark infinitesimal inflections between one accent and another—as in à or é or ô. Dieresis itself is typical of this—ü or ï—as a division of one syllable into two. In medicine the term, from the root *diachrisis/diachrinein*, refers to the diagnosis of crisis in a fever: an act of "separating and distinguishing" that requires acute attention to variations in body temperature, skin coloration, or nerve fluctuation. Third, this hermeneutic process is analogous in its own way to age-old spiritual practices such as the Ignatian "discernment of spirits" or the Buddhist method of "skillful means." It is to similar processes of diacritical attunement that we must turn, philosophically, when we encounter the faces of strangers.

Phronesis situates the incarnate experience of *aesthesis-poiesis* in the political world. In that sense, Kristeva in *Strangers to Ourselves* performs something like a poetic phenomenology as we describe it here. Her account begins poetically with vignettes describing the coming to be of the stranger and the self, and continues complete with story, reversal, and recognitions.[92] But Kristeva—much like her mentors of the uncanny, Freud and Heidegger—tends to overemphasize the priority of psychic immanence over transcendence. Freud saw the uncanny as a secret strangeness lurking within. Heidegger described *das Unheimliche* in terms of a secret call of the other *within* Dasein to return to its ownmost (*eigenst*) self. In Kristeva's case, those who acknowledge their inner strangers are more likely to become ethical and political subjects sensitive to the claims of others—neighbors, visitors, guests, immigrants. More radically still, Kristeva claims that if we recognize that we are foreign to ourselves then there is nothing really foreign outside of us at all: "The foreigner is within me, hence we are all foreigners. If I am a foreigner, there are no foreigners."[93] But what exactly would Kristeva's "ethics of psychoanalysis" entail?[94] Would it not, ironically, be the effacing of the strange itself? Kristeva shows how we are strangers to ourselves, but she does not sufficiently emphasize how there are also strangers who are *not* ourselves—and never will be. She thus misses, in our view, the excess and the self-interruption of phenomenology, the visitation of the vertical, the radical openness to alterity that escapes analysis.

In his conclusion to *Oneself as Another*, Ricoeur insists on this fundamental "equivocalness of the status of the Other," enjoining us to keep our imaginations open to an inexhaustible plurality of voices. Perhaps phenomenologists have to admit, writes Ricoeur, that "one does not know and cannot say whether this Other, the source of the injunction, is another person whom I can look in the face or who can stare at me, or my ancestors for whom there is no representation, to so great an extent does my debt to them constitute my very self, or God—living God, absent God—or an empty place. With this aporia of the Other, philosophical discourse comes to an end."[95]

Hospitality, we repeat, involves a self who welcomes and a Stranger who is welcomed. This means acknowledging both an other within myself *and* an other beyond myself. And sometimes this Other who is other than myself requires me to be open to Strangers beyond the human altogether—animal, natural, or divine.

Sorting out these differences calls for a diacritical hermeneutics of endless translation. For it is precisely because there is always something untranslatable about the Stranger (it would not be strange otherwise), that infinite translations are called for. There is never a single translation between host and guest. Something invariably remains, remaindered, inexhaustible. And it is this untranslatable kernel that keeps the Stranger strange, a guest who I can host but never contain. The real act of hospitality is to allow the Stranger to remain strange even in our own house.

Diacritical hermeneutics thus resists the lure of the perfect translation in favor of multiple translations. It solicits a "difficult"—but not impossible—art of interpretation that respects the irreducible necessity of difference. Genuine hospitality appeals to that aspect of human being that crosses languages, traditions, borders, bodies. Such crossing-over does not imply the absorption or effacing of otherness. Rather, it constitutes the true condition of hosting. Hospitality can only occur in a plurality of unique individuals; it would be unnecessary if we were all the same."[96] Yet across this difference we find our *semblables*, similar in dissimilarity, dissimilar in similarity. This is the chiasm of the Stranger that crisscrosses the cut, the chasm, the cleft between self and other. This is the stranger of the Janus-face, looking at once toward us and away, like a figure on a distant hill who seems to withdraw as she approaches.

The Stranger cleaves: binds and loosens. It cleaves to us and cleaves a space between us. It joins and disjoins, links and separates. At one moment a bridge, another an abyss. But always a twofold cleaving.

So let us be clear. Our poetic phenomenology proposes at least two amendments to the traditional account of the Stranger: first, a richer description of incarnation that intertwines *aesthesis* and *poiesis*, and second, an attention to the power of *phronesis* to navigate our concrete linguistic and political situations. Hosting the Stranger takes place in the flesh of these complex worlds. Strangers appear not just to minds but also to bodies who must deal with the marvelous or horrific, hospitable or hostile consequences of these encounters.

Strangers Encountered: Literary Liaisons

Let us take some concrete examples of diacritical discernment. We mentioned at the outset how we might distinguish between three main kinds of other: the Foreigner, the Stranger, and the Other as such. In terms of this triadic model, we described the Stranger as that hybrid persona who faces away from us qua absolute Other and toward us qua relative Foreigner. The Stranger straddles the gap between the invisible Other and the visible Foreigner. To the extent, therefore, that the Stranger appears to us as Foreigner we are obliged to practice certain acts of hermeneutic *phronesis*, that is, acts of practical wisdom which might enable us to discriminate—as justly as possible—between different categories of foreignness. This would entail identifying strangers on a scale ranging from the most elusive and unfamiliar to the most everyday and familiar. For example, the Foreigner wears many faces and appears to us in multiple ways: as enemy (hostile or hostage), as alien (resident or nonresident), as emigrant (legal or illegal), as migrant (with or without papers), as visitor (with or without visas), as new citizen (adopted, integrated, assimilated) or even, eventually, as neighbor (friendly or unfriendly). Indeed, a really refined diacritical hermeneutics might go so far as to discern foreigners within our closest friends, relatives, or siblings, even ourselves.

Existential literature provides intriguing examples of the ambivalent Stranger. Consider Beckett, who narrates obsessional scenes of unnamable, homeless vagrants; or Sartre, who explores the minds of estranged outcasts, most notably in *Nausea* and *The Sequestered of Altona*; or Camus, who pens some of the sharpest observations on the uncanny intrusion of the absurd into the ordinary. In both *The Stranger* and *The Myth of Sisyphus*, Camus describes existential events of alienation in many guises—in nature, for instance, when the habitual world makes strange with us, loses its "stage scenery" and withdraws from our grasp into an indifferent, neutral distance.[97] Or again in the most everyday experiences when humans become strange by "secreting the inhuman." Here Camus describes how "at certain moments of lucidity, the mechanical aspect of (strangers') gestures, their meaningless pantomime makes silly everything that surrounds them. A man is talking on the telephone behind a glass partition; you cannot hear him, but you see his incomprehensible dumb show: you wonder why he is alive." This unease in the face of the uncanny is not confined to unknown others in the street. It can also be an intimate lover who strikes us, suddenly, as alien and absurd. "There are days," writes Camus, "when under the familiar face of a woman, we see as a stranger her we had loved months or years ago, and perhaps we shall come even to desire what suddenly leaves us so alone." Indeed, this uncanny other can even be oneself—that "stranger who at certain seconds comes to meet us in a mirror, the familiar and yet alarming brother we encounter in our own photographs."[98] Proust, too, notes that it is often the closest loved ones whom one finds most strange, most elusive, even as we repeatedly attempt to pin them down so that we might love them objectively: "We understand the characters of people who do not interest us; how can we ever grasp that of a person who is an intimate part of our existence, whom after a little we no longer distinguish in any way from ourselves, whose motives provide us with an inexhaustible supply of anxious hypotheses which we perpetually reconstruct."[99] Proust also discovers his own "self" as estranged: "At the first instant I had angrily asked myself who this stranger was who had done me a violence and the stranger was myself, the child I once was whom the book had revived in me."[100]

Many other literary classics provide powerful descriptions of the Stranger, from Odysseus and the Phaeacians to Victor Hugo's Bishop of Digne welcoming the vagrant Jean Valjean into his home. Religious scriptures are no exception. The inaugural moments of many religions are scenes of humans encountering divine strangers—Baucus welcoming Zeus and Hermes, Abraham hosting three wanderers under the Tree of Mamre, Jacob wrestling with the dark angel, Mary confronting Gabriel.[101]

Contemporary popular culture, for its part, offers countless further examples. Think of how often big movies trade on common fantasies of alien monsters, terrorists or psychopaths who invade our homes from afar or, more frightening still, break through the masks of next door neighbors, friends and lovers. Just a few titles suffice to recall the prevalence of such themes—*District 9*, *Pan's Labyrinth*, *Men in Black*, *Sleeping with the Enemy*, *Cape Fear*, *The Exorcist*, *Scream*, *Mississippi Burning*, *Gaslight*, the *Alien* series.[102] But we might also make special mention here of the "home invasion" genre, from horror classics such as Sam Peckinpah's *Straw Dogs* (1971) to more recent films like Bryan Bertino's *The Strangers* (2008), where haunting images of shattered windows, broken door locks, transgressed thresholds, and other forms of forced entrance and violation of private space assault the viewer. Everyone will have his or her own list. In fact, the challenge might actually be to find successful movies that do *not* feature some crisis of discernment between guests and enemies. This suggests to us not an arbitrary coincidence, but a historically rooted and ramifying lineage in Western *mythos*.

With such pervasiveness, perhaps even insidiousness, hermeneutics is off duty. Hermes cannot wander far away. Close decipherings are called for, even in our most everyday words and gestures. And if it is true that hermeneutics goes all the way down, we should not, finally, ignore the inexhaustible riches to be mined from ordinary language usage (as Austen and Searle remind us). Think of such common phrases as "my mother told me never talk to strangers," "be nice to strangers," "one day you too might be a stranger in a foreign land," "when you give to a stranger you give to me."[103] Faced with the omnipresence of these motifs, it is sometimes hard to believe that human hospitality begins with the proffering of an open hand, rather than reaching for a weapon. Again we turn to Proust:

> It is not common sense that is "the commonest thing in the world"; but human kindness. In the most distant, the most desolate ends of the earth, we marvel to see it blossom of its own accord. . . . Even if this human kindness, paralysed by self-interest, is not exercised, it exists none the less, and whenever any inconstant egoist does not restrain its action, when, for example, he is reading a novel or a newspaper, it will bud, blossom, grow, even in the heart of him who, cold-blooded in real life, has retained a tender heart, as a lover of fiction, for the weak, the righteous and the persecuted.[104]

Poetics of the Stranger: Excess and Transcendence

But it is the poet who is our paradigmatic example here. Rather than continue an inexhaustible survey of philosophical, literary, and popular culture, let us conclude with two classic examples of a poetics of hospitality. (Further examples can be seen in the five poems cited before each section of this volume). Here we witness the encounter with the divine Stranger, representative of the excessive and transcendent aspect of experience that phenomenology excels at describing.

We begin with Emily Dickinson who never hesitates to offer hospitality to the divine Other in her writing. Dickinson, in poem 405, exhorts the reader to let her soul open to the new:

> The Soul should always stand ajar
> That if the Heaven inquire
> He will not be obliged to wait
> Or shy of troubling Her
>
> Depart, before the Host have slid
> The Bolt unto the Door—
> To search the accomplished Guest,
> Her Visitor, no more—

Dickinson here offers a prescription to ontology: human being should be open to the "Guest" who might from "Heaven inquire." She does not indicate the metaphysical status of this Guest; she simply describes the fact that the Guest may come and then prescribes our relation to the

Guest. Her phenomenological ontology depicts the human experience as one that always is and ought to be receptive to the unexpected Stranger. The divine Other should "not be obliged to wait." We do not need to wait for the divine to address us formally; we must merely allow our being to be unbolted. Dickinson does not include an active subject who *chooses* to open the door of existence; it is merely the case that the soul "should always stand ajar." Her phenomenology of ontological hospitality disperses agency and *pathos* between soul and environs. We might add that whether we like it or not, it simply *is* the human condition to remain ajar.

Dickinson permits the novel, divine, and strange wind to blow poetically into her expression of experience.[105] She allows the end of the poem to open itself with one of her infamous dashes, a richly ambiguous—and far from vague—gesture. Upon recognizing that incarnate experience entails being ajar, poetic phenomenology follows Dickinson's lead in allowing expression as well as perception to host the new. Accounts—*logoi*—that would describe it must themselves allow the door to the house of language to hang unlatched.

In our concluding example, we find a detailed description of what happens to the soul that has been left ajar. In George Herbert's poem "Love (III)," the Other calls, and the speaker responds hospitably. Herbert offers a phenomenology of encountering the divine Stranger. This is no arbitrary selection from among the poetic canon, but a poem that proves exemplary for at least the following reasons. The poem "comes from elsewhere" in that it takes up an instituted tradition of thinking the divine as guest. The poem, however, offers a coherent deformation of that tradition by describing *personally* the appearance of the divine Stranger. The personalized divine Stranger exemplifies the transcendent dimension inherent in the depth of incarnate experience.

This phenomenology opens with an unexpected encounter, a withdrawal by the speaker from the infinite Other, proceeds through question, and concludes with an embodied activity:

> Love bade me welcome: yet my soul drew back,
>   Guiltie of dust and sinne.
> But quick-ey'd Love, observing me grow slack
>   From my first entrance in,
> Drew nearer to me, sweetly questioning,
>   If I lack'd any thing.
>
> A guest, I answer'd worthy to be here:
>   Love said, You shall be he.

I the unkind, ungrateful? Ah my dear,
   I cannot look on thee.
Love took my hand, and smiling did reply,
   Who made the eyes but I?

Truth Lord, but I have marr'd them: let my shame
   Go where it doth deserve.
And know you not, says Love, who bore the blame?
   My deare, then I will serve.
You must sit down, says Love, and taste my meat:
   So I did sit and eat.

How can we understand this as a phenomenology? Surely it is poetic. But how does it present or dispute any of the phenomenological accounts presented earlier?[106]

Let us follow the movement of host and Stranger through the poem. Initially, the speaker ushers us into the poem. We are guests. After this recognition of Love's presence—of the divine Stranger's entrance—a reversal occurs. The speaker relinquishes his role as host to become the guest of Love. It is Love who actively "bade me welcome," the speaker recounts. Love, the Stranger, *and not the subject/speaker*, controls the terms of the exchange. Like *Mont Sainte-Victoire*, which possessed Cézanne, guiding his brush across the canvas, the divine presence possesses Herbert's speaker. On one hand, Love requires willing participation from the poet, and on the other hand, the poet must also submit to the hospitality of Love. Cézanne must rise up from his bed and head toward the mountain, yet he must then submit himself to witnessing the mountain. As a viewer, I must get up and go to the museum and stand before Cézanne's picture, but to grasp its insight, I must submit myself to the structure of perception it presents; to read Herbert's account, I actively take up the book, but to grasp his view of the divine, I allow myself to become the situation. On one hand, *you* must sit down and read the poem; on the other, you must hear and submit to the command: "You must sit down . . ." Thus, we find the active-passive, passive-active relation we have come to expect from poetic phenomenology.

Next, Herbert takes perhaps the most maligned and overused of terms, "love," and gives it new meaning. Herbert coherently deforms the prosaic term, taking up the instituted tradition of language but transforming it to accommodate new meaning. He requires a new—yet still communicable—language to describe his experience. We might think of a similar poetic estrangement in Heidegger's work: Heidegger takes apparently known and familiar terms—"death," "guilt," "conscience"—and returns them to us, having transformed them so that we must rethink the very ground of language and being. Here, Divinity is estranged and returns to us to take on a persona, a prosopopoeic face: Love.

As Levinas anticipates, the divine Stranger overwhelms the speaker, who finds he "cannot look on" Love. He physically "grows slack" at the approach of the Stranger. In further evidence of Levinas's model, Love then holds the speaker hostage: Love "took my hand" and then commands: "You must sit down." The divine Stranger approaches the poet who finds himself unprepared and unworthy. Where a poem written from Levinas's phenomenology might end here at the point in being overwhelmed by the infinite Other, Herbert's phenomenology proceeds. The poem continues via dialogue. This is Ricoeur's "difficult" exchange of dialogue, translation, and conversation that diacritical hermeneutics describes. The approach of the Stranger puts the speaker's very self into question. Herbert's speaker asks himself: Who am I? Am I the guest? Am I capable of welcome, of action?

From this putting-into-question of the self's identity, Love asks the speaker to recognize the shared life between them: to identify his own eyes as those made by Love, to commit himself to the vision that the other lives inside his very body. Like Dostoyevsky's character Zossima in *The Brothers Karamazov*, the speaker realizes himself as guilty for all, insofar as Love shares his eyes and ears.[107] The character undergoes the reversal and recognition of his true identity—a self inhabited by the transcendent Other: the self is recognized as Stranger. We witness a crucial revelation of the poem and indeed of poetic phenomenology: the transcendent inheres in the imminent. Incarnate being discloses itself as the Stranger, double-sided, visible and invisible. Human experience arises in the depth of a world, a depth that indicates the primordial, vertical dimension. This verticality structures experience. It is the "lining of invisibility" in the visible "which makes presence a certain absence."[108] The poem presents "incarnate experience" and not merely "embodied experience": incarnate experience indicates the intervention of transcendence into corporeal being, not merely the sensing of the exterior by a body. Love thus appears in the poem as a lack, as something that escapes Herbert just as surely as the other side of an object of perception recedes on the horizon as we approach it. Love overtakes Herbert impelling him to expression, like Mont Sainte-Victoire transcending Cézanne's perception, motivating him to paint this excess.

Love issues its closing command less as a gentle proffering than a firm final offer; the Stranger compels the speaker to participate in a meal. "You must sit down . . . and taste my meat." This concluding moment does not neatly resolve the encounter with the divine Stranger as one of pleasure and catharsis. The speaker's emotions are unclear. The outcome is left open. Will the speaker successfully receive Love? Will he enjoy this meal or suffer through its strangeness the way one might barely taste a dinner eaten under duress? Or will this be a moment of transfiguration in which the very activity of eating becomes divine? The poet suffers this moment: he is not at home in his own poem, his own creation. The poet has become a Stranger to himself through the event of perceiving and receiving the Stranger. The poem leaves the reader herself with an uncanny sensation of familiarity and estrangement: she knows and does not know this prosopopoeic "Love" that appears before her.

The poem ends with a command to incorporate—as in, to "make corporeal," to take into bodily being—the Stranger. We might think here of "eucharastic hospitality."[109] The speaker cannot merely witness the Stranger but must share a meal, take up the visitor's customs. Love asks to be digested: the speaker must take this strange life into his interior but without losing his own identity, participating in the mystery of generation that puzzled philosophy at least since Aristotle's *De Anima*: How can life maintain itself and yet incorporate what is other than itself? How can human being express that which transcends it? How can we speak of the Stranger whom we encounter yet, as Proust tells us, goes "beyond us"? The speech of the poem disintegrates with the arrival of this event that lies outside the written word.

It is with this mysterious event of incorporation and incarnation that phenomenology wrestles. What marks the threshold of our being? How can we speak of the depth of the world, which always beckons yet escapes us as surely as the horizon? How can we make sense of the vertical dimension of our incarnate experience, the Stranger within and without? It seems that new speech, new writing, new expression that transforms the already available language is required. We will leave it to our authors to continue the attempt.

Presentation of Texts

RICHARD KEARNEY AND
KASCHA SEMONOVITCH

The texts in this volume play host to a number of encounters with the strange. They ask such questions as: How does the embodied imagination relate to the Stranger in terms of hospitality or hostility (given the common root of *hostis* as both host and enemy)? How do we discern between projections of fear or fascination, leading to either violence or welcome? How do humans "sense" the dimension of the strange in each other, in nature, religion and poetry or in the fundamental experience of not being at home in the world—the uncanniness of being or the unconscious? Is there such a thing as a carnal perception of alterity and verticality, which operates at an affective, prereflective, preconscious level? What exactly do "embodied imaginaries" of hospitality and hostility entail and how do they operate in language, psychology and social interrelations (including xenophobia and genocide)? How do notions of empathy and imagination inform a "poetic phenomenology of the Stranger" which registers the liminal space where the Self encounters Others? And what, finally, are the topical implications of these questions for an ethical practice of tolerance and peace?

In our opening essay, "At the Threshold," we have offered a brief, critical history of phenomenological and hermeneutic studies of the Stranger. We situated our chosen term "Stranger" in relation to two of its main counterparts, the "Foreigner" and the "Other"; and we suggested that phenomenologies of the Stranger should be not only descriptive and analytic but also poetic—that is, attentive to the *poiesis* inherent in our incarnate and linguistic being. The essays which follow offer subtle and refined attention to the many Strangers—human, divine, animal and other—who appear, disappear or refuse to appear at all. This volume attempts to investigate the limit experiences of such appearing, disappearing strangers.

Part I: At the Edge of the World

In Part I, three contemporary phenomenologists, Edward S. Casey, Brian Treanor, and David Wood, interrogate hospitality as a liminal phenomenon: the relation of hospitality to place, the experience of borders, thresholds, frontiers, and portals. Casey's essay frames this section with its invocation of the Strangers Gate in New York's Central Park. This gate paradigmatically represents a permeable edge across and through which hospitality occurs. Casey and the other authors in this section reflect on other such liminal spaces where primordial decisions of hospitality and hostility take place. These edges prompt critical—in the double sense of urgent and challenging—questions in the discourse surrounding hospitality and the Stranger: Who is welcomed and who excluded? Who promises gifts and who threatens violation? Who gives the right or duty to the host to determine who crosses the line in the sand and who does not? Such sites point to the openings and closings of hospitality. Hosting involves particular limits and boundaries. As Casey puts it, "There is no hospitality in open air just as there is no hospitality in general." Or to extend the implications, politics occurs across difference, both individual and national, and not just in some universal cosmopolitan sphere. Encountering strangers—ethically or politically—takes *place*: it involves a site, either literal or metaphorical, with an interior and an exterior, a way in and a way out.

This theme of emplacement carries forward to Treanor's essay, which opens by reminding us that "hospitality is a virtue of *place*" and "always happens in a place." Our experiences of place—implacement and displacement—are precisely those that mark the preconditions for hosting the other. Informed by Aristotelian virtue ethics, environmental studies and contemporary hermeneutics, Treanor illuminates place as fundamental to being. He offers an ontology and phenomenology of space in which displacement and hospitality feature as disclosive events. Replying to Derrida's contention that hospitality is always conditioned or else impossible, Treanor suggests that different people might reply to the guest or stranger differently, according to their character and situation. Place ties a person to a "plot" on the earth but also to the "plots," stories or histories associated with a particular cultural and linguistic narrative.

David Wood's essay also turns to liminal experiences, this time of "things at the edge of the world." Wood reposes Heidegger's question, What is a "thing"? Phenomenologically revealed, things open worlds and worlds within worlds. Through a "productive strangeness," things at the edge of the world serve as sites that permit reversals and transformations. He suggests we would perhaps do better to think of ourselves as involved in an event with these strange, other-than-human faces. After dismantling our paradigm of "things," Wood moves on to provocatively address our presuppositions about the animal and human other. His essay suggests an ethics of what he calls "fractalterity" that might emerge through such reversals and estrangements; this would be an ethos that safeguards strangeness. Wood asks us, finally, to address the neglected question of hospitality to others such as animals and purportedly "inanimate" objects. He questions precisely the appropriateness of applying the term "inanimate" to these others that face us in our environments: When do we legitimately, justly attribute a soul, a *psyche*, an interiority to the "thing"?

Part II: Sacred Strangeness

The authors of Part II explore the dramatic ambivalence at the heart of human encounters with a radical alterity we might call "sacred strangeness." The sacred Stranger makes its presence known and yet withdraws from attempts at complete comprehension. Drawing on contemporary work on the theme of hospitality by Jacques Derrida, Jean-Luc Nancy, Jean Chrétien, Max Scheler, and Simone Weil, these essays interrogate the interspace between conditional and unconditional openness to the divine Stranger, raising the critical dilemma about how one distinguishes between the phenomenological "appearances" of such visitors. Do they appear as divine or demonic? Sacred or psychotic? Gracious or rapacious? This crucial task of "discerning between spirits" raises the vexed but inescapable issue of hermeneutic judgments, wagers, and risks. That challenge in turn compels us to inquire into the subtle liaisons between critical reason and embodied imagination, or indeed between faith and fantasy. How do we make *sense* of the transcendent or vertical Stranger? What kind of evidence can we invoke in this enigmatic interworld of presence and absence?

John D. Caputo shows how admitting the stranger opens humanism to transcendence. Quoting Heidegger, Caputo rebukes humanism that everywhere sees only the human and thereby deprives God and human beings alike of encounters with the Stranger. Beyond the limits of the human the divine Stranger appears to us as "trouble." God is a troublemaker, a trickster, an unexpected visitor who interrupts, disturbs, solicits, provokes. Taking his cue from both Eckhart's mystical God beyond God and Derrida's messianic religion without religion, Caputo offers a radical phenomenology of a divinely disconcerting and surprising Stranger.

Karmen MacKendrick presents an account of a sacramental ethics that is always hospitable to the strange. Drawing on various texts from Augustine, Mackey, Nancy, Chrétien, and others, she narrates a history of the sacramental in Christian intellectual history. She advocates "listening" as a primary method of hospitality, a radical openness to the strangeness of the world in its all its beautiful, destitute, and bizarre incarnations. For MacKendrick, a sacramental ethics must be practiced through deep attention to and through the corporeal.

In his essay on "incarnate experience," Anthony J. Steinbock investigates and explicates this theme of corporeality. Steinbock distinguishes between "embodied experience" and "incarnate experience" where the latter includes visitations of the vertical or transcendent. Unlike "embodied" experiences," which are "acquired" or "provoked," incarnate experiences indicate the overtaking of self by a divine Stranger. With detailed histories from Theresa d'Avila, Rūzbihān Baqlī, and Rabbi Dov Baer, he presents evidence of the multisensory manifestation of the sacred Other, arguing that mystical sensibility must be understood to include an extra "sense" of balance, harmony, and discernment in addition to the standard five senses.

Like Caputo, Kalpana Seshadri retraces Derrida's thinking. She interprets *Of Hospitality* in relation to *Aporias* and finds in both texts a story of the visitation by death. Absolute hospitality—awaiting and attending to the absolute Other—bears striking resemblance to the event of "awaiting death." Such hospitality compares to a divine "visitation" wherein the guest is uninvited and uninvitable. Seshadri cites stories of visitations illustrating and amplifying Derrida's account in Dante's biography, a poem by D. H. Lawrence—also discussed by David Wood—and the *Katha Upanishad*. Such stories iterate and reiterate, with subtle differences, the event of death, which always beckons yet never quite arrives.

Part III: The Uncanny Revisited

The authors of this section consider the Stranger who finds us not-at-home, literally or figuratively, in our place, language or history. These authors understand the strange as the "uncanny," *das Unheimliche, l'étrangeté inquiéitante,* that haunts even our most familiar experience.

What happens when we feel ourselves called by the Stranger within? When the self undergoes anxiety, when one has the uncanny sensation that the self was always already "over-there," ahead and behind, what then? This is the paralyzing situation of finding oneself "divided between two nothings," as Simon Critchley puts it. Critchley rereads the elusive discussion of the "call" of conscience in Division 2 of Heidegger's *Being and Time.* He shows that when Dasein finds itself, *sich befindet,* amidst this uncanniness, Dasein hears the stranger voice, *die fremde Stimme.* Where Casey and Treanor find the Stranger always in a place, Critchley shows Dasein to be paradoxically no place: in the gap between two nothings.

William J. Richardson responds to Critchley's essay and to the subtle differences between their respective interpretations of Heidegger, especially in *Being and Time.* Richardson reminds us of the key questions and method introduced by Heidegger through this seminal text, and then points to an alternative reading of the notion of guilt. This alternative depends on subtly different translations of "*Nichtigkeit*" and "*Unheimlichkeit,*" but also on a careful hermeneutic reinvestigation of Sophocles's *Antigone* and Heidegger's interpretation of that play. Paradigm of a paradox experienced by all human being, Antigone arrives at the home, the hearth, only to be uncannily not at home. By attending to the textual unfolding of "uncanniness" and "homeliness," Richardson refigures our understanding of both the play and Heidegger.

Who is this Stranger within, this interior haunting that makes us Strangers to ourselves in the way Antigone experienced? Freud alerts us to the hidden place in our psyches where the strange and Stranger hide, while it is Kristeva who points to the ethical and political ramifications of this split and estranged self.

Vanessa Rumble calls our attention to Kristeva's joining of self-knowledge and moral goodness and considers the implications of the related political project of cosmopolitanism. At the heart of Kristeva's politics lies the uncanny. To understand why this is so, Rumble argues that we must see the implications of Freud's turn to the death drive that destructures the boundaries within the self and between the self and others. Freud and Kristeva are hopeful that we might make "progress in Spirit," albeit for different reasons and with refined definitions of the term "Spirit." Psychoanalysis does not condemn us to a repetition of the past, Rumble suggests, but allows us to open, hospitably, to the future as to the stranger.

One such futural event is the birth of the child. What is both more familiar and strange than the birth of a child, asks Kelly Oliver? What is more uncanny? This question points Oliver to psychoanalysis and to Levinas as resources for describing children in birth as strangers and the symptomatic human reaction. Oliver illuminates Levinas's account of paternity in which a father recognizes his son as distinct, as strange, and thereby himself as also distinct and strange. Finding Levinas's account insufficient, she turns to Kristeva to supplement this study of maternity and paternity. Together, Kristeva and Levinas suggest we see giving birth as a process through which we meet an uncanny other "who is elected but never chosen." Identifying and welcoming the child-stranger reciprocally allows an identification and welcome of the self as stranger. Oliver's study demonstrates how the Stranger transcends our desire to possess and control existence.

Part IV: Hosts and Guests

In the fourth section, the authors address critical implications of the work of Heidegger, Levinas, and Derrida. By continuing a dialogue—a *dialogos,* a going through the accounts—of these thinkers, each author elucidates as-yet undiscovered resources for speaking of the Stranger.

In a subtle interweaving between the categories of Being (*l'être*) and the Other (*l'autre*), Jean Greisch invites us to explore four ways of rethinking the stranger—anthropological, ontological, ethical, and poetical. In their work on Being and the Other, both Levinas and Heidegger ask us to pose the question, "What is called thinking?" Greisch argues that between these two philosophers, we can find a middle way via poetic phenomenology. Celan and Hölderlin exemplify this way. As in the essays by Richardson and Manoussakis, the poetics of Antigone provides a thread leading us through the portal of the uncanny.

Jeffery Bloechl traces a turn in Levinas's thought that indicates a "being toward God." Bloechel finds that in his work after *Totality and Infinity,* Levinas emphasizes that hospitality to the Other involves a passivity that has been habitually covered over. Nonetheless, Bloechl asks, does not hospitality involve a certain initiative on the part of the subject? He responds that this misses the "exorbitant hospitality" demanded by the Other according to Levinas. Finally, his essay tackles the problem of gender that arises in Levinas's terminology wherein responsibility seems to rest on a binary opposition between Man and Woman. Not only does the divine Other exceed ordinary constraints, but Levinas's notion of gender also seems to transcend normal practical constraints, pointing to a sort of "impossible gender" to accompany "unconditional hospitality." Bloechl finds that all such concrete human interactions—all "concrete hospitality"—depends on a language and a situation that absolutely exceeds the subject.

So, can we apply Levinas's account of the Other to concrete situations? William H. Smith offers one such attempt in his essay on genocide. Though one might first associate Levinas's thought with the European genocide of the early twentieth century, Smith studies the Rwandan carnage in the late twentieth century. After presenting Levinas's account of the stranger, he applies this vision to a concrete case: the Rwandan genocide of 1994. The horror of this massacre lies in part in that it was committed, quite literally, "face to face" between friends and family. These events force us to ask how is it that neighbors and acquaintances could become the main perpetrators of mass murder? A phenomenology of the Stranger and the subject's hospitable or hostile response to one's own neighbor—too far or too near—is shown to be a pressing ethico-political project.

To the canonical phenomenologies of the Stranger in Derrida and Bernhard Waldenfels, Christopher Yates offers a third voice, that of the eighteenth-century religious thinker David Brainerd. Both Waldenfels and Derrida address the need to avoid both an egocentrism and a logocentrism that would reduce the other to the self or the alien to the familiar. True hospitality involves a creative response to the other, not an absorption of otherness. Yates shows how these visions of hospitality are marked by a sort of "magnetism": a mutual affection and repulsion. Brainerd's writing presents a scene in which the approach of the Stranger is fraught with an almost electric tension between invisible forces.

To conclude, we go back: John Panteleimon Manoussakis returns us to the gates of Themes where an enigmatic Stranger approaches. This anonymous Stranger draws us to the edge of language, to the limits of what permits itself to be named. Through the figure of the *Xenos*, Manoussakis illuminates Sophocles's *Oedipus Rex* as a drama that pivots on a knowledge of self that occurs by way of knowledge of the other. One can recognize the Stranger at the gates because one was once a Stranger oneself.

With that, we invite you, the reader, to imagine what follows in this volume as a banquet at which you are both host and guest. Our authors bring to the table a variety of sustaining, entertaining, and provocative offerings. Each will hopefully provide a phenomenology of the Stranger that provokes a dialogue extending beyond this brief textual symposium.

PART I

At the Edge of the World

To some of you
hesitating at this gate,
you might be better off
unknown to anyone.

Pass by every day
hurriedly.
Stay unnamed
even in the cemetery.

Enter, if you must,
by another gate
known to
God alone.

—Fanny Howe, "The Stranger's Gate"

1

Strangers at the Edge of Hospitality

EDWARD S. CASEY

Strangers at the edge? Where else would they be? The edge is their place—or equally their non-place, since the edge is no place to be: no place to be comfortable, to be identified, to have the status of a citizen or homeowner. Yet, paradoxically, the edge is also where strangers are received: it is where hospitality happens. It is the non-place where the opening of hospitable place (a place called home, country, people) emerges and where, deepened and prolonged, such place comes to stay: to last as the reliable scene and setting of hospitality. There is no hospitality in an edgeless place like the middle of a desert.

Hospitality at the edge, hospitality on the edge: hospitality as edge.

I

"Strangers Gate": these words are chiseled into the red sandstone wall next to an entrance on the west side of Central Park at 106th Street. Every major gate to Central Park has its own name. Other names, some twelve in all, are more predictable and reassuring: "Citizens Gate," "Warriors Gate." But "Strangers Gate" is rather enigmatic. The first time I saw it, walking briskly by, I was stopped dead in my tracks, staring at it in disbelief. I wondered what it was meant to signify when it was inscribed in the late nineteenth century. My best guess is that it refers to all who come to New York as foreigners: as immigrants especially but also (increasingly) as tourists and visitors. Anyone non-native is in effect a stranger, above all in *this* city with its outsize buildings and high population density, its brazen wealth chock-a-block with unalleviated poverty—Manhattan with its multilingualism and intense energies. No one feels entirely at home here, including native New Yorkers (whoever they might be). Only aboriginal "Native Americans" could rightly declare this place as "home," but they are present only as absent—nameless, not even a memory at this late historical point, only bones encountered by chance as sewer lines are newly dug. Historians of the city may refer to them with accuracy and authority; the rest of us latecomers have not the slightest clue. The most that residents of the city know now is that waves of immigrants have swept through the city from the seventeenth century to the present: the Dutch and the British, some Germans and French, and in the mid–nineteenth century African Americans and Irish (both of whom lived in close proximity in shantytowns in Central Park when it was nothing but an open plain north of the heart of the city), then tides of Eastern Europeans in the later nineteenth century, many Southerners and Midwesterners in the early twentieth century, thousands of Chinese and fewer Japanese, and more recently economic and political refugees from Central America and especially Mexico.

All of these were strangers initially—and many remain so, especially those who find employment only by doing the most menial of tasks. (It is most often undocumented Mexicans who bus tables and wash dishes these days in New York restaurants, as a moment's glance shows.) All of these peoples came as strangers in the night, and those who stayed become strangers in the day. (As if to reflect this continual strangerhood, Strangers Gate is open all day and all night.) All these strangers are odd fits, if not actual misfits, in everyday reality, never quite "fitting in." But this is also the way I would describe myself, an Irish-Swiss Kansan transplanted to New York City, even though I have lived here for some time now and am a salaried servant of the state. They, we, are strangers in the land, foreigners in the city, reminding us that "stranger" in its French root as *l'étranger* means, quite literally, someone from another country, another city—thus estranged from somewhere else, some other place.

To come from another place is to arrive from abroad—where the "broad" in "abroad" resonates with the minimal breadth that any place requires: *plat*, the ultimate etymon of "place" itself, means "flat" and "open." To be a stranger or foreigner is to come from "elsewhere," *another where* than that which is habitual or familiar: from *d'ailleurs*, as the French also say, a word in which we hear the *allos* of "other" that is equally present in the English word "alien," which becomes more of an accusation than a description in a phrase such as "alien worker," as we say with barely concealed suspicion if not outright contempt, or "foreign alien" in a wholly redundant expression that ensures that the sharp edge of insinuation turns twice in the flesh of those at whom this epithet is flung.

II

But what of the *gate* in Strangers Gate? If strangers come from a broad foreign land, an open place, to come to another land they must enter through certain gates, often stringent in their requirements for passage. "Strait is the gate, and narrow is the way" (Matthew 7:14): at stake here are not just the pearly gates of Heaven or the fiercely guarded gates of Hell. To be from abroad, *être de l'étranger*, is to move from the breadth and history of one's place of origin—even if its people have been repressed and displaced by tyrannical political regimes—into a new place, where one must pass muster in order to enter: one must first of all submit to the protocol, the *rite de passage*, of the tight gates of immigration control and (sometimes) health inspection. Even if these are successfully negotiated, other demanding gates, those of a new culture, a new language, a new people with their peculiar customs and mores, disciplines and rituals: all these await the newly admitted person.

In short, the stranger as foreigner must pass through something that has a sufficiently sturdy constitution to persist over time and to resist, by its sheer materiality or dense historicity, any merely facile passage. A physical gate is emblematic of this situation: it can be opened and closed at specific times and under certain precise conditions, which are laid down by the authority of the state and reinforced by delegated representatives of the government ("customs" officials, police, border guards). In this respect, Strangers Gate in Central Park is anomalous if not outright oxymoronic: although it is a gate, it has no gated door that can be closed and locked; nor is it ever guarded; nor, so far as I know, is it regulated by any preexisting laws of the city or state. It is in effect, an ungated gate—an always open gate.

But all gates, stringent or relaxed, possess one very basic trait: they must be, or at least have, *edges*. Edges give them definition and structure: without them, gates would be so indeterminate as not to count as gates at all. In virtually every case, gates are edges of public spaces such as lots and parks, office buildings and residences (sometimes whole residential complexes: "gated communities"), occurring at the outer limits of these spaces. Within their edges, gates provide openings in the surfaces of places and things alike. This is true no matter how restrictive they may be, how heavily guarded, how difficult of passage or discouraging of entry. Whatever their particular "coefficient of adversity" (Sartre) may be, gates will swing open in certain circumstances. The exception only proves the rule: for example, the Gate to Kafka's Castle, indefinitely barred from passage.

Gates, then, are edge phenomena: they frame spaces offering passage. They are porous in principle. To this extent, they act as that kind of edge that can be designated as a "boundary," that is, an edge that allows for traversal across it in various modes of two-way traffic. When gates are part of walls, however, they are features of "borders," which are continuous edges that can be delineated and that serve to close off or seal a nation or city—as in "the U.S.-Mexico border," otherwise known as La Frontera. A gate in a border wall such as that built recently at Nogales, Laredo, or Tijuana is thus a hybrid edge: it is a boundary-like break in an otherwise unbroken border. In the case of La Frontera, such a gate is called euphemistically a "checkpoint," which is a particular site for immigration and drug control through which one can walk or drive—if one passes inspection and has the proper papers to show.[1]

Strangers Gate, in contrast with such checkpoints, is an always open edge whose very lack of formal, state-sanctioned controls symbolizes nothing short of saying in effect: Welcome! Come on in! Enter freely and without peril! *This* gate is an edge that offers unchecked admission to anyone who wishes to walk through it. It is the very converse of the lack of welcome that is so graphically evident, and bodily sensed, at La Frontera checkpoints, which serve more as obstacles than as facilitations to passage. The long lines of waiting cars, especially those coming from the south, furnish concrete images of this unwelcoming situation. Still more telling is the anxious suffering felt in the bodies of the Mexican and Central American migrants who seek to find a way over or around the formidable wall that was first constructed as part of the all too aptly named "Operation Gatekeeper."

III

In these opening ruminations, we have been circling around a basic circumstance that we can call "the edge of hospitality." By this latter phrase I mean several things: the limit of hospitality, where it runs out; the edge at which hospitality actually happens, whether this be at a gate or a door; and hospitality as occurring at the edge—as a liminal phenomenon, a matter of thresholds in human sociality over and through which significant exchanges and interchanges, transmissions and trespasses, transpire (or, by the same token, are excluded, as when they are forbidden). I also mean the way in which hospitality does not just take place but *gives place*—offers space of a special sort—as well as hospitality itself as an edge. Let me say something about each of these factors:

1. *The limit of hospitality.* When hospitality is "conditional," it becomes the kind of thing that may *not* happen in a given circumstance. We experience this when we come to a door, hoping to be greeted but are instead turned away abruptly: the door is "slammed in our face," as we say. In this case, we have not met even the minimal criteria for admission, much less welcome. Failing to meet conditions of acceptability, we become *persona non grata*: we lack the right appearance, we have the wrong skin color, we do not have a recognizable name, or we are just unknown. We do not meet the minimal conditions for social or legal propriety, we are lacking in the *proprius*, the right ownness or identity: with the result that we are not accepted by the person who opens the door: he or she does not recognize us as one of their "own." So we are in effect *disowned* at this fragile initiatory moment. The zero limit of hospitality is reached at a glance: we are deemed unworthy to merit admission, to step through the door—where "limit" signifies the exact condition that has to be met for a stranger to be admitted.[2] (This is why we say that a situation like that at Strangers Gate in Central Park offers "unlimited hospitality": no conditions are observed, no strictures are invoked, no sanctions are levied.)

2. *Hospitality at the edge.* It is a striking fact that hospitality as an event occurs at or on an edge. There is no hospitality in the open air just as there is no hospitality in general. In this spirit, Derrida insists that even "absolute" or "unconditional" hospitality has a conditional aspect in terms of the particular laws and terms by which it is enacted: "*the* unconditional law of hospitality needs the [conditional] laws, it *requires* them. This demand is constitutive [of hospitality itself]."[3] These laws or conditions are not only legal or customary; they reflect the requirement that events of hospitality occur in circumstances of edge. By this I mean primarily spatial edges—those that obtain at the door, at the gate, on the border.

Also at stake under this heading are *bodily edges*: two or more bodies always meet in acts of hospitality, whether those of host and guest, border guard and immigrant, or among friends. But these bodily edges meet only within the terms provided by the first kind of edge, conjoining at the spatial edges of doorways and other such openings. By the same token, *cultural edges* also obtain: there has to be an edge of difference in history or language or tradition for hospitality to be an issue. Two people who share entirely a given cultural matrix do not need to offer hospitable gestures to each other—or, if gestures are exchanged, they will be perfunctory.

All such edges, spatial and bodily and cultural, enact what every edge effects: they bring together and they separate, both at once, albeit each at its own level and in its own way. Here is the bivalent basis of all hospitality, which must involve some modicum of convergence as well as separation if it is to happen at all. When there is nothing but sheer separation, we have reached the limit of hospitality, its null point; likewise, when there is nothing but fusion, hospitality also cannot happen. In either case, there is no *act* or *event* of hospitality: nothing happens at all, or else nothing that was not already the case (as in the meeting of two culturally homogeneous beings, like two "buddies" who slap each other on the back symmetrically).

Otherwise put, hospitality enacts reciprocal but asymmetrical relationships between beings who possess some means of communication and an at least minimal diversity with regard to each other: who are strangers to each other in certain significant respects. For the state of strangerhood is not confined to those we habitually designate as "strangers," that is, foreigners, immigrants, those who are unknown, etc. In the event of hospitality all parties are strange to each other in significant ways: when the door opens, the owner of the house appears just as strange to the would-be entrant as the latter does to the former. In this confrontation of two strangers, we witness the reciprocity of host and guest in the very midst of the asymmetries of power and status: "incongruent counterparts" in Kant's phrase: incongruent as other to each other, counterparts as sharing in the state of strangeness.

3. *Hospitality as giving place.* Derrida remarks that "absolute hospitality requires that I open up my home and that I give [access] not only to the foreigner (provided with a family name, with the social status of being a foreigner, etc.), but to the absolute, unknown, anonymous other, and that I *give place* to them, that I let them come, that I let them arrive, and take place in the place I offer them."[4] It is precisely because of the inherent asymmetry, the alienation, of the initial encounter of strangers that some leeway, some open space has to be proffered by the person in charge (host, owner, guard: the "hospitalizer") to the dispossessed or petitioning other: she who wishes to enter. In other words, some *room for passage* has to be allowed or provided to the entrant, the "hospitalized," keeping in mind that the English word "room" is a linguistic cousin of German *Raum*, "space." This is why the threshold always has to have a certain breadth: enough at least to step over and pass through. This breadth, as we saw earlier, entails place. Hence we speak of the "doorway" across

which movement is to be made; *way must be made*, thus *place given*, if a stranger is to feel welcome—if the stranger is to become a guest.

Place-giving is an instance of "activity in passivity," in Husserl's phrase: the giving is an activity, but what is given, room or place, is still something *there* into which one enters. It is choric in character: it is a *receptacle* in and through which hospitality happens. It is at once impassive and impersonal, for what gives place is not simply some person freely bestowing admittance to a stranger but the very space itself, its layout, as authorized by the hospitalizer.

At this level, then, we have a triad of terms: hospitalizer, hospitalized, and the place in which hospitality happens.

4. *Hospitality as edge.* What gives place, more than a person or law or custom, is *edge itself.* It is edge that is the constant among the variables we have here considered. For there would be no act of hospitality without the ingrediency of edges, their effective ingression into this act—whether these be the edges of gates or doors, bodies, or cultures. *The edge is where the action is*: this is axiomatic for the enactment of hospitality.[5] And I here mean edge not just as the point of intersection between preexisting planes (of things, places, experiences, histories) but edge as itself active: as *edge-making* or *edge-work*. This dynamic action is captured when we speak of "putting yourself on the line." Curiously, many acts of hospitality consist in just such an act, whose purport is not positioning ourselves on a laid-down or laid-out line but rather taking a certain risk, however modest, by extending oneself beyond one's habitual sense of etiquette or limits of energy in order to take an extra, unprogrammed step: a *pas d'hospitalité*. This last phrase is the title of Derrida's text, and it captures just this sense of having to step forth from comfort and security to accomplish hospitality. This stepping-forth is not just that of the person with more authority or power in the circumstance but that of *both* parties, who step toward each other—over and through an edge around which they converge. Whether the door to a house or an international border, this edge is reattested every time it is recognized or resisted, being reconstituted by each act of legal traversal or illegal trespassing. The edge of hospitality is brought into being, or brought back into being, by the scene of hospitality itself. It is always an *event*. Its being is a matter of becoming; the edge is continually made, unmade, and remade in the event of its happening.

Hospitality, often seemingly so innocuous or so formal, is anything but established. Despite its ritualistic expressions and its roots in local or national tradition, and despite the stability of the architecture (the house or wall) that may subtend it, it is something that occurs only at the extremities of existence: at the edges, as the edges: in "fractalterity" in David

Wood's suggestive term. It occurs by acts of going out—acts of radical exteriorizing. Such outgoingness is the very converse of the inwardizing that has been the great passion of the modern era: "Go within. Truth dwells in the inner man." Saint Augustine's words are cited by Husserl, the last of the great philosophical modernists; they are cited again by Merleau-Ponty, who realized that the task had become the very converse of what Husserl intended: it was to go outside the confines of conscious subjectivity, into the open of the lived world, where "everything remains" (*tout y demeure*).[6] This is not just a world chockful of edges: it is *the world on edge*.

Hospitality is a signal step in the enactment of this exteriorizing, for it entails the danger and the risk of being exposed to the other. It is not the most dramatic form of such risk, yet it contains all the basic elements of this exposure, this vulnerability: Who is that at the door? Whom (or what) will I encounter when I open it? And I, the person who knocks, whom will I confront when the door is flung open? In neither case can I know in advance; in both, we are in the grip of "the surprise of the event"[7]—the event of hospitality, just where Derrida and Levinas and Nancy, in the wake of Husserl, take us so forcefully.

IV

"A stranger stood at the gates": This familiar line, which goes back to the title of a popular poem written in the 1930s by Lewis Sharrad, "A Stranger Stood at the Gates of Hell," has lingered in the American popular imagination for a long time. Perhaps this is because of its stark juxtaposition of two disparate things that call for each other. Strangers, being unknown, call for gates—for some control and surveillance, some checking-out or checking-in on the part of whoever is in charge of the gates (in the original poem it was Satan who guards the gates to Hell). What could be more predictable, what more natural than this if strangers are presumed to be literal intruders and gatekeepers are taken to be agents of law and order? Yet, Strangers Gate in Central Park suggests a different response to this situation. In its wide-open state, this gate embodies a circumstance in which strangers, rather than being considered threatening as agents of disorder, are welcome—in which case gates need not be primarily defensive or exclusionary entities. The setup of Strangers Gate suggests that gates can be the very vehicles of welcoming unknown others, whom they embrace and usher in unconditionally. Rather than regarding strangers and gates in an oppositional standoff with each other, Strangers

Gate encourages us to think of them as engaged in a collaborative enterprise that we can designate as a circumstance of "open hospitality," in a seemingly redundant English phrase.

Just as "gate" shows itself to possess two distinctly different semantic ranges—being at once a boundary and a border—so "stranger" has a comparable ambiguity. On the one hand, a stranger is someone who is deeply alien to everything we have experienced and known, so much so that such a person is not merely foreign but truly "strange," so odd and incongruous as to upset any usual expectations we might have, even to threaten our personal integrity at some basic level. He is *atopos* (meaning in Greek both "strange" and "without place"). "He's not one of us," we mutter under our breath—or proclaim in live voice if we are Texas vigilantes spotting a *mexicano* who has slipped across the border. In this inhospitable and suspicious spirit, we seek to exclude such a person from entry into our home, our neighborhood, or our country—our part of the world, our place. We feel uneasy, destabilized in the presence of the placeless other. On the other hand, a stranger can be taken as other in a nonthreatening sense—as just "different," where this is construed as calling for our curiosity, for wanting to get better acquainted, perhaps to become friends at some point. Then we are moved to open the gates to the stranger forthwith, to welcome her or him through a passage that has become a genuine *gateway*, a porous edge that allows for ease of traversal rather than offering obstruction. We offer place to the other by opening our place to the person lacking place.

The choice is stark: either the stranger stands at guarded gates; or there is an open Strangers Gate. Either the stranger is stopped in his tracks, refused welcome; or the gate is the stranger's, being hers or his as much as the gatekeeper's.

Between these two extremes, there are many intermediate cases. One of them is the situation where we act on the basis of a principle of "universal hospitality" of the sort that Kant posited and that leads to the aporia posed by Kant's celebrated example of a killer at the door: why should we admit someone vowed to murder the very person we are harboring in our home? Kant has no humanly satisfactory answer to this dilemma: it is one of those moments where his cosmopolitanism leaves him in the lurch. In contrast, there are local traditions of hospitality in which welcome is extended on carefully constructed conditional terms: you may come in if you are a Shiite, but not if you are a Sunni. This, too, is highly problematic: if Kant's position on hospitality is too unconditional, that of a given religious or sectarian tradition is often too dependent on strict group membership.

Beyond such problematic cases, there loom many instances in which decisions of hospitality are made on pragmatic grounds: on the basis of "counsels of prudence" as Kant would call them. But then we are left with the precariousness if not the outright prejudice of individual judgment, which is certainly not reliable across a broad spectrum of cases.

My suggestion is that before trying to come up with an adequate ethic or practice of hospitality, we should begin by considering the situation of hospitality in terms of its edge character. This would mean to think of strangers as those who inhabit the edges of our domestic or national space, of gates as edges that can serve as porous boundaries or devolve into closed borders—and of ourselves (as host or guest, guard or immigrant) as called upon to recognize that we are implicated in an inevadable circumstance in which diverse edges figure and reconfigure. Although this realization will not make ethical heroes of us and even if it does not give us any infallible guide to action, at least we shall be much clearer as to the complex and subtle makeup of the circumstance. Despite its undramatic character, such an act of recognition represents a significant step forward, for it allows us to understand hospitality as at base the enactment of a unique and often urgent edge-game in which strangers present themselves at gates and in which gates are there to open or keep shut.

2

Putting Hospitality in Its Place

BRIAN TREANOR

> Hospitality . . . has to do with the *ethos*, that is the residence, one's home, the familiar place of dwelling.
> —Jacques Derrida

For the past several decades, continental philosophy has exhibited an ongoing concern with what we might call liminal phenomena, among them friendship, the gift, mourning, responsibility, forgiveness, and hospitality. Of course, to call these "phenomena" already begs the question, or at least a question, the question of whether and to what extent these events actually take place. Thinking in the wake of Jacques Derrida it is impossible to ignore, for example, the excess of the call to forgiveness over the sort of forgiveness that actually takes place in concrete situations. In the case of hospitality, this excess is apparent in the seeming tension between the unconditional law of hospitality and laws that condition hospitality in actual practice.

Thus, one significant question has to do with the relationship of the unconditional call to the conditioned response, and the nature of the tension between these competing demands. Do forgiveness and hospitality ever actually happen—that is, phenomenologically, do they ever "show up"—or must we settle with "contaminated" or "perverted" forgiveness and hospitality because the events that these names harbor, or that haunt them, are always to come (*a venir*)? Are hospitality and related concepts "liminal phenomena" or "aporetic events"? Are they possible, though difficult, or impossible? These are complex questions and a good deal of work has been done on the tension between the conditional and the unconditional; however, in either case—whether hospitality, forgiveness, and gifts are "difficult" or "impossible"—it remains the case that one of the things that ought to arise from our attention to these liminal phenomena is some insight into our actual conduct in the world. We would be remiss in our discussion of hospitality if we did not ask about actual hosts and guests, and actual moments of hospitality, if there is such a thing. So a second crucial question has to do with what hospitality actually looks like in practice. Whether hospitality is difficult or impossible, a philosophical account ought to have something to say about the way in which we actually receive strangers. These two questions—(1) the (im)possibility of hospitality and (2) what actual acts of hospitality, whether or not they are corrupted by their conditionality, look like—will be the guiding concerns for this inquiry.

Although there are important similarities between the various liminal phenomena with which continental philosophy has been concerned—all, for example, arguably exhibit the aporetic structure that so fascinates Derrida—and the sphere of one (e.g., generosity) may sometimes overlap the sphere of another (e.g., hospitality), each phenomenon bears distinguishing marks that differentiate it from others. One way to make clear this difference is to focus on an aspect of a phenomenon that distinguishes it from other phenomena. In the case of hospitality, the most convenient and useful way to do this is to examine the relationship between hospitality and place.

Hospitality is a virtue of *place*, perhaps the preeminent virtue of place. Indeed, hospitality is so deeply connected to place that it is defined by this association. Hospitality always happens in a place; it consists in giving place to another and, as such, occurs as part of a relationship between an implaced person and a displaced person. Only an implaced person can be hospitable. A displaced person, qua displaced person, can be generous, can be the giver of gifts, can be forgiving, and can be responsible, but she cannot be hospitable because she cannot give place to an other. A *host* is precisely a person who receives people into a given space or place as *guests*. Hospitality exists, if it does exist, in the relationship between host and guest. Hence the Latin *hospes*, which can mean both "host" and "guest." When the host ceases to be a host (as when she herself is displaced) or when the guest ceases to be a guest (as when she becomes a naturalized citizen or member of the family), we can no longer speak of hospitality. These conditions, as well as many others, indicate just how place-saturated hospitality is. If we fail to understand place, we fail to understand hospitality.

The Primacy of Place

Although there are other philosophical accounts of space and place, as well as associated concepts like "the body" and "landscape," the best way to begin an investigation of place is with Ed Casey's groundbreaking *Getting Back Into Place*.[1] In it, Casey argues that, while the philosophical tradition of the West has been characterized by a remarkable "temporocentrism," it is in fact *place* that most fundamentally characterizes both space and time.[2] Place, he points out, is "prior to all things" because "to exist at all as a (material or mental) object or as (an experienced or observed) event is to have a place—to be implaced, however minimally or imperfectly or temporarily."[3] We are constituted by, and in turn constitute, our places.

Indeed, Casey goes so far as to identify God with place, noting that the Hebrew name for god (*Makom*) can be translated as either "place" or "God." The primordiality of place runs so deep that it calls into question the doctrine of *creatio ex nihilo*. As he puts it, "If we ask ourselves not *what* was created or even *how* it was created but *where* creation occurred, we realize that it could not have happened just anywhere, much less nowhere."[4] The primordiality of place is supported by Jack Caputo's reading of Genesis in *The Weakness of God*. God's creation, says Caputo, was not *ex nihilo*: "Genesis does not begin at an absolute beginning. Elohim begins where he finds himself [i.e., in the *place* in which he finds himself], with co-everlasting but mute companions: a barren earth, lifeless waters, and a sweeping wind. Elohim has to play the cards he is given, to work with the materials at hand."[5] God's creation is not the creation of something out of nothing, but the calling of things to life and the interpretation of this wondrous awakening and vitality as "very good." Here is Caputo's description in total:

> In the beginning, *they are there*, wind and waters and land, barren and lifeless, the wind sweeping over the deep. . . . There they are, just there, without a word, the only noise being the heaving of the seas, the blowing of the wind. . . . Then Elohim was moved to speak to them, and by addressing them *to bring them to life*, to awaken life in them, to make life stir through their massive limbs the way one calls a sleeper to wake. *He calls them to life; he does not bring them into being*, for the whole point is that they were *there* all along, from time out of mind, in somnolence deeper and more dreamless than any sleep we can imagine. Genesis is not about being, but about life. Bare barren being is there, what was already there. The astonishing thing is that God *brings being to life*. That is the wonder, and that

life that God breathes in them is what God calls "good," which goes a step beyond being.[6]

So place, it seems, is very fundamental indeed. It is, if not the sole origin of things, at least a co-primordial constituent of the origin. Place is a sine qua non of being. Each of us here now was born into a specific place and has inhabited different places during his or her life. More radically, place (or, perhaps, pre-place-related space) was there in the beginning, in the dark of the void.

But the primordiality of place does not yet tell us about our experiences of place—implacement and displacement—and it is these experiences that are preconditions for hospitality. If hospitality requires an implaced host and a displaced guest or stranger we need to get clear on what it means to be implaced or displaced.

Implacement

Casey makes a good argument for the primordiality of place—anything that is, is somewhere.[7] However, if each of us is always already implaced, implacement seems, like being, to be a prime candidate for a concept that we neglect and forget. If place is already primordial, what does it actually mean to be implaced?

Place is a space in and from which one lives.[8] It both affects and is affected by its inhabitants, those implaced in it. Spaces become places, "implace" their inhabitants, serving to "anchor and orient [them], finally becoming an integral part of [their identities]," and making them inhabitants or natives rather than strangers.[9] Indeed, Casey seems to suggest that the particularity of implacement functions as something like *haecceitas*, or at least an important component of it; it pins us down in some particular place in the broader swath of space, situating us and shaping our unique individuality. As such, the effect of place is more than merely spatial and orienting.

> [The power of a place] determines not only *where* I am in the limited sense of cartographic location but *how* I am together with others (i.e., how I commingle and communicate with them) and even *who* we shall become together. The "how" and the "who" are intimately tied to the "where," which gives to them a specific content and a coloration not available from any other source.[10]

The addition of the "how" and the "who" to the more intuitive "where" of implacement indicates clearly the significance of place and implacement for intersubjective relationships, including, as we will see, hospitality.

But implacement is not inhabiting a space like other spaces. Because of the way that places shape and influence us, a place is, among other things, a well-known space. A place feels like home. It is comfortable, well worn, and familiar. It is predictable and secure. Place is space that is no longer alien. All these adjectives are, of course, relative rather than absolute. Things such as "comfort," "predictability," and "security" are not purely objective judgments. Places and implacement are subjective. This is because places are not simply things (a misconception, says Casey, arising from something like the natural attitude) or points in space. To know your precise location on the Earth's surface, even with the accuracy of modern GPS, is not to know your place. Places require more than mere spatial orientation. Places are *experienced* spaces of a certain sort and, as such, they have a cultural dimension, they are social, communal, and historical.[11]

Place, according to Casey, should be thought of as bounded by our bodies on one side and by landscape on the other. It is the "intimate interaction of body and landscape" that allows us to achieve orientation.[12] Together, body and landscape "collude in the generation of what can be called 'placescapes.'"[13] The landscape, as spatial horizon, exceeds place, serving as the backdrop that houses, as it were, our places. We orient ourselves within a landscape by looking for marks—natural landmarks or marks of our own making—that help to distinguish certain parts of that space from others, moving us toward implacement in the landscape. Landmarks are a way of orienting oneself in the landscape, establishing, by degrees, the sort of familiarity that we associate with proper implacement. The fewer familiar landmarks in the landscape, the less place-like it is; the more familiar landmarks, the more place-like it is.

If landscape exceeds the parameters of place, our bodies fall short of them.[14] Our bodies, too, are spatial, but we inhabit them in a way that is not entirely like our inhabitation of place. It is in and through our bodies that we engage space and inhabit our places. Indeed, many places, especially built places, are based quite directly on the body—its usual dimensions, the way in which it characteristically moves, and so on. Think, for example, of the way in which a poorly designed or poorly constructed home causes its inhabitant persistent discomfort, which in more extreme cases borders on displacement. Such a home never quite "fits" its inhabitant.[15] It is our bodies that allow us to actively participate in our implacement and orientation in the broader landscape, as Casey's analysis of Puluwatan navigation makes clear.[16] It is, ultimately, our bodies that place us "here" and most fundamentally orient us.[17] As Casey puts it,

Without the good graces and excellent services of our bodies, not only would we be lost in place—acutely disoriented and confused—we would have no coherent sense of place itself. Nor could there be any such thing as lived places [a seeming pleonasm], i.e., places in which we live and move and have our being. Our living-moving bodies serve to structure and to configurate entire scenarios of place.[18]

As the example of Puluwatan navigation suggests, our bodies' hereness is not static; our bodies allow us to journey through space and place. This process of implacement, of navigation through space and landscape by means of one's body, is dynamic. The edges demarcating body from place and place from landscape are neither fixed nor impermeable; place "overflows" both edges, toward landscape and body.

Displacement

However, if place is so ubiquitous—if it, like God, was here "in the beginning" and if we are all born into a place at our own beginnings—does it make sense to talk about displacement? Aren't we all always already in place? Quite a bit hinges on this question because it's hard to see how hospitality can exist without displaced persons, persons who have lost their place (like exiles or refugees) or left their place (like emigrants or travelers).

In an absolute sense, it may be true that total displacement is not possible, or is at the very least exceedingly rare. Recalling that it is our embodiment that ultimately grounds us "here," we have to acknowledge that

> [e]ven when we become acutely disoriented, so long as we have at least a residual sense of where we are bodily, we are never entirely unoriented in space, never wholly lost in its "undistinguishable inane," never without some vestigial hereness. Only if space itself were as intrinsically directionless, as indifferent and neutral, as it came to be regarded in the modern era, would we be threatened with anything like a complete lack of orientation, that is to say, sheer herelessness. In other words, we are never not oriented to some degree and more or less successfully in the places we inhabit.[19]

However, even if we dismiss the idea of an absolute displacement, it seems quite clear that people do experience displacements that, while less than complete, are still profoundly unsettling. Displacement becomes estrangement: a distancing, both literal and metaphorical. We can become strangers to our place—even to our most intimate place, our bodies—not only through travel but also through disorientation. Displacement happens by degrees rather than as an all-or-nothing break. Such relative displacements can be significant and represent meaningful differences between implaced and displaced individuals. Because of this, no matter how well implaced we are, none of us is ever completely removed from the threat of displacement. Our implacement is only provisional, and displacement threatens implacement at every turn.[20] This may explain why placelessness, or the threat of it, occasions such deep anxiety.[21] Place is so fundamental that displacement, even the threat of displacement, unhinges us. This is why *unheimlichkeit*, the "uncanniness" of not-being-at-home, plays such an important role in existential thought. The fear of being "lost" (i.e., without ground) appears to be fundamental to the human psyche and to our understanding of being a stranger. Even the most intrepid solitary explorer, itinerant *sadhu*, or nomadic Bedouin needs some minimal connection to place.

Because implacement and displacement are provisional and exist in degrees, we each experience both states.[22] However, there are two sorts of displacement worthy of special attention due to their influence on the question of hospitality: (1) the displacement of the stranger, and (2) the displacement of the postmodern condition. The first sort of displacement is intuitive. When we think of displaced persons, we tend to think of refugees from disasters, be they natural, social, or political. The "widow, orphan, [or] stranger" represent those who are lost, who have become displaced. But literal homelessness is not the only sort of displacement. To be homeless is to lack a primal space, either in "the literal sense of having no permanently sheltering structure [or in the sense of] being without any effective means of orientation in a complex and confusing world."[23] The first, more intuitive category of displacement is the one that occupies most accounts of hospitality; however, a second sort of displacement that we might call existential is, while less obvious, much more widespread.[24]

Cisco Lassiter claims,"[To] the modern self, *all places are essentially the same.*"[25] Though there may be accidental or incidental differences, the essence of each place has become increasingly indistinguishable from the essence of any other place. McDonald's is McDonald's, whether you are in New York, Paris, or Beijing. But this homogenization of place should give us pause, because undifferentiated space is, we saw, one of the hallmarks of displacement, which itself is characterized by the anxiety of *unheimlichkeit*. While it may be convenient to know that a Big Mac is a Big Mac, whether you are in Los Angeles or Luxembourg, it is also unsettling.

A heightened degree of displacement, as well as the anxiety and depression that accompany it, has become endemic in the postmodern era. In addition to the aforementioned existential thought on the subject, contemporary social scientists are beginning to emphasize the dangers of such detachment from place. Studies such as Robert Putnam's *Bowling Alone* chart the breakdown of community (and implacement) in the latter part of the twentieth century.

> The dominant theme is simple: For the first two-thirds of the twentieth century a powerful tide bore Americans into ever deeper engagement in the life of their communities, but a few decades ago—silently, without warning—that tide reversed and we were overtaken by a treacherous rip current. Without at first noticing, we have been pulled apart from one another and from our communities over the last third of the century.[26]

Three of the four main culprits of this trend have place-significant components: (1) the pressures of time and money, which keep us away from places (e.g., home, community) with which we would otherwise be connected; (2) suburbanization, commuting, and sprawl, with their homogenizing effects and further deleterious influence on the distances between places; (3) the effect of electronic entertainment (especially television), which detaches us from our surroundings and our fellows.[27] The rise of workaholism, urban and suburban sprawl, and isolating entertainment not only distances us from our community; it distances us from our places, leading to disconnection, itinerancy, and anxiety.[28]

Of course, no cultural shift is monolithic or unidirectional—Putnam points out that there have been movements from more communitarian to less communitarian ways of living and back again—and the contemporary breakdown of community and implacement is no exception. There are notable backlashes against the general trend toward isolation, displacement, and estrangement from our environment. Putnam's work itself ends with a call to renew community life. Reactions to contemporary existential displacement (e.g., Slow Food) are both a symptom of and a response to the problem. They are symptomatic of postmodern displacement because they are highly nostalgic—for tradition, for simplicity, or for community—and nostalgia is a sign of displacement.[29] However, they are also responses to displacement because they attempt to strengthen or restore a local, place-specific pattern of living. Whether these efforts will alter the trend toward displacement that has characterized the past fifty years remains to be seen. Nevertheless, there are a number of reasons to pay careful attention to the general trend toward greater displacement.

In terms of the current study, one significant problem with an increased experience of displacement is this: if we are not genuinely implaced, it is hard to see how we can be genuinely hospitable.

(Im)Possible Hospitality

Jacques Derrida has argued that hospitality is one of a number of key concepts in the Western tradition (examples of which we have described as either liminal phenomena or aporetic/impossible events) that are characterized by a sort of double injunction.

> It is as though hospitality were the impossible: as though the law of hospitality defined this very impossibility . . . as though the law of absolute unconditional, hyperbolical hospitality, as though the categorical imperative of hospitality commanded that we transgress all the laws (in the plural) of hospitality, namely the conditions, the norms, the rights and the duties that are imposed on hosts and hostesses, on the men or women who give a welcome as well as the men or women who receive it.[30]

Hospitality, then, exists in the tension between the unconditional law of hospitality and the conditioned laws of hospitality; the former demands open doors and borders, unconditional welcome, and radical egalitarianism, while the latter insists on some criteria for entry, rules of behavior pertaining to guests, and distinguishing between welcome and unwelcome guests.

The biblical stories of Lot and the destruction of Sodom (Genesis 19:1–29) and the outrage at Gibeah (Judges 19:22–30) illustrate the untenable nature of pure hospitality, unlimited by conditions. In these stories, it is proposed, and in the latter instance carried out, that girls or women be handed over to a mob of rapists in the name of honoring the law of hospitality. It is true that one can read something noble into the idea that hospitality extends so far as to demand that the host risks himself or his family in the name of protecting his guest, as when Victor Kugler, Johannes Kleiman, Miep Gies, and Bep Voskuijl risked themselves to hide the Frank and Pels families from deportation to Nazi death camps (Kugler and Kleiman paid for their "illegal" hospitality when they were caught). However, these biblical accounts would no doubt appear radically different, and distinctly less hospitable and virtuous, told from the perspective of the unfortunate girls and women.

Because pure hospitality is impractical, in practice the unconditional law of hospitality is conditioned in multiple ways. First, there are the duties of hosts, who, in almost all cultures, have a prima facie obligation to exhibit reasonable hospitality to guests. To the duties of hosts correspond the rights of guests. Kant claims that there is a universal right to visitation belonging to all persons "by virtue of their common ownership of the earth's surface."[31] This situation is evident in, for example, the right to asylum.[32] This first pair of duties and rights seems to strain toward the unconditional hospitality of open doors and porous borders. In practice, however, the duties of hosts and the rights of guests are in tension with the rights of hosts and the duties of guests, the latter pulling us back toward a more conditional sort of hospitality. Hosts have the right to screen guests who might harm, intentionally (e.g., criminals or terrorists) or unintentionally (e.g., carriers of certain diseases), the state or home into which they seek admittance. Moreover, the presumptive right of the guest to welcome or sanctuary can be revoked if the guest violates the rules of hospitality by, for example, committing a crime.[33]

Perhaps the most common "crime" with respect to visitation is overstaying one's welcome, which points to yet another essential condition of hospitality: hospitality qua hospitality is perforce a *temporary* situation. A guest is someone who is allowed entry, but for a limited time. Thus, for example, the "right to asylum" as currently conceived is framed by the possibilities of "repatriation" (i.e., return of the guest to whence she came) and "naturalization" (i.e., the end of hospitality because the guest is no longer a stranger but is now one of us). If a guest stays permanently, she is ipso facto no longer a guest. Of course, expatriates know that this situation is complicated by a third possibility of becoming a "permanent resident" (which, recognizing the ambiguity, Kant calls a "permanent *visitor*"[34]) possessing a green card or *carte de séjour*, which is capable of being revoked in a manner generally unlike citizenship. Nevertheless, a permanent houseguest becomes, at some point, a member of the extended family. When a guest settles down, plants roots, begins to work for her keep, and so forth, she ceases to be a guest.[35]

In any case, as Derrida points out, the very idea of rights and duties undermines the gratuity of hospitality. Hospitality cannot, per se, exist where there are "rights" of guests or "duties" of hosts.[36] If one honors the "right to asylum" in allowing a refugee to enter, we are no longer speaking of hospitality *stricto sensu*, but of some kind of economic exchange wherein the ruler of the house (*oikonomos*) opens his door under obligation, and the guest is admitted under condition (e.g., of good behavior). As Derrida points out, "to be what it 'must' be, hospitality must not pay a debt, or be governed by a duty: it is gracious, and 'must' not open itself to the guest [either invited or unlooked for], either 'conforming to duty' or even, to use the Kantian distinction again, 'out of duty.' "[37]

In addition to the conditions arising from tensions between duties and rights, and from the very idea of duties and rights applied to hospitality, there are conditions imposed by the dependence of hospitality on *place*. Hospitality depends on place insofar as it gives place—or attempts to do so, a point to which we will return—to the guest. It is a phenomenon that can only take place from a place. Only a person who is truly in touch with her place can be genuinely hospitable. In contrast, generosity, which closely resembles hospitality in certain respects, can occur without place. I can give a gift to someone who is implaced or displaced, and can do so even if I am myself displaced. But hospitality, insofar as it entails some sort of sharing of place, can take place only in place, and it requires the dissymmetry of an implaced person (the host) and a displaced person (the guest).

These various conditions are part of what Derrida calls the laws (plural) of hospitality, in contrast to *the* unconditional law of hospitality. Although the unconditional law of hospitality and the conditioned laws of hospitality are, in a sense, irreconcilable, they are also inextricably connected. Each requires the other. The unconditional needs the conditional as much as the conditional needs the unconditional.[38] Hospitality exists, insofar as it does exist, in the negotiation between the unconditional law and the conditioned laws of hospitality.

It is clear that place plays a significant role in the conditioned laws of hospitality, a role we will examine in detail. However, before doing so, it is worth a moment to consider this troubled negotiation between the unconditional law of hospitality and the conditioned laws of hospitality. In emphasizing the gap between these two laws, Derrida makes a persuasive, though not unproblematic, point about hospitality in the Western tradition.[39] Nevertheless, we might consider how this conversation could be fruitfully expanded to include non-Western religious voices.

Of Hospitality Outside Athens and Jerusalem

Despite the acknowledged interdependence of the law of hospitality and the laws of hospitality, there is a consistent tendency to denigrate the latter in favor of the former, if only by implication. The conditioned laws of hospitality (and other deconstructive aporias) are frequently referred to as "corruptions" or "perversions" of the unconditional law. This leads Derrida to characterize the asymmetry of their relationship as "tragic."[40] Such characterizations certainly have an element of truth to them, but we should be wary, or at least aware, of the way in which our position in the hermeneutic circle influences such judgments. Those of us tilling in the field of continental European philosophy, conditioned as we are by the Judeo-Christian-Islamic tradition, tend to see the conditioned laws of hospitality as a perversion of the unconditional law of hospitality rather than an appropriate pragmatic complement. Pure hospitality, generosity, forgiveness, and similar dispositions represent myriad ways that we fail to "be perfect as [our] Father in Heaven is perfect" (Matthew 5:48). We can never realize such lofty goals. And our failing is not only due to our own sinfulness (i.e., our failure to be hospitable to some determinate other here before us) but seems to follow from our very finitude. We are responsible to the other, but "there are also others, an infinite number of them, the innumerable generality of others to whom I should be bound by the same responsibility, a general and universal responsibility."[41]

Derrida suggests that the call to hospitality is one of the "primary injunctions of all the Abrahamic religions,"[42] an assertion no doubt born of his three-year seminar on hospitality, which referred regularly to "the religions of the book"—Judaism, Christianity, and Islam.[43] However, and without criticizing Derrida for focusing on these three traditions (already an overwhelming task, and one undertaken with his characteristic creativity and philosophical insight), we might remark that interreligious dialogue ought to move beyond Europe and the Near East to consider the religious imaginations of more distant traditions (Buddhism, Hinduism, etc.). Such a move will require a voluntary movement of displacement on the part of those of us implaced in Western traditions and on the part of our interlocutors from non-Western traditions, who will themselves be disoriented by the exchange. Interreligious dialogue will give rise to problems of translation, disorientation, confusion, and the discomfort associated with being displaced. But this does not make the venture unrewarding.

The tension Derrida sees between unconditioned and conditioned hospitality appears to be present in Hinduism as well, lending support to the deconstructive reading; but the Hindu context brings new wisdom and alternative interpretations to the table of interreligious dialogue. On the side of pure or unconditional hospitality, we find a call to radical hospitality in the *Taittiriya Upanishad*: "*Atithi Devo Bhava*" (let your guest be a god unto you).[44] However, on the side of conditioned hospitality we find a variety of narratives that, while not dealing with hospitality specifically, address the tension between unconditional demands and conditioned responses through the lens of Hindu conceptions of *dharma* (duty). The most famous of these accounts, though it does not deal with hospitality, is the discussion between Krishna (an incarnation of the godhead) and

Arjuna (a warrior prince) before battle in the *Bhagavad-Gita*. Arjuna surveys the opposing army and sees, arrayed across the field, many of his kinsmen; he is moved to compassion at the thought of slaying his own relatives and resolves not to fight. Krishna, however, rebukes him and argues that he must do so. Although Krishna's argument is based largely on the fact that Arjuna has misunderstood the nature of the self (the distinction between the mortal body and immortal soul or *Atman*) and of reality, he is also insistent that Arjuna must fight because it is his duty (*dharma*) given his station in life as a warrior (*ksatriya*). As a warrior it is his duty to fight rather than refrain out of compassion: "Better is one's own law though imperfectly carried out than the law of another carried out perfectly."[45] The point being that were Arjuna a different person, of a different station, in a different role, his duty with respect to his kin would be different (and, perhaps, compassion would be more appropriate).

Arguably, the way in which we ought to exhibit hospitality, like the way in which Arjuna is instructed to exhibit compassion, is dictated by our position and role in life. Just as the compassion of a warrior is different from the compassion of a holy man (*sadhu*), the hospitality of, for example, a mother of two young children is different from the hospitality of a single man. As a young man I frequently picked up hitchhikers, having done a great deal of hitchhiking myself; however, today I am much more circumspect about who I pick up, and in what circumstances, when I am driving with my two young daughters in the car. The key point here is that these differences are proper, and they *ought* to be so; "better is one's own law though imperfectly carried out than the law of another carried out perfectly." Indeed, viewed from the perspective of *dharma* these conditions themselves have a sort of divine mandate, insofar as one's caste (*varna*) and the duties (*dharma*) that go with it are the just result of actions in previous lives (*karma*). Following one's *dharma* is not a failing, corruption, or perversion. Going into battle against one's own family, passing a hitchhiker on a rainy day, or failing to open the door in the dark of night may be the result of a failure to answer the call of the other to hospitality. Then again, it may not; it all depends on one's *dharma*.

Of course, the call to unconditional hospitality is present in Hindu thought in the aforementioned *Taittiriya Upanishad*. The point here is not that Derrida's account of the tension between the unconditional law of hospitality and the conditioned laws of hospitality is baseless; rather, the point is simply that the "negotiation" between the unconditional and the conditional is likely to be different in the Hindu imagination than in the Judeo-Christian religious imagination, and that this difference provides fertile ground for rethinking the (im)possibility of hospitality. Perhaps different people *should* respond to the same *unconditional* call differently. In any case, the Hindu account of hospitality, under the influence of *dharma*, seems to offer a less "tragic," more phlegmatic account of the negotiation between the unconditional law and the conditioned laws.

Putting Hospitality in Its Place

Although Derrida's account of conditioned hospitality does lend itself to an account of place—place being one of the important constraints or prerequisites of conditioned hospitality discussed earlier—there is much more that can be said about the place-related aspects of hospitality. The key issue here is that openness (open doors, open borders, and so on), which tends to be the focus of many accounts of hospitality, is *not*, in fact, sufficient for it. Even the most unregulated point of entry, with the absence of any conditions for admittance, falls well short of hospitality. This is because mere openness is a necessary but not sufficient condition for hospitality. Hospitality is more than just admitting the other; it requires a genuine attempt to welcome the other and to make the other feel "as if" she is at home.

To be hospitable, it is not enough to simply admit the other, even without conditions. We might say that hospitality, invoking the idea of virtue mentioned briefly at the outset, must be done in the right way.[46] Real hospitality includes the openness that tends to be the focus of contemporary discussions of hospitality, but it also includes making one's resources available to the other. The host must make herself available to the guest. This should, following Gabriel Marcel's account of availability (*disponibilité*), include making one's resources—material, emotional, intellectual, and spiritual—available, or "handy," for the other.[47]

But even availability of the host and her resources is insufficient for genuine hospitality. To openness and generosity/availability must be added the attempt to help the other implace herself, even in a temporary or "as-if" manner, to help the other *feel (as-if) at home*. It is entirely possible to allow others entry (to one's home, town, or country), perhaps with few if any conditions, and yet fail to act hospitably toward them. Indeed, upon reflection, the abundance of examples of such behavior suggests that this is very common. One instance, recognizable from innumerable dramatic and comedic depictions, would be houseguests who are simply tolerated—perhaps barely tolerated and with obvious displays of being "put out" on the part of the host. The classic example of such behavior would be the extended visit of one's in-laws (though this example is complicated by the fact that while in-laws may be strangers in a sense, they are also family). Broader examples of inhospitable openness would include the integration of schools after *Brown v. Board of Education* (though the debacle at the University of Alabama, being forced, falls short on even the criteria of openness and availability) or the admittance of successive waves of immigrants—Irish, Chinese, Mexican, and so on—into the United States. In each of these cases the other was granted admittance, but they all significantly, and obviously, fall short of hospitality.

We are not hospitable if we simply throw open our doors, even if we ask no questions and allow unconditioned and unchallenged entry, simply because there is no one at the gate to question the stranger. An unmanned gate or port of entry is no more hospitable than an uninhabited house. Hospitality requires someone implaced, someone who will greet, and question, the stranger. Not all gates are checkpoints, and not all questions at the gate can be reduced to biased or bigoted attempts to exclude others, or to ethnocentric oppressions of the stranger. As Casey notes, the "primary function" of a gate is to "provide opening" rather than to exclude.[48] "Where are you from" is not always a question put to a foreigner by a police state in order to discriminate and exclude; sometimes it is a question put to a stranger by host in order to make welcome and become acquainted, to accommodate and to provide.[49]

But, even if we assume the existence of a hospitable welcome fueled by a genuinely virtuous desire to aid the other, can hospitality really make a stranger in a strange land feel as-if at home? A stranger, by definition, does *not* feel at home. To answer this we might begin by recalling that Casey tells us that nostalgia is a symptom of displacement. To this we can add Derrida's claim that "'displaced persons,' exiles, those who are deported, expelled, rootless, nomads, all share two sources of sighs, two *nostalgias*: their dead ones and their language."[50] Let us look at these two nostalgias and see if hospitality can address either one in an attempt to help implace the other.

Nostalgia for one's dead is, ultimately, nostalgia for place, for the very ground to which one is connected by virtue of one's dead family resting there: the place from which we come, the place where we belong, where our ancestors are buried and where we expect to be buried alongside them. Examples abound. The graveyard in Chamonix almost seems the family cemetery of the Simonds, so intimate is the connection of that clan to that village. Antigone, argues Derrida, is deprived of place by the loss of her connection to the final resting place of her father Oedipus.[51] The nostalgia for the place of one's "dead" is a longing for a fixed position in space; however, in contrast to the nostalgia for the immobile location of one's dead, the nostalgia of one's language, the mother tongue, is the "home that never leaves us."[52] It is the "ultimate homeland" and "last resting place."[53] Especially for the exile or the immigrant, language is often what remains of belonging when other ties to place have been severed or atrophied. It is a "mobile home" that we take with us.[54] Interestingly, the role of language in place, implacement, and nostalgia points the way, indirectly to be sure, toward identifying a genuinely distinguishing mark of hospitality. Language is the tool with which we narrate our identities and a component of implacement in space. It is the role of genuine hospitality to help the other connect these interwoven tasks: emplotment and implacement.[55]

The "mobile home of language" consists of multiple rooms. That is to say, language works to connect us to culture and place in more than one way. On one hand, there are the lexical and grammatical aspects of the language itself, which distinguish the various natural languages. However, this aspect of language is not, on its own, sufficient to constitute the sort of hominess or implacement of which Casey speaks, and on which hospitality depends. In addition to the various formal and mechanical aspects of a dialect, the home of language consists of the narratives, stories, myths, and idiomatic wisdom that together constitute anchor for linguistic implacement.[56] Narratives connect us not only to cultures but to places as well. To be at home in a language is not the result of being able to order breakfast, or even to possess the fluency to follow esoteric political debates in the newspaper. Rather, to be at home in a language is to inhabit it in such a way that its idioms, both grammatical *and* narrative, feel natural rather than forced. The former is achieved by any number of studious doctoral students; the latter, outside of one's native tongue, is rare indeed.

If implacement has a linguistic component, it would seem to follow that implacement is fundamentally narrative, which should be no surprise because our identities are tied to implacement and our identities are also narrative.

> To state the identity of an individual or a community is to answer the question, "Who did this?" "Who is the agent or author?" . . . To answer the question "Who?" as Hannah Arendt has so forcefully put it, is to tell the story of a life. The story tells us about the action of the "who." And the identity of this "who" therefore itself must be a narrative identity.[57]

However, if implacement has a narrative quality to it, then narratives can affect implacement just as they can affect identity. Paul Ricoeur argues at length, in the three volumes of *Time and Narrative* and in *Oneself as Another*, that narratives affect identity:

Unlike the abstract identity of the Same . . . narrative identity, constitutive of self-constancy, can include change, mutability, within the cohesion of one lifetime. The subject then appears both a reader and the writer of its own life, as Proust would have it. As the literary analysis of autobiography confirms, *the story of a life continues to be refigured by all the truthful or fictive stories a subject tells about himself or herself.* This refiguration makes this life a cloth woven of stories told.[58]

The refiguration of a life by narrative takes place via a threefold process that Ricoeur describes in terms of *mimesis*: prefiguration ($mimesis_1$); configuration or emplotment ($mimesis_2$); and refiguration ($mimesis_3$). Reading and emplotting a narrative allows us to see things from a different perspective. When we read stories we enter new worlds and try out new identities—worlds and identities that may, and in some sense always do, reshape the world and identity with which we began the story. Through narrative we can gain a sort of "virtual" or "as if" experience. "Stories 'alter' us by transporting us to other times and places where we can experience things *otherwise*."[59] By narrating our experience we change the way we are in the world, and this applies to implacement as well as emplotment.[60]

The role of hospitality is to aid the guest in emplotting herself into implacement—to help the guest write herself into the place, or to write the place into her story—to make her feel 'as if' she is at home (i.e., implaced). Commonplace expressions of hospitality support this claim. "Make yourself at home." "My house is your house." "We're all family here." "Have a memorable stay [i.e., one that will make a good story]." All these phrases indicate a hope that the guest, the *dis*placed other, will be successful in experiencing a degree of *im*placement. They also express a desire to help in that as-if implacement. Achieving this as-if implacement is not something the host can do for the guest; the host can only facilitate. Such hospitality is less like serving the other in the manner of an innkeeper, and even less like being hostage to the other.[61] Genuine hospitality aims to bring the guest into the rituals, rhythms, and narrative of the house, and to allow her to bring some of her own (foreign) rituals, rhythms, and narratives to the host and her house. I know that I always feel much more "at home," especially if staying for more than a day, when my hosts are not waiting on me hand and foot, but welcome me into the life of their home, allowing me to participate in the rituals and rhythms of their place (e.g., cooking, a very place-specific activity).[62] I suspect this is true of many other people as well. Although hospitality will inevitably, and rightly, involve some degree of serving the other, its essence is not the service, but successfully helping the guest to feel implaced, "as if" at home. Genuine hospitality helps the other incorporate your place into her narrative. Here emplotting takes on a double meaning: "plot" as *mythos*, the sequence of events that make up a story, and "plot" as a piece of ground, a homesite, a *place*. The work of hospitality is to help the other (guest) to integrate these two senses of plot to achieve an "as-if" experience of implacement, a *place* to rest her head though a stranger in a strange land.[63]

3

Things at the Edge of the World

DAVID WOOD

> A snake came to my water-trough
> On a hot, hot day, and I in pyjamas for the heat . . .
> And yet those voices:
> If you were not afraid, you would kill him!
> And truly I was afraid, I was most afraid, But even so, honoured still more
> That he should seek my hospitality
> From out the dark door of the secret earth.
> —D. H. Lawrence, "The Snake"

Confronted by the snake, an emissary of the strange, D. H. Lawrence is conflicted from the beginning, switching in a trice from fear and hostility to wonder and hospitality. Eventually, he throws a log at the snake, declaring, "And immediately I regretted it. I thought how paltry, how vulgar, what a mean act! I despised myself and the voices of my accursed human education."

This structure of switching or reversal appears in many places. It is found in Levinas's account of coming up against the limits of my own intentional orientation, its interruption by the face (or appeal, or call) of the Other, itself putting a strange reverse spin on Sartre's account of the effect of the Look. It is found in Rilke's description of the experience of being looked at by a tree, in the various meditations—from Plato, to Hegel, to Nietzsche and Bataille—on the significance of the sun, and in philosophical struggles over the place and status of the body—confined at different times to the position of sheer matter, burden, or instrument, and also at times released from this bondage with the recognition of its power to constitute the real. It is found in Heidegger's world-revealing meditations on "The Thing," and in his and Gadamer's reflections on the work of art.[1] In each case, a thing that begins as an object of experience becomes the site of an event of reversal and transformation in which not only is the subject implicated in an unexpected way, but the world, or a part of it, is poised for restructuration, and for the proliferation of new chains of possibility.[2]

This essay adumbrates the intriguing possibility that the world (as we call it) may be populated with beings of various sorts that in all sorts of different ways, open worlds, open onto worlds, and open our eyes to possible worlds, by interrupting this one. When Alice ventured into the rabbit hole, she discovered a world within a world. I am proposing that the world be viewed as a veritable rabbit warren, in which the entrances to these other worlds are marked by what we call things.[3] The world is no longer a collection of things, in the ordinary sense, however heterogeneous. Rather, it is a Space that enables spaces, a Time proliferating times. And *things* come to be seen as events, sites for transformation.[4]

To enter into a thing is to open up the world or worlds into which it invites us. Conceived in this way, things are marked by analogues of what physicists call event-horizons. This is the point or line at which we switch from seeing the thing as in the world, to seeing the thing as projecting, opening, or proliferating its own world, its own order of things. Or as constitutively implicated in the world in which it might seem just to be an item.

I offer here an introduction to this project, locating within this account both human and animal strangers, and indeed recurrent productive strangeness. Part of my purpose here is to argue that the ethical dimension of such reversals needs to be set within the broader context of our flickering in and out of a whole panoply of strangeness.

I

Let me begin an example of such a reversal—our experience of the sun.

It is a remarkable fact that this source of so much light should be dangerous to direct sight. We may quite properly understand this danger physiologically—that we could burn the retina. But there is another danger of a quite different order—that we may "see" something new, and disturbing, something other than what was blindingly obvious: the sun as the source of all energy, of our sustained existence, and so on. For those of us wedded to autonomy, this may be an unwelcome reminder of dependency. And for those who have come to embrace a transcendent deity, the tantalizingly ambivalent status of the sun, as both an item of furniture in the heavens, and the energetic ground of our being, might well cause a ripple of unease at least, in the decision to abandon sun worship. Maybe, for all their barbaric practices, the Aztecs were on to something. Might not sun worship be a profound practice of meditation on the deep significance of the sun, and all things solar? And there is more to come. When we look at the sun, it is true, the sun does not look back. This gives us a certain assurance of privilege. And yet our eyes—what are they? They are the evolutionary product of living on an earth flooded with light for millions of years. These things I call my eyes spring from the sun, as does every animate organism. What looks *at* the sun is a child of sunlight. This is true of me as a living being and of my eyes as essentially attuned to the sun and to the visibility it opens up.

It is easy for phenomenologists to think of the "constitutive" in a formal or transcendental sense. But here it is importantly material and historical. The event of reversal or fracture is the one in which the I/eye that sees the God/sun comes to grasp it further as the condition of its own capacity to see at all, indeed to be at all.[5] We may confidently surmise that this is a seminal event, one that ushers in further developments. Such a dependency has what I call terrexistential implications. What would it be like to welcome such a revelation? Or to refuse it? What would it be, as Nietzsche asked with regard to Eternal Return, to *will* it?

Consider for a moment one of the deepest and most difficult aspects of this dependency—our being tied up in an unthinkably deep past. The time of evolution—of life, of animal life, of human life—is unthinkably deep both because it exceeds our capacity to imagine even in terms of scale, raising really profound questions about what those limits are, and what we mean by "imagine." Can we "imagine" the Big Bang? Or the End of the World? And beyond the question of magnitude, we must also imagine our not being here, and indeed there being nothing like us on the planet. We have to peer back an interminably long way around evolutionary corners that block illumination from the distant past.

Exploring the temporal aspects of our dependency on the sun has just begun. A meditation on this opening soon realizes that our entire fossil fuel economy and way of life consists in releasing at an accelerating rate the reserves of solar energy locked up in gas, coal, and oil, burning it like there's no tomorrow.[6] We are tapping our stored solar past, as well as drinking in today's light and heat. Moreover, we know that one day, the sun will explode and the experiment will come to an end.[7]

II

The second example of reversal is the nonhuman animal. I opened with D. H. Lawrence's poem "The Snake," in which he laments his reactive violence. You could also think of Aldo Leopold's account of the light in the dying wolf's eyes.[8] Or Theodore Roethke's basking lizard, to whom, he says the stone terrace belongs.[9] The movement, the reversal, the transformation in each case is one in which the animal moves from being a part of my world, our world, to making a claim, to occasioning on my part the recognition that the animal too, in some sense, has a world, projects significant dwelling.[10] Some such experience happens when I pick up a worm crossing the path after a rain, and deposit it safely on the other side. I recognize both vulnerability and something of a manner of life, or way of dwelling on the part of the worm. In modest fashion, I go out of my way, as we say, to help him on *his* way. Something happens here, but it is mostly an accommodation of one mode of life to another. There is no threat from the worm, and he never looks back. The reversal has not yet happened; we are still on the cusp. The reversal here has many portals—we notice the spider's web, or the beaver's dam, or, as my ex-squirrel-hunting friend recalls, we watch squirrels playing on a tree trunk. In each case a concept appears on the other side of the line—home, territory, play—and we are primed for something abrupt to happen. Another friend's advice on encountering wasps is apposite here: never make eye contact, and they won't sting you. It took me a while to realize this was a joke. But this possibility of eye contact, of seeing oneself being looked at, takes us closer to the edge. The reversal happens when we see ourselves being seen, and then that we don't really understand how they see us, and then that we are as much part of their world, whatever that is, as they of ours.

This reversal through an encounter with the-other-than-human can come in ways that are all too clear. Sartre's account of the look has this abruptness about it, but being the object of the other's gaze is no mystery. In the movie *Grizzly Man*, Timothy Treadwell loses his life when he (and his girlfriend) are finally eaten by a rogue bear, after thirteen seasons of peaceful coexistence in Alaska. The director Werner Herzog comments that Treadwell just did not get it: the bears saw him as food. And when he was eaten, he became part of their world in a very literal sense. This suggests not that bears have no "as such," as Heidegger might say, but that that their version, at the very least, even if it overlaps our own, may distribute value differently. But in some ways, this reversal is still too straightforward, like man bites dog, hunter hunted. Everything changes, and yet the conceptual space is still the same. Animal fables fall under this heading. More disconcerting, and almost completing the reversal as event, is when we recognize that we may well have little or no handle on the other-than-human creature's "world." Heidegger himself seems to me to be of two minds in thinking this through. Disputing Rilke's valuation of the Open, he insists on the animal's world lacking a certain disclosedness (tied up with Truth), and he seems to go along with Von Uexkull's references to functional tone when speaking of a "disinhibiting ring."[11] These accounts make the animal's world fairly transparent to us, as a reduced version of our own. But at other times he suggests that we don't really know how the world seems to another creature.

Even that move, however, is but a stage on the way. The true reversal would come were this path to converge with the path of "What is Metaphysics?" where Heidegger speaks of the "totality of what is" slipping away from us (in Angst), the point at which we are reminded of the *unheimlich* at the heart of our dwelling.[12] The animal, I am suggesting, has this power: to relieve us of our habituated dwelling by bringing us face-to-face with a significantly different and unassimilable mode of dwelling.

III

The third case of reversal I will take is that of the other human, and here I will divide the example itself into three: the sexual other, the stranger and the enemy. The textual ghosts floating in the background here are Irigaray, Levinas (with Derrida), and Schmitt. Each of these relations marks the site of a radical transformation, or is open to such a possibility. In pursuing these three cases, I will be able to differentiate my position from one centered on the ethical opening. Moreover, I believe it will be possible to explain the misunderstanding that generates what we have come to think of as the ethical infinite.[13]

The sense of wonder is the mark of the philosopher.

—Plato

Consider first the sexual other and Irigaray's insistence that the experience of wonder properly applies to the sexual other before it applies to the cosmos, thus upending any impersonal metaphysical primacy of wonder, such as Plato proposed. Irigaray in particular alludes to Descartes's account of wonder as the first passion, being moved by our first encounter with a thing, before we know what it is. She asks that we return "this feeling of wonder, surprise, and astonishment in the face of the unknowable" to its proper place—"the realm of sexual difference"—by which, somewhat traditionally, she means the difference between man and woman. For Irigaray, wonder is the antidote to any claim to possess or control the other.[14]

How does this account fit into the schema I am proposing here? Wonder, or astonishment, is the experience that arrests, and reverses, one might say, the everyday, possessive projective orientation to the sexual other, allowing us to treat and see the other as something of a miraculous complement, as if for the first time. Here it is not that the other looks back, with the recrystallizing impact that Sartre describes in the gaze. Rather, a space of nonpossessive delight is opened up; she goes on to nominate angels as inaugurating and protecting sexual encounter as celebration, beyond any master/slave drama of domination.

Da-sein is the happening of strangeness.

—Martin Heidegger

For the second encounter with the human other, I take the example of the stranger, with an eye to Levinas's focus on the widow, the orphan, the stranger, and Derrida's meditations on hospitality. In the stranger three different dimensions come together: First the absence of knowledge: nothing is known about this person, whether he or she is to be trusted, well disposed, and so forth. Second, that the stranger is in need, being away from home. And third, it is unlikely that you will meet this person again. The appearance of the stranger may occasion no response (drive on by, don't answer the door) or a negative one (closing the door in his or her face, turning down his or her visa application). Such responses would confirm a certain default self-centeredness. But there is also the possibility of the event in which I am taken out of myself, and even moved to the point of what Derrida calls "pure hospitality"—a welcome without limit, and without checking credentials, in which I put myself (my house, my family, my country) fundamentally at risk. I see myself as hostage to the other without any consideration of reciprocity. The scales of native narcissism fall from my eyes, and I am exposed to the need of the other. I discover saintliness.

Tell me who your enemy is and I will tell you who you are.

—Carl Schmitt

For the third example I take the enemy, in which the transformation works in the opposite direction. Sometimes, seemingly from nowhere, cooperative or at least tolerant relationships with my neighbor, my friend, my compatriot, or some person or group with whom I get on well, break down utterly, to be replaced by the other acquiring the status "enemy," in extremis, to be shunned, injured, or killed. This happened in Bosnia, in Rwanda, and it happens in small ways in our streets and late-night bars everyday. It is the world of suspicion, of paranoia, in which any small event is scrutinized for its secretly hostile significance. It is a world in which Jews, communists, gays are rounded up and killed. And a world in which one state invades another sovereign state in pursuit of narrow self-interest.

To this list—lover, stranger, enemy—we could add the friend, the master, the ghost and many others. In each case, this category of the other can emerge or subside without reason, and by such transformations the world is transfigured.

The point of supplying these various examples, worked and unworked, is to demonstrate that the phenomenon of renewal and transformation in the self/other relationship is far from being restricted to the charismatically ethical cases of the other in need—widow, orphan, stranger. And the reason for this provides an ontological ground even for those privileged ethical cases, undermining Levinas's claim that ethics is first philosophy.[15] Let me now explore this thought.

IV

I have described things at the edge of the world as sites at which events of reversal and transformation take place. And that the world opened up by this whole analysis is one of fractal space and time, one in which things turn out not merely to furnish "our" world, but are open invitations to pass over into other worlds, rabbit holes. Focusing on the worlds these things open up takes us away from "subjectivity." And yet issues of that order are clearly at stake. These reversals all seem to involve a change in the direction of intentionality. Even if one wants to promote a fractal world, a space and time of discontinuous regions, one has to concede that access to such worlds is regulated by what might be called the fluency of selfhood.

I suggest that the entire domain marked by these events of reversal and transformation is generated by the combined operation of three different phenomena: (1) the primordial constitution of selfhood; (2) variable modes of identification with that self; (3) the projection of modes of otherness consistent with one's manner of self-relatedness.

We could describe these events as involving counterprojection, perhaps a cousin of the phenomenological epoche, in which we cease our thetic possessiveness, and allow ourselves to be guided creatively by what we might call play spaces. I am imagining here a generalization of Gadamer's sense of entering the space opened by a work of art.[16]

But our analysis can take another direction. If the shapes taken by the self/other relation are such as to fortify a primordially constituted self, the question remains—from what "material," with what ingredients, is such selfhood constituted? I do not want here to suggest anything very new, except to say that philosophers and phenomenologists need more regularly to take on board that the fundamental matrix of self was constitutively relational from the beginning. (See the essays by William Richardson and Edward Casey in this volume.) By this I mean that there can be no getting away from the original drama in which a human infant arrives on this earth utterly dependent on others to satisfy his absolute needs—especially hunger and sociality. The site of such needs is not yet a self, but the space in which such needs are met or frustrated is surely the original matrix of selfhood—laying down ground-level assumptions about whether and how quickly the world responds to my expressed needs, providing an original formatting to rhythms of desire and satiation, and expectations about my ability, through social interaction, to affect these outcomes. Does a breast appear when I call out for it, when I need it? In the twenty-first century, giving proper weight to these issues is no longer the special concern of psychoanalysis, but of any theory that takes seriously the layeredness of human temporal constitution.[17]

As I see it, the manner and the upshot of these transformative reversals has to do with whether and how the original "material" of self-constitution, my pre-reflexive formative relationships with my early caregiver(s), is enabling or disabling.

Let me give an example: It appears that for decades, exposing the bodies of pregnant women was actually banned from American movies under the Hays Code.[18] It has been suggested that this is because of the implied sexuality thereby betrayed.[19] But it seems just as likely that it betrays an original anxiety—that we (men, especially) who are trained as autonomous beings find it difficult to acknowledge ontological dependency. And yet this dependency is fundamental; the question is whether and how we acknowledge it. Wittgenstein declares that man is an essentially dependent being, and then adds: "And that on which we depend we may call God." Well, we may, but we may not. Irigaray clearly sees that as a displacement of a primary passion whose proper place is the sexual other. Melanie Klein, on the other hand, would see the religious as a displaced refusal to acknowledge the constitutive role of mother. And this refusal is understandable if we lack the means adequately to conceptualize the event or process of self-formation, if, that is, we insist that there must be a self there from the beginning to act *on*.

I am claiming that the domain of these topological transformations and reversals is itself made accessible/available to us to the extent that we have some sort of affective entrée to the grounds of our selfhood, one compatible with dependency, or more specifically, constitutive relationality.

At a certain level of generality, this account of reversibility clearly connects with the chiasmic sensibility that Merleau-Ponty develops in *The Visible and the Invisible*, which generalizes from the relationship between touching and being touched, between the sentient and the sensible—a broader sense of subject and world, or self/other, as mutually implicated, a condition he calls "flesh." He displaces the privilege of the eye in favor of the hand—touching and touched. In my example, the eye itself is already "touched" in the sense of materially conditioned by what it sees, in the shape of the sun.[20] What is "reversed," ruptured is the sense of the virgin birth, the uncaused cause, the autonomous subject. It is a delightful paradox that it may well be that creative autonomy is precisely something that has conditions—perhaps the good-enough mother![21]

In a way that will take us full circle, back to the sun, and the animal, I end with another case of reversal, one on a par with the Copernican revolution and one with both individual and collective significance.

Throwing a banana skin out the car window, pumping effluent into the river, tossing all the old magazines, even trying to forget one's old girlfriends, or filing away random papers under "miscellaneous," all have one thing in common—they are acts of faith in the power of Away. It used to be a place from which things and people did not come back. For the English, the rot set in when the convicts we sent to Australia returned to beat us at cricket. But right across the board these days, Away is not playing ball. We throw things "away," but the landfills are full. We pump effluent into the river, and drinking water downstream is contaminated. What used to be a straight-line has become a circle, indeed a Moebius strip. We still throw things away, but the "other" side of the strip is continuous with this side. This is a fundamental schematic reversal, a dramatic shift in the shape of world-relationality. The nurturing, sustaining world can no longer guarantee its capacity to play that role. Our toxic activity is affecting the earth's capacity to nurture and sustain us. That this could be happening is a major threat to a certain understanding of freedom and agency, one that was perhaps always mistaken.

The transformative events that erupt with a meditation on the sun, or on the animal (and on the earth), would help flesh out an evolutionary story of our constitution as humans. Coupled with the developmental story I proposed, which could be opened by a meditation on Mother, or Breast, or Infant, and we have the ingredients for a story of deep material constitutive relationality, one which would doubtless disturb the traditional poise of our autonomous agency.[22] The next question, one of ethical significance in the sense proposed by Heidegger in his *Letter on Humanism*, would be whether and how we could will—that is performatively embody—a self-understanding in which we are essentially processual, embodied beneficiaries of the evolutionary adventure, in a way that preserves rather than tries to assimilate, the strangeness.

V

This scenario of *fractalterity* would replace that of homogeneous space, either in the sense of my world, laid out before me, or that of a single space in which all world-holders find their place. The world of fractalterity is one that cannot be properly represented, but rather primes us to expect displacements, reversals, and transformations. It is in this world that strangers, gods, and monsters properly flourish, not crowded onto the same stage, as at the end of a play, but as various manners of world-opening, mobilizing, as I have said, the deepest resources by which selfhood is constituted.

Without for a moment putting in question the ethical significance of those events of self-displacement that Levinas highlights, my claim is that the capacity to break out of primary narcissism is not itself specifically ethical but ontological, and shared by events in which imagination, aesthetic adventure, and erotic delight are center stage, rather than any ethical engagement. The stranger may well be in need, demanding the bread from my mouth. But he may equally, as with the Stranger of Plato's *Sophist* (quoted by Heidegger at the start of *Being and Time*) disconcert us, question us, announce the *unheimlich*, and call on me to set out with him on a dangerous or disturbing path: "For manifestly you have long been aware of what you mean when you use the expression '*being*.' We, however, who used to think we understood it, have become perplexed" (*Sophist* 244a).

What I am proposing could be seen as radicalizing the move in *Being and Time* from a metaphysics of subjectivity to one based on constitutive world-relationality. But the version of being-in-the-world I am adumbrating here is one of fractalterity, in which we are essentially exposed to manifold ways of world-making,[23] to alien avenues, to portals of possibility. Through wonder, perhaps also through horror and disgust, we may find our friend, lover, or nation—or indeed ourselves—to be the strangest thing.[24]

Heidegger proves a rich resource here, in particular, his reading of Sophocles's *Antigone*, the first chorus of which begins, "There is much that is strange, but there is nothing that surpasses man in strangeness."[25] Heidegger will merely translate these thoughts into his own language, naming death as that "strange and alien (*unheimlich*) thing that banishes us once and for all from everything in which we are at home." Man is "always and essentially without issue in the face of death. His Da-sein is the happening of strangeness."[26] And death, indeed, is perhaps the key thing at the edge of the world.

Against Levinas, I continue to press the idea that the ethical version of expropriation via the demand of the other is not fundamental. I suggested earlier that I had doubts about infinite obligation, that it was perhaps a misunderstanding. Why do I say this? The structure of being invited, seduced, made demands of, challenged by something that exceeds any representation, is not limited to ethical demand. Indeed it captures quite well the lure of the thing, which, in projecting a world defies representation in any other world in which it is merely furniture. One could say that in the humility required to acknowledge such an excess, there is an ethical opening. But it would apply to death, to a work of art, to God or to the sun, quite as much as to the human other in need. The idea of the infinitely demanding[27] has a heroic cast to it. Derrida will ask how he can justify feeding his cat and not all the other (hungry) cats in the world, and insist that if one thought one could calculate one's obligation, one would have reduced it to an algorithm, a rule, and in effect be guilty of pursuing a good conscience. And the infinitely demanding may mislead us into giving centrality to the ethical example.

Let me try tease apart this bundle of thoughts; a number of strands are woven tightly together. First, there is the idea that my obligation is unrepresentable, second, that this obligation arises through a radical (absolute) schematic reversal in which the other is now at the center of the universe, and thirdly, that this relation to the other is asymmetrical in the sense that there can be no relation to or dealing with any demand I might be thought to make on the other (cf. pure hospitality). An incautious weaving together of these strands leads to a heroic misunderstanding. The reversal of perspective—decentering self-concern—is absolute in the sense that the Copernican revolution was an absolute. Being the center, or rotating around a center are topological options between which there is no compromise, and if we take the idea that no representation is adequate to the other and feed it into this absolute reversal of perspective, we seem to get an absolute incalculable and unfulfillable obligation to the other. There are (at least) two problems with this. The first is that while the reversal of perfect narcissism may indeed be sainthood, such a schema begins with an implausible account of our fundamental condition. Levinas is providing an antidote to a metaphysical position (Being, being-for-self, persisting in Being) without first critiquing it. On my account, the infinite is the "reversal" of an exaggerated original self-absorption.

Second, there is a deep temptation to understand the incalculable, if not exactly quantitatively, as at least able to relate to the calculable in comparative ways: "No response I make could ever be enough," as one might say, suggests we need to do more, even if that too "would not be enough." But an unrepresentable or incalculable demand does not require that conclusion. It means merely that no concept or number can ever adequately represent the obligation we suppose we have. *That* could be captured by much more modest formulas such as "doing one's best in the circumstances," "doing what seems right," "doing what felt appropriate"—none of which claims to *calculate* adequacy. To go further, on this reading, would be to evince a traumatized inability to bring any measure to a circumstance in which the investments of narcissism have been turned outward and locked onto the other.

This whole account I am giving might itself be objected to. Does not its stress on multiple, often incommensurable "worlds" encourage social isolation, political parochialism, and so forth? And surely there is at least a tension between this fractal space (and time) that would resist synthesis, and the idea that the life-support systems of the earth as a whole are in peril, and humanity with it. Does not this latter require the very unified space that our fractal vision forbids?

First, this position is not calculated to meet some extrinsic political agenda! But in fact the broad, shared recognition of a fractal universe is one that might be expected to increase tolerance by highlighting the resistance of "the world" to oversimplification. A fractal model of space does not mean that we cannot meet and talk. It would, however, be consistent with the thought that representation, political or otherwise, may not be as straightforward as we might think, or as reducible to formulas.

As far as the tension with the need for a globally unified vision is concerned, a longer story is needed. I have suggested that the recognition that there is no *Away*, that garbage returns, that the earth is a Moebius strip, is itself an event on a par with the Copernican revolution. Underlying the belief that we will need to protect and sustain the processes that protect and sustain us in particular and life in general, is the thought that while we cannot actually produce an inventory of these processes, cannot fully represent them as a whole, we can nonetheless read the signs: species loss, dead oceans, rising CO_2, the list goes on. A fractal world is compatible with being alert to and acting on critical indicators, even if the mechanisms, the processes, the subsystems they reflect are often opaque to us.

VI

This has been a trailer for a more developed project, one that articulates a heterogeneous understanding of "things at the edge of the world." It fastens on those experiences of reversal, transformation, and estrangement in which "things" conceived of in a broad sense break out of the box of a focused intentionality, and invite us (or challenge us) to different ways of worlding. Our capacity to respond to such events is not unconnected to the shape of our investment, individual and collective, in certain modes of selfhood. True autonomy recognizes its own constitutive relationality and delights in exploring the space of fractalterity. The cultivation of the *unheimlich* more generally is already of ethical significance, and precedes the ethical opening generated by the face of the other in need. The capacity for a certain self-displacement, the openness to Copernican shifts, turns out to be a condition not just for earthly delight, but also for our sustainable existence.

PART II

Sacred Strangeness

Friend, hope for the Guest while you are alive
jump into experience while you are alive!
Think . . . and think . . . while you are alive.
What you call "salvation" belongs to the time before death . . .
If you make love with the divine now, in the next life
you will have the face of satisfied desire.

—Kabir, "Friend, Hope for the Guest"

4

Hospitality and the Trouble with God

JOHN D. CAPUTO

God is trouble.

The name of God is the name of trouble, the name of a disturbance. It solicits us and visits itself upon us, like an uninvited stranger knocking on our door. It is a provocation and an interruption, venerable but dangerous, healing but quite poisonous, grounding but no less destabilizing, an ancient *arche* but very anarchical. From of old, it has perplexed us and driven us quite mad—with love and justice, with passion and rage, with madness of almost every kind. It gives the urge to kill or to risk being killed a perfect alibi. The ambiguity and undecidability are not accidental, not a simple slip or fault in an otherwise pure essence that can be cleaned up and eliminated. They are constitutive, built right in, because the name of God is the name of a limit-state, an extremity, a name in which we are driven to an extreme, our faculties stretched beyond themselves, beyond the possible to the impossible. The people of God are, for better or worse, impossible people, people with a taste for the impossible, with a taste for the worst violence and the most radical peace.

Contrary to the tendency of theology to think in terms of the divine order, and of God as the source of order, I am suggesting something out of order, that we think of God as trouble, as a source of disruption and interruption. Spinoza, following Scotus Eriugena, treated God as a *natura naturans* and *natura naturata*, and that caused both these philosophers considerable trouble in their own life times. But I want to go further and pursue the experiment of thinking of God as the source of irregularity and disordered and displaced orders, of God as *natura unnaturans* and of the world as *natura unnaturata*. God would then be the force or element in things that interrupts the current drift of "nature" and sets it on a new course, that makes things new, that renews them—for better or for worse, since there is nothing to guarantee that to make things new is to make them better.

Is it enough to speak of the undecidability of this name or might we go farther and say it is the name of undecidability itself, of the transitions and passages that transpire between things, between words and things, between words and other words? It is perhaps a name of the irreducible restiveness of our lives, of a dream and a desire, a prayer and a tear, of a restless impatience, a desire for being otherwise, which may of course make things worse, a name which houses our deepest hopes and fears. I say "a" name, not *the* name, not *the* first, last or only name. It purports to be the First Name, and in its own domain it is, which is why it causes so much trouble (and making trouble is not all bad). But it is only one of many first names in multiple domains, caught as it is in a chain of substitutions from which it can break loose only by ceasing to be a name at all.

Far from being some human projection, the name of God arises as a response to a disturbance, a solicitation, a visitation by a stranger, as an answer to the call of I know not what. It is a name we invoke, that we call upon when we are in trouble, but only because we are first of all called upon, asked to respond, provoked, for better or for worst, to either extreme. It is another case of a name we offer as a gesture of hospitality to the coming of a stranger, which makes us lives, our works and days, one among so many scenes of hospitality. If we invoke the name of God, call upon God, we call only because we are first called, even as we love because we are first loved, to which it might be added that we hate because we are first hated. That, says Derrida is the significance of the double yes, the yes, yes. The yes of the call or the solicitation echoed by the second yes of the response.

Let us stipulate, to spare ourselves an infinite analysis, that by hospitality we mean welcoming the stranger. Granted that, I am trying here to be as hospitable as possible to hospitality, to make it as welcome as possible, to make it a guest of honor. I do not want treat hospitality as a passing feature of our being, something to be included on our "to do" list when we itemize the virtues we should cultivate. I would rather say in honor of our guest of honor that hospitality is what we *are*, not (just) what we (should) do. Beyond that, I say more, for that is not yet hospitable enough to hospitality. For hospitality is also the reason that we can *never* say what we are, and why every attempt to do so comes too late, having failed to anticipate the coming of the stranger, who teaches us that things are not what we think that they are. That failure to anticipate the stranger, of course, constitutes the stranger; it is just what the stranger is, depending on what the meaning of "is" is, as Bill Clinton once famously said, when he was talking about a secret that is not the secret in apophatic theology. To say what we "are" is a way we have devised to make things easy for us ourselves, to spare ourselves trouble, which on the present occasion would mean to spare ourselves God, a visitation from God. To say who we are and to stick to it is to try to keep safe the circle of the same, which is the very definition of *in*hospitality.

Hospitality arises in response to a call we did not expect, coming from I know not what or where, whose outcome we cannot know in advance. This could be trouble, and the "could be," the "perhaps," is irreducible. For the non-knowing, please note, is constitutive of the stranger. Otherwise, there would be nothing strange. Like God: if you comprehend it, Augustine said, it is not God, not a stranger. But this is not exclusive to God. It is every bit as true of the self—*quaestio mihi magna factus sum*, Augustine also said—or of the "world," including the so called natural world, which means we cannot forget the animals. We cannot forget the animal that I am (*suis*, am/follow). That is why God and animals have a great deal in common, and why in the history of religion the one is often figured as the other, like angels depicted with the wings of birds. When Jesus goes out in the desert to pray, he is attended by angels and accompanied by the beasts of the field (Mark 1:11), which provide Jesus with hospitality in the desert/Khora.[1] Both God and animals are "strangers" that an excessive and inhospitable humanism would like to master and assimilate. Animals are en masse, we think, obtained by subtraction, "humanity" *minus* the logos that makes us their master. God, Feuerbach thought, is just us all over again, humanity doubled, in idealized alienated form. Nothing strange about either one, humanism thinks. Everywhere humanism sees only the human, Heidegger says. Everything about hospitality resists such an operation, which shows up in Derrida's amazing construction, "divinanimality," which is a strange construction if ever there were one. *Tout autre est tout autre*—that is the postmodern contribution to the medieval list of transcendentals. Each and everything is a something, is constituted by I-know-not-what singularity, or strangeness, which is the seat of the spell it cast upon us.

To the extent that I know who is coming, who is soliciting me and why, I am in command, autonomous. "Caller ID" spells the death of telephone hospitality. It contains the interruption, insures that I remain the master of the call. Then the strangeness of the strange is reduced, and the circle of the same is kept safe, reinforced, shored up.

So hospitality is more a matter of visitation than invitation, as Derrida says, more an unwelcome interruption than a planned conference.[2] Hospitality kicks into high gear when we welcome the unwelcome; otherwise we are just reinforcing the same. Just so, love builds up a head of steam when we love the unlovable, and faith when we believe the unbelievable, all of these being so many fetching variations on the possibility of the impossible. So hospitality is not possible without this impossibility, without risk, without a willingness to put oneself at risk, without putting oneself "out," outside, exposed to the stranger. The first words of hospitality are yes, yes, *oui, oui*, come, amen. But that is risky business. It could be trouble. When to resist what is strange? When to welcome it? Although welcoming the stranger involves a certain death to the self, hospitality is not supposed to be just plain suicide. I do not deny that. I just deny that there is a formula or a program that will decide for us which is which. We do not have the software yet to make this decision for us.

The trouble, the risk is irreducible. Hospitality thus is irreducibly "hosti-pitality."[3] Risky business, putting the circle of the same at risk. Without the risk, it is just more of the same. *Hostis*, the stranger, the unknown, trouble. However it is translated, *hostis* spells trouble. I do not know if this is a friend or foe, a traveler in search of lodging or a marauder. The stranger is both a venerable figure and dangerous. The stranger is maddening, like God. Undecidable, like God. Are strangers and undecidability figures of God? Or is God a figure of the undecidability of the stranger, of openness to the other? Of the riskiness that built into things, which is the condition of possibility and impossibility of moving forward.

The name of God opens up a scene of hos(ti)pitality, of an arche-hospitality that is not for all that any less anarchic. We are called upon to make room for God, to welcome God, to receive God, and then to keep our fingers crossed. We know this name will drive us mad, with justice or violence, with compassion or rage, either way, trouble. Such hospitality is not a character trait to be cultivated, not just one of several virtues, but the field in which everything we do transpires. It describes not a particular part but the very structure or movement of life, not our "essence" but the explanation for why every attempt to prescribe our essence is always already outstripped.

I am trying to begin with the name of God. Am I using or merely mentioning the name of God? Am I invoking this name or being invoked or provoked by it? I do not know, and I do not know if this distinction holds up. Whenever Derrida was asked that question, he would say, if he knew that, he would know everything.⁴ Either way, I am trying to begin with God, without forgetting that the name of God is only one of many beginnings, depending on who and when and where you are, "one possibility in the syntax and in the game of first names," as Derrida said many years ago in an early commentary on *Le prénom de dieu*, the first book of Hélène Cixous.⁵ I am trying to begin with the event that is harbored in the name of God.

I am trying to deal with trouble, liable to get into trouble, asking for trouble, *inviting* trouble, which may then pay us an unexpected call, which is an excellent definition of prayer.

Meister Eckhart Says

This scene of hospitality toward God is not something I have made up. The figure of the divine guest is reproduced throughout the history of spirituality, including the sermons of Meister Eckhart, which have long held my interest. Meister Eckhart famously said, I pray God to rid me of God, meaning I pray the God who can never be mastered and domesticated to rid me of the God whom I think I have in my sights, under control. I pray the God whose coming is always the coming of the stranger to rid me of the God who serves to keep guard over the circle of the same.⁶ I pray God to keep me hospitable to God, to the coming of the God, which sweeps me up in the groundless ground of hosti-pitality.

Meister Eckhart said, "I have begun with a few words in Latin that are written in the gospel; and in German this means: 'Our Lord Jesus went up into a little town, and was received by a virgin who was a wife.'"⁷ As usual, Meister Eckhart takes some liberties with his text, which "actually" says (that means, in the NSRV): "Now as they went on their way, he entered a certain village, where a woman named Martha welcomed (*hypedexato*) him into her home" (Luke 10:38). Luke is telling the story of Mary and Martha, widely taken in the Middle Ages as an allegory of the contemplative life and the active life. By the little town, Eckhart says, the Gospel means the soul itself, the ground of the soul, which must make itself ready for God's arrival, for the coming of God, for the event of God's advent. An advent takes place on the plane of the event. Meister Eckhart's works, both the German sermons and the Latin treatises, are all about the advent of God into the soul—about the birth of the Son in the soul, and with the readiness of the soul for this coming. As such, they belong to the thought of the event, which he stages as a scene of the hospitality the soul extends to God.

Eckhart's reading of this famous story is unorthodox, strange, defamiliarizing. Contradicting Jesus' literal assertion that Mary has chosen the better part and that Martha is distracted (Luke 10: 41–42), Eckhart privileges Martha over Mary on the grounds that Martha is superior to Mary in hospitality. Martha is busy about the many works, the many material things—meals, linens, a swept house—that are needed to welcome Jesus and make him comfortable (*vita activa*). That is not a distraction, but a gift she enjoys beyond Mary who has only one gift, who knows only how to languish at the master's feet (*vita contemplativa*). When Jesus says, "Martha, Martha," that is a sign that Jesus secretly prefers Martha because she has two gifts, while Mary has only one. Hospitality requires both gifts, a doubled yes. Mary seeks peace, as does Martha, but Martha also know that peace comes packaged with trouble.

In this sermon, the hospitable soul is said to be both a "virgin" and "wife," an aporia that Amy Hollywood has explored with great inventiveness in reference to the Beguines to whom Eckhart preached, who were themselves experts of hospitality.[8] By a virgin, Eckhart means that in order to receive God into its home the soul must be pure of all attachments, not only to worldly things but even to religious things, to prayers and fasting and vigils, which can deprive the soul of its purity and freedom for God just as easily as can worldly concerns. I can suffer for my own sake, to show what a hero of faith I am, and not for God's sake.[9] But the purity of the virgin (the "Mary" side) must be joined with the fruitfulness of the wife (the "Martha" side), with a life of works and with all the accompanying trouble of giving birth, in which the soul works not of itself, out of its own autonomy and resources, but in collaboration with God, whom it has received into its ground. So the soul must work like Martha, like a busy and fruitful wife, while also and at the same time being pure of attachment to its own works, for its sole interest lies not in being applauded for its hospitality but in making its guest welcome. The soul is trying to make a gift of hospitality, an expenditure without return, not to reinforce the circle of the same. Hospitality means welcoming the other, for example and exemplarily, God, without appropriating or compromising hospitality as a means of enforcing the circle of the same. The sermon concludes, "That we may be a little town into which Jesus may come and be received . . . may God help us to this. Amen."

Events

By the event, I mean the restiveness in things that makes things stir with something coming. Events, Deleuze says, are not what happens but what is going on *in* what happens which means that when something comes, something unexpected, that is the coming, the advent of the event. When the unforeseeable breaks out and interrupts the course of things (the Derridean sense of event), that means the event hitherto simmering as a virtuality (the Deleuzean sense) has broken out. Events are expressed in names and realized in things, which is why we are never imprisoned by names but always already delivered over by them to things and also why things are never baldly and immediately given but always already named, interpreted, construed. Thinking is conducted on the plane of the event, on an anonymous quasi-transcendental field, khoral, ankhoral, a primal site of movement and rest, life and death, joy and suffering, friend and foe, providing the groundless ground of hosti-pitality.

To meditate upon the name of God means to expose ourselves to the event that is contained in that name, to give it its head, all the while eluding the police of "religion," of the confessions and of orthodoxy that seek not to welcome but to hold captive the anarchic energy of this name. To no avail. For the name of God, like hospitality itself, contains what it cannot contain, contains the uncontainable, like the *Khora akhoraton*, which is not purely and simply isolable from *Khora* pure and simple, the nameless name in the *Timaeus*. I am not interested in "religion" but in God. "Religion" is what Meister Eckhart warns us against—fasting and vigils and observances. I go further: I am not interested in God but in the name of God. I go still further: I am not interested in the name of God but in the event that is harbored in the name of God. For the name of God, as dangerous as it saving, as life-giving as it is death-dealing, contains the uncontainable event of a provocation, a solicitation, an interruption, and a promise, to which we are called upon to offer hospitality. In a word, trouble. I pray God to rid me of God; I pray for the coming of the event promised and provoked by the name of God.

Hospitality is always hospitality to events, where event are the seeds of surprise, of what is being "harbored" in words and things, unseen and unforeseen. The several scenes of hospitality are scenes of events, in which we are taken by surprise, for better or for worse. Hosti-pitality.

The name of God is the name of a promise—and a promise cannot be made safe from a threat without being turned into a sure thing, a guarantee. That is why we ought to be careful what we pray for; we may get it. I propose that the promise that transpires under the name of God is the promise of the world itself, of the play of the world, so that to invoke the name of God is in the end a way of calling upon something embedded within the world, embedded within ourselves, in what Meister Eckhart liked to call the ground of the soul, where my ground and God's ground are the same. That means I am structured by an exposure to God even as—although this would take us off in another direction—God is structured by an exposure to the world. Deep calls upon deep, a mutual exposure, for better or for worse.

To make ourselves ready to receive this promise into our house, Meister Eckhart said, we must be pure as a virgin while being fruitful like a wife.

The name of God is a figure inscribed on the plane of the event, where it must be situated, resituated, reinscribed, like figures inscribed by the Demiurge in khoral space. As the name of an event, the name of God is entangled with the course of mundane life, with the rhythm of its joys and fears, with the terrors of the night and the exaltations of the day, which is not to say that it is any less inscrutable, any less a matter of an absolute secret, any less *tout autre*. What classical theology was searching for under the figure of the "transcendence" of God is here refigured as the provocation of God, as the provocation of the event. What was described in a certain theology as arching over or "beyond" the world is here redescribed as a modality of the world, as a way the world catches us up in its sweep, makes itself felt in all its intensity and is recorded not in high theology but in a theopoetics conducted closer to the ground.

The name of God is a venerable entry in the vocabulary of transcendence, which is a way of speaking about the coming of the other. Transcendence is not the opposite of immanence but another way to lay claim to immanence, another way the lines of force that traverse the field of immanence are intensified and made salient. In transcendence the distinctive forces of immanence are pushed to the limit, underlined, figured, and this shows up in limit-words and limit-cases, like God and death, love and hate, friend and foe. Transcendence is a category of immanence, a particular mode of immanence in virtue of which the flow of immanence forces itself to the surface. The figures of transcendence, which readily assume the form of literature or mythology, of dreams or desires, are ways of retracing the lines of immanence in imaginative form, ways of reclaiming immanence in all its richness and intensity.

We are meditating a provocation issuing from a certain recess, nestled among the obscure secrets of the world, from the secretive time of the world, which we think of as the stirring of twofold retreat. On one side, a withdrawal into a past that was never present, and on the other a withholding from the present of an unforeseeable future. The present thus is doubly displaced, doubly stretched out, pulled apart in opposing directions, opened by opposing forces. The present is thereby structured by the unpresentable so that by the present we mean the space that is opened up between two unpresentables. On one side, the present is drawn out of itself by the invitation of something promised, and on the other end it is drawn out of itself by the solicitation of something immemorial that has all along been stirring. Not time and eternity, not this world and some other sphere where time does not flow, but two modalities of time, two ways time temporalizes and the world "worlds," to deploy a couple of early Heideggerisms. Time is co-constituted by a structural too late and too early. Coiled within the settled time of the present there stirs the unsettled and unsettling time which is out of joint, which disjoins the world, which prevents the closure of the world, which the metaphysical imagination confuses with the eternal or other worldly.

One might say that this disjuncture creates an opening for the event, except that the event is the event of the disjuncture. The disjuncture is the space-time of the provocation, for what is provocative is the event. The axiom of any "ontology" of the event, were such a thing possible, is that when it comes to events, to be is to provoke. Events are not present, but what is provocative about what is present, where the tendency of the settled present is to prevent the event. We would not say that the event is, but that the event provokes. We would not say that God is but that God calls, and whether that provocation is then instantiated in some hyperbeing or other is no business of ours. The event is not what happens but what is going on in what happens, what is provocative about what happens. If we can speak of a theology of hospitality that would mean a theology of the event that takes its point of departure from the name of God, that feels about for the provocative event this name contains, without forgetting that that every names harbors a provocation, which is why any name is deconstructible. It is also important to remember that this talk of "names" is not meant to privileges nouns, or even verbs, and the inquiry made by thinkers such as Levinas, Marion, and Michel Serres into the role of prepositions is indispensable. Meister Eckhart says we must make ourselves adjectives of God, while Michel Serres says that angels operate as our prepositions.[10]

Martha, or Hospitable Agency

A provocation is not an agent; agents respond to provocations. The provocation of God is not to be imagined as something that God does, as if God were a superagent in the sky, but something that takes place in and under the name of God, which is the philosophical wisdom and realistic concession behind the adage "God helps those who help themselves." Strong theology, which is a theology of an agent-God, requires ventriloquists, people, men usually, authorizing themselves to speak in the name of God. Strong theology is megaphonics, ways men find to amplify their voice, by disguising their human all too human voice as the voice of God. Hospitality to events requires that agency be left to actual, mundane, and identifiable agents, whom no one should confuse with God and who, above all, should not confuse themselves with God. There is no more salutary offspring of the theology of events than the recognition that it is human beings who claim to do things in the name of God, which is why the history of religion is inevitably also a history of violence. God is not well described as an agent with mysterious powers to do things that for all the world seem to be the doings of more mundane powers.

But remember the agency of Martha, the wife who was a virgin, the double gift. Martha is an agent; she acts, but she acts from the ground of the soul, which is one with the ground of God. That means she is an agent mobilized in response to a provocation, to an event that is figured in Meister Eckhart in the images of the Christian narrative. The virgin part of the soul is to keep ourselves free from the illusion of an autonomous subject—that is the critique of the humanist subject—while the Martha part is to replace it with a responsible subject, an agent whose action is the agency of the other in me, a hospitable agent.

Hospitality is hospitality to the event. Theology is hospitality to the event sheltered in the name of God. God is not a powerful doer and mysterious undoer but the powerless power of the event. God does not do, undo or fail to do anything, but certain things get themselves done in or under the name of God, in response to the event that is harbored there. That is why it is futile to blame God for doing us wrong and unnecessary to exonerate God's ways before human courts. It is human beings who belong in human courts. The name of God is not the name of somebody doing or not doing something, but the name of an event that breaks open the present, for better or for worse, events such as life and death, pleasure and pain, joy and sadness, good and evil, love and hate, constituting beings both aggressive and sympathetic, which is why we are capable both of attacking and defending the stranger. In the ambiguity of this unstable middle, the proportionately ambiguous power of freedom makes its wary way. The hoary theological "problem of evil" thus has nothing to do with all the choices that a sovereign omnipotent and omniscient God could have but failed to make leaving us in our present sorry and befuddled state. The problem of evil has to do with the ambient and chaotic play of ambiguous beings, an ambience beyond mere ambiguity, since our choices rarely boil down to two. The ambience of our being is its greatest if riskiest resource.

Perhaps

Perhaps the name of God is the name of "perhaps" itself, of the quasi-transcendentality in things, which marks *être* with *peut-être*, above all with the possibility of the impossible. Perhaps God comes to mind as the name not of something transcendent but of something transcendental; perhaps not of something transcendental but of something quasi-transcendental, namely, the open-ended and restless desire inscribed in words and embedded in things, the disquieted desire inscribed in words, their *conatus*, as Spinoza called it, but not a selfish or self-aggrandizing one, which would mean to build a fortress around the same, but a welcoming and hospitable one that would expose itself to the risk of becoming. Perhaps the name of this perhaps is the name of becoming, of becoming new, of making all things new, renewing things, which is what we mean by the kingdom of God, that is, the field or plane on which the event this name harbors can transpire. Perhaps the name of God, which we have thus far characterized as trouble, is also the name of the risk of the perhaps. So much God, so much trouble and risk.

We might say, following the dizzying exchange between Cixous and Derrida,[11] that hospitality to the event turns on the undecidable play of the "might," the suggestive slippage from the powerful "might" of God, the power of God almighty, to the powerless power of the "might" as in "might be" or it "might have been," the power of a suggestiveness or subjunctiveness, of a possibility or a perhaps, of an invitation or solicitation. The theology of hospitality to the event depends upon the grammatological slippage from the indicative mood to the subjunctive mood. Theology, like deconstruction, should be written in the subjunctive, because it is all about subjunctions, modifications of the ontological into the de-ontological or me-ontological. What is disjunctive about the event appears grammatically in the subjunctive, which subverts the settled nominations and conjunctions of the present. That is why, *pace* Heidegger's famous analysis of the Anaximander fragment, Derrida locates justice, which is an interruption, a solicitation, a promise, in a disjunction or dislocation. Disjoining is the work of the event, which does not mean what the event "does," but the way the event provides the plane upon which things get themselves done.

In terms of actually getting things done, events are a weak force, a powerless power. There is no force, no power, until a response is mobilized, which fills up what is lacking in the power of the event, giving it body, where the point of the response is to make itself worthy of the event that happens to it, like Mary and Martha trying to make themselves worthy of the visit that Jesus pays them. This making itself worthy provides the entrée for an ethics and politics of the event. To speak of the weakness of God is not, then, to ascribe a failing in God, a flaw in the divine nature, as if upon closer inspection, it turns out that God is strangely missing one of the divine attributes, the way one would be missing a tooth. It is to redescribe God, the whole God, as a provocation, and as a provocation God is provocative all the way down. God is not missing something. To speak of the weakness of God is not to say that God is missing a limb or a faculty; it is simply to say that the name of God is the name of an event, of something unconditional without force, which is a matter of a "might" not might, of a "perhaps" or a "maybe," not a supreme being, where the might and muscle and actuality is to be supplied by mundane agents. That of itself ought to give pause to those who speak in the name of God, who claim to act in and under that name. They are responsible to God, responsible for God, for the being and actuality that God has in the world, for the way God comes to exist in the world. They are responsible for protecting God's good name.

Hospitality is a way to transform the world, to make all things new, which is not carried out by some invisible hand of inner necessity or by an equally invisible but transcendent hand in the sky, both of which are too heavy handed, too hard, too strong, too ham fisted to deal with events. Hospitality is rather a work of collaboration with more subtle forces, with uncontainable virtual systems, making a home for the play of events without submitting it in advance to the categories of metaphysics, which impose conditions on events. Such categories are the means we have devised to arrest the play of the perhaps. Events play together, constituting an open-ended whole, an internal complexity, a complex chaosmos, a nontotalizing chaosmotic process of self transformation, of autopoiesis, of auto-deconstruction, the complex play of perhaps.

The Inglorious Glory of the Flesh

I am willing to admit that up to now this all been a bit abstract. So let us make it as concrete as possible by pointing out that hospitality to the event takes its most elemental form as hospitality to the flesh, in all its weakness. By the weakness of the flesh I mean that while the "body" is transparent, easily forgotten or lost sight of because of the ease with which it navigates about the world, "flesh" draws attention to itself, for better or for worse, in sickness and in health, in *jouissance* and suffering. Flesh is opaque and burdensome, a site of strain and difficulty, constantly calling attention to itself, and however glorious quite inglorious. The many weaknesses of the flesh—incapacity, disability, disease and death—co-constitute the life of flesh; they do not contradict it. The weaknesses of the flesh intensify life, raising its pitch to the limits. They do not refute the provocation of God but constitute so many occasions for the invocation of the name of God, so many invitations to respond to the name of God, where the name of God means to say yes to life in all its tumult and difficulty, joy and sorrow, promise and risk. That is why it makes perfect sense to speak of a "disabled God" (Eiesland and Fletcher), or a "mortal God" (Derrida), of "the body of God" (McFague), or of a "suffering God" (Bonhoeffer), or even of the God of "indecent theology" (Althaus-Reid).[12] Difficulty, disability, indecency, disease and death itself are features of life, part of the way the multiple forms of life are etched, and not a lasting punishment for a fateful exercise of bad judgment in Eden. They no more constitute refutations of life than they constitute contradictions of the divine nature or attributes incompatible with the divine being requiring the urgent attention of theodicy. For God is the God as *natura unnaturans et unnaturata*. They are not a fall, or a sign of a fallen life, but life *in extremis*, so many twists and turns of life, bearing witness to the extremity of the event, the event of excess and exceeding that is discharged in and under the name of God and that commands our response. The idea behind the theology of hospitality to the event is to make ourselves worthy of the events that happen to us, however humbling and disabling they may seem to be. "For better or for worse" is the inscrutable and uncircumventable equation, the unavowable vow of our marriage to the flesh of the world, to the world of the flesh, where "flesh" is both the substance and the figure of this nonstable matrix, this autodeconstructive and autopoetic and primal pool.

Orthodox theology is in search of the grounds of our hope, and so it should be, so are we all, but it will not grant that these grounds are groundless grounds, that the world does not rest on something firm and transparent, some unmixed and risk free source, and to that extent it does not rest at all. Orthodoxy is the orthopedics of thought, which wants to straighten the limbs of thought. Orthodoxy is inhospitable to the stranger. It is afraid of the strange alterity of the disabled, of the different, afraid of monsters and of monstrous showings whose monstrosity is mainly a matter of looking different. Orthodoxy promises boundaries that will insure that everything within will be right and upright, safe and straight, happy and good. It will not concede the radical restlessness in things, that the world offers us multiple chances but few guarantees, that a fully grounded hope is not hope, just a good investment. Orthodoxy will not grant that to return to the source is to return to the nonoriginary origin, the originary risk, to the chanciness, the free play in things, the promise/threat, to an unnerving chaosmic mix whose unforeseeability insures that life is risky business even as we harbor hopes for things that eye has not seen nor ear heard.

The disability of the flesh is one way that flesh fleshes itself out, representing a special revelation that flesh is a constant becoming-disabled, a way that life stirs, twists and turns, part of life's multiplicity, pliancy, unfolding, part of the way life breaks up its regularities, disturbs its patterns, part of its harshness and difficulty, all of which are partners of and ingredients in its joy. *Natura unnaturata*, nature denatured, destabilized, deterritorialized, autodeconstructed, denormalized. Once we stop thinking about God as a perfect being, as an entity possessed of every possible compatible perfection, as an *actus omnium actuum*, we can begin to think in terms of the name of an event in which we seek out and affirm what we hold dear, what makes for an open ended flourishing or deeper excellence in life. The God of pure act, of actual and absolute perfection, of perfect rectitude, makes everything bent, slanted and oblique look scandalous and dark, suspicious and sinister, sinister, left-handed and sinful, the "residue of Eden," which is the best that Augustine could come up with when he considered disabled bodies, as Sharon Betcher points out.

But in a theology of hospitality, God is not an ideal, or an ideal being, or perfect act, but the name of an event in which we put ourselves at risk, expose ourselves to what drives us to the limits, to what we desire with a desire beyond desire, to what we love *per impossibile*, with prayers and tears, which are the garments of the event, the angels that announce the good news of the event. "God" is not the name of the perfect constellation and complete actualization of all possible perfection, but of a provocation, a perhaps, a solicitation, an expected visitation, an interruption, which calls us to the limits of joy and grief, like a muffled voice carried by the wind. God is figured not by the blinding sun of Platonism but by the stirring waters of the event, the face of the deep as Catherine Keller argues.[13] God does not belong to the domain of the *supra naturam* but of the *natura unnaturans*. God is not the hyperousiological I know not what of negative theology, but a call from I know not where. God is not an unlimited being but the God of limit situations. God is not an ideal of being but the ordeal of an event astir within being, an impatience within the world that pushes the world beyond itself, beyond the horizons of foreseeability, making the world risky and restless with the promise/threat. God is not a pure act but a pure interruption, not pure perfection but pure provocation, not a being but an event, the name of an event whose name I do not know, the name of a secret, of the secret sources and resources of life. The name of God is the name of a stranger who seeks a room in our home, of a coming, an advent, which we are called upon to welcome.

Such is the transcendence flesh permits, not the magical transcendence effected by a being almighty, but the transcendence of the "might" that stirs impatiently in the event, of the "perhaps" that is restlessly astir in the provocation of God.

Amen

Yes, I said, yes, come, *viens, oui, oui*—that is the prayer of hospitality, the hospitality of prayer, the prayer by which we are constituted, the prayer we are always becoming, the peculiarly postmodern prayer of a religion without religion, the passion for God in a postmodern world.

"That we may be a little town into which Jesus may come and be received . . . may God help us to this. Amen."

But without forgetting that when we pray we are asking for trouble.

5

The Hospitality of Listening

A Note on Sacramental Strangeness

KARMEN MACKENDRICK

Among the most promising-seeming possibilities for an ethics linked to theology—always a risky proposition—is that of regarding the world as sacramental. A sacramental sensibility seems, potentially at least, a way to a valuing of some aspects of the world, but not a way particularly welcoming of the strange or the stranger. But fundamental to such a sensibility, I want to argue here, is a discipline of attention, of a carefully open listening, and such an attentiveness in fact requires that we listen to what we do not already understand, what sounds in our ears and appears to our eyes as something foreign. Most briefly: attention must be paid. Or, as Jean-Luc Nancy has it, "The first hospitality is nothing other than listening."[1] Listening, though with all of our senses, is at the heart of the sacramental.

A glance at the history of sacraments, both in language and in practice, seems to make rather improbable the relation of sacramental to hospitable. *Sacramentum* first means "[A] pledge of money or property which was deposited in a temple by parties to a lawsuit or contract" and "later . . . an oath of allegiance made by soldiers to their commander and the gods of Rome."[2] The term seems to have been first used in its ecclesiastical sense by Tertullian around the year 210, roughly to render the Greek "mysterion" by which writers like Clement of Alexandria designate the "representations of sacred realities in signs and symbols . . . which only the initiated could understand."[3] In his influential early discussions, Augustine offers a useful pair of terms: *sacrum signum*,[4] making the sacrament a *sign* of the sacred; and *verbum visibile* (visible word), making the given word a sensible one as well.[5] Most of his theory, and sacramental theory generally, has focused on operant rites, but these very terms suggest the reasons that it is hardly novel to regard other things as sacramental—Christ, most frequently, but sometimes creation itself, and it is on this last that I want to dwell. As I get started here, I will specifically note what will be obvious, that I am taking and reading, in part because it is the tradition to which I am least a stranger, a specifically Christian, indeed rather Catholic, notion of sacrament[6]—but precisely in the service of seeing if it opens up at all, or if reading such signs necessarily closes off any other reading of the world—and so any other readers, too.

Sacramental rituals require some community within which their meaning is read, into which the rites themselves may initiate or further bind—in which the signs and words are shared, as if in a language. They set "us" off, it seems, from those who are not us, both those who are not initiated into the mysteries and those who cannot read the signs.[7] Lewis Mackey points out in his discussion of Augustine, "It is faith that constitutes the sign as sign. . . . How do you know that what you see or hear is language, that is, meaningful marks or noises? . . . The ambiguity of signs . . . which makes it possible for faith to regard them as such, also permits their deradication from significance."[8] Faith, then, sees signs; it is in itself a kind of semiotic will. But this would seem to close off any community of the faithful more than ever, at least if faith has already interpreted the signs, already constructed a system of propositional beliefs impervious to evidence and outsiders. If sacraments have meaning only among those who have faith in them, how could they be other than communally hermetic, deeply unwelcoming?

Perhaps fortunately for faith, or at least for those wishing to engage the sacramental philosophically, this version, whatever popular currency it may have, is hardly exhaustive. Augustine's own conversion, we might recall, is a matter not of belief—he is intellectually convinced by Ambrose's Neoplatonic readings of Christianity years before his conversionary drama—but of desire. Augustine seeks desperately not to be convinced of facts, but to be faithful in desire's direction. This is faith in the sense of fidelity, with its willingness to live in the question and uncertainty, its knowledge that all could be otherwise, its own place in the promise—and its own possibility of welcome.[9] Having faith in the reading of signs, such fidelity must also be able to speak—to read, as it were, aloud. Contemplating the curious Christian notion of divine incarnation, Nancy writes in *Dis-Enclosure* of "a faith that . . . would be nothing other than the 'courage' invoked to say the 'strange.' The strange: a divine body discerning."[10] A sacramental fidelity might help us to make sense of this—faith reads signs and perhaps what it reads, and what it says, is that very "text" of the sensible world discerned in this divinely corporeal strangeness.

There is a mysterious element to this strangeness, reminding us that in some ways the Latin marks a curious transition from the Greek. The mystery is what cannot, possibly must not, be shown; to say, behold, I show you a mystery, is not to strip the mystery away, but to show that there *is* a mystery. The *sacramentum* seems rather more fixed, indeed bound. The world read as *sacrum signum* occupies this territory between the contractual promise and the faithful mystery.

Though he might seem an unexpected source, Friedrich Nietzsche in fact sees the very possibility of promising as being at the root of ethics.[11] How, Nietzsche famously asks in his genealogy of morals, do we breed an animal with the capacity (in some translations, the right) to make promises?[12] His answer founds promise in memory and desire: to promise, we must be able not to forget, and this not out of any "mere passive inability," but from "an active *desire* not to rid oneself, a desire for the continuance of something desired once, a real *memory of the will*."[13] As active desire, this "memory of the will" is not just a recollection of having once willed, but a regathered willing. In promising is the will's own memory, the desire not to rid oneself of that desire one desired once—the will's fidelity to itself, to its desire. To read the promise of the world, then, is to read it illuminated by a desire so strong as to make itself memory.

To lead us toward some sense of what sort of mysterious promise this might be, I offer briefly a summary of some of my own recent thinking on a pair of sacramental rites,[14] the eucharist and the practice of sacramental forgiveness once called penance, later reconciliation, and popularly confession, hoping from these sacraments in the narrow sense to move us toward some sense of a broader sacramentality. The eucharistic rite and the meal upon which it is ostensibly based infold memory ("do this in memory of me") with the promise of return, and a transubstantiated presence nonetheless shot through with absence. "This is my body" calls into the moment of presence the memory of loss and the hope of recurrence. This is not a promise only about the future, but neither can it ever be wholly within the present. It does something *to* the present: it makes the present *promising*. We do not await it, not simply; we dwell in it, but in that dwelling is the awareness of the fragility of presence, the possibility, as absence meets memory, of mourning.

Forgiveness, sacramental or not, folds the future into the past as a sort of inversion of trauma: neither forgetting nor repeating the past, it instead retells the stories of past harms in a revelation of new meaning, thus releasing trauma's grip on the future. No longer needing to conform to the image of the past, futurity is reopened in its unknowableness as a space of possibility. Divine forgiveness is given in the structure of time: so long as time has not ended (and we all know what conceptual puzzles *that* would create), something other is possible. The promise of forgiveness is precisely the chance for newness, the world born again. The very mutability of the material world, its capacity to shift from one form to another, which so perturbs Platonists in general and especially Augustine in his reading of Genesis (*Confessions* 12.12 [15]), becomes here a source of hope, the possibility of being-otherwise.

So eucharistically we find the promise that the present is transformed by desire's intensity such that it will be made into memory for rewilling, for being promised again; in forgiveness we find the promise that memory itself can be made novel, and in this the future can be given its rightful uncertainty, in which alone we can rewill. In both cases, we note the formality of the promise, not just the absence but also the defiance of specifiable content.[15] In each the sacramental oath is not contractual but only promising, and joy has its sense only inextricably from uncertainty and sorrow. And this promising is the sense of the world read as promise, as well—a reading that requires us to open our idea of sense-making to various sorts of strangeness.

Perhaps what we experience and describe as "promising" here is what opens, whether what is opened is the newly revealed past, the present interleaved with mourning and joy, or the future in its restored novelty—that is, both its newness and its strangeness. This opening draws or entices us: the world without promise is foreclosed and emptied out, a space of despair[16]—as Georges Bataille has it, "the absence of hope, of all *enticement*."[17] Despair—numbered by Thomas Aquinas among the theological sins (ST 2.2.20.1)—sees a world without promise.

How, though, would a world entice us out of our despair, show itself as promising—and in so doing, obligate us in turn? It seems obvious that we would have to read it rightly, and the longest-standing answer as to how we might do that is perhaps in the Neoplatonic ethics of attention to beauty,[18] which we might not follow in its inward turn away from the senses, but can follow as far as its urge for a discipline of attention to the beautiful, a discipline both taken up and troubled in Neoplatonism's Christian versions. When Augustine pays attention to beauty—asking the beautiful things of the world where and what his beloved God is—his question is attention itself, and it is beauty that answers, beauty that simply in being declares God to him.[19] As Jean-Louis Chrétien notes, "The

Augustinian notion of beauty as a voice is in itself more persuasive than the idea that the things of the world are an occasion for us to praise God."[20] Beauty invokes our attention and provokes us to *join* it in praise, drawing us to itself as the promise of happiness, to steal a much later phrase from Stendhal.[21] But the happiness, here, is nothing distinct from the promise.

Because Augustine, more resolutely than most Neoplatonists, refuses panentheism, his vocal world is not saturated with, but traced by, the God who is nonetheless absent from it; said, but not found, in all things. Beauty remains a call that is its own and only answer. It is in this calling that it opens the world, makes the world promising. As Chrétien puts it, beauty "does not take place, [but] makes space. It does not occur in a preconstituted place from which it derives its condition of possibility, as if it were coming out on to a stage. . . . By taking place, it makes space: in other words, it causes this place, here, to arise in all its jubilant and heartrending exclamation."[22]

In an only slightly more poetic rendition, Rainer Maria Rilke opens the *Sonnets to Orpheus* with the "pure uprising" of a tree, a tree raised at once in the world and the ear by Orpheus's singing. Orpheus sings, and "everything falls silent": in the space of his song rises the space for speaking, for "fresh beginnings."[23] Place and time alike are opened by beauty and by the words of praise—sacramental words even outside the rite, in response to the world. Praise is a peculiar version of language, in which the content is revealed as much to the speaker as to the addressee.[24] It is a matter not of information but of exclamation, even of the heartrending sort; it does not inform us about the world but rather opens it newly before us. In this newness we encounter once again what is strange to us, and welcome, promising, in that strangeness. So when we praise the world in its beauty, we *join* in voicing praise; we do not describe beauty but echo it, our meaning taking its sense in and from this sudden opening before our senses; we render choral the speech (or perhaps it ought to be song) of the world.[25] We receive the promising in our astonishment—and perhaps, as Rilke elsewhere suggests, we are here just to say it, to read the world aloud.[26] But we can only thus say it if we are in fact open to astonishment, if we read in the suspension of knowing that makes astonishment possible: if, even as we say, we *listen* for what we do not already know, could not already have said—listen before we understand, without the presumption of understanding. What both allows and requires our sacramental saying is an attentive openness that likewise allows and requires us to hear the strange.

Beauty imposes upon us the peculiar obligation of the very attention to which it answers, without which we would never hear it. And beauty is, if not in fact terrifying,[27] always a bit strange: it stops us and unsettles us, makes us rearrange our perceptions, makes us see again. But even this is too simple if we think of it as prettiness that, as reward for our attention, sets us at ease, telling us that God is in his heaven and all is right with the world. Chrétien suggests that "there is within [beauty] a power which breaks presence, which separates and invites separation, a power of denudation and dispossession, a demand for itinerancy."[28] Beauty, in opening spaces, does not securely enclose us; to be invited is to be risked, too. In this strange spatializing, an ethics of beauty moves away from that Plotinian approach compelling us to turn our attention inward, there to find that all beauty is One, that alienation is impossible, and that we must be wary of too much investment in our senses. But our responsive openness to the opening—as we have known with particular vividness since Levinas—can hardly be restricted to happiness; destitution calls us too, and we are as responsible to need, to what is missing, damaged, lost in the sensible world, as we are responsive to beauty. More: it is the same openness, the same hospitable listening, that responds in us to beauty and to need, and the sacrament as promise is equally this demand.

This call of the destitute other is not quite so distant from the call of beauty (in its strangeness, belonging to the strange and the stranger) as it might seem. Beauty calls to us not merely where it rises up but also where it is not—where what should have offered the promise of happiness has been destroyed or refused or desperately damaged. To continue with Chrétien, "the distress opened in us by the devastation and growing ugliness of people, places, or things is another form of this harrowing experience of beauty: anyone who destroys beauty seems to us to be profaning, in some degree, that by which the world really is a world, containing things that demand that one stop and consider them (in the dual sense of looking at them and respecting them)."[29] To consider, to be responsive to the beauty of the world must entail vulnerability to beauty and ugliness both. Or, to invoke Rilke again, lament arises only in the space of praise.[30] We hear praise and we voice it in the double call of attentiveness, but in this synesthetic space, too, our mourning may arise, and sometimes must: we mourn where we might have rejoiced, where the promise is lost or forestalled or destroyed, cut off or walled off or simply denied.

If we are insensitive to beauty and to joy, then the call of destitution is at best an unrelieved burden of duty; if we are insensitive to woundedness and destitution, then the call of beauty is a frivolous aestheticism. We are drawn both to the work of caring for the other and to the joy of careful attention. It is in this doubleness of care and delight that we find ourselves returned to be the sign of the promise, beauty always in dispossession, in the strangeness of what rises up, that divine discerning of the flesh, of the body as "unique bearer of speech . . . the very site of any response to the appeal."[31]

The efforts to disentangle beauty and destitution, enticement and fear, joy and sorrow are also efforts to tidy the sacramental promise back into a contract fulfilled and finalized and kept, to read simple signs that inform us of a clearly defined divine entity—ideally one in which power is neatly divorced from vulnerability, one we can praise without lament. Much—probably most—of Christianity does just this, but it thus takes the sacramental firmly out of the world—thus rendering the promise unsigned, the word invisible. If we want to remain in the world—that is, if we really want any sense of the sacramental—we are recalled to attention.

We must listen to what we see, or see, like Augustine, as if in our sight the world spoke and we said it again. In attending to what calls, we hear, as Nancy reminds us, the chance of hospitality. Again, we can trace some version of this idea, hospitable listening, back to Nietzsche, who links attentive listening to hospitality in the *Gay Science:*

> This is what happens to us in music: First one has to *learn to hear* a figure and melody at all, to detect and distinguish it. . . . Then it requires some exertion and good will to *tolerate* it in spite of its strangeness, to be patient with its appearance and expression, and kindhearted about its oddity. Finally there comes a moment when . . . we wait for it, when we sense that we should miss it if it were missing; and now it continues to compel and enchant us relentlessly.
>
> But that is what happens to us not only in music. That is how we have *learned to love* all things that we now love. In the end we are always rewarded for our good will, our patience, fairmindedness, and gentleness with what is strange; gradually, it sheds its veil and turns out to be a new and indescribable beauty. That is its thanks for our hospitality.[32]

This is a lovely passage, but I would have to say, as one seldom does, that Nietzsche does not go quite far enough. Even here, beauty is strangeness that seduces us because we have not merely allowed, but carefully disciplined, ourselves to be seduced, and we remain enraptured only while, even in the comfort of its familiarity, it remains a little bit strange, a little new even in the comfort of its familiarity.

If we listen for the call with the idea that we know what we will hear—or what we will answer—we have not listened at all: "To be listening," says Nancy, "is always to be on the edge of meaning."[33] Remaining secure in knowledge of what the world signifies, we will have no idea, and no way to discern, what strangeness might arise before any of our senses. When we *listen* to another person, we listen to the call, not only of her words, but also of the world to which those words call us and in which those words respond: the world in which they have their sense, the praise into which they join. We try to hear the sense of her faith—not the list of beliefs, but the desires and delights, revoiced in praises and laments, which give sense to her world—but the only way to try to hear this is to suspend the presumptions that underpin our usual understandings. Fidelity reads signs in light of desire: the world is sacramental not simply insofar as it "is," but as it is read; in the voice of praise we not only hear, but echo, in paying attention. We listen not only for another's web of meaning, but also for the astonishment of other desires.[34]

We can attend to others' words and the world's signs only together. To have the capacity to respond to the promising, we must retain the openness that listening is, but in this opening, we must be able to hear the sign, read the visible word, across faiths yet without reducing the other to the known. In this attention to the world mutually constructed with language, there is the chance of community, of the sacrament, of the mystery: not now as the secret sign designed to seal in those who belong and exclude those who do not, but as the mysteriously promising which invites us together, invites us both to join in praise and to listen with. What we hear will be strange, as our words and others' and the world's echo and redouble one another, offering both praise for the world as it is and petition for the world as it ought to be, for beauty mourned.

We must listen, and look, and touch, and more. Divinely to discern the world is to find the divine in the sensuous; to say it, as if into being, as we see that it is good. To attend with care, as if to beauty, is not only to discern strangeness, but also even to *make* strange, to force oneself out of the known and the familiar—even in the face *of* the known and the familiar. This is what art often does, transforming rather ordinary objects and sounds and movements by the very act of presenting them for our attention. In this, in fact, is some important part of the long shift of our aesthetic sensibility away from the classical sense of an ordered and symmetrical beauty and toward a broader sense of the interesting, the surprising, the arresting, in which the Platonic sense of astonishment in the face of beauty is nonetheless retained. To welcome beauty is to welcome that making-strange, looking again at what was boringly familiar; the strangeness of art, of philosophy, of madness, and love. Even what we already saw, already knew, may hold the possibility of something else, of beginning again in wonder. In the cultivation of this wonder by the discipline of desire—not its suppression, but its attentive awakening—is also the cultivation of the hospitality of listening, with its attendant risk.

The risk is that of trusting in the promise, being seduced by the world, risking knowledge in favor of a learned and disciplined practice in being ignorant[35] of what is and of what is to come, even of the meaning of what has been; to run the risk of listening to the stranger before we know if we can understand. But there is no promise without such risk: its bond is not that of the contract, but that of possibility, the mutual, uncertain invitation that we hear in the saying of it. The discipline of attention to beauty reveals to those who practice it the strangeness of the world, its capacity to stop us and to open spaces, its promise. Such attention reveals both the astonishment of the unexpected and the devastation of possibility's foreclosure. The strangeness of the world extends to the strangeness of those we call strangers, to whom hospitality demands that we attend in both their inviting promise of happiness and the hollow spaces of their need—and that we attend not simply by looking, but by listening to a language that never quite perfectly translates, no matter how nearly we share it, a language in which, still uncertain, we just might hear and make promises.

We always have the option of refusing to make promises or to accept them, not just in a contractual sense, but also in the sense of disallowing the strangeness of others and their worlds to intrude. We have the option of finding the world uninteresting, of refusing the discipline of desire that responsivity is, by which we strengthen our will to will again, to say of desire yes, always. Without this option, the promise gives way to determinism or predestination, and the open is closed again. The world and the other, destitution and beauty, call; they do not impose with the ineluctability of logic or physics. They call to desire to attend, to faith to say the strange too: the strangeness of discerning divinely. If we accept the responsibility of response to the call, it is not simple joy that follows; it is rather the far more complicated joys entangled in the passing of time, joys that fight against our own immense capacity for inattention, self-absorption, self-certainty, and carelessness. Any community that could claim to be gathered in faith would have to remain thus uncertain, attentive, in its gathering, ritualizing not the contract, but the promise, signed not on a dotted line but throughout the sensible/spoken world.

To read aloud the world as a sacred sign is to read the promise in it: the possibility that calls to us, by which we will to continue to be called. To read the promise is to find in the actual the possibility of the genuinely unknown and unexpected, to read in an attentive discipline of desire. The same openness that lets us respond to the beauty of the world must open us, leave us vulnerable in making us responsive, not only to the ugly, but to other readings, the signs and words of other languages as they too read aloud. We must be able to hear other readings of the world even if we find them strange, even if we find *ourselves* strange. As Nancy warns us, we (philosophers especially) have discarded listening in favor of understanding.[36] To listen even where we do not understand is a demanding hospitality indeed, but it is a demand inherent in sacramental sense.

Mostly, we do not like risks and uncertainties, and we would far rather conceive of faith and community as forms of (possibly false) security and enclosure, beauty as reassurance that we belong here, others as speaking languages we already know (or need not bother learning). We are least willing to mix memory and desire, to doubly will by willing rewilling, to open ourselves to the risk of responding and the future to our own unknowing, in the face of the strange and the stranger. We hoard our sacraments.[37] We are willing to hold to the bond, but not to the promise of the possible; to the rites of the initiated, but not to the mystery; we want to respond by rote to the comfort of familiar words without having to listen, unknowing, for the call, and in it for the possibility of other voices.

And we want the response to our own calling to be, not another question, but an answer, preferably one we would have predicted. Yet answers foreclose the very mysteries that, as mysteries do, always question us. The mystery must always hold open the question, among others, of its own address—the question of who "we" are, and to whom "we" speak. Fidelity must be responsible to the hospitality of listening without knowing, and this responsibility is caught up, perhaps unexpectedly, in our right not only to make, but also to receive, promises. To will rewilling, to make memory into desire, is to insist upon the vulnerable openness that beauty makes, that desire always is.

Every promise dispossesses, or, as Chrétien puts it, "Every promise . . . receives itself and I receive myself through it, in giving itself and in order to be given, but it must receive the capacity to be given. And from whom, if not from the other (*l'autre*)?"[38] The promised community, the community bound by the promise and by faith, says the divine body discerning the promise as the always strange sign of the sacred in the world. To be promised the world must be to dwell uncertainly in it: the community is gathered only by as much strangeness as it has the courage to say, by the faith that holds open the question, by the promise received through otherness. A sacramental ethics must be always hospitable, open to the strange.

The sacramental world shows us a mystery throughout; it does not cease to call us, to seduce us, to draw us into response. In it, fidelity to desire is more important than propositional stubbornness. We tend to will only half the promise; we will not to rewill but to have our wills fulfilled once and for all. But promises do not come by halves. To live in a sacramental ethos, to see the sacred in the world, we must not only grudgingly, but joyously, will to rewill a mystery, and in it, to hear the voice of the stranger in the song of its own pure uprising.

6

Incarnate Experience

ANTHONY J. STEINBOCK

This essay concerns different kinds of experiences that pertain to corporeality. In particular, I appeal to descriptions that suggest and illuminate a unique mode of corporeal experience that is distinct from what we usually understand as embodiment. This distinction is governed phenomenologically, and not asserted speculatively or on the basis of traditionally held belief systems. It is discerned by being attentive to different ways in which corporeal experience is *given*. Thus, what guide this investigation are modes of givenness.

In speaking of corporeality, I suggest an operative distinction between "embodied" experience, where we are concerned with perceptual and epistemic bodily attunement, and "incarnate" experience, where it is a matter of what I have referred to elsewhere as vertical experience.[1] This distinction between embodied and incarnate experience is not to advocate any kind of dualism; rather, it is an attempt to be attentive to modes of givenness that are mutually informing but phenomenologically distinct.

By incarnate experience, I understand that kind of experience that corresponds to "different ways of sensing" reported by mystics of the Abrahamic tradition. These reports suggest an experiential difference between, for example, seeing physical objects and "visions," hearing acoustic sounds and "locutions," physical pains and "wounds of love," suffering and "affliction," and so on. In these descriptions, God is experienced in two ways. On one hand, God is experienced as what one could call the "divine stranger" in the sense that these experiences through which the

Holy becomes uniquely present are unfamiliar, atypical, and sometimes even unwelcome. The presupposition here is that God is outside of the individual, foreign, and only, if ever, interrupts finite experiences. What becomes clearer through the intricate descriptions of vertical experiences, however, is that these "alien" experiences are invitations to a disposition of the self, to a hospitable welcoming of the Holy by the individual, on one hand, and a realization of a radical intimacy of the Holy with the individual from the very start, on the other. This is why the mystics of the Abrahamic tradition often write of experiences that at first seemed unnatural, but then became more than natural. The revaluation of experiences within experience itself points to an inexhaustible divine "presence" as familiar, intimate, always already at the core of the individual, and hence, the experience of the Holy as "friend," "lover," "spouse," "my deepest self," and so on.

If the individual were understood as self-grounding, the Holy could only ever be at a remove, fully "alien." But the mystics, in particular, realize themselves as not-self-grounding; as such, the Holy is always at the origin of the person—hence radically intimate—but as inexhaustible and superabundant "presence," never within our grasp and strangely, mysteriously transcending.

How are we to make sense of such descriptions and experiences where corporeality is concerned? We can begin to respond to this question by noting that their givenness relates to their actuality in the sense of *Wirklichkeit*: actual as effective.

It is commonplace to think of mystical experiences as having nothing to do with the body; when we think of the body in religious experience, we often conceive of it in negative terms, like punishing the body as a means to afflict and thereby rectify the soul (e.g., in self-flagellation or fasts). But this is a very shortsighted view. By contrast, recent works have recognized the ways in which mystical experience is tied to positively to the body, for example, in the case of the erotic; it is interesting to note, moreover, that it is most often women who are sensitive to this dimension.[2] Indeed, even asceticism can have an entirely positive meaning as a way of focusing sensibility without denying the value of sensibility.[3]

In my approach, I am interested in how incarnate experience is expressed in sense experience. Further, I am concerned with how bodily experiences as incarnate experiences can open pathways to new kinds of vertical experiences, how religious practices might for example inculcate transformations of incarnate meaning, and how we might be able to speak in terms of evidence regarding such vertical incarnate experiences. It is such incarnate experience, in part, that allow us to clarify an experience as, say "religious" and not the other way around (that is, not presupposing the religious and then positing an experience as religious). So, while there is current research showing that the body is in play in mystical experience, I want to investigate more specifically the ways in which the senses "give" vertically through different kinds of experience.

Let me cite a simple but profound insight by the phenomenologist Max Scheler. In his *Vom Ewigen im Menschen*, he writes: "*Wer kniend betet, betet in einer anders gefärbten Idee von Gott, als wer stehend betet*"[4]: Whoever prays kneeling experiences God in a different way or has a differently nuanced idea of God than those who pray standing.

Hermeneutically speaking, this means that bodily attitudes are themselves expressive of religious experiencing, and bodily attitudes are ways of disposing oneself to the Holy. In addition, one's background will color the kind of visions and locutions he or she experiences. These experiences, further, will only make sense *within the sphere of religious experiencing itself* and cannot be adjudicated from outside that sphere, like from the sphere of what I call "presentation."[5]

Phenomenologically speaking, Scheler's insight suggests that the presence of God is given in multifarious incarnate manners. In this regard alone it is important to avoid reducing religious life to a change in "mental states," or to regard the presence of the Holy as mere "alteration in consciousness," or even as "mystical consciousness." It is always already incarnate.

Certainly, there are *personal* transformations that occur, and these are decisive in terms of mystical experience or more generally religious experience. But the mystics also experience the presence of the Holy in an incarnate manner, and this is all the more interesting because it is all the more neglected. This point bears on the peculiar incarnate dimension of the experience.

It would be one task to show the ways in which individual persons and collective persons can become so distinctive through religious experiences, and their systems of knowledge and practices so peculiar, that they not only have different paths to the "religious," but that they have different a priori and perhaps exclusive truths, even for only one individual or a single collective person.[6]

My observation develops a different implication. It is this: Incarnate experience alters the structure of corporeal experience. This implies that culture and tradition are responses to vertical experiences, which in turn become dispositions to their reception.[7] Nevertheless, the incarnate meaning can go beyond that culture's or tradition's significance because this givenness is the "founding" moment. Religious experience as evident in incarnate experience (not religion) is founding for culture and is rather generative of tradition, which in turn is generative of our dispositions to them.

For reasons I have noted previously,[8] I confine my remarks to the Abrahamic tradition, and in particular to primarily three exemplary mystics, Saint Teresa of Avila in the Christian tradition, Rabbi Dov Baer in the Jewish tradition, and Rūzbihān Baqlī in the Islamic tradition. Let me address givenness with respect to certain senses, then explicate some implications for incarnate experience, and then turn to the question of hermeneutics and the problem of evidence.

Reception as Presence of Holy (Givenness)

For reasons of space, it is not possible to treat each of the mystics with respect to all the senses. For the purposes of this exposition, allow me to feature briefly a certain range of experiences in each of the three mystics, though their experiences naturally overlap. In the following I mention locutions in Saint Teresa; visions, taste, and orientation in Rūzbihān Baqlī, and warmth in Rabbi Dov Baer. These are not intended to be exhaustive descriptions, but rather only suggestive markers.

Locutions

There are a plethora of examples of locutions to draw from in Saint Teresa's case, but let me begin with this one, since she reflects on the first time a locution occurred. The Carmelite writes: "You answered me, Lord: 'Serve me, and don't bother about such things.' This was the first locution I heard You speak to me, and so I was very frightened."[9] Again: "I began the hymn [*Veni Creator*]; while saying it, a rapture came upon me so suddenly that it almost carried me out of myself. It was something I could not doubt, because it was very obvious. It was the first time the Lord granted me this favor of rapture. I heard these words: 'No longer do I want you to converse with men but with angels.' This experience terrified me because the movement of the soul was powerful and these words were spoken to me deep within the spirit; so it frightened me—although on the other hand I felt great consolation when the fear that, I think, was caused by the novelty of the experience left me" (*Collected Works* 1:25.5).

In attempting to articulate the phenomenal character of these experiences, Saint Teresa makes the following discriminating observation: "The words are very explicit but are not heard with the bodily ears, although they are understood much more clearly than they would be if heard—and to try, no matter how hard, to resist understanding them is of no avail. When, here on earth, we do not want to listen to something, we can stop our ears or so turn our attention to something else that even though we hear we do not understand. In the case of these words God addresses to the soul there is no way of avoiding them; rather, even though I may not want to, they make me listen and make the intellect so keenly capable of understanding what God desires us to understand that it is not enough either to desire or not to desire to understand" (*Collected Works* 1:25.1).[10]

Notice that the quality of these locutions is not merely passive. They are received and beyond what she could have produced by herself, but they are themselves productive, active in the sense that they are *efficacious*. We read: "And behold by these words alone I was given calm together with fortitude, courage, security, quietude, and light so that in one moment I saw my soul become another. It seems to me I would have disputed with the entire world that these words came from God. . . . His words are works!"[11]

It is interesting to note that even in these infused, "supernatural" experiences, the senses are still engaged, even if the vision is spiritual. Saint Teresa contends, "This kind of vision and language is something so spiritual that there is no restlessness in the faculties or in the senses, in my opinion, by which the devil can deduce anything. Sometimes—briefly—this suspension takes place; but at other times it seems to me that the faculties are not suspended, nor are the senses withdrawn but very much present" (*Collected Works* 1:27.7).[12] Accordingly, even in experiences that accrue to us beyond our own efforts, the senses are not overcome, but as Saint Teresa attests, present in peculiar ways in the experience.

Warmth

We also find other descriptions that emphasize touch in the modality of warmth. Like others, Rabbi Dov Baer will write of the reception of God in terms of warmth (being warm with the touch of God), without this being reducible to being warmed, say, by a fire. Such experienced warmth takes place bodily, but this warmth is neither generated by an external object, nor from the individual's internal attentiveness to being warm. Such an experience he contends is a result of the Source and not due to himself or something he could accomplish. Indeed, a collateral danger of being moved to ecstasy in the contemplation of divine matters, according to Dov Baer is that the individual could believe that it is *he* who is warm with the touch of God. The result would be a kind of "egotistical lust": The individual removes the Holy from himself by becoming holy in his own sight, so much so that eventually he becomes greatly deluded and confused in values. [13]

Dov Baer's point is that such an ecstasy—the term Dov Baer uses for the presence of God—is accompanied by a transvaluation of the divine and worldly (*Tract*, 71). The more genuine the ecstasy, the more it is experienced as "being moved from one's place" in the sense of going out of "Egypt," that is, removing material and spiritual limitations (*Tract*, 77–78).[14] The efficacy of such experiences is not only that one receives God in these distinctive ways, but also that the senses are themselves transformed such that one now perceives in a radically different, vertical manner. In this way, the experience of warmth and vitality in piety—which is given as the second stage of divine ecstasy (the seventh where the whole range is concerned)—is expressive of a new orientation of the person and also of the senses. Now, writes Dov Baer, it is like "second nature" not to transgress God's will.[15] What was once held as "natural" is internally and spontaneously revalued as "unnatural" in light of the "second nature" which becomes guiding and in this sense, "first nature."

Just as we can find other senses in play in mystical experiencing for Saint Teresa, we could explore for Dov Baer the way in which hearing is given in divine modalities, how nearness and proximity are integral features in such an experience, and how in both Saint Teresa, Dov Baer, and in the next figure, Baqlī, "tears" play a fundamental role; but let me press on to the role of visions tastes, and orientation as intimated by Rūzbihān Baqlī.

Vision, Taste, and Orientation

Visions are common in certain mystical experiences. It is noteworthy that in his descriptions, Rūzbihān Baqlī, will distinguish between what he calls "visitations" (*wāridat*) and apparitions (*bādī*). Visitations, for Baqlī, are particular, for example, to the station of love, as well as to the station of longing and passion (where a station is expressive of pure gifts, "grace," and cannot be acquired by our own provocation). Visitations are said to be distinct from mere apparitions because in part the latter appear and disappear. In distinction, a visitation "enters the heart and settles in the heart, encountering the conscience." He writes: "Then his essence and attributes appeared, and he drew me until there was only a cubit between us. I looked at his majesty and beauty, and I was intimate with him, and passionate, and I remained in that state for hours."[16]

There are other evocative visions that concern the sense of taste and eating, others that relate intimately spatial directionality. For example,

Rūzbihān writes of experiences being sweet (e.g., "sweet union"), some experiences being given in taste or in aromas (like the ways food or wine are given).[17] The visitations he describes are literally "full bodied," and more than spectacles, since they have direct a participatory quality. In a striking passage, striking not only for its depth but also its erotic sensibility, Rūzbihān writes: "Then I saw the Prophet coming toward me from Medina. . . . He opened his mouth and took my tongue and mouthed my tongue gently. Then I saw Adam, Noah, Abraham, Moses, Jesus, and all the prophets and messengers coming toward me, and they mouthed my tongue. Then I saw Gabriel and Michael, Israfil, Azra'il and all the angels, and they mouthed my tongue. So [did] all the saints and sincere ones" (*Unveiling*, §146). This expresses not just a passing acknowledgment of Rūzbihān by the prophets and others, but also a personal intimacy shared by lovers, lovers who approach Baqlī from the East, that is, the orientation of Holiness.

These brief examples from Saint Teresa, Dov Baer, and Baqlī suggest that there are experiences of a distinctive order that have their own modes of givenness, given as they are in incarnate manners. Let me now draw out some implications for this dimension of incarnate experience.

Implications for Incarnate Experience

From these few examples of what I am terming incarnate experience, it is possible to outline some central characteristics. They concern the depth or level of the experience peculiar to incarnate experiencing, the sense-localization or sense-discrimination of the experience, the extension of our understanding of the senses beyond the common "five senses" peculiar to the Western tradition, the qualitative authority internal to the experience, and the evocative nature of "surplus-experience" given as incarnate.

First, while it is different for each of these mystics, and necessarily so given the uniqueness of the radically personal and interpersonal experience, it is interesting to note that for these mystics, what I am calling incarnate presence tended to occur along with the more profound experiences of the Holy. In Saint Teresa's case, for example, incarnate experience did not occur in an auditory manner until after she was well *advanced in prayer*.[18] By well advanced in prayer, I mean that locutions were experienced not at the beginning stages of acquired prayer—the presence of God that corresponds more or less to my efforts. Nor were they given in some of the later stages of infused prayer, corresponding to the second or third degrees of prayer (here working on the model of watering a garden) or fourth, fifth, or six dwelling places (on the model of the "Interior Castle"), where one might think such locutions would take place. Rather, they began within the modality of "union."[19]

I say that one might think they would take place on the levels of these earlier "acquired" experiences because if the senses are presupposed to be lower, then one might think that less advanced experiences would have bodily shape, and the more advanced ones would be free from the body. But this is not the case at all; in fact, it is just the reverse. Only at an advanced stage of prayer did Saint Teresa experience God in these incarnate ways.

Such incarnate experiences can be understood as integrated experiences, which is to say, spiritualized or divinized sense-experiences; they are not disconnected bodily, nor are they subject to quantification. They are not without the body; they are bodily, but not merely bodily; or rather, they are embodied, but not merely embodied: they are incarnate. On Baqlī's account, for instance, it is their peculiar *efficacy* that points to a distinction in the experience itself, and calls for a more explicit distinction between such incarnate and embodied experiences.

Second, these statements by the mystics obviously introduce a distinction between seeing with the eyes and a kind of spiritual seeing, hearing with the ears and a different kind of locution, and so on.[20] This may lead one to suspect that these experiences are not related to the senses or that there is a kind of dualism between the body and soul, or that these experiences are merely "metaphorical." But what we must not overlook, and what is phenomenologically interesting where incarnate presence is concerned, is the fact that these givennesses are given in such a way that they are experienced *as a locution and not, say, a vision*. That is, if they were *merely* metaphors, or if they were merely arbitrary, why would they be given with warmth rather than with balance? Why as a vision and not as a locution?

My observation here is that these intimacies are experienced in a sense modality ("where the senses are very much present," as Saint Teresa relates), and this certainly says something about the incarnate nature of the experience. Thus, even if the mystics do attempt to distinguish a locution from the hearing of a physical sound—within the same sense-sphere—the incarnate experience is still a givenness within, say, the auditory sphere, and not experienced as a vision or in an olfactory manner. The quality of an experience that is given as the overwhelming vision of God or locution from God is different from, say, the "pleasing fragrance of God." This is not nothing.

Third, on the basis of these and other experiences from the mystics, I believe we could expand our very understanding of the senses such that they would not be limited, say, to five. Taking as a basis incarnate experience, we could articulate a "sense of balance," a sense of direction, a sense of dynamics, a sense of movement, a sense of warmth, a sense of comfort. It is true that we already speak in these ways, but we have not worked out the realm of sensibility starting from incarnate experience. Would not these incarnate experiences help to clarify our embodied experiences of being in the world?[21] This is not to suggest that embodied experience would map onto incarnate experience. For example, while we could describe the embodied experience or "sensibility in general," is in the case of Merleau-Ponty as "reversible," we would not want to ascribe ipso facto the trait of reversibility to incarnate experience. In fact, on the mystics' accounts, incarnate experience appears to be irreversible and asymmetrical. Likewise, just because we detect irreversibility as peculiar to incarnate experience, we would not then merely assert that asymmetry belongs to "sensibility" as such, or as Merleau-Ponty puts it, to the "flesh" (*la chair*).

Fourth, all of these descriptions appeal to an *experiential difference* in the kind of givenness it is, and presupposes that one has the kind of experience and attentiveness necessary to recognize such an experiential difference. For example, Rūzbihān speaks of a taste remaining in his heart, a witnessing with the eye of the spirit, an authority in the locution itself that distinguishes it from other ones, or a tenor in the difference between "mundane" conversations and conversations that are of a spiritual nature (cf. *Unveiling*, §§161, 74). This is in part the role that the master plays in Jewish mysticism or the confessor in Christian mysticism—a crucial aspect for Saint Teresa, for example.

Of course, one cannot simply assume a prior experience to discern a present one, since then one could not account for how a present experience could be discerned as authentic within that present experience. This is why Saint Teresa, Dov Baer, and Baqlī implicitly appeal to the *qualitative* authority within the experience itself. For example, words are experienced as not coming from me, but as coming upon me with a force and magnitude. Baqlī writes: "I heard the word of the Truth (glory be to him) speaking from beyond these veils. It was as though I heard great peals of thunder, and great thunderbolts in this likeness. Creation and time were melting with awe of his word" (*Unveiling*, §163). It is in this respect that the detection or the discernment is and can only be internal to the experiencing itself. The corroboration of their experiences lies in the transformative power of the experience itself such that "I" become a different person through the experience, and this evidence becomes self-evidence in the lives the mystics live in service to God as love of neighbor.

Fifth, it could be objected that the mystics resort to imagery and metaphor to express this overwhelming presence of God. Ineffability would then seem to hamper any effort to describe such experiences as they record them since the experiences are never represented adequately in language. Let us leave aside the fact that description takes place inadequately even in perceptual experience since the givenness is essentially inadequate. When we observe the mystics resorting to "images" or imagery when they describe their incarnate sense experiences, it is not to be taken in the sense that the imagination is employed in the sense of conjuring fictive events. We need to note for now only that the force of the imagery of the mystics is never meant to be completely provocative, but rather evocative, so that we can possibly experience that which they experience and to help guide us along our way. Ineffability is grounded in excess or surplus, not in a lack, withdrawal, or absence. Incarnate experience is surplus or excess experience.

The problem, if it can be stated as a problem, is that there is qualitatively "too much" to be said; the presence is too ebullient. The Baal Shem Tov writes of his visions that the mouth would be worn out if he attempted to describe what he had witnessed. It is indeed noteworthy that despite the so-called problem of "ineffability," the mystics are never reduced to silence. It is due to a kind of presence that is experienced as overwhelming from their side as finite persons that the mystics are motivated to eloquence and imagery. It is not that there is somewhere an "adequate" language, and imagery and metaphor are a second best. Rather, for the mystics imagery and metaphor suggest at least an implicit awareness of language's own limits, and to the extent that it (imagery) is aware of its (language's) own insufficiency at indicating the Holy ("this is God"), imagery becomes for the mystics a "superior" mode of language. Imagery in this regard is perhaps more critical and less naïve than philosophical discourse. Moreover, it is precisely this mode of discourse that the Islamic mystics, for example, find to be "done well" and "beautiful" (*ihsān*).

Furthermore, that the mystics are never reduced to silence (which, if they remained silent, would only reaffirm the hegemony of language as indication and not evocation), is also due to the felt sense of one's own inadequacy and the anxiety of standing before the Holy and being called to forgo the demands of the self by doing the "will of God." Remoteness is predicable of real or ideal objects, and it is they that are susceptible to the kind of dialectic of being present and absent. From the philosophical/mystical anthropology I am tracking here, persons as absolute cannot be given with the relativity of objects—objects that avail themselves to the hermeneutic "as structure." Even though they are inaccessible as objects, persons are immediately and directly given in a way that cannot be subsumed under object-givenness, and this holds above all for the Holy as Person.

The Question of Hermeneutics and the Problem of Evidence

One can certainly submit an experienced presence, the givenness of the Holy in the form of "prayer" (Saint Teresa) "ecstasy" (Dov Baer) or "unveilings" (Baqlī) to interpretation. Such religious experiences are embedded in a religious tradition and in the individual's personal relation to the Holy. Saint Teresa of Avila, just to give one example, constantly attempts to "test"—after the "fact"—whether a particular givenness (say, a prayer of quiet, a prayer of spiritual delight, a prayer of rapture) is actually from God or from another source, like self-delusion, an illness, like rabies, or the devil—who would be an unwelcome stranger, a hostile enemy. This process of testing can be understood as a hermeneutical endeavor.[22]

But to say that hermeneutics at this level is called forth in ascertaining the evidence of prayer, ecstasy, and unveiling (something that we find constantly at stake in the mystics); to say that religious experience given "at the pleasure of God" is nuanced by the richness of the historical context is to my mind different from saying that the presence of God emerges only from a dialectical interplay or negotiation of meaning, that the vertical givenness in the mode of epiphany is given only through the back and forth of the interpretative enterprise (passive or active). To be sure, interpreting the presence of the Holy, and in particular, understanding incarnate experience, is a formidable undertaking. And if one wishes to call the practice of what is known generally as the "discernment of spirits" an interpretative enterprise, then I would concur. But then what one must take into account in any such designation is that there is an essential difference between the modes in which the Holy is given—the ways the mystics describe—the "authority" of the givenness, the "spontaneity" and the like, and the way in which objects are presented. If we assume that hermeneutics characterizes the field of the latter, namely, presentation, then I think we should be careful in cavalierly applying the term loosely to the former.

When we examine the quality of givenness as described by the mystics, the ones with which I deal in any case, we can say epiphany in the mode of incarnate experience has an internal clarity, power and authority, depth, as coming-from-elsewhere; it is immediate, sudden, non-anticipatable, each experience being complete, full, absolute. For them, these are qualities of the experience that could only be given in the incarnate experience itself, even though they attempt to evoke them through their descriptions and imagery after the fact. If we wish to equate the fullness of an experience with objects of presentation, then we would have to say that incarnate experience is "overfull," superabundant, and, as in the refrain of the mystics, without measure. To say that this presence is experienced absolutely and fully, however, does not mean that the Holy is exhausted in this experience; but if the experience is surpassed by an ever-deepening presence, or if it is renewed, it takes place uniquely. Further, these kinds of incarnate presence are qualified as sudden, coming on of their own accord, spontaneous, creative, immediate, without any sense of our being able to anticipate or control them. It is God who is "active" in relation to whom our participation in the experience is "passive": We do not cause or provoke these experiences; they are experienced as grace; our "activity," as it were, is receiving. But the Holy is "received" in an incarnate way such that it *alters the structure of experience itself*, and this makes a qualitative difference in how we live with others and in the world—as Saint Teresa concisely puts it, the words are works.

Accordingly, such "vertical" experiences are confirmed as authentic according to the stature of the experience itself. For example, Baqlī does not appeal to perceptual experience to confirm a different order of experience, say, incarnate experience. He neither appeals to a "proof" through rational demonstration, nor does he appeal to his own assessment of his "progress." Rather, there are "intersubjective" confirmations of his experiences, and these are given by the saints, the prophets and angels, and Muhammad himself.

Undoubtedly, such a corroboration might appear to be circular and presupposing what it should confirm. That is, if we are looking for some kind of proof that the experiences are authentic from the "outside" of those experiences—experiences that are "objective" and can be adjudicated by others as true or false—then such confirmations would appear to be just as much in question. Why do angels, saints, the prophets, and so on confirm these experiences when we might say in turn, "That is all well and good, but what tells us that *these* confirmatory experiences are themselves authentic? Do we not need another set of evidentiary confirmations to verify these intersubjective confirmatory ones? Do we not need something more 'tangible,' something that is precisely not of this religious order in order to verify this other order of experience? Otherwise, are we not just back where we started?"

The fact that Rūzbihān cites *these* intersubjective sources and not others indicates to us immediately that the verification of the said experiences is *internal to its own kind of experiencing and occurs on this level of experiencing*. There is and can be no external adjudication or justification since they can be authenticated only in the manner of this kind of experiencing. We cannot measure incarnate experience according to embodied experience. Perceptual evidence, for example, cannot authenticate spiritual experiencing; the experience of loving another or being loved by another can be "confirmed," as it were, only *within* that same kind of emotional experiencing, and not, for example, by rational reflection on the loving or any experiencing that is different *in kind*. Rather, it must be internal to or consistent with its own domain. Just as perceptual experience can only be disappointed or confirmed within a kind of "perceptual faith," such that what is given perceptually can supplant a previous perceptual givenness and accepted as such, so too can vertical experiencing only be disappointed or confirmed within the context of a religious experiencing, or here "incarnate experience."[23]

Drawing on the mystics might seem to be counterproductive in discerning basic structures of religious experience, especially where incarnate experience in concerned. How can the descriptions of such "elite" persons be taken as descriptive of our relation with the Holy, of the sense-experience of God, and as sketching, however modestly, the structures of these experiences? It is precisely the purity or refined character of their lives (and not the fact that there are either few or many) that enable us to see more clearly the essential structures of that founding interpersonal sphere. Thus, quite contrary to the mystical relations being "exclusive," "isolated," or "rare," they are instead *exemplary* of incarnate experience and of what is always already going on in that interpersonal sphere for all of us and open in principle to all of us, though for most of us it is lived rather obscurely or in a misdirected manner.

Do we have access to these experiences? Yes and no. Yes, to the extent that epiphany is happening all the time. The effort required is one of "bracketing" one's self to liberate the vertical dimension in the things themselves and in our selves; the effort is one of disposing oneself (or disposing the self, as mentioned before) so that we can *perhaps* be struck in ways similar to the ways in which the mystics themselves are struck. This disposition of the self, however, is not merely an intellectual exercise, because such a divestment of self is *lived through*, say, as humble service, which may entail what the mystics refer to as poverty, obedience, and so on. No, in the sense that many of these experiences that I describe on the basis of the mystics are themselves *beyond* the pale of our own efforts (and their own efforts) and come to the individual literally as gift or grace. In this respect, there is nothing one can do to provoke this dimension of experiencing. Indeed, as Saint Teresa of Avila instructs, it is prideful to go around wearying ourselves that we do not have these special experiences. And there is certainly no point in diluting the significance and uniqueness of mystical experiences so that we think they are simply at our disposal or within our discretion.

Still, one may object, if religious experience is so "singular," and in this context, if incarnate experience is so distinctive, one may wonder whether the so-called idiosyncrasy of the mystics is really not just a sign of their pathology, or whether psychoses are not really just what religiously inclined folks want to call mystical experiences. Can they in any way illuminate the dimension of the senses? The writings of the famed Dr. Schreber, analyzed and popularized by Freud, highlight some of the difficulties in discerning differences in such experiences.[24] For example, Dr. Schreber writes lucidly from his first-person perspective about being in direct communication with God, of having a mission to redeem the world and to restore it to its lost state of bliss, of being the recipient of divine miracles ("rays of God"), of becoming God's wife, of the assumption of passivity in relation to God, of bodily functions being evoked miraculously by God, of regarding "God Almighty" as his ally, of suffering and privation for God, etc. He also notes that his experiences exceed human understanding; the "divine revelations" cannot be expressed adequately within the confines of human language, and for this reason he must resort to "images and similes."[25] Are these not religious experiences and attempts at expression like any other we have encountered?

There were, of course, "nuances" to these experiences. For example, Dr. Schreber describes, in an attitude of both rebelliousness and reverence, God not needing to be acquainted with living human beings, since he only needed to have intercourse with corpses; he maintains that God is only "nerve"; he writes of his emasculation by God as a precondition for a new race of human beings to be created, of his "voluptuousness" as a taste of bliss, of his right to scoff at God, a right that belongs to him alone and not to others, and of his identification with Jesus Christ.

We must note several things here. First, the attempt to evaluate these descriptions, to the extent possible, is the attempt often referred to, within a religious context, as the discernment of spirits.[26] Is not Freud himself attempting this, if only in an ambivalent way? On one hand, Freud immediately situates Schreber's writings within the framework of psychopathology. His ideas are said to be of a pathological origin; he is assumed to be a paranoiac and delusional.[27] On the other hand, when Freud reduces these experiences to the order of "religious paranoia," is he (Freud) not delimiting a sphere of religious experience, *via negativa*, that is, by detecting Schreber's experiences as not *true* religious experiences?[28]

Second, within the context of religious experience the relation between the mystic and "religious paranoia" may not always be clear for us. If the mystics are "hypernormal," then what it means to be normal, as it is unfolding within human experience, is still in the process of *becoming normal*, in the process establishing norms within experience. The religious life is in this sense optimalizing, normalizing, in the dynamic sense.[29] There is not a final sense of normality already worked out in advance, outside of human experience that we could then apply to that experience. If there is a difference between the "normal" in the sense of optimalizing, and the pathological, it is a difference that lies in the integrity of the religious experience itself, and is not in its conformity to a stock set of external standards.

Furthermore, we cannot rule out the possibility that one could have religious insights, incarnate experiences, and then lose them, misunderstand them, or misinterpret their significance, not just intellectually but also at the core of one's being. It is entirely possible that psychoses be taken as mystical experiences, mystical experiences as psychoses, or genetically speaking, that mental pathologies had originated as mystical experiences.[30]

Third, religious experience as I have been explicating it, is fundamentally open, "generative" (optimalizing), and not closed. It is not susceptible to a definitive clarity. It is not only psychoanalysis or psychotherapy that sometimes wants this clarity at the risk of betraying the experiences (in the name of doing justice to them); "religious" fundamentalists also desire this kind of definitiveness such that when the "truth" is pronounced, everyone will be driven to accept it. It is within this attitude of closedness, fixity, of arbitrarily limiting experience. That is the problem. Such a limitation in the name of definitiveness (from the side of either psychopathology or fundamentalism) is a sign of arrogance at best.

Does this mean, then, that we must abandon any and all critical perspective of "discernment"? Although one cannot discern, say psychoses from mystical experiences with absolute clarity and definitiveness (since the experiences arise within generativity and have to be taken up *within* "it"), perhaps we could note some clues for discernment, clues suggested by these mystics' experiences, but nevertheless clues that do not provide a final key for dispelling the mystery in which they find themselves. For example, to repeat some of the features disclosed by the mystics and on the basis of the authority of their experiences (the mystics—whom, I admit, I identify on the whole *as* having mystical experiences or incarnate experiences—an unavoidable hermeneutical problematic), we could ask: Are the experiences expansive or narrowing? Do the experiences lead one to embrace all levels of reality or to shrink back from existence? Are the "effects" of prayer that one live in the service of God, love of neighbor, welcoming the stranger, or do they yield the shunning of others? Is there a devotion to God more than the devotion to the idea of God? Is one left cold, frustrated, indifferent, or with a sense of calm and "interior peace"? Do the experiences open one to deeper values, or limit what can appear as value? Is the attitude toward "nature" a devaluation of it through *ressentiment*, or a revaluation of it in relation to spirit? Does a later experience or insight disclose something about a former one? Is one left humble or prideful? Is one left fixated on the "communications," "visions," "locutions"? Is there service or devotion despite the "gifts"? Do the experiences tend toward the abandonment of self, or toward the attachment to self and to things?

Conclusion

The mystical experiences that I treated here are given in certain ways, and these ways are what I term *incarnate*. Incarnate experiences are distinctive bodily experiences that are "infused." They are to be distinguished from "embodied" experiences, which correspond to experiences that are "acquired" or that can be "provoked" in whatever form. Given the restrictions in this work, I remained primarily with the common bodily senses, but it would also have been possible to explore other incarnate experiences, such as the vertical experience of "tears," the erotic (erotic in the full sense) dimensions of rapture, and so forth, which could also be understood as incarnate and not "merely" as embodied.

The discernment of incarnate experiences on the basis of the descriptions provided by the mystics yielded five initial implications for our understanding of incarnate experience: they occur as infused or gifts and are not produced by our attempts to procure them (actively or passively); while they are given as irreducible to embodied experiences, they nevertheless are received within a peculiar sense-modality and identified as such; incarnate experiences are not limited to "five senses" and at least suggest a more open range of essential possibilities for embodied experiences—without, however, attempting to map the structures of one dimension of experience onto another; incarnate experiences are given with a peculiar qualitative authority and are discerned with an experiential difference; incarnate experiences are "surplus experiences," demanding evocative discourse.

Understood generatively, incarnate experiences can inform embodied experiences. This situation ushers in a hermeneutical problematic because incarnate experiences can lead to extremely different worlds—what I have called homeworlds and alienworlds—and this situation circumscribes a unique scope of issues for the matter of personal and interpersonal evidence; this matter of personal and interpersonal evidence is grounded in the reception of and openness to the Holy. Furthermore, understood in this respect, homeworlds and alienworlds (and the internal dynamics of culture and cultus) would have to be understood as being founded in incarnate experience, demanding in turn further investigation into incarnate experience for their clarification.

The Time of Hospitality—Again

KALPANA RAHITA SESHADRI

> Hostage, host, guest, ghost, holy ghost, and *Geist* . . .
>
> —Jacques Derrida

How does someone dreaming, wondering about half-forgotten stories in dead languages, (*something about a boy who seeks hospitality from Death only to find that Death is not at home and awaits him* . . .) find a door, at least a narrow passage to slip into the discursive space of the modern university where the thought of hospitality and the stranger is carried on in the language of expertise? After several tries, she might boldly settle for an interruption, a sheaf of observations: It appears that any attempt to think hospitality in relation to the stranger, is inescapably to situate it at the limit of the unknown—the ultimate border of death. In other words, there seems to be some indiscernible and subtle relation between the thought of hospitality toward an absolute stranger, and the syntagm "awaiting death." What is more, this relation seems to inform any scene of hospitality—be the other family, friend, or foreigner. And is it not the case that this resolutely unspoken relation is already at some level understood and attested to in the daily words that encircle parting, taking leave, departure, sending off—*à-dieu*?

To wonder about this relation is to recognize that no contemporary thinker (other than perhaps Levinas) has worried about this relation with more tenacity and nuance than Jacques Derrida, who nevertheless puts the term "hospitality" in play in such varied contexts that it refuses to be gathered into a single proposition. However, if the dreamer-wonderer were to pursue this relation between death and hospitality, it is to Derrida's *Apories* that she must turn, a text that when read alongside *Of Hospitality* and *Adieu à Emmanuel Levinas* yields insights—sometimes "formidable" ones.[1] But first, before plunging headlong into the impossible topic that is called "death" and the ethics that are also the essence of 'hospitality,' let us hear what Derrida says when he is issued a direct invitation to respond to the word "hospitality."

Priority of Affirmation

In *Of Hospitality*, Derrida begins by situating the question of hospitality in relation to the absolute anonymous other who washes up on the shore bereft of the cosmopolitical rights that distinguish the legitimate foreigner. The latter *xenos* is not an anonymous other, rather he or she is one with whom a pact *xenia* is made thereby alluding to "an objective morality . . . [that] presupposes the social and familial status of the contracting parties, that it is possible for them to be called by their names, to have names, to be subjects in law . . ."[2] The absolute other, on the other hand, "cannot have a name or a family name."[3] In other words, this figure would be in an oblique nonrelation to the laws of the land—as one to whom they would not apply.[4] Thus, it is with this unspeakable figure before him, facing him that Derrida raises the question of what it means to speak of an ethics of hospitality. He writes:

> [T]he absolute or unconditional hospitality I would like to offer him or her presupposes a break with hospitality, with the right to or pact of hospitality. . . . The law of hospitality, the express law that governs the general concept of hospitality, appears as a paradoxical law, pervertible or perverting. It seems to dictate that absolute hospitality should break with the law of hospitality as right or duty, with the "pact" of hospitality. To put it in different terms, absolute hospitality requires that I open up my home and that I give not only to the foreigner . . . but to the absolute, unknown, anonymous other, and that I *give place* to them, that I let them come, that I let them arrive, and take place in the place I offer them, without asking of them either reciprocity . . . or even their names. The law of absolute hospitality commands a break with hospitality by right, with law or justice as rights.[5]

In the second seminar, entitled "*Pas d'hospitalité*," Derrida refers to the ethical imperative toward the absolute other as mandated by what he now terms as "the law of absolute, unconditional, hyperbolic hospitality."[6] And this inexorable law, Derrida suggests, can even command that we transgress "all the laws (in the plural) of hospitality."[7] To focus on this constitutive transgression of ethical hospitality is immediately to acknowledge its aporetic nature—the space of a decision, and the impossibility of any decision that would make hospitality "as such" realizable. The time of hospitality then is fundamentally that of an aporia (in fact a series of aporias as we shall see)—not a problem, which implies, as he says in *Aporias* "a project [or] a task to accomplish"[8] but a "nonpassage, paralyzing us . . . before a door, a threshold, a border, a line, or simply the edge or the approach of the other as such."[9] But then, even as he elaborates the antinomy between "the singular law" and "the objective laws" as antinomy and point of aporia, Derrida, almost as a non sequitur, says quite decisively:

> Let us say yes *to who or what turns up*, before any determination, before any anticipation, before any *identification*, whether or not it has to do with a foreigner, an immigrant, an invited guest, or an unexpected visitor, whether or not the new arrival is the citizen of another country, a human, animal, or divine creature, a living or dead thing, male or female.[10]

Then he goes on:

> In other words, there would be an antinomy, an insoluble antinomy, a non dialectizable antinomy between, on the one hand, *The law* of unlimited hospitality (to give the new arrival all of one's home and oneself, to give him or her one's own, our own, without asking a name, or compensation, or the fulfillment of even the smallest condition), and on the other hand, the laws (in the plural), those rights and duties that are always conditioned and conditional . . . across the family, civil society, and the State.[11]

In the text of the lecture given a year later in 1997, entitled "Hostipitality,"[12] Derrida (with reference to Heidegger) says "before the question, if one can speak of a before that is neither chronological nor logical, in order for there to be a question there must first of all be an acquiescence, a 'yes.' In order to ask there must be a certain 'yes.'"[13] The "yes" here then functions as the trace or the remnant of that non-dialectizable antinomy as an affirmation, an acquiescence that cannot be integrated into the series that Derrida refers to from Benveniste "(*hosti-pet-s, potis, potest, ipse,* etc)."[14] It appears then that the "yes" that is prior to all questioning is the very condition of possibility for any hospitality, for hospitality to resist becoming hostility.

Farewell, Farewell!

Despite the silent "yes," and acknowledgment that "language *is* hospitality,"[15] the language *of* hospitality Derrida suggests is stymied by its own boundless finitude. One can only ever speak of hospitality in one's own language thereby subjecting every welcome to an endless translation. The stranger, the foreigner or guest must necessarily

> ask for hospitality in a language which by definition is not his own, the one imposed on him by the master of the house, the host, the king, the lord, the authorities, the nation, the State, the father, etc. This personage imposes on him translation into their own language, and that is the first act of violence. That is where the question of hospitality begins: must we ask the foreigner to understand us, to speak our language, in all the sense of this term, in all its possible extensions, before being able and so as to be able to welcome him into our country? [16]

Assuming then that question of hospitality begins (and also ends) with the precondition of translation, which severely limits the welcome, (a point that Derrida raises again in the "Hostipitality" lecture) Derrida also seem to limit the thought of hospitality to the welcome—to the act of receiving. In the lecture, he adds: "Already, as you have heard, I have used, and even used up, the most used words in the code of hospitality, the lexicon of which consists of the words "invite," "welcome," receive "at home" while one is "master of one's own home" and of the threshold."[17] But surely, this is only one chapter of the vast lexicon? Interestingly, Derrida makes little mention (in this context) of the vast vocabulary of parting and sending off that are indubitably integral to any hospitality. Without the chapter on good-byes, the lexicon of hospitality would surely be meaningless. There would have been no hospitality, and no fundamental acquiescence. What is hospitality without an appropriate send-off: "farewell," "*au revoir*," "*arrivederci*," and so on? In the English language however, it seems departures are absolute. Good-bye, which is a contraction of "God be with you," appears to send off into the unknown. There is no mention of seeing the other again, but the sentiment abounds in colloquial expressions such as "see you soon," "till we meet again," "come again," and "until later," and in the more ambiguous ones such as "ta-ta" and "toodle-oo." All languages, it appears, possess as many words of farewell as they do of welcome, if not more. This vocabulary tends to be more nuanced and responsive to the length of the intervals of absence—from a grand voyage to a brief sortie, for though an indifferent welcome can be remedied, a coarse farewell negates absolutely. Thus the fundamental "yes," if it is to preserve its function as the trace of that undialectizable antinomy that discloses the impossible appearance of hospitality as such, then it must imply not only an unconditional welcome, but perhaps more importantly the hope for the return of the guest, multiple returns. And above all, it is a "yes," an unconscious silent "yes," that implies that between the present coming and the future perfect of the return, one affirms a departure, a safe departure.

Thus, if we consider the event of departure as being equally significant to the entrance, and as subject to conditions and ambivalences between hospitality and hostility as the latter, then something of the structure of this gap between an arrival and a departure in relation to which hospitality finds its temporality begins to disclose itself. To take the scene of departure into consideration is to discern that the ethical aporia, the impossible accomplishment of hospitality pertains to its temporality—a temporality that is recursive, and returns again and again.

Perhaps a good example that attests to the ethics of hospitality as the opening of a recursive temporality can be found in Filippo Villani's biography of Dante. Unlike Boccaccio and Leonardo Bruni, who also chronicled Dante's life,[18] Villani offers anecdotal detail regarding the circumstances of the poet's death. It appears that while in exile at Ravenna, Dante was asked by his host Guido to undertake a diplomatic mission to Venice to persuade them to desist from war. Villani writes:

> This affair hastened the death of the poet; for death, in truth, visits even the illustrious ...
>
> The poet gladly accepted the charge, and after he had overcome the many obstacles that were laid in his way, arrived, with some solicitude, at Venice. But the Venetians, who were little trained in eloquence, feared the man, lest they should be shaken in their proud purpose by his persuasiveness, wherein the poet, as they had learned, was exceedingly effective. Though Dante begged again and again that he might announce his mission, they refused to give him audience. And when the poet, being denied a hearing, petitioned for carriage back to Ravenna by sea, since he was afflicted with fever, they, laboring under still greater folly, utterly refused his request.
>
> It seems that the Venetians had granted to the admiral of their naval force the full powers of peace and war, and feared that, if they

allowed Dante a safe return by sea, he of himself would be able to turn the admiral whither he wished. Surely on this illustrious city the shame of its mad folly will rest for ever, for it is manifest that this great republic was laboring under the veriest fickleness, in that she feared lest his persuasiveness should move her from that course whereon she had deliberately decided; and, what is baser still, in that she wished to banish eloquence from her city. With great inconvenience the poet, therefore, though ill with fever, made the journey to Ravenna by land, where, a few days after his arrival, he died, and was honored with a public funeral.[19]

I quote this passage at length for two reasons: it demonstrates not only that "solicitude" has no meaning and is effectively nullified if "safe passage" is denied, but also that "banishing eloquence"—that is, speech—is a violence that precedes the violence of imposed translation, which Derrida underlines. Hospitality and its failure occur in this case in the simple linearity of the journey to and from Ravenna and Venice, illustrating a silent "no"—a prior negation rather than an affirmation. Though the precise failure of the linearity is not easy to pinpoint, the example does serve to illustrate something of the impossible temporality of hospitality: From the perspective of departure, it is never simply accomplished and depends upon its repetition.

Riddle of the Door

But why does the temporality of hospitality have to be recursive in order to be ethical, and how can what is recursive be aporetic? By indicating a recursive structure to the ethics of hospitality, I do not mean to refer hospitality to a rule or a procedure that can be applied repeatedly in order to produce identical results; rather, the recursion here is the radical recursion of repetition with a difference. In other words, the recursive structure of the temporality of hospitality is best captured in terms of its paradoxical topology—a Moebius strip or a torus—where the identities of the inside and the outside, the points of origin and end, above and below are suspended. This is one of the paradoxes of hospitality, which make it possible to say, as Derrida aptly phrases it, "we do not know what hospitality is."[20] Such a temporality then is always open, radically open to what may come. The door swings upon its hinges.

The aporia of ethical (not legal) hospitality then opens us to the thought of the threshold—what might be termed as the riddle of the door. The door being neither entirely private nor public is the border of passing and trespassing, the threshold at which the question of ethical hospitality is located. In other words, just as there can be no question of hospitality without the door and the threshold, there also can be no hospitality with a door or a threshold. As Derrida remarks: "But if there is a door, there is no hospitality. There is no hospitable house. . . . This is the difference, the gap between the hospitality of invitation and the hospitality of visitation. In visitation there is no door."[21] In other words, hospitality understood as the absolute opening to the future (*a venir*) would take place only through the nullification of these two separate and opposed greetings. No doubt such nullification occurs relatively punctually whenever there is a scene of a "visitation." And visitation is of course quite different from a visit. Let us pause momentarily at this word.

Derived from the Latin *visitationem* (with all its rich connotations of sight, face, *visum*, *viso*, and so on), with the addition of a definite article, "the visitation" usually refers in a Catholic context to the visit of the Virgin Mary to the home of Elizabeth, a kinswoman, who was pregnant with John the Baptist. The event as narrated in Luke 1:39–57 is an extraordinary (perhaps paradigmatic) scene of hospitality, for it is not simply a visit between two women but a benediction and a greeting between the unborn. As an amniotic inhabitant, John the fetus not yet Baptist, sensing the sprit of the messiah who is come but is not yet born, leaps within the womb, and it is this "leaping with joy" of the difference within and from herself that Elizabeth as host receives from Mary. The differentiated temporality of this scene is truly as Derrida says in *Aporias*, that it is the guest who brings the gift of hospitality, a promise.[22] I quote the following passage, which cannot be paraphrased given the layers of possible meanings in each sentence and word—especially the word "home"—can deliver when read in the context of "the visitation":

> The at home [*chez-soi*] as the host's gift recalls a being at home [*chez soi*] (*being at home, homely, heimisch, heimlich*) that is given by a hospitality more ancient than the inhabitant himself. As though the inhabitant himself were always staying in the inhabitant's home, the one who invites and receives truly begins by receiving hospitality from the guest to whom he thinks he is giving hospitality. It is as if in truth he were received by the one he thinks he is receiving. Wouldn't the consequences of this be infinite? What does receiving amount to? Such an infinity would be lost in the abyss of receiving, of reception, or of the receptacle, the abyss of that *endekhomenon* whose enigma cuts into the entire meditation of *Timaeus* concerning the address of the *Khōra* (*eis khōran*). *Endekomai* means to take

upon oneself, in oneself, at home, with oneself, to receive, welcome, accept, and admit something other than oneself, the other than oneself.²³

Arrivant

However, let us note that Derrida is not speaking of "the visitation." He simply says "hospitality of visitation," thereby invoking the more profane connotation of the unexpected visitor. It is such an uninvited, uninvitable visitor, non-guest (the great and anonymous unwashed who wash up on our shores) that Derrida terms the *"arrivant,"* and it is with the *arrivant* that he also situates not the figure of the messiah per se but that which "exceeds the order of any *determinable* promise."²⁴ The term *arrivant* has a specific valence in Derrida's thought. In *Aporias*, he speaks of being taken aback by the uncanniness of this word. He writes:

> the new *arrivant*, this word can, indeed mean the neutrality of *that which* arrives, but also the singularity of *who* arrives, he or she who comes, coming to be where s/he was not expected, where one was awaiting him or her without waiting for him or her, without expecting *it* [*s'y attendre*], without knowing what or whom to expect, what or whom I am waiting for—and such is hospitality itself, hospitality toward the event. One does not expect the event of whatever, of whoever comes, arrives, and crosses the threshold—the immigrant, the emigrant, the guest, or the stranger. But if the new *arrivant* who arrives is new, one must expect—without waiting for him or her, without expecting it—that he does not simply cross a given threshold. Such an *arrivant* affects the very experience of the threshold, whose possibility he thus brings to light before one even knows whether there has been an invitation, a call, a nomination, or a promise. . . . What we could here call the *arrivant*, the most *arrivant* among all *arrivants*, the *arrivant* par excellence . . . surprises the host—who is not yet a host or an inviting power. . . . The absolute *arrivant* does not yet have any identity yet have a name or an identity. . . . Its place of arrival is also de-identified. . . . *Yet this border will always keep one from discriminating among the figures of the arrivant, the dead, and the revenant (the ghost, he, she, or that which returns).*²⁵

Given the undecidable difference between the *arrivant* and the *revenant*, what is a profane visitation that is not quite a visit? Let us turn here briefly to D. H. Lawrence's well-known poem about a visitation entitled

"Snake." Once again, the setting is Italy—this time, not Venice but the island of Sicily.

The poem begins with an abrupt declaration: "A snake came to my water-trough/on a hot, hot day and I in pyjamas for the heat/to drink there" The day is already extraordinary—exhausting adjectives, demanding repetition. And Lawrence is caught in the glare of the heat: he is not quite dressed for the world. Not being dressed when a guest arrives is to be caught off guard; one cannot receive a guest in deshabille. He is vulnerable in the heat. He needs water but finds he must wait, pitcher in hand, as though he himself were a "second comer." Lawrence must step aside for his guest—more precisely an uninvited visitor—an *arrivant*. However, as Lawrence watches the serene snake sip water silently "with his straight mouth" and "straight gums" a sense that this is a visitation begins to capture him. What may have been shock, impatience, or surprise gives way to a feeling of pleasure. He feels "honoured" he says, but he is also afraid. He is not sure if his sense of gladness at the snake's arrival is a sign of his cowardice, perversity, or humility. Those are the options, perhaps translatable as fear, curiosity, or passivity.

However, Lawrence says that on that blazing July day, with "Etna smoking" "the voices of education" tell him that the snake must be killed. He recalls that in Sicily the black snakes are harmless, but the gold ones are "venomous." Thus when they emerge "earth-brown, earth-golden from the burning bowels of the earth" their venom is like the scorching lava of smoking Etna. On this hot, hot day, fear dominates Lawrence. But quick on the heels of fear arrives respect, even a bite of tenderness. "But must I confess how I liked him,/How glad I was he had come like a guest in quiet, to drink at my water-trough/And depart peaceful, pacified, and thankless,/Into the burning bowels of this earth?" But the poem is not about Lawrence's encounter with the snake. It is in a sense about never being able to be, to dwell in the silent acquiescence, the "yes" of the moment of hospitality. The moment is realized too late only after it has already passed. Having let the snake drink its fill at his water trough, Lawrence even witnesses its satisfaction: 'He drank enough/And lifted his head, dreamily, as one who has drunken,/And flickered his tongue like a forked night on the air, so black,/Seeming to lick his lips . . ." Something about that lazy, complacent, thankless, satisfaction of the snake rouses Lawrence's passion. Watching it ease itself back with unhurried sinuousness into its "dreadful hole," Lawrence is overcome by something indescribable. He picks up a "clumsy log" and hurls it at the departing snake: "I think it did not hit him,/But suddenly that part of him that was left behind convulsed in undignified haste/Writhed like lightning, and was gone/Into the black hole, the earth-lipped fissure in the wall-front,/At which, in the intense still noon, I stared with fascination." A bad send-off.

Having dispatched his quiet visitor post haste, Lawrence feels remorse and regret. He berates himself: "I thought how paltry, how vulgar, what a mean act!/I despised myself and the voices of my accursed human education." Lawrence believes he has missed his chance with one of the "lords of life." In his imagination, the snake regains its majesty as one of the lords of the underworld. Lawrence has missed his chance, but chance for what? He says, "I wished he would come back, my snake." But why, what for? No doubt, Lawrence is right that he now has "something to expiate/A pettiness." But what was the chance that he missed, and why does he wish for the snake (is it this particular snake?) to return? Lawrence does not say. Perhaps, he never can, for as Derrida says *"nous ne savons pas ce que c'est que l'hospitalité*, we do not know what hospitality is."[26] There is no possibility of a shared language, and no shared time that marks this scene of arrival and departure. And if there were to be another "chance," what will Lawrence do the next time the snake comes thirsty and slithering out of the burning bowels of the earth? How will he use the "chance?" Perhaps he will simply give it its right to drink, let it depart satisfied, and not harm it. In other words, he may step aside and, though once again in pajamas, he may expose his vulnerable body to what may come. To lay the table of hospitality on the basis of not doing harm to each other can hardly serve as a dictum. And yet the poem, though it records a missed encounter marred by a shameful departure, ironically perhaps testifies to the possibility of what Derrida terms as "hospitality beyond hospitality" that remains absolutely open to a non-predicable "whatever." It appears that in this case at least, to let the visitation happen, it is required that one miss one's chance—that hospitality, as it is generally understood, fail.

However, this is not precisely what Derrida says though he seems to touch on it. Bringing us back to the thought of recursive hospitality as radical openness to the future, he writes:

> hospitality can only take place beyond hospitality, in deciding to let it come, overcoming the hospitality that paralyzes itself on the threshold which it is. It is perhaps in this sense that "we do not know (not yet, but always not yet) what hospitality is," and that hospitality awaits [*attend*] its chance, that it holds itself out [*se tend vers*] its chance beyond what it is, namely, the paralysis on the threshold which it is. In this sense hospitality is always to come [*à venir*], but a "to come" that does not and will never present itself as

such, in the present (and a future [*a venir*] that does not have a horizon, a futurity—a future with a horizon).²⁷

The relation between Lawrence's "missed chance" (and we may add that of the Venetians as well toward Dante) and Derrida's chance to come is not that the former locates hospitality in the past (after the departure) and the latter in the future (awaiting arrival). On the contrary, as chance, hospitality by definition cannot be just once; rather, it is what is indeterminable and at best recursive, in the sense that it may (have) come again. Thus, to think hospitality, one must somehow cope with its temporal paradox—that it is on one hand pure contingency and on the other hand recursive. Whether one speaks of arrival or departure, the chance of hospitality implies a necessary openness to a coming (again)—*a-venir* and *re-venir*.

With the next sentence of the preceding quotation, Derrida opens a small passage through which we can now tentatively enter the field of thought dealing with hospitality and death. The opening question was: what is the relation between the inexorable law of hospitality offered to the stranger and the syntagm awaiting death? Derrida's sentence reads: "To think hospitality from the future—this future that does not present itself or will only present itself when it is not awaited as a present or presentable—is to think hospitality from death no less than from birth."²⁸

Revenant

What does it mean to think hospitality *from* the future, and to think it not only from birth but also death? Is it that we must think not only from *the* visitation (birth) but also *a* visitation (death—the absolute stranger) where the difference between *arrivant* and *revenant* can no longer be determined? How far can we go in interpreting, understanding Derrida's insistence that the law of hospitality must be absolutely unconditional, open to whatever may come as hospitality as a hospitality toward death? What would that mean? How should it be interpreted? It is necessary to turn to *Aporias*, if only because it offers Derrida's most exacting exploration on the topic of hospitality in relation to death in terms that powerfully deconstruct the priority of the ontological over the ethical—and vice versa.

As a contribution to the conference dealing with passing through or crossing borders (*le passage des frontiers*), *Aporias* situates the thought of the border at the limit of truth, death, and property.²⁹ Not only does Derrida propose to "wander about in the neighborhood" of these topics, but he also implies a certain correlation of effects between: the notion of the border as separating a here and a there, including the "here" of life and the "there" of death; the aporia of this separation given that death can be said to be a border and to have no border; and the ethics of being open to this "experience" of aporia, which he terms hospitality. By placing pressure on the word "experience," Derrida clarifies that he prefers the term aporia to antinomy insofar as the latter term serves a context in which "law (*nomos*), contradictions or antagonisms among equally imperative laws [are] at stake. However the antinomy here better deserves the name of aporia insofar as it is . . . an interminable experience. Such an experience must remain such if one wants to think, to make come or let come any event of decision or of responsibility."[30] Derrida also reminds us that elsewhere he had defined deconstruction as "a certain aporetic experience of the impossible."[31] If every border presents an aporia between hospitality and hostility, it appears then that in this text, hospitality arises more as an experiential (existential) issue and less as pertaining to the tension between legality and a certain notion of justice. Nevertheless, Derrida does not let disappear the political and ethical valence of the aporetic border making it return again and again to unsettle the limits set by the existential analysis of death.

Derrida suggests that there are three types of border limits: those that cut between political and social spaces (territories, countries, cultures, and so on), those that separate disciplines of knowledge, and those that separate concepts—ontological concepts (humanity and animality).[32] It is this last border between conceptual determinations of death and dying that preoccupies Derrida for the majority of the text because "they intersect and overdetermine the first two kinds of terminality."[33] In the interest of brevity, I shall not discuss the text's intricate procedure of analysis, which throughout deploys the "logic" of aporia. Instead, I shall merely follow the line of thought that waits, if indirectly, upon the question of hospitality and death. To get anywhere, (which may be nowhere) we will then have to ask with Derrida "what takes place in an aporia" (65, 32)? The answer, for surprisingly there is one, is that something comes to pass, something arrives—the *arrivant* as someone or something that "makes the event arrive" (66, 33). And this event the one that concerns us most is what "arrives at the river's shore" (65, 33).[34] This *arrivant*, then, cannot be expected, he/she/it can only be awaited. Such is hospitality toward the event. And it is at this fearsome border where the ultimate event of hospitality (who is the host, who is guest?) arrives that Derrida undertakes to read Heidegger's analysis of death, deceasing, dying, perishing, ending, and so on. In particular, it is the distinction that Heidegger insists upon between dying and perishing that most interests Derrida. In other words, it is at this consequential border between the absolute propriety of dying as *Dasein*'s most proper possibility, and the complete exclusion of animals from this experience as creatures that can only (merely?) perish that Derrida situates the interrelation of hospitality and death.[35]

Derrida begins his analysis by observing that from Heidegger's perspective every discourse of knowledge that treats death—be it biology, anthropology, psychology, even metaphysics and theology—must necessarily presuppose the existential analysis of death, insofar as they must depend upon a founding concept, and that the "existential analysis of *Dasein* alone can provide this concept."[36] Derrida discerns three corollaries to this methodological decision. First, the existential analysis of death in its absolute priority and independence would recognize itself as having no disciplinary and cultural limits, yet it would maintain an un-crossable (hierarchical) one between itself and every other discourse. Second, this decision would eliminate "the politics of death," thereby ignoring modern bio-politics (genocide, bioethics, etc) and the problem of "dying well." Nevertheless, Derrida suggests that "it is not certain that Heidegger does not ultimately give us a discourse on *the best*, indeed *the most proper and the most authentic*, relation to dying: hence, *de bene moriendi*."[37] In other words, the pristine purity of the existential analysis of death is not without a trace of a certain sovereign political decisionism.

Reaching the End

The third corollary is the one that is most relevant to the question of hospitality and Derrida himself marks its salience to the text as a whole.[38] It is here that the series of nouns that serves as my epigraph appears: "it is what would make us pass, in spirit, from hostage to the host/guest and from the host/guest to the ghost. (This is the series constituted by hostage, host, guest, ghost, holy ghost, and *Geist*.) In *Being and Time*, [title is translator's addition] the existential analysis does not want to know anything about the ghost [*revenant*] or about mourning."[39] At this point Derrida reaches the dead end of dead ends, the aporia of *Aporias*. It appears that for the one wondering about the relation between hospitality and death, "mourning and ghosting [*revenance*], spectrality or living on, surviving."[40] Heidegger's existential analysis of death is a closed door; the only recourse would be to enter via the fundamental debate between Freud, Levinas, and Heidegger.[41]

Interestingly, Derrida does not plunge into that abyssal debate. Instead, he begins an impossible/possible journey to the end by undertaking an immanent critique of *Dasein*'s essence as possibility, and its most proper possibility, as death.⁴² He isolates two series of ontological statements concerning possibility: as possibility of being, *Dasein* must necessarily assume and testify to this, its own possibility or potentiality. Thus Derrida cites Heidegger who writes "with death, *Dasein* awaits itself [*s'attend lui-meme, steht sich . . . bevor*, 'stands before' in Macquarrie and Robinson] in its ownmost potentiality-for-being" (250)."⁴³ This awaiting itself, which is also Derrida's subtitle to the book, is opened up to disclose three transitive meanings, namely: one awaits oneself in oneself; or one awaits oneself as "expecting [awaiting] the other, or that the other may arrive"; this is "a notable relation to death"; or "we can wait for each other [*s'attendre l'un l'autre, l'une l'autre*]."⁴⁴ About this last modality of waiting, Derrida says:

> This reference is more heterological than ever—others would say as close as ever to the limits of truth—when the waiting for *each other* is related to death, to the borders of death, where we wait for each other knowing *a priori*, and absolutely undeniably, that life always being too short, the one is waiting for the other there, for the one and other never arrive there together, at this rendezvous (death is ultimately the name of an impossible simultaneity and of an impossibility that we know simultaneously, at which we await each other, at the same time, *ama* as one says in Greek: at the same time, simultaneously, we are expecting [the original is "*nous nous attendons*"] this anachronism and this contretemps.⁴⁵

What do these modalities of ontological awaiting—as potentiality for being, for death as *Dasein*'s ownmost possibility—have to do with hospitality? Derrida implies that in the plural reading of modalities one to three, there is a certain movement of approximation toward the border, the limit. Thus his extrapolation of the phrase "awaiting each other at the border of death" from Heidegger's phrase "with death, *Dasein* awaits itself" leads to a contretemps—a countertime, off time. Of the word "contretemps," the first definition in the *Oxford English Dictionary* refers to the terminology of fencing: "A pass or thrust which is made at a wrong or inopportune moment." Like the sorrow that follows the clumsy log thrown at the back of a departing snake, the contretemps is always a missed chance, a mischance. And insofar as we await each other "at the river's shore," knowing full well that there can be no simultaneity in arriving at this rendezvous, what we await "even together" is the mischance, the contretemps. And it is this waiting for the mischance that we can perhaps locate a certain possibility of hospitality.

The implication of hospitality in the contretemps is clarified in the second series of ontological statements on possibility that Derrida outlines. It pertains to the addition, a supplement a certain "complement of impossibility to possibility"[46] in the same sentence of Heidegger's that he has worked on in terms of the awaiting. Derrida is here focused on Heidegger's point that as *Dasein*'s most proper possibility, death is also the possibility of an impossibility. Let us recall that what is at stake here for the thinking of hospitality is the propriety of dying as *Dasein*'s (exclusive) ownmost potentiality. The "nuclear proposition" whose "gripping paradox" is rarely noted, Derrida says, sets off "successive explosions" in the "underground of the existential analysis."[47] What is this lethal proposition that we can anticipate will blast open the fortified border between dying and perishing, the properly human and the inhuman? It is in fact located in the differing modal occurrences of the possibility of impossibility.

The first occurrence of this buried explosive is detected in the sentence: "This is a possibility in which the issue is nothing less than *Dasein*'s Being-in-the-world. Its death is the possibility of no-longer being-able-to-be-there."[48] Here, Derrida underlines the relatively familiar idea of possibility or *dunamis* as constitutively both a simple being able and the *a-dunamia* of "being able" of "not being able."[49] He writes: "Heidegger does not say 'the possibility of no longer being able to be *Dasein*' but 'the possibility of being able no longer to be there' or 'of no longer being able to be there.' This is indeed the possibility of being-able-not-to or of a no-longer-being-able to, but by no means the impossibility of a being-able-to."[50]

The next more consequential work of detection that Derrida undertakes can be briefly stated. He reads a certain slippage in Heidegger's sentence from death as the possibility "of" the impossible to "as" the possibility of impossibility to imply that death as *Dasein*'s most proper possibility could well mean that this proper possibility of an impossibility is itself impossible with the consequence that the most proper becomes the least proper.[51] Thus, he writes:

> We will have to ask ourselves how (a most proper) possibility as impossibility can still appear *as such* without immediately disappearing, without the "as such" already sinking beforehand and without its essential disappearance making *Dasein* lose everything that distinguished it—both from other forms of entities and even from the living animal in general, from the animal [*bête*]. And without its *properly-dying* being originarily [*sic*] contaminated and parisited by the *perishing* and the *demising*.[52]

Different from the earlier set wherein the contretemps emerged in the awaiting, here the contretemps emerges within possibility itself. In other words, rather than being its most proper possibility, death is disclosed as *Dasein*'s improper possibility. The consequence of this reading, as he says, is *"redoubtable"* (fearsome, formidable). For it undermines the border between *Dasein*'s experience of death as proper dying and the animal's non-experience of death as mere perishing. Also, the universalizing and sovereign border that protects priority and independence of the existential analysis of death from all historical, cultural, and other differences and analyses is breached. To open the border of death and dying—to welcome every creature to enter into the ark and to depart from it (for they must both happen), there, in and upon the rivers of death, something like hospitality seems to insist itself between one and the other.

Glimpsing then this open passage, perhaps something of that half-forgotten story in a dead language may be recalled, and recounted. What was the story that was also a discourse of the boy who visits the abode of Death? Is it not the frame and the kernel of the *Katha Upanishad*?

> A powerful sage performs a grand and holy sacrifice. At its conclusion, he distributes according to custom, valuable gifts to his guests. The boy (Nachiketas) critical of his father's generosity inquires: "and to whom will you give me, father?" (He may well have asked "what is the extent of your auctoritas?") And the father: "to Death. I shall give you to Death." And so the boy travels to the abode of Death, and when he arrives, he finds that all is still. There is no one at home to receive him. Imagine: Death is not at home. He is away. So, the boy waits without water or shelter. And when Death returns to discover the unexpected and neglected guest, he hastens fearful of having offended the laws, to offer water, to remedy his lapse. He has missed his chance with this boy—Death has. And so he must grant the boy three wishes—the right to ask for anything three times. But the boy doesn't ask, he inquires. The first two are easy. Then, he has saved this one to the last. He insists, he must know, what is death? What is the secret of Death? Despite pleas, the boy refuses to yield. And Death who had long awaited this boy his disciple but had missed his chance, is held hostage. What does he do? Is there a way out?

PART III

The Uncanny Revisited

The time will come
when, with elation
you will greet yourself arriving
at your own door, in your own mirror
and each will smile at the other's welcome,

and say, sit here. Eat.
You will love again the stranger who was your self.
Give wine. Give bread. Give back your heart
to itself, to the stranger who has loved you

all your life, whom you ignored
for another, who knows you by heart.
Take down the love letters from the bookshelf,

the photographs, the desperate notes,
peel your own image from the mirror.
Sit. Feast on your life.

—Derek Walcott, "Love After Love"

The Null Basis-Being of a Nullity, Or Between Two Nothings

Heidegger's Uncanniness

SIMON CRITCHLEY

for Bill Richardson

At times, reading a classical philosophical text is like watching an ice floe break up during global warming. The compacted cold assurance of a coherent system begins to become liquid and great conceptual pieces break off before your eyes and begin to float free on the sea. To be a reader is to try and either keep one's footing as the ice breaks up, or to fall in the icy water and drown.

This is true of every page of Heidegger's *Being and Time*.[1] But it is nowhere truer than in the discussion of conscience in Division 2, which, to my mind, is the most interesting moment in *Being and Time*. I want to try and show where the ice floe of fundamental ontology begins to crack, for it is there that the questions of the uncanny and the stranger will begin to make themselves heard. At stake will be bringing the human being face to face with its uncanniness, with the utter strangeness of being human: we *are* the null basis-being of a nullity, a double zero suspended between two nothings.

As everyone who has read *Being and Time* is aware, what Heidegger is seeking in Division 2 of *Being and Time* is an authentic potentiality for being a whole, which turns on the question of the self. If Dasein's inauthentic selfhood is defined in terms of *das Man*, the "they," and this is something over which I exert no choice, then what Heidegger is after in Chapter 2, Division 2 is a notion of authentic selfhood defined in terms of choice. So, I either choose to choose myself as authentic or I am lost in the choiceless publicness of *das Man*. Heidegger's claim is that this potentiality for being a whole—for being authentic—is attested in the voice of conscience.

Ontologically, conscience discloses something: it discloses Dasein to itself.

> If we analyse conscience more penetratingly, it is revealed as a call *(Ruf)*. Calling is a mode of *discourse*. The call of conscience has the character of an *appeal* to Dasein by calling it to its ownmost potentiality-for-Being-its-Self; and this is done by way of summoning it to its ownmost Being-guilty. [2]

Conscience is a *Ruf*, a call. The call is a mode of *Rede*, a silent call, as we will see. The call has the character of an *Anruf*, an appeal that is a summons or a convocation (*Aufruf*) of Dasein to its ownmost Being-guilty. We will see below what Heidegger means by guilt, which is something closer to *lack* in the Lacanian sense or indebtedness than moral guilt or culpability. Heidegger insists that our understanding of this call, hearing this call, unveils itself as wanting-to-have-a-conscience, *Gewissenhabenwollen*. Adopting this stance, making this choice, choosing to choose, is the meaning of *Entschlossenheit*, resoluteness or decidedness or being determined or possessing fixity of purpose. Such is the basic shape of the argument in Division 2, Chapter 2 and the terminology employed.

Heidegger argues that the call of conscience calls one away from one's listening to the they-self, which is always described as listening away, *hinhören auf*, to the hubbub of ambiguity. Instead, one listens to the call that pulls one away from this hubbub to the silent and strange certainty of conscience, "The call is from afar unto afar. It reaches him who wants to be brought back."[3]

To what is one called in being appealed to in conscience? To one's *eigene Selbst*, to one's own self. Conscience calls Dasein to itself in the call. What gets said in the call of conscience? Heidegger is crystal clear: like Cordelia in *King Lear*, nothing is said.

> But how are we to determine *what is said in the talk* that belongs to this kind of discourse? *What* does the conscience call to him to whom it appeals? Taken strictly, nothing. The call asserts nothing, gives no information about world-events, has nothing to tell. Least of all does it try to set going a "soliloquy" in the Self to which it has appealed. "Nothing" gets called to (*zu*-gerufen) this Self, but it has

been *summoned (aufgerufen)* to itself—that is, to its ownmost potentiality-for-Being.⁴

The call contains no information, nor is it a soliloquy, like the ever-indecisive Danish prince. It is the summoning of Dasein to itself that occurs silently. This picks up on a remark where Heidegger writes, "Vocal utterance . . . is not essential for discourse, and therefore not for the call either; this must not be overlooked."⁵ So, conscience discourses in the mode of silence, in and as *Verschwiegenheit*, reticence, which is given an extraordinary privilege in the discussion of discourse in *Being and Time*. Reticence is the highest form of discourse. One says most in saying nothing.

The logic of the call is paradoxical. On one hand, the call of conscience that pulls Dasein out of its immersion and groundless floating in *das Man*, is nothing else than Dasein calling to itself, calling to itself by saying nothing. It is not God or my genes calling to me, it is me, myself, and I. As we will see, this logic will become more complex.

> But is it at all necessary to keep raising explicitly the question of *who* does the calling? Is this not answered for Dasein just as unequivocally as the question of to whom the call makes its appeal? *In conscience Dasein calls itself.* This understanding of the caller may be more or less awake in the factical hearing of the call. Ontologically, however, it is not enough to answer that Dasein is *at the same time* both the caller and the one to whom the appeal is made. When Dasein is appealed to, *is* it not "there" in a different way from that in which it does the calling? Shall we say that its ownmost potentiality-for-Being-its-Self functions as the caller?
>
> Indeed the call is precisely something which *we ourselves* have neither planned nor prepared for nor voluntarily performed, nor have we ever done so. "It" calls, against our expectations and even against our will. On the other hand, the call undoubtedly does not come from someone else who is with me in the world. The call comes *from* me and yet *beyond me*.⁶

This is a very interesting passage. The call comes from me, yet it calls from beyond me, "*Der Ruf kommt aus mir und doch über mich.*" It is this *über mich* (in which we find an echo of Freud's Über-Ich) that is so uncanny, that happens against my will and is something that I do not voluntarily perform. Dasein is both the caller and the called, and there is no immediate identity between these two sides or faces of the call. How do we explain this? How do we explain this division at the heart of the call of conscience that we all hear, "which everyone agrees that he hears," as Heidegger insists.[7] (Does everyone hear it? Perhaps that's another essay.)

In order to explain the division within the call, Heidegger folds the analysis of the call structure back into the care structure. The situation of Dasein being both the caller and called corresponds to the structure of Dasein as both authentic and inauthentic, as anxious potentiality-for-Being or freedom and thrown lostness in *das Man*; that is, Dasein is both in the truth and in untruth. So, insofar as I am a thrown project, I am both called and the caller. This takes Heidegger back in a fascinating way to the discussion of *uncanniness* that first appeared in the discussion of anxiety in Paragraph 40. Heidegger asks: what if this Dasein that finds itself, *sich befindet*, in the very depths of its uncanniness should be the caller of the call of conscience? This leads us to the idea of the alien or stranger voice, *die fremde Stimme*, in a way that recalls Nietzsche's 1886 Preface to *The Birth of Tragedy*:

> In its "who," the caller is definable in a "worldly" way by *nothing* at all. The caller is Dasein in its uncanniness: primordial, thrown Being-in-the-world as the "not-at-home"—the bare "that-it-is" in the nothing of the world. The caller is unfamiliar to the everyday they-self; it is something like an *alien* voice. What could be more alien to the "they", lost in the manifold world" of its concern, than the Self which has been individualized down to itself in uncanniness and been thrown into the "nothing."[8]

What might be noted here is the repeated emphasis on the word "nothing" and the general strangeness of the claim that Heidegger makes. The call of conscience is the anxious *Unheimlichkeit* of not being at home in the *Heimlichkeit* of at home, but then this "not at home" is claimed to be the *nothing* of the world (the word "nothing" appears in quotation marks in the Macquarrie and Robinson translation). The self is thrown into the nothing of the world, and into that nothing I hear the silent call that strikes me as alien.

Strictly speaking—and this is thought that I want to get at in this essay—the *self is divided between two nothings*: on one hand, the nothing of the world and, on the other, the nothingness of pure possibility revealed in being-towards-death. It is akin to Lacan's idea of being "between two deaths" in *The Ethics of Psychoanalysis*, but perhaps even more radical.[9] The self is nothing but the movement between two nothings, the nothing of thrownness and the nothing of projection. Which is to say that the uncanniness of being human, being a stranger to oneself, consists a double *impotentialization*, but I will come back to that.

Heidegger insists that the uncanny call calls silently,

> The call does not report events; it calls without uttering anything. The call discourses in the uncanny mode of *keeping silent*. And it does this only because, in calling the one to whom the appeal is made, it does not call him into the public idle talk of the "they," but *calls* him *back* from this *into the reticence of his existent* potentiality-for-Being. When the caller reaches him to whom the appeal is made, it does so with a cold assurance which is uncanny but by no means obvious.[10]

Note the cold assurance of the appeal here, the uncanniness of *kalte Sicherheit*. Uncanniness pursues Dasein down into the lostness of its life in the they, in which it has forgotten itself, and tries to arrest this lostness in a movement that Heidegger will call in the next chapter of *Being and Time* "repetition." It is only the self's repetition to itself of itself that it can momentarily pull clear of the downward plunge of *das Man*. When the self ceases to repeat itself, it forgets and ceases to be itself.

Heidegger completes this run of argument in the following way,

> The proposition that Dasein is at the same time both the caller and the one to whom the appeal is made, has now lost its empty formal character and its obviousness. *Conscience manifests itself as the call of care:* the caller is Dasein, which, in its thrownness (in its Being-already-in), is anxious about its potentiality-for-Being. The one to whom the appeal is made is this very same Dasein, summoned to its ownmost potentiality-for-Being (ahead of itself . . .). Dasein is falling into the "they" (in Being-already-alongside the world of its concern), and it is summoned out of this falling by the appeal. The call of conscience—that is, conscience itself—has its ontological possibility in the fact that Dasein, in the very basis of its Being, is care.[11]

So, the call of conscience is entirely intelligible in terms of the care structure, that is, thrown projection, of falling factical existence, and we do not need to resort to other powers to explain conscience, that is, God, as in Paul or Luther, or public conscience or "world conscience" that Heidegger deals with in the final pages of Paragraph 57.

What does the uncanny call give one to understand? Conscience's call can be reduced to one word: "Guilty!"[12] But what does Dasein's guilt really mean? It means that because Dasein's being is thrown projection, it always has its being to be. That is, Dasein's being is a lack, it is something *due* to Dasein, a debt that it strives to make up or repay. This is the ontological meaning of guilt as *Schuld*, which means guilt, wrong or even sin, but can also mean debt. To be *schuldig* is to be guilty or blameworthy, but it also means to give someone his or her due, to be owing, to be in someone's debt. *Schulden* are debts, which have a material origin, as Nietzsche argues in the *Genealogy of Morals*, and which I have tried to analyse at length elsewhere in relation to Shakespeare's *The Merchant of Venice*.[13] Life is a series of repayments on a loan that you did not agree to, with ever-increasing interest, and that will cost you your life; it is a death-pledge, a mort-gage. As Heidegger perhaps surprisingly writes, although it should be recalled that he was writing in troubled economic times, "Life is a business whether or not it covers its costs."[14] Debt is a way of being. It is, arguably, *the* way of being. This is why credit, and the credence in credit, its belief structure, is so important.

Heidegger runs through the various meanings of guilt understood as having debts, being responsible for, or owing something to another. Although this would require separate and extended analysis, it is fascinating to watch Heidegger try to separate his conception of guilt from the usual concept of guilt as responsibility to others or from any idea of guilt understood in relation to law or the *Sollen*, the Kantian ought that Hegel criticizes and whose critique Heidegger implicitly follows. Heidegger, of course, is trying to get at an ontological meaning of guilt and avoid the usual legal or moralistic connotations of the word. What he is aiming for is a pre-ethical or pre-moral understanding of guilt, or perhaps an originary ethical understanding of guilt. Can he do this? I do not know, but let us follow him a little further into some of the most difficult and radical passages in *Being and Time*.

As Heidegger tirelessly insists in these pages, Dasein is a thrown basis (*ein geworfene Grund*). It projects forth on the basis of possibilities into which it has been thrown. This is also to say, as we will now see, that Dasein is a null basis. He writes, and the German is dense and difficult to render here,

> In being a basis—that is, in existing as thrown—Dasein constantly lags behind its possibilities. It is never existent *before* its basis, but only *from* it and *as this basis*. Thus "Being-a-basis" means *never* to have power over one's ownmost Being from the ground up. This "not" belongs to the existential meaning of "thrownness" it itself, being a basis, is a nullity of itself. "Nullity" does not signify anything like not-Being-present-at-hand or not-subsisting; what one has in view here is rather a "not" which is constitutive for this *Being* of Dasein—its thrownness. The character of this "not" as a "not"

may be defined existentially: in being its *Self,* Dasein is, *as* a Self, the entity that has been thrown. It has been *released* from its basis, *not through* itself but *to* itself, so as to be *as this basis.* Dasein is not itself the basis of its Being, inasmuch as this basis first arises from its own projection; rather, as Being-its-Self, it is the *Being* of its basis.[15]

This is fascinating. The claim is that Dasein is a nullity of itself. Dasein understood as being a basis means that it does not have power over itself. Dasein is the experience of nullity with regard to itself. The potentiality for being-a-whole that defines Dasein's power of projection is revealed to be an *impotentialization,* a limit against which it runs and over which it has no power. It is the impotence of Dasein that most interests me. As we will see, it is a double impotence.

As a thrown basis, Dasein constantly lags behind its possibilities. As he writes, "In being a basis [*Grund-seiend*], that is to say existing as thrown [*als geworfenes existierend*—another of Heidegger's enigmatic formulas], Dasein constantly lags behind its possibilities." The experience of guilt reveals the being of being human as a lack, as something wanting. The self is not just the ecstasy of a heroic leap towards authenticity energized by the experience of anxiety and being-toward-death. Such would be the heroic reading of the existential analytic—and I do not doubt that this may well have been Heidegger's intention—that sees its goal in a form of *autarky*: self-sufficiency, self-mastery or what Heidegger calls in Paragraph 64 "self-constancy" (*Die Ständigkeit des Selbst*).[16] Rather, on my view, the self's fundamental self-relation is to an unmasterable thrownness, the burden of a facticity that weighs me down without my ever being able to fully pick it up. This is why I seek to evade myself. I project or throw off a thrownness that catches me in its throw and inverts the movement of possibility by shattering it against impotence. I am always too late to meet my fate. For those with ears to hear, this is a reading of Heidegger perhaps closer to Beckett than to a certain Nietzsche (but there are many Nietzsches).

Dasein is a being suspended between two nothings, two nullities: the nullity of thrownness and the nullity of projection. This is where the text gets really radical:

> Not only is the projection, as one that has been thrown, determined by the nullity of Being-a-basis; as *projection* it is itself essentially *null.* This does not mean that it has the ontical property of "inconsequentiality" or "worthlessness"; what we have here is rather something existentially constitutive for the structure of the Being of

projection. The nullity we have in mind belongs to Dasein's Being-free for its existentiell possibilities. Freedom, however, *is* only in the choice of one possibility—that is, in tolerating one's not having chosen the others and one's not being able to choose them.

In the structure of thrownness, as in that of projection, there lies essentially a nullity. This nullity is the basis for the possibility of *in*authentic Dasein in its falling; and as falling, every inauthentic Dasein factically is. *Care itself, it its very essence, is permeated with nullity through and through.* Thus "care"—Dasein's Being—means, as thrown projection, Being-the-basis of a nullity (and this Being-the-basis is itself null). This means that *Dasein as such is guilty*, if our formally existential definition of "guilt" as "Being-the-basis of a nullity" is indeed correct.[17]

Dasein is a double nullity. It is simultaneously constituted and divided around this double nullity. This is the structure of thrown projection and the ontological meaning of guilt. That is, Dasein is guilty; it is indebted doubly; it is null at the heart of its being; it is essentially doubly lacking. Thrown projection means: *das nichtige Grund-Sein einer Nichtigkeit*, the null basis-being of a nullity. And this is nothing less than the *experience* of freedom. As Heidegger writes, freedom is the choice of the one possibility of being: in choosing oneself and not the others. But what one is choosing in such a choice is the nullity of a projection that projects on the nullity of a thrown basis, over which one has no power. Freedom is the assumption of one's ontological guilt, of the double nullity that one is.

Heidegger goes on to show that this existential-ontological meaning of guilt is the basis for any traditional moral understanding of guilt (see 286/332). Heidegger's phenomenology of guilt, like Nietzsche's in the *Genealogy of Morals*, claims to uncover the deep structure of ethical subjectivity that cannot be defined by morality, since morality already presupposes it. Rejecting any notion of evil as *privatio boni*, Heidegger's claim is that *Guilt is the pre-moral source for any morality*. It is beyond good and evil. Is guilt bad? No. But neither is it good. It is simply what we are. We *are* guilty. Such is Kafka's share of eternal truth.

Heidegger brings a large number of themes discussed in this essay together in an enormously powerful way, and here we come back to uncanniness:

> The call is the call of care. Being-guilty constitutes the Being to which we give the name of "care." In uncanniness Dasein stands together with itself primordially. Uncanniness brings this entity face to face with its undisguised nullity, which belongs to the possibility

of its ownmost potentiality-for-Being. To the extent that for Dasein, as care, its Being is an issue, it summons itself as a "they" which is factically falling, and summons itself from its uncanniness towards its potentiality-for-Being. The appeal calls back by calling forth: it calls Dasein *forth* to the possibility of taking over, in existing, even that thrown entity which it is. It calls Dasein *back* to its thrownness so as to understand this thrownness as the null basis which it has to take up into existence. This calling-back in which conscience calls forth, gives Dasein to understand that Dasein itself—the null basis for its null projection, standing in the possibility of its Being—is to bring itself back to itself from its lostness in the "they"; and this means that it is *guilty*.[18]

There is an awful lot going on here. Guilt has been shown to be the innermost meaning of care, its very movement, its *kinesis*. Here and indeed elsewhere in his work, Heidegger is simply trying to think kinesis as the rhythm of existence and ultimately the rhythm of being itself. This movement, which is the movement of thrown projection, or what I prefer to call "thrown throwing off," is the structure of the call, which "calls back by calling forth." It calls Dasein forth to take over its potentiality for being by taking it back to its thrownness and taking it over.

Look closely at Heidegger's words: Dasein is the *"nichtiger Grund seines nichtigen Entwurfs,"* the null basis for its null projection. Dasein is a double nothing, a double zero. This is the meaning of thrown projection. Guilt is the movement, the kinesis of this nullity, a movement *vor und zurück*, back and forth, or to and fro, as Beckett would say. Such is the strangeness of what it means to be human, the uncanniness of being brought face to face with ourselves. As Heidegger writes in *Introduction to Metaphysics*, "Dasein is the happening of strangeness."[19] The human being is the utter strangeness of action between two nothings. The self is a potentiality for being whose sole basis, limit and condition of possibility is a double impotentialization, which of course is to say that it is also a condition of impossibility, an existential quasi-transcendental. Impotence—finally—is what makes us human. We should wear it as a badge of honor. It is the signal of our weakness, and nothing is more important or impotent than that.

Heidegger insists that Dasein does not load guilt onto itself. It *is* in its being already guilty. Dasein *is* guilty, always already, but what changes in being-authentic is that Dasein *understands* the call or appeal of conscience and takes it into itself. Dasein as authentic comes to understand itself as guilty. Which means that Dasein as potent comes to understand itself as impotent. In doing this, Dasein has somehow chosen itself: "*er hat sich selbst gewählt*," as Heidegger writes.[20] This is very interesting: what is chosen is not having a conscience, which Dasein already has *qua* Dasein, but what Heidegger calls *Gewsissen-haben-wollen*, wanting to have a conscience. This is a second order wanting, a wanting to want the want that one is, an ontic-existentiell decision,

> Wanting to have a conscience is rather the most primordial existentiell presupposition for the possibility of factically coming to owe something. In understanding the call, Dasein lets its ownmost Self take action in itself (*in sich handeln*) in terms of that potentiality-for-Being which it has chosen. Only so can it be answerable (*verantwortlich*).[21]

Thus, answerability or responsibility—which would be the key to any originary ethics or pre-moral morality—consists in understanding the call, in wanting to have a conscience. This choice, Dasein's choice of itself, in Heidegger's strange phrasing, is taking action in itself. As Heidegger will remind us at a significant later date, "We are still far from pondering the essence of action decisively." The word "action" is one that Heidegger both uses in *Being and Time* and continually reminds us that he wants to avoid. Such—as Derrida told us a long time ago—is the logic of Heidegger's avoidances. But what might action mean when conceived in relation to the double nullity we have described? What might potentiality for being mean when its condition of possibility and impossibility is a double impotentialization? To perhaps anticipate another essay, such a conception of action might be called tragic, or better, tragicomic. As one of Beckett's gallery of moribunds, Molloy, asks himself, tongue deep in his cheek, "From where did I get this access of vigour? From my weakness perhaps."[22]

9

Heidegger and the Strangeness of Being

WILLIAM J. RICHARDSON

It was sheer serendipity that brought us together, but there we were. The original question was innocent enough: "How are we to understand hospitality?" Even when sharpened into "What can phenomenology tell us about welcoming the stranger?" it still seems to intend no harm. But when the "stranger" in question morphs into the "uncanny," it takes on a weirdness that the uncanny itself suggests. For the layman, the word suggests a feeling of dread or inexplicable strangeness, seeming to have a preternatural cause, as if locked into the present by some ominous and long forgotten past. The formal nature of "uncanny" has been explored elsewhere in these pages, notably by Vanessa Rumble. That Simon Critchley and I came to address the matter independently but simultaneously was a matter of pure coincidence. That we should see the matter so differently after long years of warm, philosophical exchange is just plain weird. I propose to summarize the difference between us and conclude with a remark or two of my own.

Both of us began our philosophical search differently, in different places and at different times. For me, the philosophical search had begun earlier but changed after I first ran into Heidegger. Since then, his search has influenced my own. For Heidegger himself, the search began, as he tells us, at the age of eighteen (1907) in his final year at the gymnasium, when he was given a copy of Franz Brentano's doctoral dissertation, *On the Manifold Sense of Being in Aristotle*. There "being" translates the Greek *on*, that-which-is-the-case. Since what-is (-the-case) has many meanings,

155

Heidegger asked: What is the meaning of the "is" that is common to them all yet remains different from each so as to mean the same in each? After examining all of the major Greek thinkers, Heidegger discovered that no one had answered the question because no one had posed it in these terms, so that his question became: what is the meaning of the Is of what-is as different from its presencing in each one? This was his essential question—but only half of it. For in ignoring the question, the Greeks nonetheless continued to use "is" as if they understood what it meant. This forgetting of the question was indigenous to the question itself by reason of a certain "not" that seemed ingredient to it. Simultaneously with the being-question, then, was the question about the negativity that seemed to inhabit the asking of it from the very start.[1]

What philosophical method would lead to an answer? Phenomenology, of course, partly because in 1907 in Germany this was the only respectable game in town, partly because there seemed no better way to proceed than to take as phenomenon par excellence the one that raised the question and must already have some intimation of an answer, simply in order to be able to ask the question. But the self-concealing "not" of the original experience persevered in the method as well. Describing the phenomenological method itself, Heidegger writes:

> What is it that by its very essence is *necessarily* the theme whenever we exhibit something *explicitly*? Manifestly, it is something that proximally and for the most part does not show itself at all: it is something that lies *hidden*, in contrast to that which proximally and for the most part does show itself; but at the same time it is something that belongs to what thus shows itself and belongs to it so essentially as to constitute its meaning and its ground.
>
> Yet that which remains *hidden* in an egregious sense, or which relapses and gets *covered up* again, or which shows itself only in *disguise*, is not just this entity or that but rather the being of entities, as our previous observations have shown. This being can be covered up so extensively that it becomes forgotten, and no question arises about it or about its meaning. Thus that which demands that it become a phenomenon, and which demands this in a distinctive sense and in terms of its ownmost content as a thing, is what phenomenology has taken into its grasp thematically as its object.[2]

The "not" here that clings to a phenomenon's capacity to reveal itself is ingredient to the being of *Dasein* as well.[3]

How this analysis of *Being and Time* proceeds is familiar. The human phenomenon (*Dasein*) is described as being-in-the-world. Basic questions:

What then is "world?" what is meant by "being-in" such a world? The world itself is not a being but rather a horizon within which *Dasein* encounters other beings as meaningful. Not a being itself, world for Heidegger is essentially not-a-being, a No-thing—yet by no means absolutely nothing. To be "in" such a world involves three components of the disclosive process. The first is called "understanding" (*Verstehen*), a power to project the world of total meaningfulness (imagine a cosmic X-ray or MRI machine capable of lighting up from the inside the being-structure of everything that is because it has access to the Is of what is). The second component is called "disposition" (*Befindlichkeit*), a power to reveal in nonconceptual terms what and how things are. By the power of disposition, *Dasein* becomes aware of the fact that it is actually in the world as if thrown there with no awareness of how this came to be. This thrownness is the essential factuality (thereness) of *Dasein*, the simple fact that it is there at all. Disposition reveals not only the basic facticity of *Dasein*, however, but the fact that it is thrown among all sorts of other beings upon which it depends for its own survival—a fact described as "fallenness." Along with this goes a pervading "not"—the penchant of every being to resist the revelatory process within it by which it manifests itself as what it is. When this resistance is collectivized into a kind of group interdependence, it coalesces into the shared tendency to think and do what everyone else thinks and does, under the drifting guidance of a seductive Everyman that Heidegger calls simply *das Man*.

The third component of *Dasein*'s being "in" the world is called "discourse" (*Rede*) that actually translates the Greek word *logos*, which in Heidegger's reading means the power "to let-be-seen," particularly through language and reason. Here it means to let come to manifestation what understanding and disposition reveal.

Having discussed these basic elements in *Dasein*'s structure, Heidegger tries to think them as a whole, and with the help of an analysis of the experience of anxiety, he manages to put them into a single formula to which he gives the name "care." Accordingly, *Dasein* is "the being-ahead-of-itself-already-in (the-world) as being alongside entities encountered within the world."[4] All the essentials are there: *Dasein* as projective disclosure (*Sich-vorweg-Sein*), as thrown (*schon-sein-in*) and fallen alongside other beings within the world. What is the role of "*logos*" (the third existential component) in such a structure? To serve as the "voice of conscience" in *Dasein* as care, to let-itself-be-seen as what it is, to acknowledge and accept itself as such. This means to let it be seen as projective disclosure, trammeled by multiple forms of "not" that permeate it: as thrown, *Dasein*'s disclosive projection is not master of its origin; as thrown into the world, it is not capable of understanding the world as anything other than No-thing; as fallen it is not free from its sluggish dependence on other beings and the globalizing seductiveness of *das Man*; and finally as project-unto-end (*peras*: the outer edge of things where they both start and stop being), *Dasein* is not immortal but inescapably being-unto-limit (and for humans this means death). For *Dasein* to acknowledge all that and accept that it be so is to attend to the voice of conscience and become "authentically" one's self.

It is at this level of the analysis that Critchley enters the fray and addresses the relevant problems involved. He is interested in the nature of conscience, both as call and as content, that *Dasein* is summoned to acknowledge and that Heidegger designates as "guilt." This is where serendipity leads us both to agree and to disagree: to agree on the meaning of call and to disagree on the interpretation of guilt. Specifically, I find Critchley's interpretation in this volume of the call that comes "from me" yet somehow from "beyond me" admirable. My difficulty is with his interpretation of guilt. He begins with what I perceive to be an insufficiently critical acceptance of the English translators' translation of the German word *nicht* ("not") and the German word *Nichtigkeit* ("not-ness" or "not"-infectedness) as "null" and "nullity." As I read it, "not" denotes negation that limits something positive, "null" a negation that is unqualifiedly total. Correspondingly, *Nichtigkeit* suggests the character of being affected by, and even deformed by, a limiting "not"; nullity suggests unqualified, hence unlimited, negation of any positivity at all. Thus, for Critchley, "the potentiality for being-a-whole" which defines *Dasein*'s power of projection is revealed to be an "impotentialization," and his own preference is clear: "it is the impotence of *Dasein* that most interests me." All of this nullification results in the following summarizing formula for *Dasein*: "we are the null basis-being of a nullity, a double zero suspended between two nothings." *Dasein* is a null basis-being, that is, a being-as-basis in the sense that it has been released not through itself but to itself as a basis through which the projection takes place, but limited by the "not" of its thrownness insofar as it is not the master of its own origin. There is a "not" that is constitutive of the very being of *Dasein*.[5] "This not belongs to the existential meaning of thrownness. It itself, being a basis, includes a negativing element (*Nichtigkeit*) of itself."[6]

To clarify my own attitude toward all this, I shall cite one passage from Heidegger and one from Critchley, then add a comment of my own and move on. Heidegger is discussing the call to *Dasein* as care and writes:

> The call is the call of care. Being-guilty constitutes the being to which we give the name of "care." In uncanniness *Dasein* stands

together with itself primordially. Uncanniness brings this entity face to face with its undisguised nullity (*Nichtigkeit*), which belongs to the possibility of its ownmost potentiality-for-being. To the extent that for *Dasein*, as care, its being is an issue, it summons itself as a "they" which is factically falling, and summons itself from its uncanniness towards its potentiality-for-being. The appeal [of conscience] calls back by calling forth: it calls *Dasein forth* to the possibility of taking over, in existing even that thrown entity which it is. It calls *Dasein back* to its thrownness so as to understand this thrownness as the null (*nichtiger*) basis which it has to take up into existence. This calling-back in which conscience calls forth, gives *Dasein* to understand that *Dasein* itself, the null (*nichtiger*) basis for its null (*nichtiger*) projection standing in the possibility of its being—is to bring itself back to itself from its lostness in the "they"; and this means that it is *guilty*.[7]

I find this pretty straightforward: the call of conscience is to summon *Dasein* to come forward toward the fullness of its existence as a projection of possibilities that are limited, insofar as they are discovered to be, in fact, already thrown there. Again in this volume, Critchley, however, sees the same matter differently:

> Look closely at Heidegger's words: *Dasein* is the null basis for its null projection. *Dasein* is a double nothing, a double zero. This is the meaning of thrown projection. Guilt is the movement, the kinesis of this nullity, a movement back and forth or to and fro, as Beckett would say. Such is the strangeness of what it means to be human, the uncanniness of being brought face to face with ourselves. . . . The human being is the utter strangeness of action between two nothings. The self is a potentiality for being whose sole basis, limit and condition of possibility is a double impotentialization, which of course is to say that it is also a condition of impossibility, an existential quasi-transcendental. Impotence—finally—is what makes us human. We should wear it as a badge of honor. It is the signal of our weakness, and nothing is more important or impotent than that.

For my sense, this reduction to impotence of what seems to be no more than a limit on the power of our potency goes too far. To claim that *Dasein*'s power to be can be reduced to two zeroes that can pass their time in a kinesis between them supported only by a nothing on either side seems to make too much of too little to make any satisfying sense at all.

A word should be added here to call attention to the term "uncanniness" in these texts. It appears here in the oblique, as if belonging to a broader background that is supposed but not addressed. Rooted in the German word for home (*Heim*), Heidegger's use of the German word (*Unheimlichkeit*) means not-at-home-ness, estrangement of whatever kind. The strangeness that he imputes to *Dasein* signifies the unique prerogative of *Dasein* under the guise of its openness to the Is (being) of what-is (beings) that derives from its existential structure by which *Dasein* is both ontic and ontological at once: "*Dasein* is ontically distinctive in that it is ontological."[8] In the texts cited, uncanniness refers to *Dasein* in the most abject form of its finitude: thrown, fallen and under the sway of *das Man*. The terminology will return.

So much for Heidegger's sense of the "uncanny" in 1927. Flash forward to 1942. Much had happened in between: to the world (the outbreak of World War II); to Heidegger personally (the disastrous experiment of 1933); to his way of thinking through the famous self-described "turn." We cannot follow him through all that but one clear symptom of the turn in his thinking was a fresh interest in the poet, Friedrich Hölderlin (1770–1843). In Hölderlin, Heidegger found a fellow wayfarer whose effort to respond in poetic terms to what he called the manifestation of the "Holy," Heidegger found closely similar to his own effort to think the meaning of being. There are several essays from this period (notably "Homecoming/To Kindred Ones," and "Remembrance") that describe the poet's formation as a poet.[9] Born close to his roots, the poet typically experiences the need to journey abroad and let his talent mature under foreign skies. Eventually, he will return home to be near to the Source of his poetic gift and come to fullness of his talent by being "at home" in nearness to that Source. Heidegger's abiding interest in Hölderlin was in someone who could help him understand what it meant to be truly "at home" near to the Source of language in its origins. In 1942 Heidegger gave a full semester course on Hölderlin's hymn "Der Ister" ("The Danube") where, in part, he tunes in to Hölderlin's own dialogue with another poet of comparable stature, namely Sophocles. The basic text of that discourse is the first choral ode of Sophocles's tragedy *Antigone*.[10] Serendipitously enough, the theme of the first ode turns out to be the meaning of "uncanny." We will restrict our attention to what Heidegger adds to our understanding of this theme only.

Recall the bare essentials of *Antigone*, the play: Oedipus is gone, Eteocles and Polynices, his two sons, have just slain each other in mortal combat, and Creon, their uncle, has assumed complete political charge.

For Eteocles, he orders a funeral with full military honors; for Polynices, there will be no burial at all. Creon commands that Polynices's rotting corpse become the food of birds, animals, and creeping things, because he had been a traitor to his country. As an act of defiance, Antigone buries Polynices anyway. Creon is enraged at the news, not knowing it was she who was responsible, and he orders the sentry who brings the news to catch and bring the culprit to him immediately, or else. As the sentry leaves, the chorus enters and sings the following ode, after which Antigone will be brought in as prisoner:

> Manifold is the uncanny, yet nothing
> more uncanny looms or stirs beyond the human being.
> He ventures forth on the foaming tide
> amid the southern storm of winter
> and crosses the surge
> of the cavernous waves.
> And the most sublime of the gods, the Earth,
> indestructible and untiring, he wears out,
> turning the soil from year to year,
> working the ploughs to and fro
> with his horses.
>
> And the flock of birds that rise into the air
> he ensnares, and pursues
> the animals of the wilderness
> and of the ocean's surging waves,
> most ingenious man.
> He overpowers with cunning the animal
> that roams in the mountains at night,
> the wild-maned neck of the steed,
> and the never-tamed bull,
> fitting them with wood,
> he forces under the yoke.
>
> And into the sounding of the word
> and swift understanding of all
> he has found his way, even into courageous
> governance of the towns.
> And he has pondered how to flee
> exposure to the arrows
> of unpropitious weather and its frosts.
> Everywhere venturing forth underway, experienceless without any way
>   out

he comes to nothing.
The singular onslaught of death he can
by no flight ever prevent,
even if in the face of dire infirmity he achieves
most skillful avoidance.

Craftiness too, as the work
of his ability, he masters beyond expectation,
and if he falls on bad times
other valiant things succeed for him.
Between the ordinance of the earth and the
order ordained by the gods he ventures:
Towering high above the site, forfeiting the site
is he for whom non-beings always are
for the sake of risk.
Such shall not be entrusted to my hearth,
nor share their delusion with my knowing,
who put such a thing to work.[11]

Before addressing the ode directly, Heidegger situates his interpretation by recalling the opening conversation between Ismene and Antigone in Act I, after Ismene had tried unsuccessfully to dissuade Antigone from her plan. "You leave this to me and to that within me that counsels the dangerous and the difficult," says Antigone. What is that? "*pathein to deinon touto*," she replies. Heidegger translates: "to take up into my own essence the uncanny that here and now appears" (lines 1–6). In a sense, the whole of his interpretation is there. He explains:

> *pathein*: this is not passive acceptance or mere toleration. It means a true experiencing, an enduring and suffering, so to speak, that he translates himself as a "taking up into one's own essence."[12]

As for *deinon*, Heidegger offers a summary of his own rich elucidation of this term:

> We can more or less delimit the range of the *deinon* as follows. It means three things: the fearful, the powerful, and the inhabitual. Each time it can be determined in opposing ways: the fearful as that which frightens and as that which is worthy of honor; the powerful as that which looms over us, and as that which is merely violent; the inhabitual as the extraordinary, and as that which is skilled in everything. Yet in its essence the *deinon* is neither merely the fearful, nor is it merely the powerful, nor merely the inhabitual, nor any of

these according to merely one side; nor is the *deinon* simply all these heaped together. What is essential in the essence of the *deinon* conceals itself in the originary unity of the fearful, the powerful, and the inhabitual. What is essential to all essence is always singular. The full essence of the *denion* can therefore unfold itself only in something singular. In translation, we have rendered *to deinon* "the *Unheimliche*, the uncanny." The word is not meant to indicate some further meaning in addition to these previously mentioned; rather it is meant to name all of them together, and, indeed, not by bundling them together in an extrinsic manner, which is linguistically impossible and nonsensical. Rather it is meant to name them in such a way that the term "*das Unheimliche*, the uncanny," as it is to be understood in what follows, grasps the concealed ground of the unity of the manifold meanings of *deinon*, thus grasping the *deinon* itself in its concealed essence.[13]

And then there is *deinon touto*. The estrangement (*deinon*) that Antigone faces goes farther than her ontological structure that characterizes all humans. It involves her history, too. Daughter of an incestuous marriage, sister of the naïve Ismene and of two brothers that killed one another, one of them left unburied in shame as a traitor, Antigone alone was left to bear the ignominy of it all, and whatever shame remained. This sort of thing is "nothing that human beings themselves make but rather the converse: something that makes them into what they are and who they can be."[14] The *deinon* she assumes is "that against which nothing can avail, simply a matter of her destiny."[15] Finally, add to all this the decision to bury Polynices.

By any standard, then, Antigone is utterly estranged and unhomely, uncanny in every way. Taken in the sum, then, the *deinon* Antigone faces includes: her ontological (congenital human) structure, her historical destiny and her existential choice. But what does the ode have to say about all this? For Heidegger, the ode presents a paradox that must be resolved. On one hand, it presents a picture of human uncanniness in terms of the clear record of success (man's adjustment to his physical environment, man's developments of language, thought, and culture, man's resourcefulness in dealing with the contingencies of life despite the risks involved). All this success is not without its downside of course (death, in particular, remains inescapable), but by and large the record is astonishing. And Antigone, since she is the principal focus of the play, may be considered a paragon of its success. Yet at the same time, the chorus will have none of it, Antigone notwithstanding: "such will not be entrusted to my hearth,/nor share their delusion with my knowing/who put such a thing to work." How explain, Heidegger asks, this paradox?

Prescinding from theoretical issues about the nature and function of the Greek chorus and the kind of knowing it may lay claim to, Heidegger focuses his attention on the "hearth" that the chorus apparently has access to, tracing the origin of this word back to an ancient Greek word *estia* implying fire as a source of both heat and light. It can attract human beings around it to constitute a center for interaction and kind of "home" for them. This suggests to him that being itself may be poetized as such a home. With a little bit of help from Plato, Heidegger describes it in this fashion:

> The hearth is accordingly the middle of beings, to which all beings, because and insofar as they are beings are drawn in the beginning. This hearth of the middle of beings is being. Being is the hearth. For the essence of being, for the Greeks, is *physis*—that illumination that emerges of its own accord and is mediated by nothing else, but is itself the middle. This middle is that which remains as beginning, that which gathers everything around it—that wherein all beings have their site and are at home as beings.[16]

In this context, the orientation of beings toward being suggests a way in which being homely is grounded. In this sense, the reference in the ode to being unhomely may be taken as an intimation of what it means to be attentive to the homely and to risk belonging to it. I take homely here to mean "being at home" through nearness to the hearth and unhomely as being at a distance from the hearth, through ignorance, disregard or mere forgetfulness. In this way, "being unhomely" may show itself as a not yet awakened, not yet decided, not yet assumed potential for being homely and becoming homely. It is precisely this being unhomely that Antigone takes upon herself. Her facing up to this *deinon* is her supreme action as a singular human being. This action is the movement and "drama" of becoming homely. In becoming homely, being unhomely is first accomplished. And this is not merely in the sense that in becoming homely, being unhomely comes to its conclusion; rather, Antigone's becoming homely first brings to light the essence of being unhomely. "Becoming homely makes manifest the essential ambiguity of being homely."[17] Now to become homely in this way is "what Antigone herself calls *pathein to deinon touto*, passing through this being unhomely amid all beings. In Antigone's taking such being unhomely into her own essence she is 'properly' unhomely,"[18] which means she is becoming homely too.

In any case, the closing words of the chorus conceal within them, as Heidegger sees it, a suggestion of that risk not yet taken by Antigone, but it is accomplished in the tragedy as a whole. Antigone herself is the supreme risk within the realm of her *deinon*. To be this risk is her very essence.[19] How did the actual taking of the risk come about?

It is hard for us to imagine what kind of life Antigone had led in the Thebes of its day before the events of the play. Antigone herself tells us all we know and it has to be enough. In the opening scene she says to Ismene: "There is nothing—no pain,/our lives are pain—no private shame, no public disgrace, nothing I have not seen/in your griefs and mine."[20] Full of anger and shame, she already had something smoldering inside her, waiting to burst into flame, when Creon's proclamation against Polynices supplied the spark. Whether one could speak of her mood as "not yet awakened, not yet decided, not yet assumed potential for being homely and becoming homely" is moot. She was surely ready for drastic action when the time came.

The next we see of her is when the sentry brings her in captive. Creon is shocked and outraged. Words are few: "Do you deny you did this, yes or no?" "I did it. I don't deny a thing." "Were you aware a decree had forbidden this?" "Of course I was. Everybody knew. It was public knowledge." "And still you have the gall to break this law?"

> Yes. It was no Zeus that bade me this
> Nor was it Dike, at home amongst the gods below,
> who ordained this law for humans.
> And your command seemed not so powerful to me
> that it could ever override by human wit
> the immutable unwritten edict [that comes from] beyond the gods.
> Not just now, nor since yesterday, but ever steadfast
> this prevails. And no one knows from whence it once appeared.[21]

Here she puts into words loud enough for Creon to hear her yes to *pathein to deinon touto*, a total act of the whole self. The rest of the drama is but an orchestration of them.

The clarity and force of her choice came not from herself alone but from some Source that attunes all human beings as human beings. It follows not merely human ordinance. What determines her action here has been encountered nowhere before, yet has already appeared before all else without anyone being able to name a particular being from which it has sprung forth. It is to that which is unconcealed in this way that the essence of Antigone belongs. To embrace it as such was the essence of her risk.

"To be sheltered within and to become homely in what is thus unconcealed is what she herself names *pathein to deinon touto.*"[22]

What can we say to conclude? The analogy between Antigone's defiance and *Dasein*'s achievement of authenticity (the "self-assured, anxiety ridden freedom-unto-death"[23]) is clear enough. Equally clear it seems to me, is the fact that Antigone's ultimate risk in acknowledging this supposes as a structural basis something more solid than two zeroes supported by two nothings, one on either side. Thrust toward being (*Seinkönnen*), even though thrown and fallen-unto-death, Antigone was strong enough to make a final choice among the options still available to her and remain faithful to that choice up to the very end. Clearly, she lamented the losses involved, but there is never a sign of regret for the choice itself.

There is some gain, too, in a clearer sense of what Heidegger understands by the uncanny. For the phenomenologist of 1927, the uncanny was the irreducible strangeness of being human, inasmuch as *Dasein* enjoys a privileged openness to the Is of whatever is. The focus at that time was on the finitude (the irreducible "not") of that openness (thrown and fallen-unto-death) with an emphasis on what it would mean for *Dasein* to respond authentically to the call of conscience to accept itself as such. After the turn in his thinking, the rigorously phenomenological style of *Being and Time* shifted into a differently rigorous hermeneutic style of the later years (e.g., "Hölderlin's Hymn 'Der Ister,'" 1942). Here the uncanniness (not-at-homeness) of *Dasein* in *Being and Time* is thought in terms of the unhomeliness of the inexperienced poet who becomes awakened to the possibility of becoming at home in nearness to being, the Source of his poetic gift. The model of such transformation would be Antigone herself, whose acceptance (*pathein*) of her own uncanniness (*deinon*)—at once ontological, historical, and existential—offers an example of one who truly (*kalon*) came to the fullness of her self.

Is there some gain for us in all of this? Surely there is a gain in seeing the sometimes cerebral phenomenological analysis of *Dasein* in *Being and Time* transformed into the flesh and blood features of a human being plunged into a life situation (mythical or not) that was uncannily complex. There is gain, too, in being forced to realize that peripheral issues persist and remain to be addressed: for example, the nature of Antigone's freedom (however limited) in making her choice, the nature of the "action" that concretizes it, and the nature of the responsibility it engenders—all of these suggested in the Heidegger texts cited by Critchley.

But is there any gain in our understanding of the uncanny? Certainly Heidegger strips it of any romantic dress. But he guards the essential strangeness of *Dasein* as both ontic and ontological at once. This accounts for the not-at-homeness of the *Dasein* of *Being and Time* and the unhomeliness that may become at home with being that the *Antigone* analysis shows to be possible. How precisely welcome the stranger that appears under the guise of the uncanny? The present reflection suggests this: at the heart of the human mystery is the "not" that marks its finitude and permeates being human, whether host or guest, from the start. This is the root of the ambivalence that lets the stranger be either friend or foe in the end. How then welcome such a stranger? The way we welcome the "not" in ourselves: with eyes wide open and whatever wary wisdom we can muster.

And one final gain: Heidegger for once leaves us with some sense of hope. "What is worthy of poetizing in this poetic work is nothing other than becoming homely in being unhomely. Antigone herself is the poem of becoming homely in being unhomely. Antigone is the poem of being unhomely in the proper and supreme sense. . . . Perhaps what is essential and only to be poetized in this way, namely, the potential of human beings for being homely is even the highest thing that the poet must poetize."[24]

And tomorrow is another day.

10

Progress in Spirit

Freud and Kristeva on the Uncanny

VANESSA RUMBLE

> The Egyptian Moses had given to . . . the people a more highly spiritualized notion of god, the idea of a single deity embracing the whole world, who was not less all-loving than all-powerful, who was averse to ceremonial and magic and set before men as their highest aim a life in truth and justice.
>
> —**Sigmund Freud,** *Moses and Monotheism*

In the penultimate chapter of *Strangers to Ourselves* (1989), Julia Kristeva distills the "political and ethical impact of the Freudian breakthrough."[1] Surfacing at the close of an invigorating cultural (and classically Kristevan) romp through political, literary, and philosophical history, carrying us from dawning awareness of sexual difference ("the first foreigners: women") to Jewish, Greek, and Roman representations of autochthony and otherness, and finally to Enlightenment thinking on universalism, her remarks on the uncanny in Freud signal our entry into a domain decisively shaped by Kristeva herself: that of politics and psychoanalysis. "The ethics of psychoanalysis implies a cosmopolitanism . . . of a mankind whose solidarity is founded on the consciousness of its unconscious."[2] The appearance of the Freudian concept of the uncanny in this context suggests that the goal of this movement is in a sense its starting point.[3] The movement toward cosmopolitanism involves, in Kristeva's presentation, the working through of the most primordial psychic connections —the remnants of the earliest yeas and nays, the projections and identifications from which the conscious "self" emerges. What binds us to one another is the shared wound of separation. Kristeva's repeated attention to this theme in the 1980s and subsequently is, I argue here, representative of a "return to Freud" which is distinctively her own.

Writing in the aftermath of Derrida's provocative exploration of nationalism in *De l'esprit: Heidegger et la question* (1987), Kristeva sees Freud's ethical legacy as entailing the interrogation of boundaries both within and external to the subject:

> The uncanny would thus be the royal way by means of which Freud introduced the fascinated rejection of the other at the heart of that 'our self,' so poised and dense, which precisely no longer exists ever since Freud and shows itself to be a strange land of borders and othernesses ceaselessly constructed and deconstructed.[4]

Like Freud, Kristeva circles, ever and again, the vexed connection between ethics and the unconscious, between ethico-political ideals/imperatives and the "split" human being whose aspiration to autonomy is forever undermined by the force of the Freudian discovery. If the task of psychoanalysis becomes in this way interminable, Kristeva seems confident of its bearing: "If I am a foreigner, there are no foreigners."[5] Welcoming the foreigner is a function of coming to terms with disintegration, or, in terms less stark, with finitude and opacity. Recognizing the subject as forever divided—limited in agency, incapable of self-knowledge, etc.—we can "promot[e] the togetherness of those foreigners that we all recognize ourselves to be."[6] Kristeva's claim is not so much that acknowledging unwanted aspects of oneself allows one to stop saddling others with these same traits. Taking ownership of disavowed impulses is not the real issue. It is the unconscious itself that is a standing affront to the dream of self-mastery, and it is this dream of mastery that must encounter its limit, again and again, in the blind eyes of Oedipus. If finitude can be or is in some manner decisively accepted, then foreigners need no longer bear the onus of somehow having violated wholeness, purity, and omnipotence; "foreigners," then, need no longer be made to pay for the disappointments of the natives.

Viewed in this light, Kristeva's formula for solidarity—the insight to be gleaned from psychoanalysis—is but a particular mode of representing and wrestling with finitude. That host of "modern" and "postmodern" thinkers (Nietzsche, Heidegger, Blanchot, Levinas, Derrida, and Butler come to mind) who have struggled, with poetic and conceptual force, to underline the acceptance of human mortality and human limitation, would not find psychoanalysis's song about the illusion of autonomy and the modesty of our claims to self-knowledge strange or foreign. The difficulty we have embracing the stranger and the other, our tendency to violate this other, is not unrelated to the difficulty we have embracing the cold possibility of a universe that does not extend to us the promise of temporal protection and eternal life: both offend our self-regard. What, in Kristeva's eyes, is peculiar to the psychoanalytic response to this exigency?

At this point, a skeptic might well wonder whether psychoanalytic practice or theory is likely to succeed in extracting solidarity from consciousness of finitude. The skeptic might pause over Kristeva's apparent disregard of Freud's sober observations of human nature: "One must be humble and hold back one's sympathies and antipathies if one wants to discover what is real in this world. . . . We lay a stronger emphasis on what is evil in men because other people disavow it and thereby make the human mind, not better, but incomprehensible."[7] Even prescinding from the question of whether human aggression in all its aspects (among these the tightening of individual and national boundaries in the interests of domination) is not rather reinforced by the encounter with finitude,[8] Kristeva's joining of self-knowledge and moral goodness calls out for further exploration. Placing in question both the individual's sense of boundaries and the economic limits on the hospitality of nation states and the generosity of its citizens, her challenge to the status quo is a radical one. Indeed, Kristeva locates the challenge that psychoanalysis poses to individualism as a successor to the "religious or rationalist" universalizing tendencies that individualism has displaced. The possibility that Kristeva's call for cosmopolitanism might prove itself to be less revolutionary audacity than complacent narcissism cannot be gainsaid. At times the Bulgarian-French philosopher whom Barthes dubbed "*l'étrangere*"[9] exhibits a puzzling assurance that "the other without," if welcomed and nourished, will return the favor,[10] a confidence which seems to neglect the reality and the "difference" of this other.[11] Kristeva is well aware of the risk that utopian aspiration resolves itself into support of the status quo, but does she succeed in skirting this risk?[12]

Kristeva's object, whether her concern be with politics or psychoanalysis, art or feminism, melancholy or motherhood, is the site of transformation. Her privileging of Freud's essay on "The Uncanny" (1919) in *Strangers to Ourselves* can be understood as a gesture in the direction of this transformative space.[13] In the notion of the uncanny, and the related affect of anxiety, we have a fruitful meeting point of infant and adult, of subject and other, of conscious and unconscious, of philosophy and psychoanalysis. Kristeva sets up shop in the no man's land of the *Unheimlich*, that space of ultimate familiarity and unsettling absence, as though it were the most fertile space possible for thinking and living. What makes Kristeva unfurl the banner of "the uncanny" in the middle of a discourse on philosophy, politics, and a hope that goes by the name of cosmopolitanism? Addressing this question affords a glimpse of what, in both Freud and Kristeva, might bode for "progress in spirit."

Taking Kristeva's notion of the uncanny as clue, we turn back to Freud's halting formulations of prehistory in the attempt to grasp the nature of the hope they both express for (human) spirit. While their hopes for humanity might appear to be grounded in quite disparate visions of human reality, common elements present themselves. The hope that Kristeva associates with psychoanalysis and the Freudian notion of the uncanny calls for a reading of the place of the latter in Freud's sociopolitical thought. This issue, which is the central concern of this essay, allows us to broach the question, so crucial to an understanding of Freud's work: Does his social-political thought minimize pre-Oedipal ties, or does it, however obliquely, accord these a fundamental role? Particular attention is given to texts in which Freud's metapsychology—his reading of the basic drives—is paired with his reflections on the question of meaning in history.[14] We treat principally *Group Psychology and the Analysis of the Ego*, *Civilization and Its Discontents*, and *Moses and Monotheism* before returning to Kristeva's case for an ethics of psychoanalysis. I suggest that Freud's turn to the death drive and his concomitant reformulation of the Oedipal complex, with its new emphasis on identification and primary narcissism, are central to understanding the significance of the uncanny, both in the context of Freud's thought and as it relates to Kristeva's conception of an ethics of psychoanalysis.

Progress in Spirit

If Kristeva's reading of history points to the possibility of progress in our capacity to live with others ("without ostracism but also without leveling"), Freud's own sketch for a philosophy of history, as outlined in *Moses and Monotheism*, shares in this hope for progress. But if Kristeva's account is one of boundaries recognized as permeable and changing, Freud's hope, early and late, is based on his stern insistence on measure and limit. Framed as a progression from animism (an attenuated form of narcissism) to religion (a further attenuation of narcissism) to scientific objectivity (the defeat of narcissism and rise of objectivity),[15] "progress in spirit," he proclaims, relies on the vanquishing of narcissism. In the final work published in his lifetime, *Moses and Monotheism*, this emphasis on "acceptance of difference" (whether it be called "objectivity," "truth," or "reality-testing") remains primary, and he ties its accomplishment explicitly and repeatedly to the rejection of the magical thinking associated with infantile narcissism: "The Egyptian Moses had given to . . . the people a more highly spiritualized notion of god, the idea of a single deity embracing the whole world, who was not less all-loving than all-powerful, who was averse to all ceremonial and magic and set before men as their highest aim a life in truth and justice."[16] What Freud calls "progress in spirit" (*Fortschritt in der Geistigkeit*) is, it would seem, the fruit of the rejection of the belief in spirits (*Geister*, in *Totem and Taboo*)—spirits who in one way or another could be bribed—in favor of an impersonal "spirit" of justice and truth. If, in Kristeva's view, benevolence toward the foreigner entails a felt awareness of one's early and intimate ties to others and the ongoing implication of others in one's "inner" subjectivity, Freud's goal seems premised on attaining the maximum distance from this near fusion.

Were this the final word on the matter, the relation between Kristeva and Freud would be but a study in contrasts. But the notion of *Geist*, which Freud claims for the Jews, points an avenue (or a hidden path) for rapprochement with Kristeva's concerns.

Moses and Monotheism lauds the Hebrew tradition as one of progress in *Geistigkeit*—a progress that consists in a movement away from (proto-Romantic) belief in a spirit-animated nature. Here, as earlier in *Totem and Taboo*, Freud's contention is that belief in the omnipotence of the individual's thoughts and wishes becomes translated into an investigation into the invisible forces of nature. Only gradually, according to Freud, does this force come to be viewed as impersonal:

> Human beings found themselves obliged in general to recognize "intellectual [*geistige*]" forces—forces, that is, which cannot be grasped by the senses (particularly by the sight) but which nonetheless produce undoubted and indeed extremely powerful effects. . . . This too led to the discovery of the mind [*Seele* (soul)] as that of the intellectual [*geistigen*] principle in individual human beings. . . . [T]hey [then attributed] the soul [*Seele*] which they had discovered in themselves to everything in Nature. The whole world was animate [*beseelt*]; and science, which came so much later, had plenty to do in divesting part of the world of its soul once more; indeed it has not completed that task even today.[17]

The progression depicted here repeats the trajectory outlined earlier in *Totem and Taboo*. But the positing of "*Fortschritt in der Geistigkeit*" as the outcome of the process raises a question concerning the nature of the step (*schritt*) forward, as spirit (*Geist*) survives even in the word Freud chose for the triumph of de-souled mind over matter. As we will see in what follows, the evolution of Freud's metapsychology and his understanding of the Oedipal complex render questionable the possibility of the definitive "achievement" of this detachment.

Freud's choice of the term *Geistigkeit* as the singular designation for Jewish accomplishment has, of course, a polemical angle. He wrests the notion of *Geist* from the cultural heirs of Herder, Hegel, and Goethe and claims it for the Jews.[18] *Moses and Monotheism* lends itself to a reading oriented toward its historical urgency, that is, as, on one hand, an account of the roots of anti-Semitism, and on the other, a veiled diatribe against National Socialism.[19] Our emphasis here, however, is on the question of the persistence of/return of "Geist" in the "highest" reaches of cultural achievement. In this approach, readers of Kristeva will find intimations of her lifelong interest in joining the earliest forms of meaning-making (Kristeva's notion of the semiotic, so intimately associated with the body's energy and rhythms) to subsequent symbolic formulation. Similarly, the role played by the notion of *Geistigkeit* in *Moses and Monotheism* may be read, I argue, as a clue to the significance of early object relations in Freud's thought. Spirit's *wissenschaftlich* exertions in the realm of theory are conditioned by ties that were anything but lifeless.

Freud's work is haunted at a number of junctures, and not only in *Moses and Monotheism*, by the specter of early object ties. How is this "haunting" made manifest? In much the same way as the latent wish in a dream—through discontinuities in manifest content, unexpected or unmotivated turns of argument, telling omissions—and most particularly through the recurring perplexities which trouble Freud's theorizing, bringing him ever and again to the effort of rethinking and reformulation.

Initially, the charge that Freud does not attend adequately to early object relations may appear doubly unfair. He addresses on a number of occasions the causes for belief in spirits (of the dead, in *Totem and Taboo*, and of ghosts/automatons/doppelgangers in "The Uncanny"). In each instance, his explanation draws from his theorizing on narcissism/early object relations.[20] Nonetheless, at critical theoretical junctures—particularly those concerned with the psychodynamics underlying religion, morality, and civilization—Freud routinely deflects attention away from the mother/infant bond.[21] His description of the intrauterine state as one of "absolute self-sufficient narcissism"[22] captures in a nutshell Freud's baseline ipso-centrism.[23] His creative reworking of the drives and his introduction of the death instinct signal nonetheless the force of the very phenomena that his ipso-centrism would exclude. Freud's account of what makes for "progress in spirit," for meaning in history, is dependent on the early object relations whose supersession he desires. The theoretical crisis that underlies Freud's thematization of the uncanny marks the emergence of this theme. Both the reconceptualization of the drives and the substantial reframing of the Oedipal complex, which are roughly contemporaneous with his reflections on the uncanny, are witness, however indirectly, to the primary and unsurpassable significance of "the other" in the life of the individual.[24] Three texts are the focus of attention here: (1) Freud's account of the Oedipal complex in *Group Psychology*, (2) his remarks on the oceanic feeling in *Civilization and Its Discontents*, and (3) his understanding of the past and future of the Jews in relation to their leader Moses in *Moses and Monotheism*. In each of these texts, a moment of indifferentiation between subject and other, which might be called uncanny, comes to the fore. Anticipating the dialogue with Kristeva's thought, it may be said that *if* Freud's thinking about early object relations is decisive in shaping his drive theory and his presentation of the Oedipal complex, then the key role Kristeva accords the uncanny in her reflections on psychoanalysis and ethics is not only justified but also in accordance with the momentum of Freud's own work.

An Uncanny Metapsychology

As we have noted, Freud's tendency to downplay pre-Oedipal relations is not all pervasive: *Three Essays on the Theory of Sexuality* (1905), with its emphasis on early development, is a case in point. But the implications of early object relations are grasped first in "On Narcissism" (1914) with Freud's attention to the gradual coalescing of the ego through early projections and identifications. The essay is pivotal for Freud's metapsychology and for his subsequent appropriation by Lacan and Kristeva. "On Narcissism" disrupts the distinction between self and other on which the first drive theory rested: a libido that can be transferred from (nascent) subject to object and back again cannot be squared with Freud's earlier understanding of the neurotic as torn between ego and object "instincts." The very notion of self-preservation as a basic drive (the ego instinct) is problematized by Freud's growing awareness of the shifting boundaries of the self—that is, by the fact that the "ego" to be preserved is by no means given at birth. Faced, then, with the prospect of a pansexualism that would render his own position indistinguishable from Jung's, Freud works out a new theory of a fundamental opposition between the energies of life (*Eros*) and death (*Todestrieb*).[25]

Freud's new drive theory may provisionally be read as replacing the early division of ego-instincts and object-instincts with an opposition between the drive toward individuation and drive toward merger. While libido was initially conceived as inexplicably "driving" one well-delineated monad toward another, *both* drives are now seen to condition the genesis of the subject—a subject now decentered by these forces. The distinction between self and other which was to define the terms of the most basic human conflict is not only abandoned: the theory of life and death drives places the emergence of the (ever-shifting) boundaries of the self at the very heart of Freud's metapsychology. The drives are no longer forces acting upon/within a clearly delineated self. Long before Kristeva's assertion of an ethics rooted in the experience of the uncanny, the subject is understood as bound up at its very "core" with the workings and being of another.

Freud's theory is remarkably similar to the split posited by Schopenhauer between a supra-individual will possessing ultimate reality and a principle of individuation that has its home in the realm of appearance (the former serving as the model for Freud's largely unconscious "*Es*," the latter as analogue of Freud's well-armored ego, itself a precursor to Lacan's imaginary).[26] A telling difficulty appears, however, in the attempt to specify which of the newly conjured drives, life or death, is to correspond to merger, and which to individualization. The initial aligning of the death instinct with self-preservation, a component instinct "whose function it is to assure that organism shall follow its own path to death,"[27] suggests that the death drive is linked to individuation and the erotic drive to fusion. Ultimately, though, this equation proves untenable, and for the same reason as the metapsychology based on the opposition of ego and object instincts: both presuppose a discrete subject.

Eros is said to have as its purpose the combining of "single human individuals, and after that families, then races, peoples and nations, into one great unity, the unity of mankind."[28] Both the infant at the mother's breast and, later, a person in love, exhibit the "feeling of indissoluble bond," the unity of ego and object,[29] which is the trademark of Eros.[30] The instinct of death is, by contrast, an awkward conglomerate of impulses—toward biological death, toward inertia and conservation of energy, and toward aggression, mastery, dissolution, and destruction.[31] Once Freud abandons the awkward attempt to classify self-preservation as in the service of a death drive, he must confront a Thanatos that, like Eros, disrupts the distinctions that prevail in the land of the living. Struggling to produce an example of a death instinct—and coming up short—Freud exclaims in wonder that the whole situation "creates a positively mystical impression"![32] The ability of examples to illuminate the terrain is brushed aside:

> The two kinds of instinct seldom—perhaps never—appear in isolation from each other. . . . It must be confessed that we have much greater difficulty in grasping that [death] instinct; we can only suspect it, as it were, as something in the background behind Eros, and it escapes detection unless its presence is betrayed by its being alloyed with Eros.[33]

The uncontainable libido, upon which the first drive theory came to grief, manifests itself here in an Eros so thoroughly (in)fused with death that the latter rarely or never appears apart from the former. Indeed, it is ultimately difficult to determine which term, death or Eros, is the greater friend of fusion (or disintegration and abjection, to borrow from Kristeva). Eros works for the merger of infant/caregiver, lovers, and ultimately citizens, and so on. Death also serves to unify the individual with a more encompassing force.

Freud's reflection on the nature of the fundamental drives point to a never-finally-fixed demarcation of self and other. There is an element of the uncanny in this metapsychology, in which (empirical) definition of the drives—whose conflict is to found human culture—remains so elusive. It is difficult to avoid the conclusion that the fundamental drives posited in *Beyond the Pleasure Principle* (1920), stemming from his 1914 reflections on narcissism and the libido's labile investments, share the indeterminacy of inner and outer that marks the experience of the uncanny. In spite of Freud's repeated protest against Jung's instinctual monism, "eros" and "death" give the impression of inseparability. Freud ponders the possibility of aligning his two basic drives with the love/hate ambivalence of object relations in Oedipal dynamics.[34] But, the reader may wonder, what precedes the degree of individuation required for love and hate?

Crossroads of the Oedipal

Freud's reformulation of the fundamental drives leads to an understanding of Oedipal dynamics as less a tale of rivalry and usurpation in the familial trio than a privileged site for the inscription of desire (usually presupposed in the Oedipal narrative). Though Freud offers no detailed overview of the relation between the Oedipal complex and his metapsychology, the revised theory of the drives comes to be mirrored in Oedipal dynamics now understood as encompassing early object relations. In *Group Psychology*, he makes room for an Oedipal complex that does not involve the decisive cut with the maternal (or early object relations of all forms) proclaimed later by Lacan under the heading of the symbolic. Kristeva, in *Tales of Love,* is quick to see the implications of this shift, a shift that makes possible her use of the uncanny in constructing an ethics of psychoanalysis.

In *Group Psychology and the Analysis of the Ego,* the publication of which followed close on the heels of the metapsychological innovations of *Beyond the Pleasure Principle,* identification/mimesis, "the earliest expression of an emotional tie with another person"[35] comes to play a key role. Identification no longer represents merely a belated response to Oedipal frustration but may be understood as itself a party to the conflict:

> Identification is known to psycho-analysis as the earliest expression of an emotional tie with another person. . . . It fits in very well with the Oedipal complex, for which it helps to prepare the way. . . . It [identification] behaves like a derivative of the first oral phase of the organization of the libido, in which the object that we long for and prize is assimilated by eating and is in that way annihilated as such. The cannibal, as we know, has remained at this standpoint; he has a devouring affection for his enemies and only devours people of whom he is fond.[36]

Freud's claim is that a boy's (more mature/differentiated) love for his mother is balanced by a pole of identificatory love/hate, described as a kind of devouring love, for the father. Noteworthy here is the fact that the relation to the father is described as ambivalent, not *in consequence of* the rivalry associated with desire for the mother, but prior to it. This more primitive form of "identificatory" affection is a devouring love that is ambivalent "from the first":

> At the same time as this identification with his father, or a little later, the boy has begun to develop a true object-cathexis towards his mother. . . . He then exhibits, therefore, two psychologically distinct ties: a straightforward sexual object-cathexis towards his mother and an identification with his father which takes him as his model. The two subsist side by side for a time without any mutual influence or interference. In consequence of the irresistible advance towards a unification of mental life, they come together at last; and the normal Oedipus complex originates from this. The little boy notices that his father stands in his way with his mother. His identification with his father then takes on a hostile colouring and becomes identical with the wish to replace his father in regard to his

mother as well. Identification, in fact, is ambivalent from the very first; it can turn into an expression of tenderness as easily as into a wish for someone's removal.[37]

Note the startling formulation here of the birth of the Oedipal complex: two relations (not yet thematized as "relation") coexist side-by-side "without mutual influence or interference." Then, "in consequence of the irresistible advance towards . . . unification [*infolge der unaufhaltsam fortschreitenden Vereinheitlichung*]," they "come together at last." And the immediate result of this coming together? A conflict, a sundering: "the normal Oedipus conflict originates from this." Or, we might say, the birth of the subject.

Upon examination, and as was the case with Freud's definition of the drives, the terms of the Oedipal conflict remain elusive, particularly insofar as one attempts to delineate the roles of "mother" and "father" in the scene. In the passages from *Group Psychology* quoted earlier, ambivalence has its primary source not in the incestuous feelings toward both parents, with attendant dual rivalry, *but rather in the fact the relation toward both the "father" and the "mother" exists simultaneously on two planes or registers*: the one oral, the second more differentiated. The young boy's relation to the father is described in terms that would commonly be viewed as derivative from his relation to his mother: as *oral*. But the child's relation to the father cannot, of course, be limited to one of early identification: the father takes on the role of freeing both the male and female child from absorption in the mother's world/desire. At the same time, the child's relation to his mother is not solely one of "straightforward sexual object-cathexis," but always bears the resonance of early oral ties. On this reading, the Oedipal complex is less a tale of painful rivalry than a scar which marks the impossibility of "full" translation between two registers of experience with each of two parents—a recurrent point of crisis (and the terrain of both Freud's and Kristeva's notion of the uncanny).

Freud's increasing emphasis on identification as intrinsic to Oedipal dynamics leads to an interpretation of the latter as a critical meeting point of infant and adult ways of loving, wanting, and "thinking." Early "objectless identifications"[38] meet more fully differentiated object relations. The maturation that was to result from the drama of love, rivalry, loss and identification is replaced by a crisis at the heart of the self, a crisis that is manifest in our relating to others at one and the same moment on radically distinct planes. Freud's fanciful conjuring, in *Civilization and Its Discontents*, of a Rome that could be viewed in a single instant in its successive historical incarnations is an apt figure for the psychoanalytic project, that is, for the psychic strata it would bring to light.³⁹ The Oedipal juncture marks the emergence of the other as distinct, a "moment" in which identification with the other yields, or for the most part yields, to the separation necessary for desire.⁴⁰ It remains conflictual, its objects both within and external to the subject, a site of discontinuity as well as ongoing transformation. The juxtaposition, found in Freud's *Group Psychology and the Analysis of the Ego*, of (1) an Oedipal complex with increased emphasis on pre-Oedipal identification as one of its components and (2) the role of suggestion/hypnosis in the enrichment or impoverishment of group life, will lead us back to issues tackled by Kristeva under the heading of the uncanny.

As indicated, Freud's presentation of the Oedipal complex in the early 1920s is increasingly concerned with the role of identification in Oedipal dynamics. In a 1919 letter to friend and analyst Sándor Ferenczi, Freud links, as if in one breath (1) the composition of the essay "The Uncanny," (2) the completion of *Beyond the Pleasure Principle*, with its fundamental revision of the theory of drives, and (3) the working out of the argument of *Group Psychology and the Analysis of the Ego*.⁴¹ The unnamed common denominator in all these instances is the provisional nature of the ego's boundaries, both in early object relations, as these boundaries form, and in dimensions of group behavior. If the concern with early object relations in "The Uncanny" is patent, these relations are no less central to the revised theory of drives, to the revisioning of the Oedipal complex, and to the uncanny pitfalls and transformative possibilities of social existence.

The evolution of Freud's thinking, and his continual return to the question of the birth of conscience, is an ongoing encounter with and reinterpretation of the Oedipal complex. This ever unresolved crisis between fusion (disintegration/abjection) and individuation bears within it a certain moral drama which, at its extremes, appears either as capitulation to unconscious urges or submission to a life of arid principle.⁴² Suffice it to say that the possibility of living a moral life ("a life in truth and justice") is related, within *Group Psychology*, to the ongoing negotiation of the Oedipal drama.

Oedipal Conflict as *Nachträglichkeit*

The ever conflictual, ever unresolved Oedipal dynamics can now be seen to mirror the vision of human life that Freud presented so powerfully in *Beyond the Pleasure Principle*. There, the conflict between life and death was portrayed as divided between, on one hand, the forces of anticipation, striving, futural projection, representative of the drive of Eros toward ever more complex unities, and on the other hand of stasis, nostalgia, and so on—the domain of the former "ego instincts." The temporal dimension of the conflict leads us to the phenomenon known as *"Nachträglichkeit."* Translated as deferred, or delayed, action, *nachträglichkeit* represents *in nuce* an amalgam of these two modes of experience, one timeless, the other caught up in the flow towards a future. Through the action of *nachträglichkeit*, as described by Freud in "Screen Memories" (1899), past traumas reemerge continually in ongoing experience, like ripples from a timeless center. Correspondingly, current repressed concerns reshape the past in a continuing process of revision and construction.[43] The phenomenon occurs not only in marked instances of trauma but is inherent in the manner in which we all, of necessity, view past, present and future. Psychic traumas and their effects in ongoing experience merely magnify everyday features of conscious life. Charles Shepherdson makes the universality of the phenomenon evident in his depiction of "the traumatic event—the very advent of the ego":

> The experiences of war and other traumas do not belong to past time. They continue to intrude upon the present, blocking the experience of the here and now, and asserting themselves in place of immediate experience—as if blinding the subject and interrupting vision with a kind of memory that does not appear as "memory," ... so that the subject's own experience is lost....
>
> As the very structure of the "mirror stage" suggests, the traumatic event—the very advent of the ego—takes place before the subject is able to bear witness, ... and because it stands at the origin in this way, "before" the subject, we can only conclude that the trauma was never present to the subject as such, and this is why it cannot pass away or belong to the past, as a present that once was. Because it does not belong to the past, moreover, the traumatic event is constantly expected to return from the future, like a catastrophe that is about to occur—a catastrophe (like object-loss in Kristeva's text) that must be avoided at all cost.... As Blanchot says, "We are on the edge of disaster without being able to situate it in the future: it is rather always already past, and yet we are on the edge or under the threat, all formulations which would imply the future—that which is to come—if the disaster were not that which does not come, that which has put a stop to every arrival."[44]

Though Shepherdson's description of *nachträglichkeit* draws on the later theorizing of Blanchot and Lacan, it is implied already in the structure of an Oedipal complex linking (1) early identificatory relations "prior to the advent of the ego" and (2) "true object cathexes" that presuppose an ego already on the scene. As is clear from Shepherdson's quote, the structure of *nachträglichkeit* is a quasi-transcendental condition of consciousness—it is not restricted to instances of trauma. As the reference to Kristeva suggests, it is related to the psychic processes of attachment and separation, and it pertains to the threat of object loss (as well as the obverse threat, that of capitulation to and engulfment by the other, dubbed by Kristeva "abjection").

The conflict that goes by the name of Oedipal is thus mirrored in *nachträglichkeit*'s disruption of linear time. The tragic resonance of this vision of human existence, torn between striving/accomplishment and timeless union with a solicitous/enveloping other, appears in a phenomenon as basic as our need for sleep. The phenomenon of sleep testifies, in Freud's eyes, to our inability to tolerate, uninterruptedly, "the world into which we have come so unwillingly."[45] "Thus by being born we have made the step from an absolutely self-sufficient narcissism [Freud's take on prenatal existence] to the perception of a changing external world. . . . And with this is associated the fact that *we cannot endure the new state of things for long*."[46] A world that is not moved by our desires, not governed by "spirit," a world that is dead, is not to be borne. We prefer a universe in which the laws of nature show themselves to be in harmony with our own sense of necessity, as well as with our deepest wishes. Neither condition coincides with Freud's view of reality. Yet our simple need for sleep shows that the triumphal march of increasing separation from the other—from narcissism, through religion, to science, as depicted in *Totem and Taboo*—has suffered a decisive setback. The hypnotist's command to "sleep" and the parent's lulling a child over the threshold to sleep testifies to the subject's ongoing juggling of separation and connectedness at the most elemental level. Any reading of the Oedipal complex that overlooks the imperative nature of this need, or that implies a decisive arrival at an object relation beyond the sway of narcissism, does not do justice to the intersection of individual psychology and group psychology that Freud brings to light in *Group Psychology*. Julia Kristeva's work of cosmopolitanism relies explicitly on this "uncanny" intersection of individual and social.

Freud's understanding of the promise and risks of group existence is tied to a culture's careful negotiation of immersion in group life versus individuation and responsibility:

> In the course of our development we have effected a separation of our mental existence into a coherent ego and into an unconscious

and repressed portion which is left outside it; and we know that the stability of this new acquisition is exposed to constant shocks. In dreams and in neuroses what is thus excluded knocks for admission at the gates. . . . It is quite conceivable that the separation of the ego ideal from the ego cannot be borne for long either, and has to be temporarily undone. In all renunciations and limitations imposed upon the ego a periodical infringement of the prohibition is the rule; this indeed is shown by the institution of festivals.[47]

The parallel drawn here between psychic and social structure is prescient. Neither the primal repression of id nor the parallel separation of ego and ego ideal can be endured without respite. In the absence of cultural mediation through which the ego ideal is relaxed and the repressed comes to expression (Freud's example in this instance is carnival), the conflict that is the life of the subject threatens to become insupportable. Failure to judge these stakes properly, Freud warns, can lead to a hypnotist/leader's usurpation of, and the citizen's abdication, of the ego ideal. Instead of the fresh air of carnival (with its passing joy and cruelty), a more enduring, and ominous, substitution of an external object/leader for one's ego ideal occurs. External authority usurps internal authority.[48] An uncanny event indeed, and a potential that Kristeva recognizes as ever-present—most decidedly when no art/religion/psychoanalysis capable of bridging the realms of sensual and intellectual is on hand.

Already in *Group Psychology*, it is clear that the conflict between "progress" and nostalgia involves discomfort and unease. In *Civilization and Its Discontents*, where this battle is described in terms of civilization and its costs, Freud notes a universal desire for "consolation," which he himself is unwilling to provide. Thus he shuns, in 1920, the possibility of a leadership that he later, in 1938, will shoulder. In what follows, we trace the fate of fusion and differentiation in the larger socio/political arena treated in *Civilization and Its Discontents* and *Moses and Monotheism*.

Civilization as Discomfort and as Destiny

Civilization and Its Discontents, written in 1929, paints a sobering picture of the price of civilization's restrictions on human freedom. Its account of culture and conscience paves the way for the final attempt to view religion and ethics in light of (pre-)Oedipal conflict in *Moses and Monotheism*.

As is so often the case in Freud's texts, the reader is solicited for help in solving a mystery (just as the analysand is called on to help unveil the riddles of pathology).[49] In the case of *Civilization and Its Discontents*, the riddle, introduced in Chapter IV, concerns the extent of the strictures placed on sexual impulses by civilization, since these strictures would seem to exceed the necessities associated with the survival of the group. At first, there is little sign of early object relations or of the uncanny in this drama. The proposal is that sexual expression is limited in order to form larger collectives that serve the interests of the group. Sexual desires must yield to the necessities of work. The mystery surrounding social controls on sexual expression appears resolved—the conflict that characterizes the civilized ego is one between libidinal and self-preservative drives (id versus ego "instincts," the first drive theory).

The question is abruptly reopened in the next chapter, and the mystery deepens: how are the impracticable moral ideals of love of neighbor and love of enemies to be accounted for? Why is sexual satisfaction postponed in favor of the pursuit of impossibly exalted ideals, ideals unrelated to the goal of bringing bread and game to the table? The stage is set for the (re-)introduction of what "people are so ready to disavow": the reality and power of human aggression, a scandal that Freud well knew far exceeded his "revelations" regarding infant sexuality. It is the death drive (introduced nine years earlier in *Beyond the Pleasure Principle*) that necessitates the massive diversion of sexual energy to "aim-inhibited" affection, which is to bind the members of society. Such inhibitions leave the individual frustrated and uneasy (we return to familiar ground), and "civilization" is for its part bound in the vicious cycle of inhibiting sexual expression as a means of "binding" aggression, while the resultant frustration and aggression necessitates still further tightening of sexual mores. It is not only the call of the hearth that opposes larger social organization, but also the stirrings of an enigmatic "death drive."

With the introduction of the death drive, however, the emphasis on society's regulation of its members gives way to questions concerning the origin of conscience and guilt. The death drive complicates the understanding of individual freedom thus far elaborated in *Civilization*. Not only must "civilization" limit aggression and sexual expression in order to make social existence possible, but individuals are also themselves divided in their aims—"prior" to the reach of stern parents and oppressive cultures, infused with a uncanny strangeness associated with death. The death drive accounts for both the need for social controls and the individual's capacity to enforce them. Freud's account of the primal horde (in chapter VII of *Civilization and Its Discontents*) is invoked in order to account for the "original sin" of a guilt whose "fatal inevitability"[50] exceeds any cultural exigency. The myth of the primal horde and of the internalization and transmission of this event to subsequent generations, intended to address this anomaly, exposed Freud to charges of Lamarckism. Whatever the outcome of scholarly debates on the matter,[51] it is clear that the tale of the primal horde is to bridge the tie, at the level of the unconscious, between the individual and the race; as such the issue emerges prominently in *Totem and Taboo*, *Group Psychology*, *Civilization and Its Discontents*, and, last but not least, *Moses and Monotheism*.

Though Freud understands guilt to be fueled by the energy of the thwarted aggressive instincts,"[52] these impulses are internalized, we are told, not only due to the individual's encounter with parental aggression, but also, and importantly, because of the individual's love of/identification with the figures of authority. Freud's concern, in preceding chapters, to confront the reader with the scope of human aggression—to persuade the reader that the opposition between civilization and erotic impulses is necessitated by the presence of this menacing leviathan—is here balanced by an account of conscience (and of the Oedipal complex which gives rise to it) as bound up with "the part played by love."[53] Prior to Freud's discussion of the death drive in the sixth chapter of *Civilization and Its Discontents*, he alludes to this anomaly:

> The sexual life of civilized man is notwithstanding severely impaired. . . . Sometimes one seems to perceive that it is not only the pressure of civilization but something in the nature of the function itself which denies us full satisfaction and urges us along other paths. This may be wrong; it is hard to decide.[54]

Ambivalence gives rise to conscience; internalization of moral principles, Freud makes clear, is not a function of external aggression alone.[55] The central role accorded ambivalence and identification in Oedipal dynamics thus reflects the theoretical advances made in *Group Psychology*. The psychic mechanisms underlying the life of the individual and the group are not as discrete as Freud's description of the individual's rebellious desire for freedom would suggest.

The Oceanic

As we have seen, *Civilization and Its Discontents* raises the question of the rationale for and consequences of civilization's vigorous regulation of the lives of its members. A first-time reader of the text confronts, in addition, an apparently minor perplexity in the text's first pages, one that serves to embed the larger issues of culture and conscience (the battle of life and death, at the level of macrocosm and microcosm) in early object relations and the theme of the uncanny. The uncanny, as we have seen, reveals individual conflict at its most fundamental level as bearing within itself a social dimension; viewed in this light, chapter I of *Civilization and Its Discontents* has the potential to qualify the account of conscience offered in its subsequent chapters.

Freud is a master narrator, with such a keen awareness of the likely objections to his claims that these are typically tackled prior to the unveiling of the latter. But *Civilization and Its Discontents* opens in a seemingly haphazard way, in a debate with novelist/pacifist Romain Rolland over the source of religious feeling. Rolland's claim is that religious feeling has its source in an oceanic feeling (*ozeanische Gefühl*), "a feeling as of something limitless, unbounded." Freud ultimately dismisses this feeling as the source of religious belief, but not before dedicating almost the entirety of the first chapter of *Civilization* to an inquiry into its source. Why the concern with this naturalistic, feeling-based account of religious faith? Or, put differently, what is the significance of the oceanic feeling, given the fact that Freud treats it as a red herring on the quest for a drive-based account of religious belief? The red herring plays a suspiciously prominent role in the work, and one casts about, automatically, for the unnamed considerations that would warrant this. Freud does mount a memorable diatribe against Christianity later in the book, its target being the demand for "universal" love of neighbor.[56] Might Freud's examination of the oceanic feeling and his rejection of this feeling as a basis for religious belief serve also as a rejection of the oceanic feeling as the basis for a naturalistic ethics (that is, an ethics understood as a direct expression of human sentiment)? The oceanic feeling, preceding as it does the capacity for renunciation, for consciousness of freedom and individuality—is related to the phenomenon of the uncanny.

The espousal of the death drive in *Beyond the Pleasure Principle* (1920) was heralded by the essay on the uncanny (1919). *Civilization and Its Discontents*, the work that, subsequent to *Beyond the Pleasure Principle*, offers the most sustained case for the death drive, opens with the vivid sensual tones of the oceanic feeling, a feeling that, like the uncanny, involves the ego's uncertain boundaries.

> An infant at the breast does not as yet distinguish his own ego from the external world as the source of the sensations flowing in upon him. . . . [Later] the ego detaches itself from the external world. Or, to put it more correctly, originally the ego includes everything, later it separates off an external world from itself. Our present ego-feeling is, therefore, only a shrunken residue of a much more inclusive—indeed, an all-embracing—feeling which corresponded to a more intimate bond between the ego and the world around it.[57]

Freud goes on to note that "this primary ego-feeling" may persist and exist "side by side with the narrower and more sharply demarcated ego-feeling of maturity."[58] It is this phenomenon of dissonance—of partial "regression to a time when the ego had not yet marked itself off sharply from the external world and from other people"[59]—which Freud ties to the uncanny in his paper of 1919.[60] Though the uncanny and the oceanic feeling are distinct states of mind, with the uncanny associated with anxiety, and the oceanic feeling with comfort and security, both derive from the capacity to revive in some form earlier feeling states and earlier forms of object relations. The Oedipal complex, as it was presented in *Group Psychology and the Analysis of the Ego,* marked the gap between two different and untranslatable registers and served as the point of departure for an account of the vicissitudes of individual responsibility. Here, too, the phenomena of the uncanny and the oceanic are brought into association with moral endeavor.

The subjective feeling of the oceanic might appear a plausible source of religious feeling and, more generally, a source of cultural and ethical ties. The account of the oceanic feeling as the residue of early stages of ego development does nothing to diminish this plausibility. But, however plausible the association, Freud is not inclined to embrace oceanic fusion as the fount of human empathy. His treatment of the oceanic more likely represents, at least in part, some form of preemptive strike—an attempt to discredit the possibility of basing an ethics on nonconflictual sympathy and fellow-feeling. He is concerned to reign in and render questionable "excessive" ethical aspiration. Freud is eager, for this reason, to cast Christian ethics as impracticable—too sublime, too dismissive of the human.[61] The possibility of a universal oceanic feeling that could be seen as bolstering and legitimating the lofty aspirations of Christian ethics would not have been welcome. At all events, the oceanic feeling is dismissed as the source of religious feeling ("the oceanic feeling became connected with religion later on"[62]), and the religious urge is instead said to arise out of awareness of danger and a desire for powerful paternal protection. Taken as a sole support for the Christian injunction to universal love, the oceanic feeling does not do justice to the fact of aggression.

The question remains whether the oceanic feeling serves only a negative function in the text, a warning against conceptual error (the notion of an unmediated moral sense based in sympathy). Freud's discussion of the long-preserved psychic strata by which he accounts for the oceanic feeling calls to mind the distortions and temporal anomalies surrounding *nachträglichkeit* and tied to what would later be referred to as the split subject. If, in Freud's eyes, the conflict between love and death in the cosmic macrocosm and the psychic microcosm is the crowning insight of *Civilization*, the oceanic feeling and conflicts surrounding its repression or resurgence introduce and frame this larger drama. The question of societal organization and the basic drives that govern it are introduced by a discussion of the forces that govern the first stirrings of difference in the ebb and flow of mother/child. As indicated in the discussion of Freud's metapsychology in section II of this essay, the opposition of love and death drives may be viewed as eclipsed by the presence, in *both* drives, of a potential for unification/fusion and its opposite. If the oceanic feeling is not compatible with the model of ethico-religious experience centered on the dictates of a patriarchal religion, the extensive treatment granted the phenomenon troubles the waters, casting doubt on the adequacy of the treatment of religion and morality that followed. Can any cogent account of ethics emerge from the neglect of early object relations? The continual return of the tale of the primal father (mother?), also in the penultimate chapter of this text, would seem to indicate that it cannot.

In the concluding pages of *Civilization and Its Discontents*, Freud ponders the outcome of the supraindividual conflict between eros and death. Will the forces of love and unity prevail, or will destruction (of self and other) carry the day? In this context, Freud maintains a strict neutrality. Earlier, in the first chapter of the text, Freud had observed: "I cannot think of any need in childhood as strong as the need for a father's protection."[63] But Freud refuses, in the closing lines of *Civilization and its Discontents*, to fill the place of this consoling father/prophet:

> For a wide variety of reasons, it is very far from my intentions to express an opinion upon the value of human civilization. I have endeavoured to guard myself against the enthusiastic prejudice which holds that our civilization is the most precious thing that we possess or could acquire and that its path will necessarily lead to heights of unimagined perfection. I can at least listen without indignation to the critic who is of the opinion that when one surveys the aims of cultural endeavour and the means it employs, one is bound to come to the conclusion that the whole effort is not worth the trouble, and that the outcome of it can only be a state of affairs which the individual will be unable to tolerate. My impartiality is made all the easier to me by my knowing very little about all these things. . . . Thus I have not the courage to rise up before my fellow-men as a prophet, and I bow to their reproach that I can offer them no consolation: for at bottom that is what they are all demanding—the wildest revolutionaries no less passionately than the most virtuous believers.[64]

Having broached the implications of aggression as a fundamental drive, Freud refuses to pronounce upon the future of the battle between love and hate. Whether "the whole effort [of civilized existence] is . . . worth the trouble" is a question we children of the race may direct to fathers and prophets, but not to Freud. At least not in 1928. Freud's attempt to carve out a position of neutrality in the pitched battle of love and hate and his shying away from the role of prophet is reflective, in my eyes, of an unwillingness to acknowledge at this point the ongoing and never fully surpassed pull of early object ties—ties that are deeply formative of our ethics and religion.

The elements to which have attended thus far—early object ties, a richly multivalent Oedipal complex, and its role in Freud's accounts of primal history and the founding of culture—all come to be cast in compelling form in the monumental retelling of the story of Moses, the Egyptian stranger, imposing his uncanny Aten religion on the wandering tribes of his chosen. This is to become Freud's final dramatic assessment of object loss, mourning, and "progress."[65] The staging of the encounter with the primal father, the instauration of the law, and the destiny of the Jewish people suggest a reading of early object ties as ever implicated in cultural striving and accomplishment. The insight is expressed with striking economy by Freud's understanding of the post-exilic deity of the Hebrew tribes as an amalgam of the impartial and transcendent deity of Akhenaten, whose universal ascendancy reflected the compass of Egyptian rule, and his fiery, boundary-breaking Hebrew counterpart. The God of measure and the god of trespass/fusion are unaccountably joined. How the journey from these early ties is imagined—as traumatic cataclysm and exile, or as spontaneous unfolding—is key to drawing out the ethical bearing of psychoanalysis.

Trauma and Monotheism

Begun in 1934 and published in the year prior to Freud's death, *Moses and Monotheism* (1938) was not calculated to win admirers for Freud. The central theses of the work, that Moses was an Egyptian and that the Jewish people were *his* creation—"chosen," that is, by Moses rather than by God, can scarcely have appealed to fellow Jews as comfort in dark times. Freud maintained that monotheistic belief originated in Egypt under Akhenaten's reign and that it excluded "everything to do with myths, magic, and sorcery."[66] Set apart by its "clarity, consistency, harshness and intolerance,"[67] the religion of monotheism failed to receive poplar support and was abandoned after Akhenaten's death. Moses, an aristocrat, and perhaps a member of the royal household, left Egypt at this time in hopes of founding a new kingdom and restoring worship of the Aten god. He chose the Semitic tribes of Goshen for this purpose, leading an exodus from Egypt with Canaan as its goal. Freud claims that, ultimately, the Aten religion was as unpopular among the Semitic tribes as it had been among the Egyptian people. The Jews rose up against Moses and killed him. Subsequently, these tribes, bearing now the traumatic memory of crime against their leader, joined other Jewish tribes of the region between Egypt and Canaan, and these tribes unified under a new leader, Moses of Kadesh. "Domineering, hot-tempered and even violent,"[68] this Moses forged a new religion from elements of both Egyptian monotheism and the Midianite worship of Yahweh, which on Freud's account resembled the Canaanite worship of storm-god Ba'al and his attendant deities. This is the story told in Essays I and II of *Moses and Monotheism*, composed prior to Freud's emigration to England.

The final essay tells the story of a gradual "return of the repressed" among the Jewish people, that is, the return of the "original" Egyptian monotheism, with its refusal of idolatry and stringent ethical demands. According to Freud, the repressed memory of the murder of Moses, itself an echo of the murder of the tyrannical father of the primal horde, returns repeatedly in the history of the Jews, particularly during times of historical hardship, *bringing with it the monotheistic religion to which he adhered*.[69] The Prophets gave form to this "return of the repressed" as they "tirelessly preached the old Mosaic doctrine—that the deity disdained sacrifice and ceremonial and asked only for faith and a life in truth and justice."[70] The progress in spirit (*Fortschritt in der Geistigkeit*) that Freud attributed to the Jewish people was due to the ever more powerful resurgence of this foreign god, demanding a turn away from the senses and an obedience to a transcendent deity (a turn marked in male flesh by circumcision). A gap thus exists between Moses's original presentation of monotheism to "his" people and their eventual affirmation of its precepts. Monotheism's break with sensuality is here presented as a past event that nonetheless remains on the horizon—a promising menace, like any threatened return of the repressed. But in this case the repressed is our very capacity, limited as it may be, for measure, for objectivity, for justice. The gap between monotheism's first "arrival" (glimpsed? rejected!) and its never fully accomplished re-cognition is the space of the wandering in the wilderness. The *nachträglich* quality of trauma could hardly be more plainly cast; and here this "belatedness" concerns *the very reception of our humanity*. Let us look more closely at the manner in which Freud projects this connection between trauma and the ethico-religious field.[71]

The dualities in Freud's account of the transmission of monotheism are striking: the original "Apollonian" Moses, murdered by his people and succeeded by a fiery "Dionysian" Moses; and likewise the two "Judaisms"—the strict monotheism of the Egyptian Moses and the subsequent "compromise" in Kadesh with forms of worship resembling Canaanite polytheism—are salient.[72] As these doubles proliferate, one begins to suspect that they are joined in some manner—the Egyptian Moses, whom Freud identifies as a pacifist, and the warlike Midianite Moses; the god Aten, transcending nature and sense, and the boundary-destroying volcano god Yahweh.[73] Doppelgangers all. Freud's account of the way in which monotheism is to be retrieved repeats this uncanny association of violation and purification. Freud claims the Egyptian pacifist god is only recalled through a return of the repressed, and the repressed in this instance was murder. The "progress in spirit" for which Freud wishes to argue is described as the victory of intellectuality over brute force. This victory recapitulates at the cultural level the outcome of the Oedipal complex through the instauration of the law, the twin prohibitions of exogamy against incest and murder. In *Moses and Monotheism*, however, it is the murder of Moses that makes possible the resurrection of monotheism from the depths of memory—uncanny, strange, as any renunciation.

In a nutshell: there are two traumas in the text: murder and monotheism. They are as closely implicated as the boundary-crossing instinct of life and the arid separation of the death drive, which themselves, as we saw, eventually confound their own determination. The drives of life and death, serpentine in their weaving (section II), the "crossing" of identification and individuation in the Oedipal complex (section III), and the final and intimate association of murder and monotheism are discomfiting.[74] If we were to substitute a crossing of familial sexual boundaries (incest) for murder, or if, more generally, we were to replace "murder" with the urge to merge with the other, then we might say that the exhortation to lead a life of "truth and justice" has as its complement a drive that, in however different forms, crosses boundaries. Whether this is a fiery deity, a violent Moses, or the mother of childhood is unclear. It would not be first time that a violent masculinity conceals something quite other. The inseparability of Freud's fiery bloody god of immanence and the transcendent upholder of justice points to a reality at the core of any psychoanalytic ethics. Just as in *Civilization and Its Discontents*, the battle for morality and justice seems quite closely tied to something going on in the nursery.

In the first Prefatory Note to Essay III of *Moses and Monotheism*, written from Vienna, with the German invasion imminent, Freud writes of his hesitation to publish the work, speculating that what is "preserved in concealment will some day . . . venture without danger into the light." And this was a return of the repressed that was doubtless of great personal interest for Freud. When he communicated the outline of his theory to Lou Andreas-Salomé, she responded by drawing attention to the work's anomalous optimism:

> Hitherto we have usually understood the term 'return of the repressed' in the context of neurotic processes: all kinds of material which had been wrongly repressed afflicted the neurotic mysteriously with phantoms of the past, because in them he sensed something primevally familiar, which he felt bound to ward off. But in this case we are presented with examples of the survival of the most triumphantly vital elements of the past as the truest possession in the present, despite all the destructive elements and counter-forces they have endured. . . . Whatever strange things may have gone on in the soul of primitive man, which seem to us in later times from our more enlightened standpoint to be so obviously archaic and distorted, these things nevertheless include elements of psychical power which later receded behind intellectual, emotionally weakening forces.[75]

It is unclear whether Andreas-Salomé and Freud would agree as to the identity of the "triumphantly vital elements of the past" to which she refers. In Andreas-Salomé's account, both the ghastly trespass and the sublime law seem to be included under the heading of what is "vital." In any case, Andreas-Salomé has not failed to note that Freud, who earlier refused to pronounce upon the worth of civilization, takes up in these pages the position of one who offers the ambiguous consolation that in *Civilization and Its Discontents* was withheld. To be human is to be cultured, riven at the core by an uncanny event, itself neither of nature nor of culture. Torn out of nature, though never removed from the ebb and flow of her timeless approach.[76] Becoming one with "his people," Freud abandons his agnosticism regarding the future. Acknowledging the world-historical importance of single individuals like the great man Moses, he grapples with his own fame and intellectual legacy with the tempered pride and candor of one about to die. Seeing the fragility of his own life, of his life's work, and of his fellow Jews; seeing the terrible fragility of culture itself, he at last sides with the endeavor of culture and humanity, with all it entails; and he announces with sibylline assurance the ambiguous condolence culled from a life of thought: morality will return, and with it violence, too; but morality will return, ever and again from the ashes.

Tales of Love

In the introduction to this essay, we asked how the cosmopolitanism advocated by Kristeva, and linked by her to psychoanalysis, would differ from a more generic coming-to-terms with finitude. We asked, more particularly, why Kristeva associates her undertaking with Freud's work on the uncanny, which seems concerned more with aesthetics than with ethics. We have seen that Freud's 1919 essay on the uncanny brings to the fore experiences and affects associated with the ego's unstable boundaries, as well as the relationships out of which the ego emerges. The essay signaled major changes in Freud's theory of drives and his understanding of the Oedipal complex, which in turn generated, in *Group Psychology*, *Civilization and Its Discontents*, and *Moses and Monotheism*, a meditation on what we might call the vicissitudes of culture.

If the significance of early object relations in Freud's metapsychology is open to debate, they are unquestionably the central focus of Kristeva's trilogy *Powers of Horror* (1980), *Tales of Love* (1983), and *Black Sun* (1987).[77] In *Tales of Love*, Kristeva argues that primary narcissism, with its pre-objectal "relations," lies at the core of all object relations. She draws support for this view from Freud's "On Narcissism":

> Freud seems to suggest that it is not Eros but narcissistic primacy that sparks and perhaps dominates psychic life. . . . For Freud, as we know, binds the state of loving to narcissism; the choice of the love object, be it "narcissistic" or "anaclitic," proves satisfying in any case if and only if that object relates to the subject's narcissism in one of two ways: either through personal narcissistic reward (where Narcissus is the subject), or narcissistic delegation (Narcissus is the other; for Freud, the woman). A narcissistic destiny would in some way underlie all our object choices, but this is a destiny that society on the one hand, and the moral rigor of Freud on the other, tend to thrust aside in favor of a "true" object choice.[78]

Kristeva maintains that "narcissism" is by no means an original or primal state, but a "supplement." She cites in this connection Freud's distinction between a primal "autoeroticism" and narcissism—which can only be elicited by "a new psychic action [*eine neue psychische Aktion*]."[79] This supplementary action allows Kristeva to claim that narcissism is a state which surpasses the mother-child dyad and involves, already, the triadic structure normally associated with Oedipal relations: "That observation [of a new psychic action] endows narcissism with an intrasymbolic status, dependent upon a third party but within a disposition that chronologically and logically precedes that of the Oedipal Ego. It prompts one to conceive of an archaic disposition of the paternal function, preceding the Name, the Symbolic, but also preceding the 'mirror stage' whose logical potentiality it would harbor."[80] Not surprisingly, Kristeva makes her difference from Lacan explicit at this point, introducing an "imaginary Father" who is to make possible both relation and signification: "the emptiness that is intrinsic to the symbolic function appears as the first separation between what is not yet an Ego and not yet an object."[81] Narcissism, Kristeva claims, is the "screen" for this emptiness, its double.

Though her terminology is daunting, it is clear Kristeva rejects what she takes to be Lacan's violent separation of the symbolic from the sensual "communication" of mother and infant. In the case studies cited in *Black Sun*, the analysand's affectless speech is read as a sign of (1) what Lacan formulates as "lack of lack," a failure of decisive separation from the primal caregiver or (2) an all too decisive sundering of this bond. The analysand's aimless and disjointed speech becomes, particularly in Kristeva's work in the 1980s and thereafter, a symptom at once social and individual. Just as Kant claimed that a coherent moral life requires postulating an eventual union of virtue and happiness, Kristeva shows that human thriving requires that the language of the body can be drawn toward the aspiration of the spirit.[82]

How is an ethics to be elicited from Kristeva's reading of narcissism? Citing Freud's account of identification in *Group Psychology* as the "earliest expression of an emotional tie [*Gefühlsbindung*] with another," she joins identification (*Identifizierung*) and empathy (*Einfühling*).[83] Stating that she does not wish to embark on "the impossible quest for the absolute origin of the capacity for love as *a psychic and symbolic capacity* [emphasis mine]," she shifts the domain but takes up the quest: "The question actually bears on states existing on the border between the psychic and the somatic . . . within analytic treatment itself."[84] Rather than leave this intersection between body and psyche at the abstract level, she draws the thread through the loom:

> Let me simply note that becoming *as* the One is imagined by Freud as an oral assimilation; indeed he links the possibility of archaic identification to the "oral phase of the libido's organization . . ." Nevertheless, one might well wonder about the notional slippage

that takes place between the "incorporation" of an object, or even its "introjection," and an *Identifizierung* that is not on the level of "having" but locates itself at once on that of "being like." On what ground, within what material, does having switch over to being? While seeking an answer to that question it appeared to me that incorporating and introjecting orality's function is the essential substratum of what constitutes man's being namely, language. When the object that I incorporate is the speech of the other—precisely a nonobject, a pattern, a model—I bind myself to him in a primary fusion, communion, unification. An identification. For me to have been capable of such a process, my libido had to be restrained; my thirst to devour had to be deferred and displaced to a level one may well call "psychic," provided one adds that if there is repression it is quite primal and that it lets one hold on to the joys of chewing, swallowing, nourishing oneself . . . with words. In being able to receive the other's words, to assimilate, repeat, and reproduce them, I become like him: one. A subject of enunciation. Through psychic osmosis/identification. Through love.[85]

What Kristeva presents here is the unfolding of human relations, at the intersection of the somatic and the psychic, as the simultaneous unfolding of signification.

When Kristeva locates the source of cosmopolitanism in the anxious, uncanny space of narcissism—that "limit of advent-and-loss of the subject"[86]—those looking for social change may well despair. In its concern with the past, psychoanalysis is charged with foreclosing the future: "Kristeva's ethics must turn on 'going over the course of projection-identification,' which makes the other an integral part of the same, if it is to be an *ethics* of psychoanalysis, and so must remain without real otherness or futurity."[87] The assertion that psychoanalysis is concerned with the past overlooks the *nachträglichkeit* that characterizes not only traumatic experience, but also all experience. The notion of trauma as a past event contradicts the force of psychoanalytic practice, which aims not at recreating a fixed past, but at a creative enactment of a never-before-present event. Freud and Kristeva associate the possibility of progress with this "return" to a past never before experienced. Winnicott's name is pertinent here, as he located the capacity for symbolization in the transitional space created in the gradual separation from the "mother." If this space is one of trauma, it is also characterized as a potential source of lifelong creativity and spontaneity. The sort of creativity which allowed Freud, at the end of his life, to assume his Jewishness—his given. If experience in general and trauma in particular both witness to an event and a subject which is neither past nor present; only the future remains for its advent. The troubled waters of the present, individual and social, call out for it. The necessity of the journey to the past in psychoanalysis may reflect the fact that, limited as we are, the future must be sewn, at least partly, of the stuff we have on hand, stuff that, from the beginning, at the beginning, was shared. This does not guarantee that the door to the stranger will be open. Nothing does. But it makes the welcome possible. A cause for celebration.

The Uncanny Strangeness of Maternal Election

Levinas and Kristeva on Parental Passion

KELLY OLIVER

In his essay "The Uncanny," Sigmund Freud describes the uncanny as what is concealed and frightening in the familiar and agreeable or vice versa.[1] He moves from discussing animated dolls, the Sandman's fear of losing his eyes as castration anxiety, doubles and mirrors, fear of death, dear of the dark, to the mother's body. In general, he attributes uncanny sensations to castration anxiety (whether from seeing the mother's "castrated sex" or as symbolically represented by pecked out eyes) and the return, or repetition, of repressed childhood fears or desires.[2] Specifically, he links the uncanny to the reanimation of that which has been passive, whether that means the feminine become active (including dolls, the maternal body, feelings of helplessness, and boys adopting the feminine position in relation to their fathers), or the reversal of a drive from passive to active through the return of the repressed (which can also be the return of a repressed feminine desire or fear of the activated feminine).[3]

Freud suggests that psychoanalysis itself is uncanny insofar as it "lays bare hidden forces" and thereby makes the familiar seem strange.[4] Certainly, the foundational fantasy of Freudian psychoanalysis, the Oedipal complex, condenses all of the uncanny elements he describes into one image of a son who unknowingly and helplessly fulfills or repeats prophecy by killing his father/double, marrying his mother (thereby returning to the uncanny "home of all human beings") and then symbolically castrates himself by gouging out his own eyes.[5] This uncanny incestuous family becomes the basis of the "family romance" imagined as foundational to human subjectivity. Because of their status as doubles recalling their parents own childhood and thereby reactivating repressed fears and desires, and because of their own sexual and aggressive drives, infants are born into this uncanny Oedipal struggle. Ambassadors of the uncanny, infants appear as "animated dolls," as triggers for castration anxieties in both fathers and mothers (insofar as they are torn from mother's bodies), as reminders of repressed childhood fears, and certainly as evidence of the uncanny place that is every human being's "first home," the maternal body and mother's sex.

On this psychoanalytic model, infants are subject to a primary trauma, namely the necessary breaking up of their primary bond with the maternal body for the sake of the social, which gives birth to desire. All desire comes back to this nostalgic longing to return to the "first home," the time before time, before the beginning of individual history, which is to say, the bond with the maternal body. This is the melancholy and uncanny fantasy of the Freudian child. But, what of the parent for whom this little person emerges on the scene as both someone so familiar and yet so strange?

What is more uncanny than the birth of a child? The child appears out of its mother's body, with which it has been one, as a double, as kin, as the most familiar, yet as unique, as strange, and as unpredictable. Even if the child is wanted, *this* child has not been chosen; *this one* cannot be planned. No one (cloning aside) can choose who his or her child is or who it will become. Choosing to have children is not choosing to have this one unique child; that is a choice that happens always and only retroactively. This is the strange "choice" that is no choice of paternal or maternal election whereby a parent elects to have this very child whom he or she cannot ever anticipate. Even if a parent imagines its child as an extension of itself, a mini-me who will actualize all of its unfulfilled dreams, the child is other, and therefore all the more uncanny in these instances.

In this essay, using Emmanuel Levinas's notion of paternal election and Julia Kristeva's notion of maternal passion, I will discuss the uncanny retroactive choice to have *this particular* child. Both Levinas and Kristeva suggest alternatives to the Freudian Oedipal model of child-parent relations. Yet, their discussions complement each other not only because Levinas focuses on paternity and Kristeva on maternity but also and moreover because for Levinas paternity points to an "absolute future" or "infinite time," while for Kristeva maternity points to the "lost time" of a "time before time." Furthermore, although both discuss fecundity in terms of passion or Eros, Levinas sees love for the child as the telos of this passion, while Kristeva maintains that dispassion for the child is the seat of love. Yet for both, the child is the ultimate stranger who recalls us to the stranger within ourselves, or the alterity by virtue of which we become subjects.

Levinas and Paternal Election

Emmanuel Levinas proposes a notion of paternity that cannot be reduced to law or castration threats but must be a promise. He proposes an ontology of paternity that takes us beyond the Freudian psychoanalysis of paternity, which he claims reduces sexuality and paternity to pleasure and egology. The promise of paternity is not recognition of yourself in the other, but rather a promise of nonrecognition, of strangeness, of an open future, what he calls infinity. The promise of paternity is not the Freudian promise that the son will inherit his father's power or his father's relationship to a mother-substitute. It is not a promise from the past, a promise that returns to itself. Rather, the promise of paternity, as Levinas describes it, is a promise of an open future, the promise that the son is to his father. The child appears as a stranger that invites, even commands, the hospitality of the Levinasian ethics that puts the stranger, the widow, the orphan first and holds my own subjectivity hostage to that other. But, with the child, it becomes even clearer how the father's sense of himself as a subject with that Husserlian sense of ownness comes through his relationship with this other who is both him and radically not him. It is this uncanny relationship to the stranger who is my kin that displays the structure of hospitality that returns me to myself for the first time vis-à-vis Levinasian ethics as first philosophy.

Although Levinas suggests an analogy between death and paternity, fatherhood requires neither murder nor sacrifice. If anything, it is the death of egology and the acknowledgment of a future to come, a future that does not include me. Paternity does not reestablish the Hegelian battle of the wills, each seeking recognition from the other; nor does it return us to a battle of wills that reinscribes the subject and turns the self back onto itself even in the operation of self-dispossession and abandonment. Rather, paternity opens up a different structure of subjectivity that exposes the self onto the other. Paternity is a special case of alterity that can inform all other relations. Levinas suggests that it is the only relation in which the self becomes other and survives.

For Levinas, paternity begins with Eros and fecundity. Yet, Eros and fecundity are ontologically anchored in paternity. Eros is possible because of sexual difference, which is neither a contradiction between two different terms or sexes nor a complementarity between two different terms or sexes. Eros is an event of alterity, a relationship with what is absent in the very moment at which everything is there. Even in an experience that seems to completely fill the universe with itself the caress seeks something other. The caress is not directed toward another body; rather the caress is directed toward a space that transcends through the body and a time that Levinas describes as a future never future enough.[6] In the erotic relationship the caress is directed toward the future, the forever and always of promises of love, a future that is never future enough to fulfill such promises.

The relationship with the other is such a promise, a promise that cannot be fulfilled, a paradoxical promise whose fulfillment would destroy the promise. And this promise is time. For Levinas, time is not constituted as a series of nows; it is not constituted in the present or by an ego. Rather, time is the absent promise in the relation with the other; it is the not-yet, the always still to come. It is the time of love, the infinite engendered through finite beings coming together. "Love seeks what does not have the structure of an existent, the infinitely future, what is to be engendered."[7] Love seeks what is beyond any possible union between two. Love seeks the "transubstantiation" that engenders the child. Engendering the child is an inherent element in the structure of the erotic relationship; the erotic relationship is defined as fecundity. The caress and voluptuosity are analyzed within this context of fecundity. Paternity opens the masculine subject onto infinite time and returns him to the ethical relationship.

In the masculine erotic relationship as Levinas describes it, the other beyond the subject's control is the feminine other; fecundity necessitates a relationship with a feminine other. This feminine other is a prerequisite for moving outside of oneself: "But the encounter with the Other as feminine is required in order that the future of the child come to pass from beyond the possible, beyond projects. This relationship resembles that which was described for the idea of infinity: I cannot account for it by myself, as I do account for the luminous world by myself."[8] The transubstantiation of the father by the son is only possible by virtue of the feminine other. Man needs woman to beget a son. More than this, the infinite time opened up between father and son through paternity is possible by virtue of the movement through the cyclical, nonlinear, time of the feminine. Paternity moves the (male) subject outside of time through the mediation of another time, the cyclical time of life. Paternity conquers "father time" by moving through the feminine.

Levinas suggests that paternity opens the subject onto infinite time in various ways. The discontinuity of generations brings with it inexhaustible youth, each generation replacing the one before it. In addition to this chronology that stretches indefinitely through time, the ontology of paternity sets up the subject within infinite time. The space between the father and the son opens up infinite time. Not only the discontinuity of generations which promises continued youth, but also the transubstantiation of the father in the son opens the subject to an other. "[T]he father discovers himself not only in the gestures of his son, but in his substance and his unicity."[9] In this way the father discovers himself in the son and yet discovers that his son is distinct, a stranger.

Through the transubstantiation of the I, Levinas says that paternity accomplishes desire. It does not satisfy desire, which is impossible, but accomplishes it by engendering it and by engendering another desiring being, the son. Paternity engenders desire, which is the infinite time of the absolutely other. The time of the other is infinite as compared to the finite time of the self. In relationship with the child, the subject is opened onto infinity: "The relation with the child—that is, the relation with the other that is not a power, but fecundity—establishes a relationship with the absolute future, or infinite time."[10] Paternity, with its generation and generations, literally opens onto infinite time, a time beyond death. That future is the infinite desire that is present as a desire for desire itself infinitely extended into a future that is never future enough. What Levinas calls "goodness" is associated with the infinity of desire engendered by paternity. "In paternity desire maintained as insatiate desire, that is, as goodness, is accomplished."[11] And, paternity is the link between desire and goodness, Eros and ethics. Erotic desire is accomplished (since unlike need, it can never be satisfied) in engendering a son, a son who embodies desire. In this sense, desire engenders itself.[12] The desire of the caress in the erotic relationship, then, is ultimately resolved in paternity: "This unparalleled relation between two substances, where a beyond substances is exhibited, is resolved in paternity."[13] From the beyond, desire, two substances create another desiring substance, the son.

More than the continuation of the substance of the father in the son, as the word "transubstantiation" might suggest, paternity is a form of transubstantiation of subjectivity itself. Paternity transforms subjectivity from the subject as "I-can" who sees himself as the center of meaning and values—the constitutor of the world—to a subject beholden to, and responsible for, the other. This form of transubstantiation takes us beyond substance. The subject or "I" is not a substance, but a response. The paternal subject is not Husserl's, Sartre's or Ricoeur's virile "I-will" or "I-can" but a response to the other who opens up a radically different time, a time beyond the "I-will" or "I-can." Levinas says that the relationship with the son through fecundity "articulates the time of the absolutely other, an alternation of the very substance of him who can—his transubstantiation."[14]

The relationship of paternity is unique in that the I breaks free of itself without ceasing to be I.[15] It is the only relationship in which the self becomes other and survives. The I breaks free of the ego, of what ties it to itself, so that it can reach out to another, even become another, become other to itself. This process of becoming other to itself opens up the possibility of beyond its own possibilities, an openness to an undetermined future. "Fecundity is part of the very drama of the I. The intersubjective reached across the notion of fecundity opens up a place where the I is divested of its tragic egoity, which turns back to itself, and yet is not purely and simply dissolved into the collective. Fecundity evinces a unity that is not opposed to multiplicity, but, in the precise sense of the term, engenders it."[16]

On Levinas's analysis the father discovers himself in the gestures, the substance, the very uniqueness of his son. This discovery of himself in the son is not recognition; the father does not recognize himself in his son, but discovers himself, finds himself for the first time. Thus, paternity engenders the father as much as it does the son. And fecundity gives birth not only to the son, but also to the father. In relation to his son, who is both himself and not himself, the father discovers his own subjectivity. As he realizes that his son is distinct, a stranger, he discovers that he too is distinct, even a stranger to himself.

Rather than establish the equality between, or mutual recognition of, father and son, or brothers for that matter, Levinas's notion of paternity establishes the uniqueness of the subject in relationship with the other. The father/son relationship is not one of law-bound recognition, but of outlaw singularity. What Levinas calls "paternal election," which chooses from among equals, makes unique precisely by recalling the nonuniqueness of the equals among which this one was chosen. The father chooses the son after he has had no choice. His love elects this particular child in his uniqueness as the loved one, the one meant to be. In this regard, Levinas suggests that all love for another person must approach paternal love insofar as that love elects the loved one from among all others. This love makes the loved one unique, and makes this love necessary rather than contingent. This love is not just for a limited time only, but is for all time, for a future never future enough, for infinite time.

At this point, we might wonder why the relationship with the lover does not provide the same kind of uniqueness as the father-son relationship. There are several reasons: first, the feminine lover is neither radically other nor the same and both are required for the uniqueness identified with the father-son relationship. It is as much the son's sameness as the son's difference that engenders the uncanny otherness experience by the father in this relationship. Moreover, while the man chooses his mate, he does not choose his child, except after the fact, through paternal election. It is this choice that is not a choice that makes paternal election even more uncanny than sexual difference and the relation to otherness inherent in the caress. The father's subjectivity itself is made uncanny and thereby transformed through this relationship with an other who is him and not him. Levinas emphasizes that it is the otherness of the son that pulls the father out of himself toward infinity. Yet it is the sameness of the son that allows the movement without shattering the father's subjectivity altogether. Ultimately, it is the uncanny familiarity between father and son that allows for the father to discover himself and his uniqueness through his son. The father identifies with his son, but not because they have the same DNA. Indeed, it seems that in an important sense Levinas's notion of paternal election is born out of traditional views that while the mother of a child is undeniable, fatherhood remains a question. Yet, paternal election makes this biological question irrelevant. It is not just the biological substance of the son that makes him like and unlike his father; rather it is because the father both calls and is called by his son. The father chooses this son and that election makes them both unique; in turn the son's uniqueness makes the father unique. Through their relationship, they both are singular. Yet, the discovery of their singularity has its basis in their uncanny familiarity and their love.

The father is his son, and yet the son is a stranger to the father, and the paternal relationship makes him a stranger to himself. For Levinas, desire is possible only in a relationship with an absolute other. Paternity engenders desire and thereby returns the erotic relationship to the ethical. It is important to note that the fact that he is a son is not what makes him unique; he is unique because he is this son chosen from among brothers. All children are brothers, but only this one is my son. Elsewhere I ask, could the transubstantiation of the father take place in relation to a daughter?[17] Would the father discover himself in his daughter's substance, gestures, and uniqueness? Or, is she too strange? Too uncanny? Obviously, without sexual difference—without daughters, mothers, and wives—the uncanny sameness between father and son cannot maintain itself. Yet, within Levinas's world, girls and women remain extraneous to this most strange, loving, and infinite paternal relationship. They appear as a means to an end, the traditional immanence that gives birth to transcendence.

Kristeva's Maternal Passion

Kristeva gives an explanation for girls and women's extraneousness to patriarchal culture. A strange explanation to be sure, she argues that women's "extraneousness" to, and "extravagance" within, the phallic order are the result of their primary bisexuality that puts them in the impossible situation of wanting it all. As we know, on the Freudian model, girls have a much more complicated development in relation to the Oedipal complex than boys do. Girls have to change both their erogenous zones and their love objects, while boys do not. Both boys and girls are primarily attached to their mothers. But whereas in "normal" heterosexual development boys are encouraged to have mother substitutes as love objects, girls are not. On Kristeva's account girls can reactivate their primary relationships with their mothers by becoming mothers themselves. Their own experience of pregnancy, childbirth, and mothering, put them back in touch with the "lost time" of their own infantile bond with the maternal body. Kristeva rejects Freud's theory of penis envy as the reason why women can find fulfillment in motherhood. It is not, as Freud maintains, that through motherhood women gain phallic power through their child, but rather because repressed desires for their own mothers are rekindled. For Kristeva, the baby is not a substitute penis but rather an antidote to what she calls "feminine fatigue," which comes from women's "extraneousness" and "extravagance," which takes great efforts to negotiate. Kristeva, contra Freud, reverses the direction of desire from mother to baby and suggests that we all want the same thing: What do we want, whether we are women or men? We all want our mommies. This is why she suggests that both men and women look for mother substitutes in their mates.

Reading Kristeva, it seems as if women's "*étrangeté*" (which can mean foreignness, strangeness, or extraneousness), and their "extravagance" comes from the fact that within heteronormative phallocentric cultures, they are in the impossible position of wanting their mommies and their daddies in one and the same love object.[18] Their desires are extravagant because they want it all, they want both sides of the "dual universal," as Kristeva says, that is humanity. At the same time, their desires are perversely extraneous to the reproduction of the species, which traditionally has been their place in the sun. Kristeva suggests, if she does not say, that the cause of both women's extravagance and their extraneousness is their fundamental bisexuality.

Following Freud, Kristeva identifies two phases of the female Oedipal development: What she calls "Oedipal prime" is an attachment to the mother that leads to both an identification with the mother and a desire for her. What she calls "Oedipal two" (*bis*) changes the girl's love object to the father and to the law. Now, the girl wants to be the best at following his rules. By so doing, she protects her mother/self insofar as the fantasy of the child being beaten is not she but rather some bad boy. In *This Incredible Need to Believe*, *Hate and Forgiveness*, and a recent lecture, Kristeva rereads Freud's "A Child Is Being Beaten" as an account not only of individuation and sexual differentiation, but also of the inauguration of human civilization à la Freud's band of murderous brothers in *Totem and Taboo*.[19] She argues that from the perspective of the little girl, moving from Oedipal prime to Oedipal two, the girl protects herself from incestuous arousal by masochism and then by concentrating on others (which, I would say, may amount to the same thing). For the girl, the prototype of the beaten other is the victimized castrated mother (with whom she both identifies and refuses identification). She tries to protect this ambivalent object of her affection by looking for others to take her place in the beating fantasy, especially boys or men. As Kristeva describes it, in Oedipal two, the little girl displaces her incestuous desires for her father (which only barely covers over her desires for her mother) onto language and thought. Kristeva calls this "the extravagant capacity of sublimation that all humans possess but which, I, little girl, work hard to excel in better than anyone else."[20] Tired from fighting not only their own extraneousness to the phallic order but also the victimization of their beloved mothers, they suffer from "feminine fatigue." Kristeva describes this feminine fatigue as the result of a bisexuality that has not been worked through. Unable to choose between mother and father, to take sides once and for all, this woman is exhausted from walking the fence. She wants to please her father and that is why she excels at his game, although she uses it against him to defend her mother, even if she is what Kristeva calls a "crazy mother." "We are not all psychotic," says Kristeva, "but we can all be crazy. Crazy for one another (men and women, women and women, men and men) because we are crazy for our crazy mothers."[21] It turns out, however, that some are crazier than others for those crazy mothers. Too invested in pleasing the father with their intellectual pursuits to be her, yet too loyal to her mother's craziness, to her depression, to be him. Confused about who to be and therefore about who to love. Wanting to be everything and to love and be loved by everybody, an extravagant and ultimately exhausting desire.

Kristeva imagines a "cure" for feminine fatigue in motherhood. She maintains that woman's extraneousness or strangeness to the symbolic order is manifested in a specific way during pregnancy and motherhood, particularly in the mother's relation to the infant.[22] And pregnancy and motherhood are ways of working through the passion that makes us speaking beings, the passion that makes us human rather than animals.[23] Maternal passion, she argues, is a prototype of all human passion. Following Jean-Didier Vincent, she defines passion as specific to man in it requires reflexive consciousness and the capacity for encountering the other. Passion is the crossroads or interface between emotions, which are bodily or somatic and shared by all vertebrates, and reflexive consciousness, which is the result of both the symbolic pact that founds human civilization (that is to say, the murder of the father and substitution of the totemic animal) and the formation of the unconscious as a result of the repression of this criminal act upon which the pact originates. In other words, passion is both what makes human experience uncanny or strange and allows us to live with that strangeness.

Of course, Kristeva's rereading of *Totem and Taboo* complicates Freud's story. In *Powers of Horror*, she emphasizes the brothers' incestuous desires for the mother;[24] in *Sense and Nonsense of the Revolt*, she emphasizes the pleasure in the totemic feast that operates as counterbalance to the horror and guilt;[25] and in her recent work, *This Incredible Need to Believe*, she emphasizes the incestuous desire for, and identification with, the suffering father, the father who is being beaten to death.[26] Unlike Freud, Kristeva focuses on Eros and *jouissance*, rather than on the guilt and murder, in the totemic feast and its repetitions. Moreover, even when it is about the father, for Kristeva, it is also and always about the mother and the pleasures and horrors of her body. This is why maternal passion is a prototype of passion from the side of the child, the father, and the other more generally. But it is from the side of the mother herself that Kristeva locates the essence of human passion.

In a chapter of *Hatred and Forgiveness* entitled "The Passion According to Motherhood," Kristeva says, "allow me to take the mother's side" and proceeds to describe "the extraneousness of the pregnant woman" as the narcissistic withdrawal wherein "the future mother becomes an object of desire, pleasure and aversion for herself." In this state, which Kristeva claims is not unlike "possession," the pregnant woman is "incapable of taking into account an existence separate from her own."[27] She is completely absorbed by emotions invested in her own body as the "hollow" habitation of a future love-object that she will have to allow to become a subject. Here is how Kristeva describes this maternal progression toward what she calls the "miracle" of love:

> [It] begins by the passion of the pregnant woman for herself: her destabilized "self," a loss of identity, because divided by the intervention of the lover-father, and, through this intervention of the

other, inhabited by an unknown third party—an embryo, a fetus, then a baby, a child, though for the moment an indiscernible double. . . . This first stage of the passion turned within is followed by the mother's passion for the new subject that will be her child, provided he/she ceases to be her double, but from whom the mother *detaches herself* to allow the child to become an autonomous being. This motion of *expulsion*, of *detachment*, is essential. Thus, the negative immediately inhabits maternal passion.[28]

This move from self-absorption to love of the child and then eventually release or weaning of the child is the "miracle" of maternal passion because the mother embodies both passion and dispassion, or passion and working-through passion. On Kristeva's account, then, it is not primarily passion that is uniquely human, but rather dispassion or the sublimation of passion, which is essential to maternal passion as successful mothering. She describes the "miracle":

> Miraculously ("miraculously," because even though it seems impossible, this alchemy manages to take place, and consequently, humanity exists, thinks, speaks, lives), motherhood is a passion in the sense that the emotions of narcissistic attachment and aggressiveness, filtered through reflexive consciousness and through the unconscious that speaks of Eros and Thanatos, are transformed into love (with its more or less attenuated correlate of hate). I would even say that in this experience of motherhood, passion takes on its most human aspect, which is to say, the furthest from its biological foundation, which nevertheless accompanies it (the famous drives of attachment and aggressiveness), and that it takes the path of sublimation without ceasing to be a passion. . . . It is in motherhood that the link to the other can become love.[29]

Several features of Kristeva's account are particularly noteworthy. First, she describes pregnancy and motherhood as the most human activity insofar as it is the furthest from mere biological functioning. Clearly, this claim is antithetical to traditional views of women's role in reproduction, which, as we know, has been and continues to be seen as a matter of biology, even animality. And while it is akin to de Beauvoir's suggestion in *The Second Sex* that human females are more oppressed by their relation to reproduction than female animals because they can reflect on the experience, Kristeva, unlike Beauvoir, valorizes maternity. In addition, maternal passion is quintessential to human passion because it can be a form of working through conflicting emotions of attraction and aversion, which are the result of animal drives, by turning them into the human passions of love and hate. On this account, animals are incapable of love and hate because these so-called feelings require reflexive consciousness and expression in language and therefore go beyond mere feelings in the technical sense in which emotions are opposed to passions. Yet, the transformation of emotion or bodily drive into passion or sublimated drive is only the beginning of maternal passion. Its telos is the detachment or dispassion required for weaning the child and helping it become autonomous. And this simultaneous holding onto and pushing away is what is truly distinctive—and strange—about human passion embodied most dramatically and dynamically in maternal passion. This is why Kristeva says that there is no good mother except the one who lends herself to matricide, echoing her earlier provocation from *Black Sun*, "matricide is our vital necessity."[30] She also claims that the good enough mother loves "no one" because her passion is eclipsed by her detachment, which leads to her "serenity." Passion, then, is essentially uncanny.

Interestingly, Kristeva claims that psychoanalysis can perform the same structural modifications of optimal motherhood: "I said: *without a relationship to maternal passion*, it being understood that motherhood is a biological and symbolic process and that analytical, self-analytical, or sublimatory work can arrive at the same structural modifications. I am emphasizing the structural experience of motherhood: I am not fundamentally 'pro-birth.'"[31] There is something about the structure of motherhood, then, that can be emulated in analysis, something that can move the woman through the borderline state that is her inherent bisexuality and becomes explicit in pregnancy, toward "serenity." This serenity, which may seem to echo Freud's oceanic feeling, from the side of the pregnant woman, actually explodes the illusion of oneness and wholeness in order to love passionately and yet let go of that love to embrace life. Like childbirth, analysis (and writing, art and mysticism) can bring "a time of new beginnings and rebirths and a certain serenity." For Kristeva, however, the serenity of rebirth is always and necessarily the uncanny experience of both holding and letting go that opens us up to transformation.

But it is not just the mother's relationship with the child that makes motherhood transformative. In addition, it is the woman's relationship with her own mother through her experience of childbirth and motherhood that makes motherhood one way of dealing with the fundamental bisexuality of the bivalent female Oedipal complex. Through motherhood, a woman identifies with her mother and fuses anew that incestuous bond in a socially acceptable way. In this way, motherhood opens onto a past that has been repressed and can now be reactivated; in Freudian terms, this is a reactivation of a passive past, a feminine and maternal past, the reanimation of which is particularly uncanny. In this regard, Kristeva's reactivation of the role of the mother, maternity, and childbirth within the discourse of philosophy and psychoanalysis is itself uncanny; like the dutiful daughter who wants to please her father by playing by his rules and yet cannot give up her allegiance to her mother, Kristeva's theory of maternal passion straddles the uncanny threshold between paternal law and maternal jouissance.

In addition to reactivating the passive feminine now become active maternity, Kristeva suggests that in motherhood, the woman returns to her own childhood and "unconsciously relearns her mother tongue" by teaching her child to speak. She thereby revises not only her relation to her mother, but also her relation to language. Rather, than find her self-extraneous or foreign to the phallic order, as a mother teaching her child to speak, she is essential to it. Through the baby talk she shares with her infant, she reconnects words, affects, and bodily sensations, which also reconnect her with a "lost time," the time of infancy, the time of Oedipus prime. Again, maternity connects the mother to her past, but to a past that is prior to time, to a time before time, that is both her sensuous relationship with her own mother's body and her sensuous relation to sounds, particularly the sounds of the body become language. Baby talk is a "sensorial language" that allows the mother to find "the conjunction of her symbolic and carnal essences." Baby talk remains symbolic even while foregrounding the semiotic element of language, particularly as it relates to the relationship between the maternal body and the infant, and maternal body and the lost time of her loving bond with another woman's body.

Insofar as it is outside of linear time, this "lost time" is reminiscent of the time of infinity invoked in Levinas's account of the paternal relation to the son. In both cases, there is something monumental about the relationship with this uncanny other who is both me and not me that propels us out of clock time and into the time of our erotic carnal existence as beings who mean. Yet, for both, a movement through time is necessary to realize, if never once and for all, the meaning of this carnal existence in relation to the other, the stranger, that most uncanny of creatures, this particular beloved child. Thus, Kristeva concludes: "the very structure of maternal experience favors this metabolism of passion into dispassion" through the place of the father, time, and the acquisition of language, all three of which provide the distance necessary for detachment required for turning passion into dispassion. In a sense, then, motherhood and analysis shared the same goal, namely, to turn passion into dispassion through sublimation. We need to give up love, or at least estrange ourselves from it, in order to find it beyond craziness and in serenity. In other words, we find love only by becoming strangers to it. Passion as sublimation comes through dispassion and distance, the distance that Kristeva suggests makes us human—and makes human experience uncanny. Alluding to Colette, Kristeva reassures us, "The dispassionate humanity reborn from this experience would not necessarily be boring or robotic. Perhaps it would simply have a gay, varied, and plentiful lucidity. And it would preserve the laughter of love: to the point of making light of love itself." In her earlier work on Female Genius, Kristeva suggests that perhaps motherhood is the antidote to the increasing atomization of human experience insofar as maternal creativity engenders human individuals through both nature and nurture.

In "Fatigue in the Feminine," Kristeva compares this creative mother to a "good fairy": "Nothing is impossible for a mother who succeeds at her psychical bisexuality: a tireless 'good fairy,' she does not notice that she is depleted in the small cares lavished on her loved ones." It seems, then, that motherhood is a strange antidote to both feminine fatigue and hysteria insofar as the woman is exhausted and perhaps even sick, but does not notice. Kristeva gives the example of a woman who was taking care of her mother who had Alzheimer's and her son, who was operated on for a brain tumor, a woman who was so busy taking care of others that when she fell and broke her ankle she felt no pain or fatigue. At this point, we may wonder whether this tireless good fairy is just another form of maternal sacrifice and why Kristeva embraces this model so familiar to us from cultural stereotypes of the good mother, who sacrifices herself for her children. Perhaps, this good fairy mother is the one who needs to be weaned, not only for the sake of her children's autonomy, but also for the sake of her own. After all, Kristeva does insist that it is through not only her passion but also her dispassion that the mother can be a model for human passion at its best.

Kristeva suggests that, like Colette's mother Sido, the "ideal" mother has to turn away from her children to tend her own flowers, so that she too can bloom. Describing writing as another antidote to feminine fatigue, and Colette's writing in particular, Kristeva says, "No fatigue in this writing, through which a gigantic feminine Self loves itself in the French language (for the first and last time?), Sido's maternal language, consuming flora and fauna, cacti and cats, the dimensions of the universe. Flowering, continual rebirth." Kristeva suggests that the structure of motherhood, like the structure of writing, art and analysis, is not primarily about giving birth but about rebirth, and the cyclical time of flowering and dying off necessary for life.

In a sense, then, both Kristeva and Levinas suggest that giving birth to one's child leads to a process, which is necessarily ongoing, of being born and reborn oneself, through this uncanny stranger who is elected but never chosen. This strange relation requires relinquishing any illusions of control or identification in order to love this other who is "my child" but never mine. The process of negotiating—or better yet, undergoing or suffering—the passion and dispassion that constitute the Eros of paternity and maternity, can awaken the uncanny stranger within the parent. The arrival of the little stranger gives birth to an uncanniness that disturbs the parents' sense of self-control, self-identification, and self-ownership. For Kristeva, this awakening of the stranger within is a process of rebirth that comes through various forms of sublimation not limited to maternity or paternity.

Yet, it is Levinas who reminds us that the little stranger, this newcomer born out of the bodies of women, can be chosen only after the fact, which is to say as a gift beyond any economy of exchange or reciprocity. The structure of maternity and paternity when they approach the ideals described by Levinas and Kristeva, the ideals of Eros and love beyond sovereignty and self, teach us that even as we try to repress or ignore them, we do not choose the others or otherness that calls to us, but we can elect to embrace it. Although we may not choose the stranger, we can embrace him or her. For both Levinas and Kristeva, an encounter with the stranger takes us out of linear clock time, out of the ordinary time of daily routines, and propels us into what Levinas associates with the infinite time of transcendence or what Kristeva associates with the lost time of an archaic past, a time before time. Face-to-face with the stranger, as Levinas might say, pulls us out of ourselves and the time of historical existence and into the immensity of the now of eternity, what for Kristeva is grounded in the sensuousness of a bodily encounter, a caress, that aims not for the future in any causal sense, but rather for a time beyond past or future understood as cause and effect and toward the monumental time of bodies in love, an encounter in and through the strangeness of our carnal existence become meaningful.

For both Levinas and Kristeva, each human being must come to terms with his or her own uncanniness, his or her own strangeness, which is to say the ways in which experience is not his or her *own*. Acknowledging, if not embracing, the stranger within is necessary not only to find meaning in life but also to love and cherish others and otherness. For it is only by virtue of these others and otherness that we come to ourselves as subjects, if always only provisionally and in process. Moreover, it is only by virtue of these others and otherness that human passion is born. If we can elect to love this particular child whom we have not chosen, and who appears all the more uncanny in those moments we imagine we have, can we not also elect to love other others, not in spite of, but because of, their uncanny strangeness? Can we not extend our obligations and hospitality to strangers who are not our kin?

PART IV

Hosts and Guests

This being human is a guest house.
Every morning a new arrival.

A joy, a depression, a meanness,
some momentary awareness comes
as an unexpected visitor.

Welcome and entertain them all!
Even if they are a crowd of sorrows,
who violently sweep your house
empty of its furniture,
still, treat each guest honorably.
He may be clearing you out
for some new delight.

The dark thought, the shame, the malice,
meet them at the door laughing and invite them in.

Be grateful for whatever comes,
because each has been sent
as a guide from beyond.

—Rumi, "The Guest House"

12

Being, the Other, the Stranger

JEAN GREISCH

If philosophizing is not merely a matter of attending to everything, including things that are of no vital concern to us, but rather requires that one become conscious of what one is doing when one engages with questions, then we must start by recognizing in what way and under what conditions the question of the stranger can become a properly philosophical one. How does the stranger enter into philosophy?

Let me voice a preliminary scruple: What permits us in the first place to affirm that the philosopher necessarily encounters the question of the stranger?

Consider Wittgenstein's *Tractatus Logico-Philosophicus*. Should we take offense at the fact that in its meticulous concern for the intrinsically *conceptual* requirements of philosophy, this work never broaches the question of the stranger? This example suggests that the notion of the stranger is not primarily of a *conceptual* order at all. The "stranger" does not find a place among first-range philosophical concepts such as "the Absolute" or "alienation." At first glance, the philosopher seems to have nothing more to say than what is already contained in the common-sense definition of the stranger: a stranger is one with no home of his or her own, who comes from elsewhere, who does not speak my or our language. Once we have given this homely definition, it seems that there is nothing more to be said and that all more sophisticated descriptions or definitions are otiose. Some might even recall Wittgenstein's remark, commenting on the *ethical* significance of his *Tractatus*: "Above all avoid transcendental chatter when everything is as clear as a slap in the face." When, in the course of everyday life, we encounter the stranger as a political refugee, a dissident or an exile, we need no "transcendental chatter" whatsoever, because what we are dealing with here is indeed as clear as a slap in the face.

Having marked this clear contrast between concerns with concept and definition and the ethical problems raised by a real encounter with strangers, we need to take a closer look at the philosophical problems that the stranger nonetheless continues to pose. My title, "Being, the Other, the Stranger," indicates that the stranger poses a question in both the ontological and the ethical realms, and challenges us to rethink the articulation of the two realms. The order of appearance of the three terms "Being, the Other, the Stranger" does not imply any hierarchical priority. We could start with the third term, which the anthropologist places in the foreground of his investigations and questioning. A philosopher interested in the ethical problems of "the good life" and of "strong evaluations" in Charles Taylor's sense, would no doubt start with the second term. The important point is that neither the ontologist nor the ethicist can elude the problem of the stranger. Regarding ontology the question is whether or not, as is increasingly suspected in continental philosophy, it is condemned to lose sight of the stranger.

Is there *one* problematic of the stranger, or are there many? It seems to me that the problem must necessarily be approached from several angles. It is not at all certain that there is an encompassing point of view that allows us to consider all these problems at the same time. It seems rather that we must distinguish several types of questioning, each one of which refers to a specific realm: the political, the ethical, the phenomenological, the ontological, and perhaps even the theological.

My intention is nevertheless to ponder under what conditions these "regional" problems can be reconnected with the fundamental question which philosophy is obliged to put to itself: *What is called thinking?* This question, to which Heidegger dedicated one of his last lecture courses, in which he showed that it can be understood in at least four senses, invites us also to consider the question of the stranger from several points of view: the "anthropological" distinction between the "The Near and the Far"; the distinction, both "ethical" and "metaphysical," between the self and the Other or "Sameness" and "Otherness"; and last, the "ontological" distinction between "One's own and the Foreign."

The Near and the Far: The Anthropological Axis

In twentieth-century philosophy, one frequently encounters the suspicion that "philosophy"—that is, a discursive practice born in a specific culture and historical age—falls prey to an "ethnocentrism" and a "logocentrism" that are radically incapable of recognizing the stranger as such. This logocentrism vainly attempts to control the margins of philosophy, keeping the stranger at bay.[1] In temporarily putting aside the problematic link between ethnocentrism and logocentrism, let us first consider this concept of ethnocentrism. It must be restored to the science that forged it, namely ethnology[2] or cultural anthropology. It is the irreplaceable contribution of this discipline to the problematic of the stranger that I have in mind when referring to the "anthropological axis." Claude Lévi-Strauss, since his travelogue *Tristes Tropiques*, has ceaselessly commented on the professional risks intrinsic to this discipline, risks that are directly concerned with the problematic encounter with the stranger, his "strange" behavior, life form, beliefs, rites, ways of dwelling, and so forth.

The anthropologist leaves his country and his home for long periods of time, exposing himself to hunger, sickness, and sometimes danger. He surrenders his customs, beliefs, and convictions to a profanation to which he becomes an accomplice when he assumes, without mental restriction or ulterior motive, the forms of life of an alien society. He practices integral observation, beyond which there is nothing except—and it is indeed a risk—the complete absorption of the observer by the object of his observation.[3]

The philosophical result of this anthropological adventure is that it obliges one radically to rethink the problem of the universality of human nature. The anthropologist's choice of his object of investigation—"primitive" society—itself already has a philosophical implication, as Lévi-Strauss admits in subscribing to Merleau-Ponty's formula: each time the anthropologist "comes back to the live sources of his knowledge, to that which, in him, acts as a means of understanding the cultural formations most remote from himself, he is spontaneously indulging in philosophy."[4]

If, on the very ground of anthropological fieldwork, philosophical questions are born from assuming the dialectic of near and far, then everything depends upon the professional philosopher's ability to pay attention to the questions that arise here. These questions concern the concept of identity itself, whether of the individual or of a culture. In this respect, one should recall that Lévi-Strauss's conception of anthropological research is beholden to a specific philosophical patronage, that of Jean-Jacques Rousseau.[5] In the eyes of Lévi-Strauss, a remark in the *Discours sur l'origine de l'inégalité* may be read as a prophetic announcement of a not yet extant human science, ethnology: "the whole world is covered with nations of which we know only the names, yet we dabble in judging the human race."⁶ Rousseau already has an insight into the true stakes of this passion for the far-off: "When one wants to study men one must look around oneself; but to study man, one must first learn to look into the distance: one must first see differences in order to discover characteristics."⁷

Such a passion for the far-off supposes, as Lévi-Strauss notices, a singular relation—almost paradoxical—to the near, and demands a new relation to oneself: "the systematic will to identify with the other goes hand in hand with an obstinate refusal to identify with the self."⁸ This is why "confessions," whether published or expressed in private diaries, so frequently accompany the careers of great anthropologists. Lévi-Strauss himself does not hesitate to apply to his own anthropological vocation an affirmation by Rousseau, which at first glance seems only to concern the psychological profile of the latter: "here they are, then, unknown strangers, non-beings to me, since *I* wished it so! And I, detached from them and from everything, what am I? This is what I *must* find out *first!*"⁹

If we want to understand what is really at stake in the accusation that Western thinking suffers from ethnocentrism, we must first ponder the problematic and still relevant presuppositions of anthropological research, Fundamentally, it is the problem of cultural identity and difference. The problem is that "the diversity of cultures has rarely appeared to us for what it is: a natural phenomenon, resulting from the direct or indirect relationships between societies. They rather tended to see in it a sort of monstrosity or scandal."¹⁰ This scandal has also left its mark in philosophy, which was ethnocentric, each time that its own discourse about the world of others, their values or their language, reflected that "repulsion when faced with ways of living, believing, and thinking alien to us."¹¹ Such repulsion is the essence of ethnocentrism.

But insofar as philosophy is linked to a particular cultural context, has it not paid a tribute, often a heavy one, to ethnocentrism? Incontestably, this has been the case, even if philosophy's concern for the universal provided it with the critical means to resist this temptation. The widespread "culturalist" discourse of our times naively thinks that it is capable of digesting all cultural differences, and thereby believes itself to be definitively beyond the ethnocentric temptation, ignoring the truth-claims that any cultural system will convey. This is why it resembles the "country of culture" satirically evoked by Nietzsche in his *Zarathustra*:

> In truth, you could wear no better masks than your own faces, men of today. Who could *recognize* you?

> All scrawled over with hieroglyphs of the past, themselves penciled over with new ones, you have well concealed yourselves from any interpreters of the signs.
>
> And though one be a prober of mind and heart, who can still credit you with a heart? You seem formed by colors and pieces of paper all glued together.
>
> All periods and peoples colorfully adorn your sails; all customs and faiths speak flamboyantly in your gestures.[12]

It is not yet certain which of the two temptations—the "ethnocentric" or what I would like to call the "folkloric" temptation—betrays the more profound misunderstanding of the stranger. Regarding the first temptation, the question is not only to know if and when philosophy succumbs to ethnocentrism. The more pressing question consists in asking whether, by *its very constitution*, philosophy is not vowed to ethnocentrism. If it is formulated in these terms, the question of ethnocentrism leads to that of "logocentrism." But this question can only be developed within a context that is no longer directly "anthropological," as it has been defined thus far.

"One-for-the-other": The "Ethical" Axis

At first glance it may seem surprising so closely to associate the critique of logocentrism with the question of ethics. But if we agree to take this term in its Levinasian meaning, which never concerns morality codified in rules but the very founding of responsibility toward the other, then the derivation becomes legitimate. Levinas, as much as Heidegger, asks a radical question: "What is meant by the intelligibility of the intelligible, the signification of meaning; what does reason signify?"[13] This question can no longer be delimited in a "logocentric" fashion, that is, according to the economy of a logos that is *gathering* and assembling everything.[14] The "eccentric" point from which the originary relation between transcendence and intelligibility becomes thinkable is the discovery of responsibility for the other. What link is there between this discovery and the problem of the stranger? Insofar as all of Levinas's analyses bring us back to the epiphany of the face (and depart from it), it could seem that this insistence on the irreducible alterity of the face turns our attention away from the true problem of the stranger. The stranger as such has no face; from the moment that he or she is "faced," the stranger is already more than a stranger, a potential neighbor.

This standard interpretation of Levinasian thought, which would make of it but a minor ethical variant of a classical, personalist topic, is due to a fundamental misunderstanding which would effectively reduce the problematic of the stranger to the general category of alterity. In identifying the "one-for-the-other" with the originary matrix of all meaning, Levinas forces personalist philosophies of alterity to undergo a much more radical turn. We can express it in the following formula: "the other who looks at me [*qui me regarde*]" is first the *stranger*, irrespective of his or her proximity or objective distance. And it is only if he or she is first recognized as this stranger who troubles me to the point that I must consider myself his or her hostage that he or she can become my fellow and, as such, as Levinas says in varying a famous Augustinian formula, "more intimate to me than myself."[15]

This discovery that the other, be he or she near or far, stranger or traveling companion, is always already *assigned* to me, takes effectively place when we encounter the face of the other. Even the most anonymous face "regards" me. This transcendence cannot be effaced, even if nothing is so easy to crush as a face, as torturers know only too well. The great "ethical" merit of a film such as Claude Lanzmann's *Shoah* consists precisely in its attempt not to confront first the distressing documents, but rather the gazes of the victims, the torturers, and the witnesses with their unbearable quality. To speak of a "transcendence" of the other's face here recalls another Levinasian formula, a "meaning without context":

> The face is signification, and signification without context. I mean that the Other in the rectitude of his face, is not a character without a context. Ordinarily one is a "character": a professor at the Sorbonne, a supreme court justice, son of so-and-so, everything that is in one's passport, the manner of dressing, of presenting oneself. All signification in the usual sense of the term is relative to a context: the meaning of something is in its relation to another thing. Here, to the contrary, the face is meaning all by itself.[16]

This quote allows us better to understand the paradoxical link that Levinas's "ethical" reflection establishes between that which, according to common understanding, is the "closest"—the "face"—and the farthest off—the stranger. The stranger is "the one over there," anonymous and faceless.[17] If the true "revelation" of the face concerns a "meaning without context" then one must precisely recall that the "mystery" (but also the "problem") of the stranger consists rather in presenting itself as a "meaning without context." This is why the topic of the stranger crisscrosses the whole of Levinas's analyses and does not allow itself to be isolated as a regional problem. This is also why it questions philosophy's self-understanding. It turns not only against the ontological philosophy of Heidegger, but also against phenomenological thought. Levinas wishes to recall phenomenology not only to a pre-reflexive consciousness but also to a more originary passivity, more "passive than any passivity," which can be expressed only in terms of "bad conscience."[18] What is essential to this "bad conscience" is that it precedes all accusation. In his inimitable language, Levinas writes: it is the "reserve of what is not invested, of the unjustified, or of the 'stranger on the earth,' according to the expression of the psalmist. This bad conscience is a reserve of the one without a fatherland, or of the one without a home who dares not enter."[19]

What is most remarkable in this attempt, but perhaps also least often noted by commentators, is that this understanding of alterity, which in a certain sense determines the concept of the stranger, is incompatible with the classic definition of relation. To define the fundamental ethical situation as "meaning without context" necessitates rejecting "logical" or more existential language about the relation in order to substitute for it that of the "plot" [*l'intrigue*] of alterity. To say that all relation to the other is possible under the condition of the "mystery" that links us one with the other, obliges us to inscribe the relation to the stranger within the very heart of alterity.

But why does this description of the mystery of alterity turn back so massively against ontology, and against Heidegger's ontology in particular? One of the most abrupt formulations of this critique assimilates it with the disillusioned discourse of the biblical Qohelet, for whom there is nothing new under the sun. Ontology would thus be the discourse where "everything is absorbed, sucked down and walled up in the same."[20] We could say that this world-weariness is the price that ontology must pay for its refusal to admit a "meaning without context" and its desire to inscribe all meaning into the largest possible "context," namely the *world*. Ontology has at its disposal no lever permitting it to surmount this universal boredom: "except the other whom, in all this boredom, we cannot let go . . . it is because responsibility for the Other is transcendence that there can be something new under the sun."[21] It is because the ontological discourse locks up the stranger in the already-given familiarity of Being that it is incapable of *welcoming* her/him as a stranger.

According to Levinas, the ethical question that places the other under the rubric of the stranger is always already insinuated within ontological discourse. The representation of the logos-gathering must thus give way to a new understanding of the relation between transcendence and intelligibility. When Levinas speaks of an *insinuation*, he points both to the way the stranger becomes present to us ("worming his or her way into the midst of our communities") and to a form of speech and of thought that finds its hyperbolic expression in the writings of Jacques Derrida. Levinas, too, explicitly claims this *insinuating* character for his ethical thought: "a thought more thoughtful than the thought of being, a sobering up that philosophy attempts to say; that is, which it attempts to communicate, and this, if only in a language that ceaselessly unsays itself, a language that insinuates."[22] But does this insinuating character of ethical reflection, being achieved within the register of "recanting" (*dédire*), not require that we transcend the massive opposition between an ethical and an ontological discourse, which would condemn them to just glare at each other for all eternity?

There is another reason for going beyond this opposition. From Franz Rosenzweig, Levinas inherited the struggle against an idealist thinking of totality and systematization. It would be rash to carry over this polemic to the ontological thought of Heidegger. Before identifying the fundamental point of divergence between Heidegger and Levinas, one must recognize that they share the same fertile soil, that of Husserlian phenomenology. If one ponders the phenomenological analyses of *Totality and Infinity*, one notices the presence of a dialectic that moves between alterity in its most irreducible, transcendent, and "foreign" sense on one hand, and on the other the recognition of "being at home" somewhere, of "dwelling," of enjoyment. These latter traits found a sphere of belonging that renders possible the welcoming of the other and the stranger. This is why an overly hasty summation of the dialectic as opposing the Same and the Other cannot account for the complexity of the phenomena envisaged.

In pursuing this dynamic of transcendence to the very end, one can perhaps consider the following hypothesis: inasmuch as the ancient henologies and meontologies needed ontological affirmation in order to gain their momentum,[23] could we not say that in a certain sense the ethical insinuation is never so strong as when it is faced with a consistent ontological discourse, and that it dissipates its power when it supposes itself to be the sole occupant of the entire realm of the thinkable, something that Levinas never claimed?

Before pursuing this hypothesis, it is necessary to examine the ontological discourse itself by asking what place it reserves for the stranger.

One's Own and the Foreign: The Ontological Axis

Does ontological discourse dissolve the "plot" (*l'intrigue*) of alterity so as to substitute for it adherence to Being? To respond to this question I now turn to a specific ontological discourse, that of Martin Heidegger. I will consider just two important crossroads of his thought that refer directly to our question: first, the problematic of the stranger on the level of the ontological program of an existential analysis; next, the "dialectic" of one's own and the foreign contemporary with the thought of *Ereignis*.

Strange(r)ness

The suspicion that Heidegger does not pay sufficient attention to the "strangeness" of the other is not a recent one. In his book *Das Individuum in der Rolle des Mitmenschen*, Karl Löwith already chastised Heidegger for his existential analytic, where to a certain degree the other disappears to the benefit of the world.[24] Is this critique justified, or does it rest upon a misunderstanding? Even if one may regret that Heidegger did not dedicate a thorough analysis to ethical being-with-the-other, it must be recalled that he never claimed that the existential analytic was supposed to be a substitute for a fully elaborated anthropology and even less for a moral philosophy. There is no a priori prohibition against developing the Heideggerian analyses in the direction of a social *Lebenswelt* phenomenology, like that of Alfred Schütz, for example, in which the discovery and recognition of the other as stranger would have its rightful place.[25]

Beyond this false problem, we must restore the existential analytic to its true aim, namely the elaboration of a fundamental ontology. Here one discovers, surprisingly, that the question of the stranger is directly involved with the question of the meaning of being. The introductory and, in one way, fundamental indication of this problematic is the following: "*Dasein ist ihm selbst ontisch am nächsten, ontologisch am fersten aber vorontologisch doch nicht fremd.*"[26] A dialectic of the near and the far thus seems to be constitutive of the ontological program of an existential analytic. No doubt, a Levinasian philosopher would object that this already reveals an ethical failure to appreciate the stranger. But is this certain? What prohibits us from referring the encounter with the other, under the guise of stranger, to a more fundamental dialectic? The feeling of a "disturbing strangeness" (*das Unheimliche*) to which Freud devoted a study[27] remains at the horizon of any encounter, be it ever so undemanding, with the stranger. Nothing in this feeling prohibits a priori pondering its ethical stakes as Julia Kristeva does in her book: *Strangers to Ourselves*.

Above all, nothing in the existential analytic allows us to envisage *Dasein* as a subjectivity solidly ensconced in its certainties that refuse to be troubled by others. In order to characterize the very strangeness of the question of Being that strikes *Dasein*, Heidegger quotes Saint Augustine's question, "*Quid autem propinquius meipso mihi?*" and likewise the response: "*ego certe laboro hic et laboro in meipso: factus sum mihi terra difficultatis et sudoris nimii.*"[28] In exposing itself to the very strangeness of the question of Being, *Dasein* experiences a "disorientation" analogous to the experience of "culture shock" that the anthropologist undergoes in his own territory.

We can equally note that within the existential analytic itself Heidegger prepares an open space for the anthropological dialectic of the "near" and the "far" that I have attempted to analyze above. In the eleventh paragraph of *Being and Time*, Heidegger takes up the ethnological, but also the philosophical, problem of understanding the way of life of those people called "primitive." In a much more acute fashion than Cassirer, Heidegger attends to the stakes of such an undertaking. Specifically, because for Heidegger the ethnologist cannot take refuge behind the conceptual apparatus of a "philosophy of symbolic forms," the confrontation takes place between *Dasein* and *Dasein*, between my vision of the world and that of the stranger. The philosopher, who knows that the existential analytic itself requires pre-ontological testimony in order to confirm its own analyses, knows that only another *Dasein*—for example one which presents itself by way of myth—can bring these to him and that these "projections" are more decisive (from the point of view of an existential analytic) than the most sophisticated theoretical constructions of the human sciences.

The key question will then be the following: is there a privileged "place" where the strangeness of the question of Being can be experienced? This question can only be received if one accepts that the ontological interpretation requires that we distance ourselves from the ordinary interpretation of reality (the real identified in the mode of presence characterized as presence-at-hand [*Vorhandenheit*]).[29] Here we discover the decisive role of an affect, which has the privilege of placing *Dasein* before the entirety (*Ganzheit*) of its existence: *Angst*. Paradoxically, this affect individuates *Dasein* in the extreme, making it become most acutely aware of its "ownness" (*Jemeinigkeit*), and at the same time it becomes aware of its radical exposure to the world. Apparently all seems to confirm that this analysis revolves around an "existential solipsism." But Heidegger notes that this "existential 'solipsism' is far from the displacement of putting an isolated subject-Thing into the innocuous emptiness of a wordless occurring, that in an extreme sense what it does is precisely to bring *Dasein* face to face with its world as world, and thus to bring it face to face with itself as Being-in-the-world."[30]

The analysis of this "situation" (*Befindlichkeit*) privileges a "language game" that will remain at the horizon of all later Heideggerian ontology. It is to this "language game" (or family of language games) that Freud likewise refers in his work *Das Unheimliche*. Angst, when it is put into words, announces itself: "in anxiety one feels '*uncanny*'" (*Es ist einem unheimlich*).³¹ These words reveal a mode of being for which there is no (or no longer) a being-at-home (*Nicht-zuhause-sein*). This experience is necessary in order to discover that being-in-the-world means always more than occupying a place or finding oneself ensconced somewhere. The "dwelling," the sphere of the familiar that excludes the stranger, constantly risks making us forget that the very sense of Being prohibits us from definitively establishing an "entrenched position." In this sense, one could say that for Heidegger the ontological condition of possibility for the recognition of others as strangers is to accept the primary fact that existence itself is not reassuring: "*Das beruhigt vertraute In-der-Welt-Sein ist ein Modus der Unheimlichkeit des Daseins, nicht umgekehrt. Das Unzuhause muss existenzial-ontologisch als das ursprünglichere Phänomen begriffen werden.*" ("That kind of Being-in-the-world which is tranquillized and familiar is a mode of Dasein's uncanniness, not the reverse. From an existential-ontological point of view, the 'not at home' must be conceives as the more primordial phenomenon.") The "apocryphal" translation of *Being and Time*, by Emmanuel Martineau, introduces here a neologism that highlights the link between the strange and the stranger: "that kind of Being-in-the-world that is tranquillized and familiar is a mode of *Dasein*'s uncanniness [*l'étrange(ère)té*], not the reverse. *From an existential-ontological point of view, the 'not at home' must be conceived as the more primordial phenomenon.*"³²

The Hearth Is Being

Even after the 1936–38 turn in the question of Being, the topic of strange(r)ness does not disappear from Heideggerian thought, even though the link with the affect of Anxiety, which individuates *Dasein*, distends itself in order to make room for a more ontological problematic of originary temporality and the "destinal" history of Being (*Geschick des Seins*). Even more than the first ontological program, this stepping outside what metaphysics can think may awaken the worst suspicions. Within this perspective I propose to examine a central proposition of the postmetaphysical "ontology" of the later Heidegger: "Being is the hearth" (*Der Herd ist das Sein*). Since in Greek mythology, the goddess Hestia is the guardian of the hearth, I call this the "hestiological" determination of Heidegger's postmetaphysical ontology, which revolves around the core notion of *Ereignis*."³³ The sentence "*Der Herd ist das Sein*" holds a central position within Heidegger's 1942 lecture course dedicated to the interpretation of Hölderlin's fluvial hymn "*Der Ister*" (the Danube).³⁴ What makes this course particularly interesting for our problematic is that it is crisscrossed with a meditation on the dialectic of one's own and the foreign.

The course was delivered in 1942, the year of the Battle of Stalingrad. Between the lines of the course we may glimpse a questioning of the policies of occupying foreign territories (*Siedlungspolitik*) and even of deporting foreign populations (*Umsiedlung*).[35] Rightly or wrongly, Heidegger opposes to this neither an ethical discourse about the respect due to strangers nor a political discourse about the difference between fascism and democracy, but rather asserts his conviction that the xenophobic politics comes from afar and that it has a metaphysical significance. It is one of the manifestations of the will to power as metaphysical principle. This is why Heidegger affirms that the absence of questioning concerning politics and the emergence of totalitarianism do not rest "as naïve minds would think, on the accidental arbitrariness of dictators, but is founded on the metaphysical essence of modern reality as such."[36]

If the origin of totalitarianism has such distant causes, one may obviously ask whether a principle exists that permits us to stand up against it.[37] According to Heidegger it is nothing other than the discovery of originary temporality by Hölderlin and its expression in his river-related poems. This in why the preliminary remark that gives access to the hestiological orientation of ontology is that which defines the very being of rivers: "the river is a site of errancy. But the river is equally the errancy of the site."[38] This is a good example of Heideggerian chiasmus, which is the fundamental figure of his thought, directly according with ontological difference.[39]

To live, to travel, the sacred character of the "lands of refuge": Heidegger mobilizes all these significations in order to determine the meaning of the "sites" in question. When one remembers that the project of a postmetaphysical ontology is stated as a "topology of being,"[40] one understands the scope of the ontological affirmation: "the river brings man into his own and keeps him there."[41] And it is this "dialectic" of the same and the other, one's own and the foreign, that defines "the historial [*l'historialité*] of historic man."[42]

All this seems to confirm the Levinasian suspicion that ontological difference, which Levinas depicts as "the amphibious nature of Being and being [*de l'être et de l'étant*],"[43] completely obscures the face of the other as stranger. Yet it is on the basis of this preliminary formulation that Heidegger envisages a strange meeting between two poets, Hölderlin and Pindar. Why Hölderlin? Why Pindar? What is the necessity of this dialogue? Hölderlin, the poet of rivers, acknowledges in his own poetic speech the degree to which he is animated by the enigma of the stranger:

Ein Zeichen sind wir, deutungslos

Schmerzlos sind wir und haben fast
Die Sprache in der Fremde verloren

A sign are we, without interpretation
Painless we are, and have almost
Lost our speech in foreign parts.

Heidegger's lecture course ends with this very quote, which anticipates his later development of the question "What is called thinking?"[44] This strange "dialogue" between the Greek and the German poet is necessary insofar as it manifests the truth of the historial.

Becoming familiar (*das Heimischwerden*) is a passage through the foreign (*das Fremde*). If the becoming-familiar of a humanity bears the historicity of its history, then the law of the confrontation of the foreign and of one's own is the fundamental truth of history, from which truth the essence of history is uncovered.[45]

This dialectic of one's own and the foreign must be kept in view if one is to avoid the misunderstanding that the hestiological determination of ontology shelters cognition from, or entrenches it against, the stranger. Heidegger's entire argumentation in this course shows the contrary. This is particularly evident when one examines the anthropological counterpart to the formulation: "Being is the hearth." In fact, this affirmation necessitates a certain understanding of the human being. But which one? That of a selfhood peacefully at rest with its certainties and its *conatus essendi*? To the contrary, the secret of Being can only be revealed to one who fully accepts its unreassuring character troubling in the extreme to one's own destiny. It is particularly the destiny of Antigone, threatened with exile from the city, with being driven from her home, that Heidegger has in mind.

Vielfältig das Unheimliche, nichts doch
Über den Menschen unheimlicheres sich regt.

The uncanny is manifold, yet naught is more uncanny than man.

It is thus that Heidegger chose to translate the famous verse "*polla ta deina kouden anthropou deinoteron pelei*" from the chorus of Sophocles's *Antigone*.[46] This translation runs the risk of a certain violence, as Heidegger admits. Against Hölderlin, he chooses to translate more "poetically" "*to deinon*" not by "the monstrous" (*das Ungeheure*) but by "the uncanny" (*das Unheimliche*). For only this translation evokes the relation that exists between the uncanny strangeness (*unheimlich*) and homelessness (*unheimisch*).[47] This translation favors the connection between anthropological and ontological statements.

Here another implication of the problem of the stranger appears that I can only mention in passing, but that would merit a separate investigation. It is the hermeneutical problem of translation and its stakes. Heidegger affirms that the goal of his translation is to aid "in hearing within the chorus the murmur of the source of Hölderlin's hymnic poetry, even if only distantly."[48] We have here the admission, perhaps somewhat veiled, that involved in all hermeneutical relations—be it in the work of translating from one language to another or in historical understanding of a past era—is the problem of the relation with the stranger.[49] In a political context, marked at its highest point by the obsession with an absolutely pure, national language free from all foreign contamination, Heidegger defines what one could call the ethical stakes of the act of translation:

> An historical people *is* only from dialogue between its language and other languages. . . . Thought according to a historical meditation [*Besinnung*], translation is a confrontation with the foreign language for the sake of appropriating one's own.[50]

Antigone, threatened with becoming a foreigner to the city, "knows" (but in what sense?) that she must embrace her destiny: *pathein to deinon*. This is the highest means, that for Heidegger contains nothing of the heroic in the banal sense of the word, to experience the uncanny, unreassuring character of the human condition. If she is able to do so, it is because she likewise possesses the essential knowledge (*phronesis*) about (being at) home and dwelling: "all knowledge of *deinon*, of strangeness, is brought, led, clarified, and joined by the knowledge about (being at) home."[51]

Such "knowledge" about residences and residing can be stated only poetically,[52] to the point that this knowledge alone decides as to the mutual belonging of poetry and thinking. The statement "Being is the hearth"[53] is ontological and poetic at the same time. Only a line of thought that refuses to engage in this originary relation will think that Aletheia and Hestia, the two guardian divinities of the ontology of the later Heidegger, are simply rhetorical figures. In fact the reverse is true: the forgetfulness of Being consists in the progressive effacement of the hestiological and aletheiological dimensions of ontology. Forgetfulness of Being is the increasing inability to conceive of Being as home. It results in an ominous interpretation of history: "For history is nothing other than this return home."[54]

I conclude this analysis with a final remark which would also deserve a much longer development: the hestiological characterization of ontology (and the relation of one's own and the foreign that arises from it) is alone capable of providing a space to welcome the *Divine*, in other words, of thinking the relation between humans and God (or Gods) according the paradigm of the hospitality rendered to the stranger. This hospitality, which itself can only be articulated poetically, loses all its meaning if one does not acknowledge that the other name for the disturbing strangeness of Being itself is, in fact, the *Sacred*.[55]

The Meridian

If the preceding considerations do not totally eliminate the distance between the ethical and the ontological approaches to the problem of the stranger, they will at least allow a better understanding of what is at stake in this very distance. Must we go no further than this somewhat disillusioned remark, or may we envisage yet another possibility of having ethical reflection on the stranger and ontological thought on strangeness intersect? My thesis, no doubt a bit rash, is that art may play this role if we conceive of it outside of traditional aesthetic categories. This is what Paul Celan undertook in his famous Darmstadt speech, "The Meridian," a text of particular interest to us in that Levinas drew on it to dispute the priority of ontological thought. I cite Levinas's key statement: "What is strange is the stranger. Nothing is more strange nor more foreign than another man, and it is in the clarity of utopia that one reaches man external to all anchorage and homeliness."[56]

Even if this affirmation corresponds well to Celan's idea of the ultimate goal of poetry, it risks obscuring Celan's reflection on the function of art, with which it is consonant. Celan's meditation bears upon Georg Büchner's description of the wanderings of the isolated poet, Lenz. The encompassing topic of art, for Celan, is not the contemplation of the other's face, but of something more disturbing: the automaton or the puppet. Only in accepting this addition of artifice does art assume its irreplaceable role: making me a stranger to myself, it gives rise to a distance that at the same time opens a path that leads me away from myself, toward a strangeness that exposes me to the world and to the other.[57] All true encounters with the other in his or her otherness must be willing to go by way of this strangeness. Poetry that places me as a stranger to myself (*befremdetes Ich*) necessarily seems to be "hermetic." "Do not reproach us for lacking clarity," says Celan, citing Pascal, "since this is what we claim!" And he adds: "That, I believe, is the obscurity that, if not congenital, is at least ordered to poetry, from a remote or foreign region that it itself perhaps projects, with a view to an encounter."[58]

The strangeness of the poem thus defined presents two aspects. The first is its hermetic appearance, as speech that runs the risk of being dumb, of being without voice (*Atemwende*). Here Celan uses the same expression as that which guides Heidegger's interpretation of Angst: "*es verschlägt . . . den Atem und das Wort*" (It leaves one speechless and breathless).⁵⁹ Second, such poetry is an act of utopic hope, which makes the label "hermetic" inappropriate. Even though "the poem always speaks only of its own, its most intimate cause," Celan suggests,

> it has always been among the hopes of poetry to speak as well, precisely in this manner, of a *foreign* cause—no, I can no longer use this word—precisely in this manner of *the cause of another*—who knows, perhaps in the case of a *wholly other*. This "who knows," at which I have arrived, is the only thing that I can add to the old hopes, from myself here and now.⁶⁰

In thus envisaging the possible encounter with the other and the wholly other, Celan is in accord with the Levinasian perspective. His conception of poetic speech is incompatible with a correspondence of speech and Being, which would lose sight of the singular angle of inclination of existence articulated in every poem.⁶¹ Given this particular perspective, Celan's *Meridian* also intersects with the fundamental theme of Hölderlin's "Ister":

> When one thinks about poems, does one travel such paths with poems? Or are these paths only detours? Detours from you to you? Yet they are also at the same time, among so many other paths, paths on which speech finds voice, they are encounters, paths of a voice to a perceiving you, creaturely paths, perhaps projects of existence, a sending oneself forward to oneself, in search of oneself. . . . A sort of return home.⁶²

Here poetry as "*eine Art Heimkehr*" is strangely consonant with the Heideggerian affirmation: "every history is a homecoming," in the same way that there is a correspondence between Celan's formula that defines the ontological vocation of poetry: "The real is not simply there, the real wishes to be sought and won"⁶³ and the Heideggerian formula: "poetry is the 'discovery' of Being by speech."⁶⁴ In this sense, but in this sense only, Celan's "Meridian" enables us to surmount the dichotomy between the ontological and ethical aims of poetic speech, between the disturbing strangeness of Being and the ethical "obsession" with the stranger.

This intersection needs to be expressed in the poet's own words. Here one might consult all the poems that Celan grouped in the collection *Die Niemandsrose*. Among the numerous stylistic particularities of these poems, I note only the way the language of the stranger (Yiddish, Hebrew, but equally Russian and Latin) invades the space of Celan's German, the mother tongue that he never wanted to renounce. The penultimate poem of this collection, "*Und mit dem Buch auch Tarussa,*" describes the entire itinerary of Celan's exile and already mysteriously evokes what will become the place of his death. As an epigraph to this poem Celan has placed a citation (in Cyrillic script) of Marina Tsvetaeva: "All poets are Jews." The sentence from which this comes is as follows: "In the most Christian of all worlds all poets are Jews." The meaning of this definition of the poet, so near to and so far from Hölderlin's, can only be discovered in reading and hearing the poem itself, of which I simply cite one passage:

> Of
> a tree, of one.
> Yes, of it too. And of the woods around it. Of the woods
> untrodden, of the
> thought they grew from, as sound
> and half-sound and changed sound and terminal sound, Scythian
> > rhymes
> in the meter
> of the temple of the driven,
> with,
> breathed steppe-
> grass written into the heart
> of the hour-caesura—into the realm,
> the widest of
> realms, into
> the great internal rhyme
> beyond
> the zone of mute nations, into yourself
> language-scale, word-scale, home-
> scale of exile.[65]

—Translated by T. Gregg Monteith and Joseph O'Leary

Words of Welcome

Hospitality in the Philosophy of Emmanuel Levinas

JEFFREY BLOECHL

I

Emmanuel Levinas signals the importance of hospitality for his approach to ethics and religion about two-thirds of the way through his first major work, *Totality and Infinity*:

> No human or interhuman relationship can be enacted outside of economy; no face can be approached with empty hands and closed home. Recollection in a home open to the Other—hospitality—is the concrete and initial fact of human recollection and separation; it coincides with the Desire for the Other absolutely transcendent.[1]

The French text calls for a pair of significant nuances not easily discernible in English translation. To begin with, where the translation twice gives us "recollection," the original has *"recueillement,"* which suggests something more like collection or gathering-together. This alternative translation, moreover, is in keeping with Levinas's general theme in the section where this passage appears: "Dwelling," in the sense of settling into a perspective or abiding in a time and place. One only supposes to dwell in solitude, when in fact solitude is, according to some of the earliest passages of the work, a dimension of separation between oneself and the Other person. The alleged solitude of dwelling is thus in fact constituted by a form of blindness to the discrete presence of an Other, and by an intimacy that is lost on the one who is bent on his own concerns. All of this may be detected by attending to the fact that the human world is a world that is already cultivated, or if one prefers, already domesticated. Levinas's image is provocative: "the other [*l'Autre*] whose presence is discreetly an absence, with which is accomplished the primary hospitable welcome which describes the field of intimacy, is the Woman [*la Femme*]."² And "the woman," Levinas immediately adds, "is the condition for recollection, the interiority of the home, and inhabitation."³

We will return later to this assimilation of hospitality and the feminine, and we will ask about the conditions under which a single gender is invested with discretion and thus a certain reserve that are the essential condition for what will undoubtedly qualify as charity and respect. Let us also foresee what will be at stake when we do come back to the problem: to contest certain features of Levinas's notion of hospitality will be at the same time to put in question the account of ethics that accompanies it.

A second nuance of translation concerns the word "Other." This nuance is twofold. On one hand, "Other" translates "*Autrui*," which is distinctly personal, as opposed to the nonpersonal "*autre*." On the other hand, the capitalized "Other" is faithful to Levinas's capitalization of "*Autrui*" in some passages, including the one with which I have begun. Throughout Levinas's work, and according to no readily discernible pattern, he variously capitalizes or does not capitalize both "*autrui*" and "*autre*." Translators, for their part, have sometimes proposed a consistency that the original text seems not to display. In *Totality and Infinity*, Alphonso Lingis, having secured Levinas's agreement, always capitalizes instances of the personal "*autrui*" and never capitalizes instances of the nonpersonal "*autre*."⁴ Needless to say, this decision implies a specific interpretation of the philosophy itself, and not only its terminology, at the very least because it erases from view an ambiguity that may prove to be unavoidable or even essential. A complete account of these difficulties, both in Levinas's texts and in their English translations, calls for a separate exercise, but as concerns the theme of hospitality, it does seem safe to venture the following: what appears in Levinas's French as *Autrui* and is rendered in the English translation as Other invokes a personhood whose otherness is more than adjectival and thus more than relative. This in turn takes us to the religious heart of what Levinas takes to be the ethical relation, in a conception of otherness, precisely as revealed in a human face, that is strictly *absolute*. And this suggests that hospitality, as the defining feature of a relation to the other person as other person is not only ethical, as many would readily agree, but also—again in the strict sense of the word—*religious*. It is not evident to me that those for whom Levinas would be first and finally a fundamentally will have grasped the proper force of his position: being in the world is not only being for the other person, but also—and most deeply—being toward God.

These few considerations give us only a preliminary understanding of Levinas's conception of hospitality. Let us try to go further.

I have already mentioned that the reference to "hospitality" is found in a section that deals with "dwelling" (*la demeure*). It is there that Levinas proposes that being in the world is always and already being in a relation with other people. Perhaps it is useful to reawaken our sense of just how new will appear to those who come to it after a thorough schooling in the philosophy of Heidegger. And after all, are we not generally inclined to side with Heidegger, generally inclined to think very much the opposite of what we hear from Levinas—that is, to think that our primary relation is with the world, and that our relations with one another are grounded and played out there, rather as if the world is the stage on which the drama of freedom and responsibility is enacted? For Levinas, the true meaning of the world is defined by relations of responsibility between a subject and her neighbor, or as he puts it in *Totality and Infinity*, between the Same and the Other. It is well known that this designation of intersubjectivity by Sameness and Otherness is crucial to the whole of Levinas's thinking. When he calls the subject "the Same," he characterizes our natural and spontaneous way of being by involution and insularity. Left to its own devices, the subject remains centered on itself. In that mode, he writes time and again, I live as if the meaning of my own actions is determined solely by my own freedom, and as if the meaning of everything I encounter is determined finally by my capacity to recognize and comprehend it; I live, in short, as if life simply is as I find it. And even if to a considerable degree or for long stretches of time this may well work for me, it nonetheless forgets, from start to finish, the great richness of dimensions that I do not recognize or comprehend, and that are not under my control. Levinas's word "Same" is thus also a name for the world such as the subject has emptied of every hint of the incomprehensible. Among these is the otherness of the Other person. Indeed, the otherness of the Other person would not be merely one instance of an otherness that is generally excluded by ego-centered life of the subject, but in fact the sole otherness that is truly, absolutely other. Whereas the otherness of objects is only their surplus over any single perspective on them, the otherness of other people consists in an "exteriority" that could never be captured by any perspective or collection of perspectives because it is inhabited by a perspective of its own. For Levinas, the interhuman relation is a relation of Same and Other, in which the Same does not have access to the Other in her inwardness—which is to say, not only in *her* experience of *me* (as Husserl and Sartre had noticed before Levinas), but also in her desire, her restlessness, and her suffering.

This means that everything done for oneself and everything centered on oneself—from rudimentary experience to aggressive self-assertion—presupposes and excludes the otherness of the Other person. The Other, in what Levinas takes to be a very real sense, is always already there; and the subject, as Same, has always already excluded and forgotten her. To gather things to myself—to project and exploit an economy of resources—is to seize a place for myself, to make myself at home, and to address the world as if good-for-me—without considering whether it might also or even first be good-for-the-Other-person. It is from within this economy of resources and the relation to the world that it involves, that there arises the question of welcoming the Other person.

It now stands to reason that Levinas invests so much in the face of the other person. In the face of the Other person, he famously contends, the subject meets a dimension that defies comprehension. The face thus shocks, but also awakens and teaches. Whereas previously I had been absorbed in my own concerns, without cause to truly question their supremacy, now I am called to see that the Other person, too, inhabits this world I had taken as my own. Before solitude is community, and before self-indulgence is the need and desire of my neighbor, in fact already urging itself upon me in the disturbance that his or her nearness brings to the world I inhabit. Some of Levinas's most forceful, even strident proposals follow directly from here: home, as my place in the world or under the sun, is pretense if not usurpation; economy, as system of self-concern, is thoughtless self-indulgence, and freedom, as unlimited power of initiative, is the very being of forgetfulness and suppression. Hospitality, if hospitality there is, will evidently be the defining feature of a just distribution of goods, a new ethics and politics attuned to original plurality, and an authentic conversion to a responsibility for the Other person that would be prior to every form of responsibility for myself. It hardly needs to be said that this hospitality calls for nothing less than a reversal of everything belonging essentially to the subjectivity of the Same. Nor is it surprising to find, barely a decade later, in *Otherwise than Being, or Beyond Essence*, that the very subjectivity of the subject is composed of an "obsession by the neighbor."[5]

II

What, on this account of our subjectivity, would it mean to welcome the Other person as truly other? The possibility would have to be explored along two lines of inquiry—one that studies the event in which the subject might truly welcomes the Other without doing violence to her otherness, and one that studies the conditions under which such a welcome could occur without destroying the very subjectivity of the subject. The former inquiry seems to have preoccupied Levinas up to and including *Totality and Infinity*. I have already touched on its central feature: the face of the Other person confronts the subject with an otherness it cannot incorporate into its own understanding, so that the very meaning that is accorded to that person is already a response to her face. The first moment of hospitality is a gathering-together of oneself and one's very world, under the arresting presence of the human face. My world becomes truly a home when it becomes available to me as what I can either keep for myself or offer to this Other person. But this alternative is not merely a question of my freedom. It belongs among Levinas's subtler accomplishments to have discerned that the claims of the stranger can immediately instill in us a peculiar comfort: the moment an Other person crosses my threshold, I am called to put aside all of my apparently endless private concerns and rest in the certainty that here and now I must attend to the needs of my guest. Yet this cannot be the peace of complacency and oblivion, for then the needs of the Other person are reduced to a tonic for the restless soul, in which case the otherness of the Other becomes only a function of the sameness of the Same. If for Levinas hospitality delivers genuine peace, this must a peace that is found only in caring for the Other person, in welcoming her into one's home and indeed one's very identity. Hospitality requires me to become one-for-the-Other person.

But this idea, this account of what it is to catch sight of the face of the Other person and awaken from self-absorption into hospitality, requires Levinas also to show that our being is not in fact defined by the activity that drives personal initiative and comprehension, but instead by a passivity that our most natural tendencies cause us to cancel out and forget. This is increasingly the concern of his works after *Totality and Infinity*. I am first and always exposed to the approach of another person, even as everything else in me seems to conspire to cause me to think otherwise. Moreover, this is one occasion where the persistence of a theme has required a revision of the argument: it is not until the second chapter of *Otherwise Than Being or Beyond Essence*, and by way of a remarkably painstaking study of Husserl, that sensibility becomes not only the medium of the subject's relation with the elements but, already anterior to that, the site of an exposure to the other person. According to this, the final Levinas, each of us is disposed to the eruption of the Other person even and already where we are most likely to think that a certain grasping is inevitable: in our very sensing, by which the neighbor, like everything else, would necessarily be defined from one's own perspective at the very moment of contact. This can be stated in terms that touch directly on the theme of hospitality: according to Levinas, it is impossible to welcome the Other person as truly other unless passivity is a condition of our very sensibility. And were that to prove untrue, then it would be necessary to think that what we call hospitality does not go all the way to welcoming the other person without certain conditions or qualifications.

The inquiry could not be conducted at a deeper level—not without proposing to leave the domain of consciousness itself, or at any rate not without abandoning consciousness as the essential reference for phenomenological inquiry. What Levinas calls "sensibility" is the level and the *topos* in which the unformed material of external things meets and is woven into the primitive flesh of consciousness itself; in sensibility sensing and sensed are already found together. To go further, to seek a distinction between them and thus a single soil that would precede them, would be to move beneath the original and originating contact of self and world, which is to say beyond the possibility of meaning itself. So is sensibility, as the primordial entanglement of self and world, fundamentally active or fundamentally passive? On Levinas's reckoning, philosophy in the Western tradition has generally privileged the latter (activity) over the former (passivity), preferring to take its bearing from the notion that human sensing already contains within itself a rudimentary intuition of what we eventually comprehend as a particular thing. For such a philosophy, what we grasp in sensation is already on its way to disclosing within itself an essence or idea of which it is a concrete instance.[6] For such a philosophy, in other words, sensibility is already dominated by act, by an intuition of an essence. Sensing, in short, is always already on its way to knowing. Now this does seem to place sensibility under the domination of activity rather than under the sign of passivity, since everything is oriented to the specific act of intuiting an essence in the sensed.

As it happens, Levinas contests only the *privilege* accorded to activity, but not its necessary and in any case inevitable role in the constitution of meaning. Prior to the act in which we intuit an essence in the sensed, there is necessarily the passivity by which the sensed gives itself to our sensing. But with equal necessity, the act of intuition immediately ensues, for there can be no question of one without the other. The movement of consciousness and the constitution of meaning presuppose and give expression to this alternation of passivity and activity at the heart of sensing. And this alternation, which is lived time itself, must evidently be the final horizon for all meaning. According to Levinas, consciousness, considered now in the fullest sense, is forever in the process of responding to a prompt that comes from before and outside itself, activity is forever in the wake of passivity, and passivity is thus in an important sense our ultimate condition.

All of this would mean that each of us is exposed to the approach of things—including the extraordinary thing that is the human face—before we assign them a meaning relative to the other meanings to which we are already accustomed. Finally, this exposure, as the condition of a "surface" that must somehow be passive before it can be committed to any act, would be the condition of a subject to whom the Other person can reveal himself as truly Other, whereupon arises the question of a hospitality capable of respecting that otherness as indeed absolutely Other.

For Levinas, an answer can be found only in language. The simplest expression of meaning, he has contended, is occurs in a transition from passivity to a claim that already responds to the approach of the Other, and in that sense bears witness and even proclaims.[7] To make raw data yield an idea, to address a particular datum as an instance of a concept, is to pair it with a word. Meaning is constituted in the form of a phrase that has the basic form of "I take this to be that." We may immediately ask whether such a claim, or even the very existence of words themselves, do not already indicate a profound intersubjectivity. Language is already dialogue, even if sometimes in the diminished form of a dialogue with oneself. This is both its weakness and its greatness. If language, and for that matter meaning itself is an endless dialogue, then it is prevented—we are prevented—from ever settling into the power of an unquestionable assertion. At the same time, language is also an inexhaustible source of questions, and therefore of a challenge to every accretion of power. In the philosophy of Levinas, language is the very working of ethics, as meaning is born in a response to the proximity of an Other that is already an arrogation of privileges for the one who speaks. Is this tension not to be found at the heart of hospitality such as even Levinas would have us understand it? It is true that the presence of a neighbor at my door puts me unexpectedly in question. But it is also true that in the simplest act of recognition, in which I welcome her presence into my awareness, I am already on my way toward reclaiming the initiative. And unless a degree of initiative truly falls to me, it cannot be said that hospitality is offered.

III

The foregoing concern was certainly not lost on Levinas. But the questions of whether and how to commit oneself to the needs of the stranger are to be referred to what he calls "justice," the domain in which priorities and norms are mobilized only after sensitivity to the proximity of those needs has already rendered us ethically responsible.[8] And this invites us to consider a distinction between the ordinary hospitality that follows established norms and issues in time-honored practices, and the exorbitant hospitality that cannot rest on any set of norms and is not satisfied with any range of practices because they always enjoin limits for the responsibility that commands it. We have already recognized the conception of passivity that this requires, and reviewed the lengths to which Levinas must go in order to defend it. Perhaps now we can conclude that the price of true hospitality would be fidelity to this passivity that "does not revert into an assumption"[9]—or better, that what is called for is nothing less than limitless self-effacement and a patience that must be literally without end (for Levinas, "patience" is the unique passion of responsibility).

Evidently enough, this invests hospitality with a considerable *ascesis*. Not only does the face of the visitor, according to some of Levinas's best-known claims, dispossess the subject of every presumption, but that same subject must also endeavor to maintain itself in that state. The visitor estranges me, as host, from myself and I for my part must "posit myself as deposed of my sovereignty."[10] What can this mean, in the final account, if not that hospitality entails accepting and embracing as my authentic condition a relation to the Other person—as stranger and as neighbor—by which I have always already received him or her into my presence before even recognizing what he may need, let alone considering whether it is possible or even desirable that I provide it? It is no longer possible to avoid the matter of gender: *Is this not what we have already seen Levinas reserve for the attitude and comportment of Woman?*

Let us pause over this. On one hand, hospitality, responsibility and indeed the very possibility of goodness are aligned with Woman. On the other hand, Woman is defined as if antithetical to act and power, which as Levinas defines them, answer to what our popular culture sometimes associates with male aggression and testosterone. One is thus inclined to think, partly against someone like Simone de Beauvoir, that Levinas does not so much reduce Woman to the other of man as he does assimilate Woman to the ethical subject that has surrendered its claim to anything like "masculine privilege."[11] Whether one speaks of Womanhood or of ethical subjectivity, Levinas has in mind a possibility that is available to, and indeed commanded of male and female alike. "Woman" is not the counterpart of gendered man, but of Man as agent of power, violence, and the claims to sovereignty from which they emanate; thus, Man in a sense that is called into question by the approach of the stranger, or the presence of a visitor at the door. Of course, this does not resolve the problem of gender that many commentators have observed to hang over the whole of Levinas's *oeuvre*, but it does bring it into better focus: the possibility of genuine hospitality and thus also, more generally, of what Levinas is willing to admit as true responsibility rests on a binary opposition between (he calls) Woman and (what I propose to call) Man,[12] such that a positive value is assigned to the former and a negative one to the latter. In terms of Levinas's texts, this means that what *Totality and Infinity* calls "Woman" is the immediate predecessor of what in *Otherwise Than Being or Beyond Essence* becomes the ethical subject. Hospitality is a capacity and an accomplishment of Woman, but "Woman" is the proper name of subjectivity insofar as ordered to responsibility and the Good.

To center Levinas's conception of hospitality on the question of gender is to invite an extended reflection on its relation to politics, since of course all social action depends on some version of privileges for certain roles over others, whether they are determined by biology, society, or metaphysics. Derrida has often drawn attention to a hiatus between Levinas's ethics of absolute responsibility and the politics in which concerted action becomes possible, no doubt wishing to supplement the ethical pressure Levinas places on politics with claims for any number of political exigencies that would in turn press upon the ethical. With regard to the matter at hand, one may simply wonder whether the ethics of absolute responsibility and perfect hospitality does not in fact require and depend on a conception of gender that is impossible to sustain without recourse to the political domain that Levinas would have us submit to ethical critique. Is it possible to embrace and act on distinctions such as "Woman" and "Man"—or if one prefers, welcoming and welcomed—without the support and guidance of a set of practices that already tell us how to distinguish the terms of an essential difference?

Yet politics cannot have the final word in any analysis of these difficulties. For there is no denying that the practices by which an act becomes meaningful are themselves the bearers of an order in which meaning is itself possible. It would not be an overstatement to suggest that Levinas has sometimes motivated by an urge to grant any primacy to precisely this sort of order—to what, for example, Lacan has called the symbolic, to which the subject must submit as the necessary condition for acting on articulate desire.[13] Let us follow Lacan at least to this one question: is not the inevitable recourse to "Woman" itself received from the fact of language, and indeed from the fact that it is always in some way ordered? Perhaps it is true that to serve the Good is in the final account to offer hospitality to the neighbor who is also stranger and enemy. Perhaps it is also true that the price for doing so must finally be an abnegation without limit. Yet none of this ever ceases to appeal to the words by which Woman would distinguish herself from Man, even if only to put Man before herself—words by which mute gestures and an indeterminate future would be transformed into the gift of service and the work of hope. And if this is so, then we are left with the thought that concrete hospitality, the welcome that is more than an abstract idea or a well-intentioned thought, rests in no small measure on the intelligibility of words that are neither mine nor yours alone, but the milieu in which we sometimes find one another in pursuit of these important matters.

Neither Close nor Strange

Levinas, Hospitality, and Genocide

WILLIAM H. SMITH

At the outset of *Totality and Infinity*, Emmanuel Levinas defines the Other (*l'Autrui*)—the overarching theme of all his work—in terms of the stranger. He writes:

> The absolutely other is the Other. He and I do not form a number. The collectivity in which I say "you" or "we" is not a plural of the "I." I, you—these are not individuals of a common concept. Neither possession nor the unity of number nor the unity of concepts link me to the Stranger, the Stranger who disturbs the being at home with oneself. But Stranger also means the free one. Over him I have no *power*.[1]

For Levinas, then, we might say that to encounter the Other is to encounter the stranger, and that this encounter with the strange is essential to all interhuman contact: the stranger is the absolutely other, one that I do not have at my disposal, a being that is not wholly "in my site" or under my control.[2] To encounter the stranger is to encounter another source of freedom, another source of world-constitution or world-disclosure, to put it in Husserlian or Heideggerian terms respectively. Of course, what is distinctive about Levinas's phenomenological account of the Other is his claim that our relationship with the stranger is not exhausted by epistemological or ontological investigations; rather, for Levinas, our relation to the stranger—and therefore the nature of intersubjectivity itself—is fundamentally *ethical*.

Indeed, for Levinas, to encounter face of the stranger is to be called to ethical responsibility: "We name this calling into question of my spontaneity by the presence of the Other ethics. The strangeness of the other, his irreducibility to the I, to my thoughts and my possessions, is precisely accomplished as a calling into question of my spontaneity, as ethics."[3] To encounter the stranger is to encounter an ethical demand, to discover in the face of another human being the demand that I account for myself and my actions. This defining feature of all intersubjective relationships—the ethical relation as a mode of critique—constantly puts me in the position of being both responsible *to* and *for* the stranger that faces me. In a long but important passage, Levinas describes this dual responsibility:

> The face with which the Other turns to me is not reabsorbed in a representation of the face. To hear his destitution which cries out for justice is not to represent an image to oneself, but is to posit oneself as responsible, both as more and as less than the being that presents itself in the face. Less, for the face summons me to my obligations and judges me. The being that presents himself in the face comes from a dimension of height, a dimension of transcendence whereby he can present himself as a stranger without opposing me as obstacle or enemy. More, for my position as I consists in being able to respond to this essential destitution of the Other, finding resource for myself. The Other who dominates me in his transcendence is thus the stranger, the widow, the orphan, to whom I am obligated.[4]

In this way, for Levinas, when I encounter the face of the stranger I find myself in the position of being both less and more than the Other: I discover not only one who can command my allegiance, a superior, but also one who does so by calling out for aid as a dependent. The Other is simultaneously one to whom something is owed—who can judge me—and yet one who depends on my generosity to subsist. The stranger is a kind of being who is powerful by being powerless, one who "exceeds my powers infinitely, and therefore does not oppose them but paralyzes the very power of power."[5] The expression of the Other—the face of the stranger—can command me, can call me to justice, not because of the Other's worldly position of power, but because of the Other's *ethical resistance* to power. As Levinas puts it, the relation between the I and the stranger is incommensurate with the exercise of power; it is not a relation with a very great resistance, but with something absolutely other.[6]

My aim in this essay, in addition to adumbrating Levinas's phenomenology of the stranger, is to direct Levinas's phenomenological account of the Other toward one of the most vexing moral problems of the twentieth century: the problem of genocide. My thought is that Levinas's notions of the stranger, the welcome, and the face allow us to rethink genocide and its conditions of possibility. Such a move is not unanticipated by Levinas himself. As he memorably remarks: "The Other is the sole being I can wish to kill."[7] For Levinas, the epiphany of the face announces both the possibility of ethical responsibility and the possibility of total destruction; even as it calls for moral respect, the face also represents a temptation to murder.[8] If this is true, as Levinas indicates, if the face of the stranger is not only the first occasion for *hospitality*, since to acknowledge the Other is to welcome his expression,[9] but also the first opportunity for *hostility*, since I can wish to kill only an existent absolutely independent from me—that is, the Other who can sovereignly say no to me[10]—then the face of the stranger is the original locus of both the first ethical action and its opposite. It is with the face, then, that the attempt to understand the possibility of genocide ought to begin. If Levinas is correct about the primacy of ethics and the essential ethical dimension of all interhuman relationships, then the face of the stranger is the primordial site for both moral goodness and radical evil. And what is genocide if not the possibility of radical evil?

In what follows, my thesis is that Levinas's phenomenological descriptions of hospitality and the face of the stranger enable us to have a fuller appreciation of what is at stake in genocide. More specifically, I shall argue that the possibility of genocide lies in the refusal to acknowledge the Other either as a *neighbor* (close to us) or as a *stranger* (a guest).[11] Following Levinas, my claim is that genocide tries to annihilate the primordial ethical expression of the face that is the foundation of every social relationship. Although a full phenomenological account of genocide is too large an undertaking for this piece and must be developed elsewhere, I believe Levinas's phenomenology of the stranger will allow us—as a start—to reimagine the purpose and intent of genocide: it is the attempt to eradicate the demand for moral respect that exists between all strangers and neighbors, between all friends and enemies. In the end, I shall suggest that Levinas points the way toward avoiding genocidal events in our future. If radical evil is made possible by our failure of attention—or worse, our intentional obfuscation—of the essential features of our encounter with the strange, then perhaps it is only if we can see the other as strange in a particular sense—a stranger that teaches—that we can hope to prevent genocide in the twenty-first century.

The essay is divided into two sections. The first part will be devoted to a reading of Levinas's notion of the stranger and the related ideas of hospitality and the face. The second portion will attempt to apply this model of the stranger to a concrete case: the Rwandan genocide of 1994. As I shall describe, the features of the events in Rwanda push our usual attempts to understand genocide to the limit. Above all, the Rwandan genocide underscores the urgency of our need to answer the following question: How is it that apparently "ordinary" individuals—neighbors, friends, and acquaintances—could become the main perpetrators of mass murder? We can begin to see a means of answering this question, which burns so brightly in the case of Rwanda, with the phenomenological resources supplied by Levinas.

Levinas's Phenomenology of the Stranger

There are three distinctive aspects of Levinas's phenomenology of stranger that, in my view, have direct bearing on the problem of genocide: Levinas's account of the face, the asymmetrical nature of the ethical relationship between the I and the Other, and the intrinsic connection between the stranger, the I, and hospitality. Allow me to briefly describe these basic components of the Levinasian position.

The Face

The experience Levinas calls "the face" represents the ground of morality itself; the face gives us an unavoidable reason to act in a moral fashion.[12] As indicated at the start of this essay, the face is simply Levinas's way of describing an essential feature of any interpersonal relationship: to encounter another person is at the same time to encounter a fundamental demand for ethical responsibility. One cannot encounter another person without experiencing this claim, without recognizing the moral status of the other. First and foremost, however, one must understand that the face is a linguistic phenomenon and not an object of cognition or perception as is often thought.[13] The face, he writes, "expresses itself" and "the first content of expression is the expression itself."[14] In other words, the face both founds language[15] and is the first word of any language.[16] Because the face is the ground of language, it is also the ground of all human sociality. As a result, insofar as we are in community with others and share a meaningful world with them, we are always in the position of having previously assented to the demand for ethical responsibility represented by the face.

Crucially, for Levinas, no Gyges—or one who wishes to be like him—can avoid the claim of the face: "The face opens the primordial discourse whose first word is obligation, which no 'interiority' permits avoiding."[17]

What the face expresses, most fundamentally, is "you shall not commit murder."[18] That is, the face speaks of a primordial demand for moral respect, a call that emerges from the concrete exigencies of the Other's circumstances. As Levinas writes:

> The transcendence of the face is at the same time its absence from this world into which it enters, the exiling of a being, his condition of being stranger, destitute, or proletarian.... This gaze that supplicates and demands, that can supplicate only because it demands, deprived of everything because entitled to everything, and which one recognizes in giving (as one "puts the things in question in giving")—this gaze is precisely the epiphany of the face as a face.[19]

Clearly foreshadowed here is the connection between the face, hospitality and the gift. But also indicated is in this passage is the ethical claim that emanates from the other's expression, broadly conceived. In this case, the "expression" of the face is captured in the supplicating gaze of the stranger. To recognize the stranger is to recognize this claim of the face, or "to recognize a hunger," as Levinas puts it; this hunger in turn puts into question "my joyous possession of the world" and calls for some recompense on my part.[20] Whatever my response may be, I cannot explain away the prior claim of the face; I cannot go on just as before after being claimed by it: whatever I do will either be moral or immoral, as seen in light of the ethical demand of the face. In sum, then, the face represents the ethical norm of the moral order: it is an invitation to self-responsibility, an invitation that flows from our recognition of a prior ethical responsibility to the stranger who faces us.[21]

Asymmetry

Also distinctive of Levinas's position, in contrast to most contemporary moral theorists, is that he eschews egalitarianism in his account of ethics. He writes:

> The relation between me and the other commences in the inequality of terms, transcendent to one another, where alterity does not determine the other in a formal sense.... Here the alterity of the other does not result from its identity, but constitutes it: the other is the Other. The Other qua Other is situated in a dimension of height and of abasement—glorious abasement; he has the face of the poor, the stranger, the widow, and the orphan, and, at the same time, of the master called to invest and justify my freedom.[22]

The stranger approaches from a "dimension of height," as one who is "lord" and "master" in Levinas's ethical metaphysics because the Other takes up the place previously occupied by God in the history of philosophy.[23] Levinas provocatively uses these theological tropes—including the biblical figures of the poor, the stranger, the widow, and the orphan—not in order to ground morality on religion, but in order to indicate the unassailability of the other's moral authority, or more precisely, the non-reciprocal nature of our moral indebtedness to the Other. The purpose of utilizing religious imagery is not to assert that the Other is God, but to highlight the radical moral authority the Other possesses. Indeed, for Levinas it is only through the asymmetry of our relationship with the stranger that we can begin to think of our relationship to the divine. As he writes, "To posit the transcendent as stranger and poor one is to prohibit the metaphysical relation with God from being accomplished in the ignorance of men and things. The dimension of the divine opens forth from the human face."[24] It is our relation with other human beings, he claims, "that give to theological concepts the sole signification they admit of."[25]

The upshot of these claims, for our purposes, is that to be who I am—a free self in the world—means to have always already been enjoined by the Other and to have assented to the legitimacy of the Other's authority to command me. As Levinas puts it:

> The accomplishing of the I qua I and morality constitute one sole and same process in being: morality comes to birth not in equality, but in the fact that infinite exigencies, that of serving the poor, the stranger, the widow, and the orphan converge at one point of the universe. Thus through morality alone are I and the others produced in the universe.[26]

To be an I is to be infinitely responsible to the Other, a responsibility from which I cannot be released and which grows deeper the better I fulfill it.[27] For Levinas, it is only as this responsible self, as one who responds to the demands of the stranger, that I am brought to my final reality.[28] In this way, the asymmetrical nature of the basic ethical relationship accomplishes two things for Levinas: first, it shows that I am always responsible to the stranger, and second, that my obligation to the stranger is irrecusable, that I cannot shirk my responsibility—my responsibility always belongs to me and me alone. Thus, the inequality of our fundamental ethical relation to the Other implies that we are *always already* responsible to Other, and therefore, that we must take responsibility for the stranger that we encounter in the here and now.

Hospitality

In the preface to *Totality and Infinity*, Levinas asserts, "This book will present subjectivity as welcoming the Other, as hospitality."[29] As we have just seen, to be a self in the fullest sense for Levinas is live up to one's ethical responsibility to the Other. In fact, for Levinas, to be such an ethically responsible self is to welcome the stranger; as he puts it simply: "The subject is a host."[30] Like Heidegger, Levinas contends that to be a subject is to dwell in the world, or in Levinas's case, to inhabit the world by separating oneself from the elements. But in an explicit effort to distance himself from Heidegger, Levinas argues: "To dwell is not the simple fact of the anonymous reality of a being cast into existence as a stone one casts behind oneself; it is a recollection, a coming to oneself, a retreat home within oneself as in a land of refuge, which answers to a hospitality, an expectancy, a human welcome."[31] Thus, to be a subject is to inhabit a space that is suited for a welcome; to dwell as a subject is to have a home that it is ready to be shared with the Other. As Levinas writes:

> The "vision" of the face as face is a certain mode of sojourning in a home, or—to speak in a less singular fashion—a certain form of economic life. No human or interhuman relationship can be enacted outside of economy; no face can be approached with empty hands and closed home. Recollection in a home open to the Other—hospitality—is the concrete and initial fact of human recollection and separation; it coincides with the Desire for the other absolutely transcendent.[32]

For Levinas, to be a self is fundamentally to have the capacity for hospitality, to have the ability to welcome the stranger to one's abode. Indeed, one cannot dwell, one cannot be a subject, without this possibility, for "the possibility for the home to open to the Other is as essential to the essence of the home as closed doors and windows."[33]

In addition to establishing the essential features of the dwelling, however, Levinas also means to remind us of the ethical valence of language by emphasizing the necessary connection between subjectivity and hospitality. For him "the essence of language is goodness, or again, the essence of language is friendship and hospitality."[34] If we recall that for Levinas to produce oneself as an I is to take up language or to express, we can now better understand the interconnection between language and hospitality intimated above. Language is essentially connected with hospitality because in language one attempts to share the world with the Other: language is "the very passage from the individual to the general, because it offers things which are mine to the Other. To speak is to make the world common, to create commonplaces."³⁵ Thus, in speaking to the Other, in responding to the expression of the stranger, I offer my world—my dwelling—to the Other. Here language is the medium of our relation, which, as Levinas promised from the start of his work, is an ethical one: "The relationship between the same and the other, my welcoming of the other, is the ultimate fact, and in it the things figure not as what one builds but as what one gives."³⁶

However, the very same capacity for hospitality engendered by language also entails the possibility of shutting out the Other, of being inhospitable. As Levinas notes, "this possibility of forgetting the transcendence of the Other—of banishing with impunity all hospitality (that is, all language) from one's home, banishing the transcendental relation that alone permits the I to shut itself up in itself" is simply the logical consequence of the I's ability to separate itself from the Other.³⁷ Even though the transcendence of the Other is what first allows the I to become a subject—it is the expression of the face that gets language under way, and language that allows for separation of the I—the I remains free to refuse the stranger. While it is true that "I can recognize the gaze of the stranger, the widow, and the orphan only in giving or in refusing," nothing in my recognition of the stranger's gaze guarantees I will respond ethically: "I am free to give or to refuse."³⁸ In the end, then, Levinas's notion of hospitality recognizes the twin capacities of the subject as host. To possess a dwelling—which is also to speak, to use language—is on one hand to have the possibility of welcoming the other; and yet, on the other hand, this very same capacity entails the possibility of forgetting the Other, of closing one's home to the stranger and the poor despite their destitution. This possibility of shutting up the home—this inhospitality—is the first step toward hostility, even though both capacities of the subject stem from the same source: the face of the stranger, or more precisely, the expression of the face that is the first word of language.

With this characterization of Levinas's phenomenology of the stranger complete, let us now turn our attention to the problem of genocide in the hope that Levinas's analyses might allow us to understand its inner workings in a clearer fashion.

The Problem of Genocide

During the mid-1990s, events took place in Rwanda that continue to defy human imagination. The Rwandan genocide of 1994 is unique among the cohort of post-Holocaust genocides—and here one can recall Cambodia (1975–79), Iraq (1987–88), and Bosnia (1992–95)—if not for its brutality, then for its intimacy. Such a characterization may seem malapropos in the context of an atrocity, but what distinguishes the genocide in Rwanda is that it was perpetrated with remarkable closeness, by killers who were known to their victims and vice versa. Incredibly, the killing in Rwanda was conducted almost entirely face to face with machetes and the other tools of an agrarian society; it was not mechanized and did not depend on technological sophistication; it was extremely personal, hand-to-hand and neighbor-to-neighbor. Consider this description of the event:

> [In the spring of 1994], in a tiny, landlocked African country smaller than the state of Maryland, some 800,000 people were hacked to death, one by one, by their neighbors. The women, men, and children who were slaughtered were of the same race and shared the same language, customs, and confession (Roman Catholic) as those who eagerly slaughtered them.[39]

Most now know that the violence in Rwanda was perpetrated by the majority Hutu ethnic group on the minority Tutsi group; however, it is less widely known that the Hutus killed the Tutsis despite the fact that the groups occasionally intermarried, lived in the same communities, and typically knew members of each group by name. On the morning of April 7, 1994, the day after a plane carrying Rwandan president Juvénal Habyarimana was shot down, the killings began with the assassination of the prime minister, Agathe Uwilingiyamana, a moderate Hutu, along with other key political figures. Just days later, energized by the withdrawal of UN peacekeeping forces, the Hutu extremist militias (*interahamwe*) organized the systematic killings of Tutsis in the countryside. In the Nyamata district, a region of 153 square miles where French journalist Jean Hatzfeld would later conduct interviews with a group of Hutu *génocidaires* convicted for their role in the killings, the population fell from 119,000 to 50,500 over the next hundred days; within six weeks, nearly five out of every six Tutsis in the area had been killed.[40] The stunning speed and efficiency of these massacres and the fact that they were carried out primarily by farmers using machetes, not by military personnel with guns, makes the task of understanding such acts all the more difficult.

Even this brief description of the events in Rwanda is sufficient to present us with a host of unsettling questions. Under what conditions could such unbelievable atrocities by committed by ordinary individuals? How could such violence emerge between neighbors, between those who were not enemies before the killing began? Or perhaps even more pointedly, what forces can transform a neighbor—a person well known to me, a fellow human being—into someone of nonhuman status to be liquidated at the first opportunity? How can neighbors become sufficiently inimical to one another so as to permit the transformation of everyday hospitality into radical hostility, indeed, into wholesale slaughter?

As I indicated at the start of this essay, my thesis is that the possibility of genocide lies in the refusal to acknowledge the Other either as a *neighbor* (close to us) or as a *stranger* (a guest). More specifically, using the phenomenological tools provided by Levinas, I believe genocide involves the attempt to obliterate the demand for moral respect embodied by the face of the stranger. In order to explore this possibility, I will use Hatzfeld's interviews with a group of the killers in Rwanda; each of the killers grew up among Tutsi families in the Nyamata district of Rwanda and knew their victims well. And yet without the threat of bodily harm, with only the coercion of a widespread anti-Tutsi public sentiment and a modicum of official oversight, each of them became willing and unapologetic participants in genocide. How could this happen?

Certainly part of the explanation must be that those in power in the Hutu community saw, with the death of Habyarimana, an opportune moment to assert a long-held political and social agenda. The departure of the international community, particularly of the UN peacekeepers who pulled out of Rwanda on April 7, signaled for the organizers and participants in the genocide a tacit agreement to their social agenda. More than that, it released them from any moral system other than their own: the Hutus were now free to repel the Tutsis from their dwellings, to shut the doors and windows of their homes to the stranger. Consider this testimony from the killers:

> Ever since the plane crash, the radio had hammered at us, "The foreigners are departing. They had material proof of what we are going to do, and they are leaving Kigali. This time around they are showing no interest in the fate of the Tutsis." We witnessed that flight of the armored cars along the road with our own eyes. Our ears no longer heard murmurs of reproach. For the first time ever, we did not feel we were under the frowning supervision of whites. Other encouragements followed that assured us of unchecked freedom to complete the task. So we thought, Good, it's true, the blue helmets did nothing at Nyamata except an about-face to leave us alone. Why would they come back before it's all over? At the signal, off we went.[41]

The plane crash signaled to the Hutus not only an opportune political moment, but phenomenologically speaking, it also presented them with the chance to redraw the lines between guest and enemy. The Tutsis—always the minority group, and thus permanent "guests"—were no longer to be tolerated; they were now enemies, and prior hospitalities were now to become open hostilities. It is here that the possibility of genocide seems to emerge: in the twin capacities of the host for hospitality and hostility. The face of the stranger, which previously called out for moral recognition, now identifies the Other as a threat, an obstacle, or an enemy. One needs only a means of disseminating this social program—in low-tech Rwanda, the radio—and an audience ready to accept it—a Hutu majority harboring fifty years of resentment—and suddenly one can begin to understand how the idea of genocide could move from an unspoken subtext to a brutal reality.

In fact, it seems that members of the rank and file in Rwanda had no explicit plan to kill the Tutsis, at least at first; in the absence of any international force to turn them away, they simply got caught up in doing "what one does," in this case, following a plan that came down to all Hutus from higher up the chain. Terrifyingly, it seems to have been inarticulate social cues combined with the posture of authority adopted by the organizers rather than explicit coercion that inspired the killers to put their neighbors to death. Consider these reflections (italics mine):

> When you receive firm orders, promises of long-term benefits, and *you feel well backed up by colleagues*, the wickedness of killing until your arm falls off is all one to you. I mean, you naturally feel pulled along by all those opinions and their fine words. A genocide—that seems extraordinary to someone who arrives afterward, like you, but for someone who got himself muddled up by the intimidators' big words and the joyful shouts of his colleagues, *it seemed like a normal activity*.[42]

> This gentleman I killed at the marketplace, I can tell you the exact memory of it because he was the first. For others, it's murky—I cannot keep track anymore in my memory. I considered them unimportant; at the time of those murders *I didn't even notice the tiny thing that would change me into a killer*.[43]

For the perpetrators, it seems there was concealing of the face that was aided by a general loss of self in a shared public activity. These everyday killers were simply taken up into what Levinas might call a collective "Same." The Same, for Levinas, stands for the ego's tendency to define the Other in its own terms, to appropriate what is other to its own concepts and ends, creating a "totality" of meanings that always refer back to the I. In this case, the participants simply adopted a shared ideal—a "totality" that redefined the Hutu-Tutsi relationship—and by taking up this program, they became individuals "reduced to being bearers of forces that command them unbeknown to themselves."[44] These men did not lose the ability to see right from wrong; they were simply given permission to stop caring about it. Suitably prepared for the event, and given the appropriate authoritative motivation, they lost track of themselves, their prior commitments, their previous responsibilities; once they entered the role that was offered to them, they had no more decisions to make—their new position did not require them to think about what they did, only to do it. In Levinasian terms, they became functionaries of the Same: the meaning of their actions was defined not by their previous relationships, but instead was derived from the totality they served. Under the hegemony of the Same, Levinas notes, "the meaning of individuals (invisible outside of this totality) is derived from the totality."[45]

Thus, what went unnoticed by the killers was who they had become: murderers. This loss of self-possession, which entailed an equal loss of answerability, obscured for them their primordial obligation to the Other. Given Levinas's critique of the sovereign Cartesian self, it might seem odd to suggest that the killers were able to participate in genocide because they lacked a sense of self-possession or self-ownership. But such a suggestion seems to be supported in part by Levinas's reflections on the transformative nature of violence. As he writes: "violence does not consist so much in injuring and annihilating persons as in interrupting their continuity, making them play roles in which they no longer recognize themselves, making them betray not only commitments but their own substance."[46] That the killers found themselves unrecognizable during the genocide—that they betrayed not only their commitments but also themselves—seems to be confirmed by their testimony.[47]

In addition, it seems the genocidal social milieu not only concealed from the perpetrators the true nature of their new practical identities—that of *génocidaires*—but also served to transform those they knew well into strangers of a peculiar sort—strangers without the status of persons. Consider these descriptions (italics mine):

> At the beginning we were too fired up to think. Later on we were too used to it. In our condition, *it meant nothing to us to think we were busy cutting our neighbors down to the last one*. It became a goes-without-saying. They had already stopped being good neighbors of long standing, the ones who handed around the *urwagwa* [beer] can at the *cabaret*, since they wouldn't be there anymore. They had become people to throw away so to speak. *They no longer were what*

they had been, and neither were we. They did not bother us, and the past did not bother us, because nothing bothered us.[48]

In truth, it came to me only afterward: I had taken the life of a neighbor. I mean, at the fatal instant I did not see in him what he had been before; *I struck someone who was no longer either close or strange to me*, who wasn't exactly ordinary anymore, I'm saying like the people you meet every day. His features were indeed similar to those of the person I knew, but nothing firmly reminded me that I had lived beside him for a long time. I am not sure you can truly understand me. I knew him by sight, without knowing him. He was the first victim I killed; my vision and my thinking had grown clouded.[49]

Here we find the line that forms the title for this piece: in genocide, the victims are for the perpetrators neither close nor strange, neither ordinary nor completely unknown. To encounter their victims as either close (a neighbor) or as strange (a guest) would have motivated different action by the killers; it would have forced a moment of decision. Such an encounter would have forced a recognition of the Other's face, compelled the perpetrators to acknowledge the moral standing of their victims and the demand to treat them with respect. However, the perpetrators' unthinking commitment to their Hutu brethren took away their need to decide why or on what basis they did what they did: the new role they played simply permitted them to kill the Tutsi—those familiar strangers, those neighbors now nonpersons—since the Tutsis were now individuals to whom nothing needed to be justified any longer.

Such actions would never be possible, however, without an obliteration or covering over of the ethical demand of the face. The contribution of the organizers of the genocide in Rwanda was precisely to enact the suspension of the face; their job was to transform the face of the Other into a demon. Here the organizers exploited the dual significance of the face discussed earlier: recall that the face is not only an ethical injunction that stops me in my tracks—as you do when you call out my name—but also an occasion for murder. The role of the organizer was to transform this epiphany of the face into a request for extermination. This is done through fear, intimidation, and the infusion of moral disregard for the Other as a matter of everyday affairs. Again, listen as the killers speak:

We feared the authorities' anger more than the blood we spilled. But deep down we had no fear of anything. I'll explain. When you receive a new order, you hesitate but you obey, or else you're taking a risk. When you have been prepared the right way by the radios and the official advice, you obey more easily, even if the order is to kill your neighbors. The mission of a good organizer is to stifle your hesitations when he gives you instructions. For example, when he shows you that the act will be total and have no grave consequences for anyone left alive, you obey more easily, you don't worry about anything. You forget your misgivings and fears of punishment. You obey freely.[50]

Killing is very discouraging if you yourself must decide to do it, even to an animal. But if you must obey the orders of the authorities, if you have been properly prepared, if you feel yourself pushed and pulled, if you see that the killing will be total and without disastrous consequences for yourself, you feel soothed and reassured. You go off to it with no more worry.[51]

Yet even the killers themselves admit that the ethical demand of the face remained present beneath the "fine words" of the organizers. In fact, it seems the killers knew that the ethical demand of the face could never be removed from any interhuman encounter. As Levinas puts it: "The eyes break through the mask—the language of the eyes, impossible to dissemble. The eye does not shine; it speaks."[52] In Rwanda, the organizers gave the perpetrators a reason to eradicate this "speech"—the face of the Other—when it appeared, yet the eyes of the Other could not be silenced by the slogans and slurs were intended to cover them. The face claimed the killers despite the efforts of their superiors:

> Still, I do remember the first person who looked at me at the moment of the deadly blow. Now that was something. The eyes of someone you kill are immortal, if they face you at the fatal instant. They have a terrible black color. They shake you more than the streams of blood and the death rattles, even in a great turmoil of dying. The eyes of the killed, for the killer, are his calamity if he looks into them. They are the blame of the person he kills.[53]

In Rwanda, Tutsis were called "cockroaches." The meaning of this epithet is clear: the Tutsis are parasites to be eradicated from the earth. Yet the eyes of the victim are the calamity of the killer precisely because they cannot be constrained by this "mask," neither by the "fine words" of the organizers nor the carefully cultivated sense of disgust the killers sought to maintain for their victims: the eyes break through the illusion that this "animal"—a Tutsi turned up in the swamp—is not a human being.[54]

Conclusion

Though admittedly incomplete, the analyses above already provide an indication of the explanatory power contained in Levinas's phenomenology of the stranger. It is not difficult to see the parallel between Levinas phenomenological descriptions of the face and the remarks made by the killers in Rwanda; their reflections testify not only to their own experiences, but also to the depth and trenchancy of Levinas's phenomenological insight. Clearly, Levinas opens the path for us to propose a new phenomenological account of genocide and the conditions that make it possible. For our purposes here, however, it is enough to note the way in which Levinas allows us to understand the problem of genocide in a more penetrating fashion. If the possibility of genocide is the possibility of radical evil, then radical evil is not, as Kant thought, the selfish ill-will; rather, radical evil is, as Levinas at least partially suggests, the refusal to take up one's ethical responsibility to the Other: it is the decision not to see in the other someone *close*—and so my neighbor—or someone *strange*—and thus, my guest. Radical evil is not the choice to put oneself above the moral law, but the failure to recognize the moral law that all strangers carry within them.

We would be remiss, however, if we conclude this piece before we consider how we might prevent genocide in the future. Despite our vigilance, according to many sources the first genocide of the twenty-first century has already taken place.[55] Again, I think that Levinas can assist us. How can we prevent genocide? Levinas suggests that we can do so only by thwarting the capacity for radical evil within ourselves, that is, only by resisting the temptation to push others into that nonperson netherworld—neither close nor strange—where they are forced to live without moral status; it is only by taking over our ethical responsibility to the other as *our own*, by respecting the moral law within those with whom we share the world that we resist radical evil and so undercut the possibility of genocide. Thus, we must see in the stranger not an occasion for animosity, but an opportunity for teaching. We must learn, as Levinas suggests, to be *taught*. To welcome the expression of the stranger, "to approach the Other in conversation," as he puts it, is "therefore to *receive* from the Other beyond the capacity of the I, which means exactly: to have the idea of infinity. But this also means: to be taught."[56] When the Other appears as teacher, when the stranger is not shunned but welcomed, then perhaps we will be in a position to live up to our promises with respect to genocide. To achieve this, Levinas tells us, would be to open the door to a genuine peace between human beings. Peace is not achieved by superior strength, but in learning from the stranger, in the welcome, in a hospitality that is only realized in moral activity. If we mean to end genocide, then it is to this ideal that we ought to aspire, as Levinas writes:

> Peace therefore cannot be identified with the end of combats that cease for want of combatants, by the defeat of some and the victory of others, that is, with cemeteries or future universal empires. Peace must be my peace, in a relation that starts from an I and goes to the other, in desire and goodness, where the I both maintains itself and exists without egoism. It is conceived starting from an I assured of the convergence of morality and reality.[57]

15

Between Mourning and Magnetism

Derrida and Waldenfels on the Art of Hospitality

CHRISTOPHER YATES

> My royal king Menelaus—welcome guests here,
> sons of the great as well! Zeus can present us
> times of joy and times of grief in turn . . .
>
> —Homer, *Odyssey IV*

Plutarch recounts a scene in the life of the Athenian lawmaker Solon (sixth century BC), when another Greek sage, Anacharsis, has come to visit: "Anacharsis, coming to Athens, knocked at Solon's door, and told him, that he, being a stranger, was come to be his guest, and contract a friendship with him; and Solon replying, 'It is better to make friends at home,' Anacharsis replied, 'Then you that are at home make friendship with me.'"[1] In his *Les Misérables* (1862), Victor Hugo describes the moment in which Jean Valjean, a convict, arrives unexpectedly at the home of Monseigneur Bienvenu, the bishop of Digne. After receiving his wayward guest, Bienvenu remarks:

> This is not my house; it is Christ's. It does not ask any guest his name but whether he has an affliction. You are suffering; you are hungry and thirsty; you are welcome. And don't thank me; don't tell me that I am taking you into my house. This is the home of no man, except the one who needs refuge. I tell you, a traveler, you are more at home here than I; whatever is here is yours.[2]

In what follows, I will consider the manner in which two recent thinkers, Jacques Derrida and Bernhard Waldenfels, take up threshold scenes such as these, moments at the doorstep of our identity in which the arrival of the stranger, the guest, indeed even the enemy upsets the balance of our egocentric existence. My aim is to clarify how and why these thinkers attend to such a threshold by concentrating on the phenomenological disclosure of a difference between what is relative and conditional, on one hand, and what is absolute and unconditional on the other. Grasping this distinction at the heart of hospitality serves to position us, theoretically and concretely, in a scene marked by the tension between magnetism and mourning. Though distinct in their approaches, Derrida and Waldenfels invert our everyday understanding of hospitality: it is not we, as hosts, who are masters of the scene, but we who are very much in question in a provocative way.

The Literary Trope and the Matter Itself

Hospitality concerns the figure of the stranger, a figure which, according to Richard Kearney, "frequently operates as a limit-experience for humans trying to identify themselves over and against others."[3] It is a figure in whom and with whom a singular event occurs. Returning to our opening scenes, the Athenian encounter occurs against the backdrop of a tradition for which Zeus, as Homer tells us, is the god of guests (*Xenios*), the deity who will avenge the rights of strangers.[4] The French moment occurs against the backdrop of a biblical tradition for which Yahweh is the God of sanctuary and refuge, the sovereign who supersedes civil authority.[5] One need not read far to discover that Western history and literature are replete with such moments where hosts and guests are caught up in the drama of hospitality, moments that, as Jacques Derrida puts it, "testify without end in our memory."[6] Scenes of hospitality consist in a turbulence of arrival and demand, rights and recognition, and the sense that something inherent in the space of a mere threshold implicates all parties in a larger event—a crossing or collision that is already underway in, as, and even before a word of greeting is uttered. One could thus say that the question of the stranger, the other, the foreigner constitutes something of a perfect storm for inquiry at the limits of theoretical and practical philosophy. But it is important from the start to bear in mind that Waldenfels and Derrida do not purport to fetishize the "Other" or sanctify a glib universalism of precious identities where all beliefs, customs, and codes are welcome and one. They are led to the question of hospitality by that same species of necessity that compels rigorous thinkers to address lingering blind spots in our wisdom traditions and in our everyday social intercourse. And the virtue of their approaches to thinking hospitality to its limit is that we are reminded of how this event of the stranger, this interruption already housed in layers of everyday gestures and interactions, is pregnant with a disclosive summons to our fundamental being and personhood. Falling somewhere between Emmanuel Levinas's attention to the irruption of the Other at the heart of the self by way of the transcendent demand of the *face*, and Jean-Paul Sartre's description of the shame one feels when ensnared in the other's *gaze*,[7] our consideration of the art of hospitality begins with the simple recognition that the stranger or guest is, as Waldenfels reminds us, "never simply one among others."[8] As Friedrich Hölderlin famously noted: "we are a conversation" (*seit ein Gespräch wir sind*), and as Paul Valéry similarly observed: "The Other, the like of me, or maybe my double, that is the most magnetic abyss."[9] Such statements occur at the depth of a reflection on the matter of hospitality, and yet remain proximate to the everyday experience of this matter. So what do we mean when we speak of hospitality as an event, a limit situation, and a threshold? How is it constituted and what kind of meaning or "sense" does it carry?

From the level of concrete experience we may observe that hospitality is simply that qualitative category employed to describe the instant in which boundaries are crossed. There are the mundane manners comprising a handshake, a welcome, a crossing of paths or glances, a knock on the door. There are also the more formal, regulatory, or dramatic cases in which hospitality is somehow organized and authored in a calculated way: an official gathering, a diplomatic visit, a border crossing through Customs, a furlough, and so on. To be sure, there are even those instants or situations in which hospitality is coerced as an unwelcome interruption, or worse, a violation: *Let me in! Give me your purse! I'm not leaving until . . .* The expansive range of hospitality's qualitative aspect belies the banality of the term's ordinary usage. Encountered, intended, or demanded, hospitality denotes a scene of crossing that might just as soon catch us off guard as go according to plan. "What is strange," says Waldenfels, "emerges by befalling us, amazing us, frightening us, or tempting us."[10] Indeed, the "sense" of this threshold event is more varied, dynamic, and elusive than a superficial case study in intersubjectivity, social-political identity, or ethics would allow.

Accordingly, Derrida and Waldenfels bring a methodological and hermeneutic caution to the question of hospitality in an exemplary way. The caution has to do with an awareness of how we, standing in the aftermath of modern philosophy, may be inclined to regard the matter on the basis of certain epistemic and ontological assumptions. This means that having made the decision to allow the everyday scene of hospitality to "stand out" as a peculiar phenomenon, we cannot submit to its singular integrity without performing a simultaneous check on our cognitive habits. Accordingly, Waldenfels and Derrida treat the question of hospitality according to the spirit of *phenomenological* methodology. Like other challenges to the modern epistemological dichotomy between subject and object at the center of conscious knowing,[11] phenomenology is interested in the acts of *intentionality* by which a so-called object is constituted in cognition.[12] Made famous by Edmund Husserl in the early twentieth century, and extended toward the field of hermeneutics by thinkers like Martin Heidegger and Hans-Georg Gadamer, phenomenology appreciates the interpretive nature of "knowing"—for every intuition (or direct awareness) of a given object there is already a framework of prereflective intentions shaping the disclosure of that object. This does not mean that the "meaning" of the coffee mug, for example, is intrinsically adrift in a sea of subjective prejudices, but rather that the mug is perceived as a coffee mug on the basis of its cooperation with the transcendental structure of cognition. Mental acts such as judgments and beliefs color the way things appear for us, and to some extent enable given things to appear in what would otherwise look to be their singular nature.

Phenomenology, then, is interested in *describing* the event of appearance or disclosure—analyzing the facets of our own comportment to an entity or matter (*Sache*) and the item's corresponding cooperation. The actual existence (the "what") of an object is not in question so much as the concrete "how" or "as" through which such an existence happens before us. In terms of a given entity, idea, or even a person, for example, phenomenological reflection endeavors to account for the *givenness* of the matter, the primordial awareness Husserl terms *Evidenz*. The working possibility thus amounts to a retrieval of the immediacy of experience, an articulation of how, before all theoretical assumptions and determinations, human consciousness is intrinsically involved in the world it grasps. To do this one must set aside (via what Husserl calls an *eidetic reduction*) transcendent or explanatory principles in order to explore more immanent principles given as *evidence*. The problem is that such restraint, more often than not, goes against the grain of our prereflective habits.

Inverting the "Natural" Order of Encounter

Waldenfels advances this cautionary reduction by putting in question the issue of one's "standpoint" in regarding the alien. "For centuries," he explains, "we find only what I call a *relative* kind of alienness, dependent on a limited standpoint or on early phases of development." In an Aristotelian sense, this means that "only an alien *for us* is accepted, but not an alien *in itself*." There is an unquestioned self-referential basis by which the stranger, foreigner, or alien (as *xenon, alloion*) "is domesticated . . . adapted to and integrated into one's own house or home." The scene of crossing is predetermined in a vertical, not horizontal, way.[13]

Beyond mere self-interest, this tendency is rooted in the reign of a *logos* that privileges rational likeness—the rational Greeks absorb the irrational Barbarians, for example, into their logocentric scheme. Order trumps otherness. And the historical diagnosis informs the present predicament: even though the guest "who comes from the outside embodies strangeness in a preeminent sense,"[14] we tend to understand hospitality and subsume the stranger before us in accordance with "the reign of sense," a normative attachment to "existing orders" and conceptual homelands which render the alien an "*alter ego*."[15] This tendency operates in real time as well as in the time of reflection that means to account for the threshold's crossing after the fact. There is, Waldenfels explains, "a kind of *egocentrism* that reduces the alien to the own," and this is "complemented by a *logocentrism* centered on the logos as a set of common goals or rules, reducing the alien to the common."[16] In short, we tend to approach the stranger or the guest on the basis of ourselves, of who we are, where we are, how the household or worldview is arranged, so to speak. Waldenfels calls this *relative strangeness*, a tendency toward subordination and neutralization,[17] which, though often preconceptual, must be eliminated from any inquiry set on capturing the sense of hospitality. Waldenfels accounts for this development thus:

> The fact that the phenomenon of the alien has finally crossed the threshold of problematization goes back to a double mutation in Western culture, a mutation in modern *rationality* on the one hand and in the role of the modern *subject* on the other hand. Reason as an all-encompassing order and the subject as the central figure are the two points of attack. Apart from that, the two maintain a strained relation with each other: reason stands for what we have in common, whereas subjectivity has at least in part to do with what belongs to me as an individual. In any case, radical alienness enters the scene only under the condition that alienness reaches the core of Being and the heart of the self. Consequently, reason or order dissipate, and the subject becomes decentered. . . . [In this way,] it is only in the 20th century that the question of alienness or otherness becomes a central philosophical issue. . . . The alien emerges as a

peculiar phenomenon which does not simply yield to the general logos of the phenomena.[18]

In view of such remarks, it is fair to say that the scene of a "threshold" signals a parallel threshold in inquiry itself.

Derrida, too, is mindful of this "strained relation" between reason and subjectivity, and orients his own discussion of hospitality by disclosing the specific question "of" the foreigner already implicit in texts by Plato and Sophocles. Derrida believes the tradition of *conditional hospitality* is manifest in the assigned place of this *question*. The issue has to do with whether or not "the foreigner were first of all *the one who* puts the first question or *the one whom* you address the first question."[19] Who, in fact, authors the interrogative nature of the scene? In Plato's *Sophist* the Foreigner (*Xenos*) puts in question the authority of the Parmenidean *logos*. In the *Apology*, Socrates, who is on trial, puts in question the legal rhetoric and authority of the Athenian assembly, as though he were a foreigner to the rights and reasons of political hospitality and justice: "I am . . . simply a stranger to the manner of speaking here."[20] He is of course no stranger in the basic sense of the word, but the Assembly has already laid conditions on his status, conditions which the philosophical vocation of Socrates cannot meet.[21] Derrida uses this scene to illustrate the contingencies with which "the question of hospitality begins."[22] He wonders: "must we ask the foreigner to understand us, to speak our language, in all the senses of this term, in all its possible extensions, before being able and so as to be able to welcome him into our country?"[23] For the Greeks, the question of a foreigner's name may well have been the first conditional interrogative. A foreigner with a proper name would be entitled to certain legal rights of hospitality. Hugo's Valjean approximates this very point, even to some extent apologizing for his name (as a "convict"), and yet the Bishop, upon receiving him, elides the formalities of a contractual hospitality by deferring to a more transcendent (in this case Christian) milieu of welcome.

What the precedents for legal hospitality otherwise show us, according to Derrida, is more often than not a predetermined limitation on the scene of arrival and crossing. When the welcoming party asks the questions, as it were, hospitality is always already conditional. By contrast, there is for Derrida an *absolute hospitality* that, once recovered, should put such questioning in question,[24] just as Waldenfels means to recover the "decentering" afoot beneath the pretensions of vertical welcome. Derrida frames the distinction by explaining that "one of the subtle and sometimes ungraspable differences between the foreigner and the absolute other is that the latter cannot have a name or a family name; the absolute or unconditional hospitality I would like to offer him or her presupposes a break with hospitality in the ordinary sense, with conditional hospitality, with the right or pact of hospitality."[25]

This distinction—"absolute other"—already denotes something exceeding the everyday manner in which the stranger is received. Waldenfels entertains a similar distinction when he speaks of something beyond a mere alter ego: a "surplus of otherness or of heterogeneity which exceeds the given order may be called *extraordinary alienness*."[26] He has in mind those "zones of the chaotic . . . cross-roads and transfer-points through which alienness continues to invade reason and order" that put me in mind of my own strangeness[27] and place before my constitutive "consciousness of the other" (*Fremdbewusstsein*) the trembling sense of a *hyperphenomenon*.[28] In both thinkers, then, the reflexes of "relative strangeness" or "conditional hospitality" obtain in front of an Otherness that infuses the scene of the threshold with a horizon irreducible to any native *logos* and the proprieties it grounds. Before jumping to any moral or ethico-juridical decisions about how to welcome this horizon, the challenge for philosophy is to *think* it—that is, to receive the very sense of this absolute, extraordinary disclosure.

The Event and Its Provocations

It is now apparent that relative strangeness and conditional hospitality are Waldenfels's and Derrida's terms for the manner in which the scene of hospitality subsists under a potentially shortsighted interpretive scheme. These are our "natural" ways of encountering or objectifying, the stranger, the foreigner, the alien. Extraordinary alienness and/or absolute hospitality are phrases denoting what the scene may in fact actually be or require. Our alertness to such a reorientation suggests that an ethical sensibility is assigned to the theoretical labor before (and perhaps so that) a practical philosophy of the stranger may be attempted.

It is this sensibility that returns us to the meaning of hospitality as a disclosure, and to the conception of the threshold as an *event* (*Ereignis*, *événement*)[29] that should be allowed to stand out in full relief against the backdrop of an otherwise ordering momentum. For both thinkers, an attunement to the eventful nature of hospitality allows one to witness what actually is a scene of disordering, inauguration, and the reformulation of the very paradigms by which we conceive of space and self. Such an attunement is a labor of description and imagination alike. Hospitality is a topographical and ontological recovery underway. Waldenfels remarks that the "power of events we are referring to depends on the basic fact that their effects are earlier and stronger than any attempt to interpret, to explain or to change them."[30] The figure of the guest "appears as a preliminary shape of a radical strangeness that exceeds the limits of the fixed order. Hospitality constitutes a transitional phenomenon that no one can get past but which allows for many different responses."[31] Waldenfels thus turns his attention to "the frictional surfaces which allow us to ignite sparks on the concept of event" and indwell "this gulf between order and what is ordered" such that we might witness the manner in which the "extraordinary which characterizes the foundation of order returns to precisely the order it inaugurates."[32] The philosopher and his audience are, so to speak, affected by the subject matter as one "turns the event into an 'Event.'"[33] Critical thought does not calculate so much as concentrate and anticipate, and herein lies the artistry.

Derrida likewise speaks of the event of hospitality as a "situation of the absolute arrival," that is, "the arrival of the arrival."[34] Concerning the foreigner, he asks "What is meant by 'going abroad', 'coming abroad'?" so as to concentrate on the *frontier* as a space and happening that is already "caught in a juridico-political turbulence, in the process of destructuration-restructuration, challenging existing law and established norms."[35] Derrida thus colors the event of the threshold as a moment bearing the quality of undecidability, the revelation of an antinomy between duty and welcome—something like a classically trained artist on the brink of abstract expressionism: "it is as though the laws (plural) of hospitality, in marking limits, powers, rights, and duties, consisted in challenging and transgressing *the* law of hospitality, the one that would command that the 'new arrival' be offered an unconditional welcome."[36] Again, we ourselves, who wish to "understand" the "meaning" and shape of hospitality, though without the distancing instruments of calculation and categorization, are implicated in the subject matter. Waldenfels's "frictional surfaces," when pushed to their descriptive limit, spell a story of "transgression." And the operative site of the transgression is, for both thinkers, our natural or default (though by no means "original") standpoint of separation between "inside" and "outside," ego and other (noted above). This point may be further specified: following Husserl's study of "affection," Waldenfels holds that "behind intentional acts, ascribed to a subject as their author or source, there appear events that we undergo, something which happens to us. Those events belong neither to a first-person perspective as an act I perform, nor to the third-person perspective as an objective process registered or effected from the outside."[37] With the arrival of the stranger, the door between what is mine and theirs "remains slightly ajar."[38] Identity turns out to be contingent, not authoritative.[39] Alert to the legal ethos by which conditional hospitality seeks to manage such an unsettling border event, Derrida describes how the contractual avoidance of such transgression masquerades as "justice." The situation of Oedipus in Sophocles's *Oedipus at Colonus*, for example, is outside the law of Thebes, and Antigone's longing to mourn her father illustrates her allegiance to a justice that is higher than, and thus anathema to, the positive law. The confusion of inside and outside thus happens on the concrete level of embodied space, on the juridico-political level of law and duty, and also on the level of norms that exceed identity, citizenship, and ethos. "We will always be threatened," says Derrida, "by this dilemma between, on the one hand, unconditional hospitality that dispenses with law, duty, or even politics, and, on the other, hospitality circumscribed by law and duty."[40]

With these tensions and destinations in view, we still ask: what is at work in this moment of "decentering," "undecidability," and overall "shaking of order"?[41] Without losing sight of the differences that may obtain in such a moment, one could say that the phenomena at work in hospitality render it a moment of *provocation*. A phenomenological attunement to the event pairs the lived experience of provocation (in the moment) with a more absolute and ontological provocation. For Waldenfels, this quality is parsed in terms of an alternation between pathos and sense, and demand and response. The way into this model follows the aforementioned concerns about "sense": "everything that appears as something has to be described not simply as something which receives a sense, but as something which provokes sense without being meaningful itself yet still as something *by which* we are touched, affected, stimulated, surprised and to some extent violated. I call this happening pathos, *Widerfahrnis* or af-fect, marked by a hyphen in order to suggest that something is done *to us*."[42] But as we have already begun to see, where the stranger or alien is the appearing entity the pathos is heightened and elides any static designations of what is simply "alien to myself" (*Ichfremdes*);[43] the hyphen in "af-fect" denotes our feeling caught up in an event that exceeds, overwhelms, and even preempts our spheres of self-reference: "the otherness or the alienness of the Other announces itself . . . in terms of pathos, of a specific *Fremdaffektion*. We are touched by others before being able to ask who they are and what their behaviour or their utterances mean. The Other's otherness, which overcomes and surprises us, disturbs our intentions before being understood in this or that sense."[44] When Odysseus arrives on the Phaeacian island of Ogygia and is discovered by Princess Nausicaa, Nausicaa's friends take flight yet she stands firm in the turbulence of the moment and remarks:

> But here's an unlucky wanderer strayed our way
> and we must tend him well. Every stranger and beggar
> comes from Zeus, and whatever scrap we give him
> he'll be glad to get.[45]

The urgency of pathos surmounts the need for understanding. As an unknown and unnamed foreigner, Odysseus may very well be an embodied *path*ogen or perhaps a *path*way to realizing a higher justice. Nausicaa frets not over the undecidability of the situation, instead opting to wager on the affective provocation.

The task is to understand how such pathos is productive. Specifically, Waldenfels speaks of a *"birth of sense out of pathos,"* a birth that is, however, "not free of labour."[46] In other words, *Fremdheit* (otherness, alienness) names a kind of limit experience, an "affectation by the Other" that "overcomes us as *wirkende Wirklichkeit*"—"as effective reality preceding the conditions of possibility analysed by transcendental philosophy and specified in terms of rule systems or codes."[47] From the point of view of phenomenological description this is structural, but from the point of view of experience at the threshold it is felt as a disquieting demand. Following Levinas more than Martin Buber, the threshold is not an egalitarian face-to-face encounter, but "an inclined plane on which it is always the Other who occupies the upper part, the height" and it is I who am overcome by the demanding asymmetry.[48] My resulting agitation has to do not only with the sight of the foreigner at my doorstep, but also, and more precisely, with the revelation of what Maurice Merleau-Ponty calls an "original from elsewhere" whose very arrival portends an awakening of sense in my worldview but not of my own designs.[49]

For Derrida, the provocation in hospitality again concerns the interrogative nature of the scene. Who am I, now, in this being of hospitality? On what basis do our delimitations of the frontier—our translations of the refugee or stranger—subsist? The political as well as subjective realms are provoked by that disclosure of the unconditional, a higher law or justice that interrogates all our conditional measures of hospitality. Derrida is better known for his attention to the way in which the "meaning" of our language and speech assumes an accepted milieu of signification; with hospitality the deconstructive notion is the same: insofar as our legal codes, border controls, and personal conduct assume a milieu of justice in order to substantiate the preservation of a homeland or home, the operative "meaning" of such justice ought to measure itself against the demands of absolute or unconditional hospitality. To be sure, the provocation manifests itself in a disarming and laborious way. Juridico-ethical hospitality trembles before the call of hyperbolic hospitality. The provocation of the threshold is experienced as a "collision between two laws, at the frontier between two regimes of law,"[50] what Kristeva describes as a confrontation between moral and political reason.[51] Playing on the very terms proper to the conditional realm, Derrida likewise contends that we are provoked to give "right" to the unconditional and intervene in the here and now in the "name" of the unconditional. This does not mean that the necessities of a legal framework must somehow forsake all conditional measures—one cannot jettison the practical challenges abiding in visas, work permits, and identification numbers. Indeed, absolute unconditional hospitality, like radical strangeness, is impossible to preserve and enact, for we can never do enough to render justice, just as we can never translate another language or network of beliefs perfectly. Still, however, the interrogative provocation is present every time hospitality is, in the strict sense, "given," and by electing to undergo the trial that is always already underway we may well become all the more mindful of our complacency in treating the guest in a relative, conditional, or dogmatic way. It is misleading, after all, to believe that my home and hearth are intrinsically my own; they are "mine" on the basis of contract and custom, but the veracity of these very norms is already based on a higher justice that supersedes and, on occasion, interrupts my ipseity.[52] Here again Odysseus is a fitting example. Upon his return to Ithaca he must assume the identity of a beggar on the outskirts of a home that was once his own. He is received first by his "loyal swineherd" Eumaeus, who, not knowing it is Odysseus, nevertheless grants him the same unconditional welcome as Nausicaa:

> It's wrong, my friend, to send any stranger packing—
> even one who arrives in worse shape than you.
> Every stranger and beggar comes from Zeus
> and whatever scrap they get from the likes of us,
> they'll find it welcome . . .[53]

The coming reinstatement of Odysseus in his lawful home, together with the revelation of his identity, is premised on the swineherd's deference to a higher justice manifest in a scene of pathos. What Homer presents in the order of events is also true in the order of priority.

The Root of All Things and the Realm of Tears

These two approaches to the provocative shape of hospitality are obviously similar. Neither purports to be a practical (that is, moral) philosophy of otherness. But in their phenomenological submission to the "matter" (*Sache an sich*) of meeting between host and guest, both Waldenfels and Derrida exhibit the ethical scope of the threshold. Their calls for a bracketing of our self-referential or objectifying ways of thinking and inhabiting hospitality cannot help but imply an "ought" for inquiry and experience alike. And their descriptions of the demand made manifest in the scene of hospitality would seem to compel a moral telos for our *being* provoked. But even if we remain impatient for a formulaic "ought" to emerge from this extensive description—something akin to a rulebook for otherness—Waldenfels and Derrida would have us remain in the decentered state of provocation and undergo a final stretch in the restructuring of "sense."

What is ignited by the frictional play of self and other, inclusion and exclusion, is, for Waldenfels, an illumination of the threshold as a space of the "between" (*Zwischen*)—what he elects to call a "magnetic field."[54] What does this mean? Adhering to the provocations of pathos and demand (noted above) is a topographical disclosure that amounts to an "initiation into 'another state' . . . that we never leave behind."[55] The stranger or alien is not simply an appearance of difference and, as extraordinary, is never reducible to any "as such" entity. The alien in fact inaugurates a space of *"incarnate absence"* (*leibhaftige Abweseheit*) between ownness and alienness. The space of the threshold consists in an "as" that never concedes to an "is"—like a phrase that never translates—a sense or *logos* "drawn from the phenomenon itself" wherein "absence, distance or inaccessibility constitute alienness or otherness."[56] No doubt this is a peculiar incarnation. The between incarnates an "irrevocable elsewhere," something of an original responsiveness before and beyond all attempts at symmetry. It is an "intermediary realm" (*Zwischenreich*)[57] in which my pathos doubles back through my freedom, a repetition of the extraordinary at the root of all "order" *in* "the order it inaugurates."[58] Radical strangeness, says Waldenfels, "touches the 'root of all things'" and is thereby "not thinkable without reconceiving reason, the subject, and intersubjectivity."[59] The challenge in thinking this sense of the between thus amounts to a thinking of that which constitutes constitution itself—the sense of sense itself. Remarkably, this suggests that the radical strangeness that haunts every scene of hospitality marks a collision that is also a collusion from which a species of "meaning" arises. To characterize this singularity of the between as a magnetic field is to emphasize the dynamism of a productive, yet unresolved, contradiction—like a conversation that proceeds by way of interruptions, sometimes circling back through the question with which it began.[60] The magnetism of the between, then, is that heterogeneity that bears on both parties, of which both parties are potentially aware, and through which the "uncanny" (*das Unheimliche*), diachronic nature of our dialogue "stirs me up in my very core, where I am at home."[61] The iterability of the between and the irreducibility of the threshold together comprise an adventure in meaning that ignites my creative response to the other (as my stranger, my host) without pretending any ontic end or beginning.[62]

I find an example of such magnetism in an unlikely historical and literary source: the diaries of eighteenth century evangelist, David Brainerd. Edited by his friend, Jonathan Edwards, Brainerd's diaries document his missionary journeys among the Native Americans (the Delaware Indians in particular) in New Jersey. Wedged within his many accounts of failed and fruitful conversion attempts, there is a curious encounter between Brainerd and a minister of the traditional Delaware faith in 1745. Brainerd describes their meeting as follows:

> But of all the sights I ever saw among them, or indeed anywhere else, none appeared so frightful . . . as the appearance of one who was a devout and zealous reformer, or rather restorer of what he supposed was the ancient religion of the Indians. He made his appearance in his pontifical garb, which was a coat of bears' skins, dressed with the hair on. . . . He advanced toward me with the instrument in his hand that he used for music in his idolatrous worship, which was a dry tortoise shell, with some corn in it, and the neck of it drawn on to a piece of wood, which made a very convenient handle. . . . When he came near me, I could not but shrink away from him, although it was then noonday, and I knew who it was, his appearance and gestures were so prodigiously frightful. He had a house consecrated to religious uses, with divers images cut out upon the several parts of it; I went in and found the ground beaten almost as hard as a rock with their frequent dancing on it.[63]

The superlative nature of the meeting first consists, then, in a fearful provocation. One can imagine Brainerd's fright before this stranger's appearance, as well as the astonishment he surely felt in crossing paths with his precise vocational and ethnic double. The scene renders Brainerd a guest to another's ministerial project, and he crosses a threshold which itself bears witness to ardent religious worship. There is a heterogeneity of two ministers and two ancient religions. Brainerd continues:

> I discoursed with him about Christianity, and some of my discourse he seemed to like, but some of it he disliked entirely. He told me

that God had taught him his religion, and that he would never turn from it, but wanted to find some that would join heartily with him in it; for the Indians, he said, were grown very degenerate and corrupt. . . . Since that time [of the Delaware's own perceived calling] he had known God and tried to serve Him; he loved all men, be they who they would, so as he never did before. He treated me with uncommon courtesy, and seemed to be hearty in it. . . . I perceived he was looked upon and derided among most of the Indians as a precise zealot, that made a needless noise about religious matters; but I must say, there was something in his temper and disposition that looked more like true religion than anything I ever observed amongst other heathens.[64]

Three elements of this description are remarkable for the "magnetism" they reflect. First, there is the fact of a dialogue whereby both parties seem to articulate and embody their dynamic contradiction. Second, there is in the Delaware minister a doubling of the loving, reform-minded, and under-valued shape of evangelism felt and sought by Brainerd himself. Third, Brainerd confesses his own affectivity arising within this scene of welcome. The stranger stirs him in his spiritual core, touching the divine root of his religious sensibility as if to mystify and affirm Brainerd's own "sense" of spiritual meaning in an undeniable way. Host and guest remain fundamentally apart, and yet fundamentally intertwined. It is a fantastic and wholly unexpected interruption in the normal course of Brainerd's travels, one in which he finds himself welcomed and inspired by the priestly embodiment of that which he means to convert. Brainerd's report pays the minister the highest of all evangelical compliments, and yet the remaining polarity is evident in Brainerd's use of the term "heathens" to classify his host.[65]

Derrida would likely agree with Waldenfels's account of the "between" and would concur with the implied assertion that a focus on the field of "intentionality" at work in the magnetic space (no matter how rigorous) is "not enough"[66] to account for the pathos of the threshold. Brainerd's ministerial intentions in this scene were shaken, though he appears to have been unable to sustain his own reciprocal welcome in an unconditional way. We begin to understand how it is that a phenomenology of intentionality, says Waldenfels, "does not solve the riddle" of the between but rather "opens an immense field of questions."[67] What would have transpired, for example, had Brainerd remained with his host and danced upon the same dirt? Is there cause to expect or hope for as much, wagering on a deeper manifestation of religious sense?

For Derrida, the ongoing restructuring of "sense" consists in the provocations of absolute, unconditional hospitality we have noted. Here too there is a concentration on "doubling," though with an added measure of pathos and reckoning. Drawing again on the predicament of Antigone, Derrida emphasizes *mourning*, not magnetism. Antigone is a "hostage" to the conditional hospitality of Thebes, even while (and on account of the fact) she wishes to "host" the body and memory of her fallen father. In this way she fulfills Levinas's assertions that "the subject is a host" and "the subject is a hostage."[68] And it is the denial of her intended mourning that causes her to weep: "She weeps for her mourning, if that is possible."[69] Her paralysis, Derrida seems to say, echoes the paralysis one feels when striving to utter an oath that exceeds the realm of speech. Antigone's entrapment in legal norms is, in effect, an entrapment in the language of local sense. Her only recourse to a higher justice is to exchange language for tears, the measures of sense for those of mourning. Says Derrida: "This interiority of the heart, this invisible speech, that is what comes to the tears."[70] Mourning is what happens when faced with the impossibility of answering an unconditional call. Antigone mourns her inability to transgress a paradigm of citizenship on behalf of an oath to the absolute. The magnetic field cannot coordinate to sanction her familial hospitality. But, as in the case of Antigone, we too should hope to run the risk of honoring the unconditional even if it results in mourning. Returning to the more basic conception of the threshold, Derrida allows himself this moral exhortation: "Let us say yes *to who or what turns up*, before any determination, before any anticipation, before any *identification*, whether or not it has to do with a foreigner, an immigrant, an invited guest, or an unexpected visitor, whether or not the new arrival is the citizen of another country, a human, animal, or divine creature, a living or dead thing, male or female."[71]

But should we always say yes? Even to the thief or oppressor? Derrida's statement is easy to misunderstand. Though it is true he fails to treat adequately the question of our discernment and the necessary conditions we may apply in hospitality, his meaning is that we should say yes as far as we are able—"before" any determination, indeed, but not in lieu of any determination whatsoever.[72] His exhortation is rooted in his appeal to the "sense" stirred up by the disclosure of the absolute and unconditional Other, and he maintains this emphasis because he is all too aware of our inclinations to defer this awakening. Derrida's Antigone portrays such affirmation in a stirring way, but what we have observed in the case of Brainerd illustrates the difficulty in knowing how far we may expect the duties of one "zealot" to remain bracketed before those of another. Still, by saying yes, if even for a moment, we honor the fact that otherness is not a manageable variable in a stable moral equation. "Yes" is an affirmation that we too are in question, that we are stewards and not owners of the house, that our laws and beliefs are not beyond the reach of reform, and that the "heathen" before me may perhaps be a brother apostle.

In sum, we have seen that both thinkers take the appearance of the guest or stranger as a drama of interrogation. Namely, it is an interrogation of ourselves. A reminder that we have always already been interwoven with the foreigner, and that our household, our realm, our borders are not, per se, realms in which we play master in any dogmatic way. Absolute unconditional hospitality, like radical strangeness, is impossible to preserve and enact. We can never do enough to render justice. The point seems to be that if we are nevertheless now mindful of this impossibility, we will be all the more alert to our complacency in treating the guest in a relative or conditional way. This phenomenological deconstruction of the scene of hospitality discloses the genuine starting point for the practical moral decisions that must follow as we carry on in our concrete roles as selves, citizens, and stewards of immanent and transcendent paradigms of identity. There is no perfect formula for solving the riddles of interreligious difference, immigration, or interventions in sovereignty disputes, for example. But perhaps we will make room for the disorderly, make less of exclusivity or antagonism, and make a point, with Derrida, of "mourning" the deferral of unconditional justice.

The Stranger in the Polis

Hospitality in Greek Myth

JOHN PANTELEIMON MANOUSSAKIS

> That, following one of the directions it takes, is the question of the foreigner as the question of the question. Does hospitality consist in interrogating the new arrival? Does it begin with the question addressed to the newcomer (which seems very human and sometimes loving, assuming that hospitality should be linked to love—an enigma that we will leave in reserve for the moment): what is your name? tell me your name, what should I call you, I who am calling on you, I who want to call you by your name? What am I going to call you? . . . Or else does hospitality begin with the un-questioning welcome, in a double effacement, the effacement of the question *and* the name? Is it more just and more loving to question or not to question? to call by the name or without the name? . . . The question of hospitality is thus also the question of the question.
>
> —Jacques Derrida

The Question of the Question

By the gates of Thebes the stranger has no name. For to be given a name, or to give oneself a name, is to identify oneself as someone, and therefore as not a stranger anymore. Naming the stranger amounts to depriving him of his strangeness and appropriating him to the familiar, to ourselves. A stranger who can be named by this or that name is no longer strange. He is already within. Even before he enters my city or my home, he has entered my language: as Levinas says, "language *is* hospitality."[1]

By the gates of Thebes, the stranger without name and thus outside language, is only an enigma. An enigma is received by an exchange of enigmas. The city responds to the stranger standing by its gates by mirroring back to him the enigma that he is. We know that the enigma is really about the stranger himself. He *is* the enigma. And the answer given is meant, at the end, as a description of the stranger himself: "man."

For the stranger to arrive at the city and, therefore, to language, he must first pass through a confrontation with his origin, an event that takes invariably the form of an encounter with the father—the patronymic being, of course, a form of naming, perhaps more fundamental than one's own proper name—in the double possibility of recognizing him or failing to do so. The stranger's father, like the stranger's name, has remained for a long time now forgotten or unknown. It should be noted that the moment of *anagnorisis* for Oedipus is not only the knowledge of his proper father (Laius) but more importantly, through that knowledge, the revelation of himself (*auto-anagnorisis*).

Having received admission by means of the name of the father (*le* nom *du père*), the stranger can now enter the city, that is, the realm of his desire, where desire can be desired, ventured and ultimately satisfied in the person of the regal mother/monster (Jocasta). That the object of the stranger's desire does not exist except as a fantasy of the imaginary is sometimes said explicitly but to no avail. Furthermore, the object of the stranger's desire is always banned by a prohibition (*le non du père*) that is made manifest invariably as a risk of death at the hands of the Theban Sphinx. Desire is marked by death and having one's desire realized means that one is prepared to risk one's life.[2]

Oedipus Rex is about the question of the stranger's name and the *nomos* (law) of hospitality. The figure of the stranger, the foreigner, is not only without a name but also, and as long as it remains anonymous and unknowable, without law as well. The law is primarily that of language— what is *legal* is what belongs to *legein* and to *logos*. Without language, or rather *outside* language, the stranger is at once anonymous and a-nomos.

Community Without Otherness

Sophocles makes the plague the incentive moment of his play *Oedipus Rex*. A plague has befallen the city, and the elders have gathered outside the royal palace to ask for the intersession of their king. Of course, a plague is not just any disease: it is an infectious disease—that is a disease that manifests itself not through the single individual. Plague, for Sophocles as later for Camus, does not affect so much the individual *qua* individual as individuals in the plural—insofar as one belongs to a community and precisely *on account of* that community. The plague is a sickness of the community, of the city (that is, the *polis*). In fact, one could say that the plague is a *political* disease.

Further, the dialogue about a certain sickness reflects a sickness in the dialogue. Reading carefully the exchange that takes place between the chorus and Oedipus in these first pages of the drama, one comes to realize that it has only the semblance of dialogue, for it proves to be no more than an echoing monologue. Oedipus speaks but what he says returns to him, as his own reflection. The chorus says nothing that Oedipus does not already know (as he admits, v. 58); and in fact he has already done what the chorus came to suggest (vv. 41–43). Moreover, there is that reflexivity of sickness between city and king on which Sophocles insists (by repeating the same word three times within the space of two verses). Thebes is sick but "no one is more sick," as he declares, (vv. 59–61) than he himself—this reciprocity stops short only before revealing the real nature of that relationship, that is, if Thebes is sick that is *because* Oedipus is sick. Finally, there is the "*homou*" of verse 64 that brings city and king together into a solid amalgamation, the result of which is a Theban Oedipus and an Oedipal Thebes.

Oedipus's sickness is, of course, not that of the plague—for Oedipus, at this stage of the drama, knows of no community, he has no other and therefore he is the individual *singulare tantum*—his is the sickness of his own identity. I mean the sickness inscribed in his very name—for Oedipus's name is, quite literally, the name of disease ("swollen feet"). Sophocles connects these two diseases—the disease of the individual, that is, the self-enclosedness in sameness, and the disease of the communal that has projected evil outside itself in some mythical Other, in this case the Sphinx, and makes the one the manifestation of the other. The Sphinx as hybrid monster of woman and animal is the scapegoat ostracized to the gates of the city. If, in other words, Oedipus infects Thebes with his disease, this is because this Thebes is established on the Oedipal expulsion of evil, the exclusion effected by Oedipus solving the Sphinx's enigma. But, conversely, if Oedipus is sick this is because he cannot trace his identity to a time beyond his triumph—a triumph of reason—over the enigma posed by the Sphinx.[3] In resolving the riddle of the monster Sphinx Oedipus deprives her of her secret Otherness. He slays the estranged stranger at the gates of Thebes. He destroys the strangeness of alterity itself.

Let us try to clarify this complex point. Both king and polis are formed on the same twofold basis: the exclusion of otherness and, what comes as a result of this, the self-enclosure within sameness. Nowhere is this better illustrated than in Oedipus's encounter with the Sphinx. If the chorus has gathered to ask for Oedipus's help, and if Oedipus is so determined to provide it, this is because he rescued the city from the primeval strangeness of the Sphinx. For both the city and its king, the eradication of that strangeness (a temporal eradication, in any way, that is, a deferral of their encounter insofar as the mystery of the Sphinx returns later transformed as the plague) is a point of reference that determines who they both are. This city is precisely a city liberated from the enigmatic strangeness of the Sphinx by a stranger (Oedipus) whose strangeness consists precisely of being *not* a stranger but rather a native of the land he visits for, as he thinks, the first time. The Sphinx, on the other hand, stood at the borders of Thebes and thus she had defined the very boundaries between the city and what was other than the city—the city's other. That topological function was also transposed to another level: the Sphinx functioned as the symbolic presence of evil, very much like the Serpent in the Garden of Eden.[4] By threatening with death anyone who would prove unable to solve her enigma—the enigma that she herself was—she also stood as a reminder of that ultimate limit of death. By solving her puzzle, Oedipus had not only explained a riddle but also defended the city against the evil other, the stranger, the foreigner, the outsider. In doing so, Oedipus becomes a new founder of this "suburban" Thebes where what is evil is identified as what is other.[5]

The forgetfulness of otherness thus lies in the constitution of the *polis*. It is precisely this new identity that Oedipus evokes in his opening address and it is of this identity that the chorus reminds him as they plead *that he remains the same*. This telling request comes from the priest's lips (v. 53) and expresses a veiled anxiety about change—the same anxiety that Oedipus would try to ward off by declaring, when it would be too late, that "nothing can make me other than I am" (vv. 1084–1085). The exclusion of otherness is completed with the imperative that one remains the same, in recognition, perhaps, that otherness and evil might lie ultimately within oneself.[6]

In that recurring sameness, bereft of the possibility of opening up to what is other, time runs as a continuous present, a *nunc stans*. The enigma of the Sphinx, as we will see later, had opened up for the city the horizon of time—in fact it was nothing less than an invitation to think man's existence as stretching from past to future, to think the present as a present offered by the past for the sake of a future and to think the one in terms of the other, to see, that is, the past under the light of the future. Having solved the enigma of time, Oedipus closed his being and that of the city in the present—and thus they live, as Creon aptly says (vv. 130–131), trapped in the isolated now. Asked why the city did not investigate the death of Laius, he says "we were compelled to attend to instant needs" that is, to an instantaneous present that unfolds into a series of "nows" without ever forming a memory, namely, a past. It is precisely from the past that both Oedipus and Thebes are alienated ("we were compelled to let slide the dim past"). And it is this very past—in the form of disease—that returns now to plague the present.

The Double Self

The "dim past" that the city was compelled to let slide is more specifically spoken of in Greek as *t'aphane*, that is, the things invisible. Oedipus's answer in the next line is one of those celebrated moments of intentional ambiguity that the Sophoclean irony builds on: *ego phano* can mean either "I will reveal [these invisible things]" that is, "I will make apparent what now remains unapparent"; or it can mean "I will be revealed." In fact, *Oedipus Rex* does both: what the future reveals is precisely the past, and Oedipus is shown as being equally implicated in both. One could, then, speak of two Oedipuses: the Oedipus that lives in the present and for the present, oblivious of the past and without a future, and the Oedipus of the future when he will come to realize his past. It is such a double Oedipus that the great soliloquy of verses 216–275 presupposes, if it is to be effective. The Oedipus of the present curses the Oedipus-to-come, an Oedipus ignorant of himself turns against an Oedipus gifted with the knowledge of his ignorance. One needs to notice here that Sophocles makes the former—Oedipus of the present—nothing more than a figment of Oedipus's imagination, while the latter—the Oedipus to come—is bestowed with reality.[7]

There is a moment in the play where these two Oedipuses meet each other, and therefore a moment when, proleptically, the future meets the present. Teiresias enters the stage exactly as Oedipus will later exit it: blind, led by a child, knowing the truth. Already in the beginning, the audience is given a fast-forward glimpse of the end. Teiresias is the future of Oedipus. As such, as Oedipus's future, he has the power to effect the first break on the solid surface of Oedipus's imaginary, self-created identity. That crack occurs precisely at verse 437 when Oedipus asks: "who are my parents?" Oedipus's question is about his past, though this past cannot be recognized unless it returns, in the guise of a future, to his present. The question about his beginnings will signal his end and thus the promise of a new beginning.

Oedipus introduces himself as soon as verse 6 of our text with the phrase: "Oedipus, renowned to all." Apart from a certain sense of pride, this self-proclamation conceals the real problem that is precisely that of his identity, insofar as Oedipus is "renowned to all" but *unknown* to himself. The reply of the priest (vv. 31–38) gives us a glimpse of Oedipus's self-established identity: Oedipus is the city's redeemer. The reference here is to the Sphinx. As we saw, the farther back into his past that Oedipus can go at this stage, the oldest memory that he can recall of himself is his triumph over the Sphinx's enigma. The encounter between these two strangers, the Sphinx and Oedipus, becomes the birth-moment of the latter's imaginary identity. This is the very moment when Oedipus gives birth to himself—it is no accident that immediately afterward he would replace his father, quite literally, by taking his father's place on his mother's bed, becoming as it were, his own father and thus, in a way, fatherless.

Oedipus, at this point, is only the person who was able to solve the Sphinx's enigma. What distinguishes him, in other words, from the rest of the people and makes him to be "the best among men" (v. 46) is precisely his ability *to think*. Oedipus is not a Hercules. He doesn't labor with physical strength. Nor is he an Odysseus, winning the day by his personal skill and persuasion. Oedipus is solely a thinker. But what kind of a thinker? The answer lies in the enigma. The Sphinx asks:

> What is that animal that
> In the morning walks on the four,
> At noon on two feet
> And at the evening on three?

Oedipus's answer was only a word: *man*. A word that, strangely, referred back to him, insofar as he *was* his answer. In retorting against the monstrosity of the Sphinx with the humanity of man, one could feel tempted to say that Oedipus becomes the first humanist, and in doing so solely with confidence in his reason, he also becomes the prototype of a rationalist as well.[8] If, however, Oedipus succeeds in solving the Sphinx's puzzle, this is because he thought of a particular characteristic of man and his existence: he conceived of man in his *timely* manifestation—of the human being as projected in the horizon of time, for it is precisely time that the three periods of the day—morning, noon, and evening—indicate. Oedipus thinks of man as that being that persists in temporality—he thinks, in other words, of *being and time*. Oedipus gives the ancient monster a *modern* answer and thus he fittingly becomes not only father of himself but also father of that fatherless epoch that is called modernity. Oedipus has given birth not only to himself but also to the mind—to himself through the mind. Oedipus's answer means this: *I think* (for I am able to think the enigma that I am) *therefore I am*. Oedipus the philosopher. In order to do so, however, he had to conceal the very irrationality that lies at the root of reason,[9] the chaos that is always prior to order,[10] and to reduce "man" to an abstract, empty concept. The Sphinx was nothing else but Oedipus's own, at once irrational and evil element, externalized and made *other* than him by being projected on the other, in order precisely to avoid recognizing it as his own. Such unrecognized evil, however, remains inescapable (or, if one prefers, unforgivable). Indeed, not only does it return in the form of the plague but also with the urgency of a responsibility that demands to be assumed insofar as it has now been made public.

An indication of that self-made identity was given at the beginning of the drama when Oedipus names himself. If he can give himself his name that is because he has first given himself to himself. As with our names, our identities are given by others. To receive a name is to recognize that you have a beginning (the two events almost coincide, the giving of a baby's name follows shortly after the baby's birth). By refusing to receive a name, Oedipus indicates his refusal to accept his beginnings—for that we would have to wait until the very end of the drama, for at the end his beginning will be revealed and accepted (it is only at the end that the beginning can be recognized). For now, however, Oedipus remains "anarchic" that is, without *arche*, in a semblance of eternity, for without beginning he is also without end, that is, without boundaries. This unlimited self, a self that knows no limits or limitations, cannot but be an imaginary self.

Oedipus, as an infant, is exposed to exteriority, an exteriority symbolized first by his expulsion from the paternal house and, furthermore, by being left on Mt. Cithaeron to die (vv. 1170–1180). This exposure constitutes undoubtedly a traumatic event of which he has no memory and yet, in a way, he is constantly reminded by his very name. His name, after all, is the name of that trauma in the literal sense ("Oedipus" means "the one with swollen feet," and trauma is the Greek for "wound"). His self-made identity can be explained as an imaginary construction in which he finds rescue from that painful exposure. His identity is imaginary insofar as it denies the trauma of his infancy. It is an imaginary identity because it does not take account of the beginning (*arche*); it *fakes* anarchy. Therefore, Oedipus's identity is determined by two parameters: expulsion of otherness and self-insulation in sameness. It is this and nothing more that the Delphic oracle says, translating it as it were in the language of a double crime, when it prophesized that Oedipus will kill his father and sleep with his mother. Patricide and incest are forms of violence directed toward the Other. They are pathological attachments to the Same, symptoms of Oedipus attachment to being the same as himself.

Oedipus's fatal encounter with his father at the crossroads outside Thebes signifies that every murder is potentially a patricide for every Other is always the parental Other—the Other who gives birth to me since I cannot be my own origin. Similarly, every returning upon oneself (*cor curvum in se*) constitutes a form of incest. Jocasta is for Oedipus an other bereft of otherness; an other upon whom I have projected my own familiar image, that is, my expectations, my feelings, myself. Such a projected "other" is nothing but a mirror that reflects back my own reflection and therefore my relationship with such an "other" is deeply incestuous. The recognition of this double crime will break down the imaginary self and will "give birth" to a new identity ("this day will give you birth and kill you;" v. 438).

The First Moment of Recognition: Evil

From this perspective, the actual "carrying out" of this double crime is irrelevant, for, in a sense, patricide and incest have been committed long before they take place and when they occur; they are only symptomatic—a delayed manifestation, so to speak—of Oedipus's patricidal and incestuous identity. It is crucial to recall that Oedipus executes both acts *precisely* as a result of his desperate, and, by all accounts, sincere effort to avoid them. It would be a mistake to read the inescapable crime in terms of some fatalism. Oedipus cannot avoid the double crime as much as he cannot avoid who he is—and if he *is* the crime that he commits, even prior to committing it, this is precisely because he wants to avoid being who he is.

In fact, it is only after he has fulfilled the Delphic prophesy that Oedipus can escape his criminality. Thanks to the double crime, Oedipus's identity is now both externalized and realized and thus the possibility has opened up for him to recognize himself. It is curious but telling that Sophocles is not interested in the crime itself but only in its *recognition*; that is why he sets both plays, *Oedipus Rex* and *Oedipus at Colonus*, after these events. No wonder, then, that the only person who can see Oedipus's relationships properly is the seer Teiresias who, precisely by being blind to the present, can perceive what remains for most invisible (*t'aphane*), that is, the future and the past.

Oedipus's knowledge of himself depends on his knowledge of others (for example, he will fully know who he is only once he comes to know that his wife is also his mother). However, we have seen how Oedipus invented himself on the basis of the exclusion of otherness. The first step toward recognition of otherness takes place through a double confrontation, first with Teiresias and then with Creon. The irruption of hostility at this stage is to be counted as a positive development for it signals, for the first time in the drama, Oedipus's awareness of the other as other. So far Oedipus had refused to enter into any relationship with another—even that of hostility. In doing so, he had refused himself the very possibility of relationship insofar as the first step of a genuine relation with the other cannot but be hostile. If the other is truly other and not another me, he, or she appears as *other* than me and therefore my first recognition of the other cannot be anything but oppositional. At this initial stage, I still have the option to (1) express my hostility toward the other (fear, scorn, hatred, disgust, indifference) and thus acknowledge his otherness, even if it is in these negative terms; or (2) avoid hostility for the sake of badly understood "respect" that, in the name of tolerance and acceptance, creates a homogeneous community without otherness and thus without the possibility of relation (i.e., the image of the plague that befalls the city in the opening of the tragedy). Between these two options, the refusal of hostility is worse for, by assuming for itself the good prematurely, it can lead nowhere but must remain stagnant, inauthentic. In the words of G. K. Chesterton: "The next best thing to really loving a fellow creature is really hating him. . . . The desire to murder him is at least an acknowledgment that he is alive."[11] Under this light, "love thy neighbor" (Matt. 12:13) is the same commandment as "love thy enemy" (Matt. 5:44) *for the first enemy is the neighbor* until love transforms that very enemy into a neighbor, truly understood.

Conclusion

Finally, and by a way of conclusion, I would like to speak also of Oedipus as one meets him in Sophocles's later work *Oedipus at Colonus*. By the gates of Athens, Oedipus is, once more, a stranger. The gods have led him here to die, a stranger among strangers, by granting him death's absolute hospitality: a death without a tomb, marked by no tombstone, engraved by no name: a nameless death. Without the *nomos* of funeral customs and without name, Oedipus becomes in Athens the perfect stranger inscribed within the realm of the *polis*, interred without any markings, not even that of a corpse or a relic. A stranger perfectly strange.

Prior to his death, Oedipus is received in Athens by the city's legendary founder and hero, Theseus. As Derrida notes, the encounter between Oedipus and Theseus is an encounter between two strangers that are not strange to each other, for they both have experienced the status of a stranger.[12] Wandering, for a moment, beyond the text of Sophocles, we can follow the lines of their past as they converge into the bond of *xenia* between Pelops, Theseus's maternal ancestor, and Laius, Oedipus's father. Oedipus's family curse, the curse of the Labdacides, originates at a time when Laius was received as King Pelops's *xenos*. The institution (*thesmos*) of *xenia* or *hospitium* imposed a set of certain well-defined rituals on the two men who were so bound: the exchange of gifts was certainly one of the most predominant of these rituals, as it was also the ethical responsibility of the *xenos* for his host's sons, and vice versa; a responsibility to be compared only to that of paternal duties.[13] Laius, however, having fallen in love with Pelops's son, Chrysippus, raped and abducted him. The crime was not so much that of pederasty but rather that of the violation of the sacred *xenia*; indeed in a way that was tantamount to incest (Chrysippus ought to have been like a son to Laius). Chrysippus's brother, Pittheus, was to become the father of Aethra, Theseus's mother. So both Oedipus and Theseus are linked by Pelops, who, in turn, was himself the reason of another violation of *xenia* (in this case of *theoxenia*) committed by his father, Tantalus, who deceived the gods by cooking and serving his dismembered son as their meal.[14]

By all accounts, *xenia* predated the formation of the *polis* and thus constituted a pre-political network of relationships between mostly men of equal status. The mythology developed around the person of Theseus signals the institutionalization (*thesmos*) of the prince's claim to power as it is related by the story of Theseus's retrieving his father's symbols of power, namely his sandals and sword, from the place that Aegeus had laid them down (*thesmos*), hidden under a rock.[15] Theseus's return to Athens and his subsequent recognition as rightful ruler of Athens, his reorganization of the Athenian *demes* on the modern model of *synoecism*, sets the foundations of the democratic constitution of the *polis*. All this is encapsulated in his encounter with Oedipus at Colonus. If the political *synoecism*, the "dwelling-together" of foreigners, was made possible, it was thanks to the symbolic acknowledgement of the foreigner in the middle of the Athenian *polis* in the form of the blind Oedipus.

The overlapping stories of Theseus and Oedipus complicate Theseus's extension of hospitality to the blind Theban king. Does Theseus render to Oedipus the hospitality that is due to him by their ancestral bond of *xenia* established between their families, or in spite of it? Is the reception of Oedipus the *xenos* restoring the economic exchange of hospitality that had been repetitively and compulsively violated by their fathers, or is it transcending it, moving, as it were, beyond the quid pro quo exchange among friends towards what Derrida would call an absolute hospitality? The answer to these questions remains the work of future readings.

Notes

At the Threshold: Foreigners, Strangers, Others
Richard Kearney and Kascha Semonovitch

1. We might also note that our inquiries here are largely about differences between Strangers—human, animal, or divine—rather than about the "strange" as such, a category that covers many impersonal experiences related to nature, animate or inanimate. Perhaps, of all the phenomenologists we deal with, it is Merleau-Ponty who most readily extends the description of strangeness beyond human others to include other forms of sentient and insentient beings in nature. (Think, for example, of his account of Cézanne's painterly relationship to Mont Sainte-Victoire.) The notions of uncanny strangeness—as analyzed by Heidegger, Freud, Kristeva, or Lacan—are still related to the experience of the human in its encounter with Being or the Unconscious. Dasein's experience of the uncanny is its experience of its *own* nothingness, while the psychoanalytic notion of the *das Unheimliche* is the return of one's *own* childhood traumas in the guise of uncanny phenomena. In both cases, strangeness is a feature of immanent, if hidden, human experiences. It is not an encounter with nature as such. Behind the "strange" the "stranger" still lurks, even when it is a stranger to ourselves.

2. Here we intend "ambiguity" in the rich sense that Heidegger and Merleau-Ponty used it, not in the weak sense of mere "ambivalence." See Merleau-Ponty "Interview on 'Man and Adversity,'" *The Merleau-Ponty Reader*, ed. Leonard Lawlor and Ted Toadvine (Evanston, Ill.: Northwestern University Press, 2007), hereafter cited as "Interview."

3. Martin Heidegger, *Being and Time*, trans. John Macquarrie and Edward Robinson (New York: HarperCollins), 176.

4. Julia Kristeva, *Strangers to Ourselves*, trans Leon S. Roudiez (New York: Columbia University Press, 1991), 214 n 14.

5. Merleau-Ponty, "Interview," 236.

6. Martin Heidegger, *Fundamental Concepts of Metaphysics*, trans. William McNeil and Nicholas Walker (Bloomington: Indiana University Press, 1995), 6.

7. Plato, *Apology*, 17d, cited in Jacques Derrida, *Of Hospitality*, trans. Rachel Bowlby (Stanford: Stanford University Press, 2000), 19. Derrida notes that Socrates claims a special "foreigner's right" in his speech.

8. Peter Carey, *Oscar and Lucinda* (New York: Vintage Books, 1997), 325.

9. In the *Fundamental Concepts of Metaphysics*, Heidegger describes how certain concepts "are taken rather as *indications* that show how our understanding must first twist free from our ordinary conceptions of beings and properly transform itself into the Da-sein in us"; 296–297.

10. Edmund Husserl, *Cartesian Meditations*, trans. Dorian Cairns (The Hague: Nijhoff, 1973), sec. 62; hereafter cited as CM.

11. Ibid., 108.

12. Ibid., 110.

13. Ibid., 111.

14. Paul Ricoeur, *Oneself as Another*, trans. Kathleen Blamey (Chicago: University of Chicago Press, 1992), 333; hereafter cited as OA.

15. Husserl, CM, 150.

16. Ibid., 111.

17. Dan Zahavi, *Husserl's Phenomenology* (Stanford: Stanford University Press, 2003), 113. Zahavi (157 n 36) strongly critiques Ricoeur's reading and declares that it rests on a misunderstanding of constitution. For further discussions of Husserl on intersubjectivity, see also N. Depraz and Dan Zahavi, eds., *Alterity and Facticity: New Perspectives on Husserl* (Dordrecht: Kluwer, 1998).

18. Zahavi, *Husserl's Phenomenology*, 113.

19. In Ricoeur's words, we realize how the other "belongs to the intimate constitution of . . . sense"; OA, 329.

20. Ibid., 326.

21. Appresentation is understood here as a "non-originary presentation" (*Vergegenwärtigung*); Husserl, CM, 115.

22. Ibid., 109.

23. Let us try to put Husserl's complex phenomenological analysis in another way. The self experiences the other in a primordial intuition of the non-primordial. (The phrase is Edith Stein's in *On the Problem of Empathy*, a doctoral thesis directed by Husserl in 1916.) The other as other can never be primordially given. Our immediate sense of the other is of someone who escapes us even as we seek to empathize with that person over there. My only immediate experience is of me "here," in my flesh, but I can project what it is like for the other to be in her flesh "over there." As Ricoeur puts it, "Here we reach the paradoxical core of the other's mode of givenness: namely, that 'intentionalities directed toward the other as foreign (*étrange/fremde*), that is, as other than me, *go beyond* the sphere

of ownness in which they are nevertheless rooted"; OA, 333. See also Richard Kearney, *Strangers, Gods and Monsters* (New York: Routledge, 2003), 79, 248; and more recently, Daniel Birnbaum, *The Hospitality of Presence: Problems of Otherness in Husserl's Phenomenology* (Berlin: Sternberg Press, 2008).

24. Husserl, CM, 110.

25. Ibid., 114–115, our italics.

26. Ricoeur, OA, 333.

27. Ibid.

28. Emmanuel Levinas, *The Theory of Intuition in Husserl's Phenomenology*, trans. André Orianne (Evanston, Ill.: Northwestern University Press, 1973), 155.

29. Levinas critiques Husserl and Heidegger alike in *Totality and Infinity*. Husserl's primordial sphere is one more instance of "what we call the same," and in Heidegger coexistence still "rests on . . . comprehension"; *Totality and Infinity*, trans. Alphonso Lingis (Pittsburgh: Duquesne University Press, 1969), 67.

30. Emmanuel Levinas, *Time and the Other*, trans. Richard A. Cohen (Pittsburgh: Duquesne University Press, 1987), 83.

31. It has even been claimed that Husserl emphasizes just as much as does Levinas the essential inaccessibility of the Other and that "Husserl and Levinas are mainly phenomenological allies, not opponents"; Soren Overgaard, "On Levinas's Critique of Husserl," in Dan Zahavi, Sara Heinamaa, and Hans Ruin, eds., *Metaphysics, Factity, Interpretation* (Dordrecht: Kluwer Academic Publishers, 2003), 116.

32. See *Totality and Infinity* for this history. See here Bernhard Waldenfels's critical reading of Levinas in "The Other and the Foreign," in *Paul Ricoeur: The Hermeneutics of Action*, ed. Richard Kearney (London: Sage, 1996), 111–124; and "The Experience of the Alien in Husserl's Phenomenology," *Research in Phenomenology* 20 (1990): 19–33. Waldenfels develops an important distinction between a "relational alterity" (where the self is open to the Other as such) and a "relative alterity" (where the Other is reduced to our consciousness as an Other-for-us). See also here the important critical analysis by Robert Bernasconi, "The Alterity of the Stranger and the Experience of the Strange," in *The Face of the Other and the Trace of God*, ed. Jeffrey Bloechl (New York: Fordham University Press, 2000), 66ff. See finally our own discussion of this critical literature and the crucial discussion of Husserl's phenomenology of the Other by Levinas, Ricoeur, and Derrida in "Aliens and Others" in Kearney, *Strangers, Gods and Monsters*, 70–82 and 246–250.

33. See "Diachrony and Representation," in *Time and the Other*, 108. For Levinas's description of "host" see *Totality and Infinity*, 299; for his description of "hostage," see *Time and the Other*, 109. Both Ricoeur in *Oneself As Another*, 338, and Derrida in *Of Hospitality*, 135, 139, remark on this terminological shift in Levinas.

34. It is Heidegger who reminds us that when Dasein is disclosed as "*solus ipse* . . . this existential 'solipsism' is far from the displacement of putting an isolated subject-Thing into the innocuous emptiness of a worldless occurring,"

Being and Time, 247. Dasein is disclosed *not* as isolated thing but comes "face to face with itself as Being-in-the-world," with its dispersed and relation character. Ibid.

35. In *The Second Sex*, Simone de Beauvoir criticizes Levinas for fetishizing the feminine as an other so intangibly Other (to male experience) that actual women are deprived of subjectivity. Women, too, retorts de Beauvoir, are selves as well as others, subjects who relate to others in their own right.

36. See Derrida, "Violence and Metaphysics," in *Writing and Difference*, trans. Alan Bass (Chicago: University of Chicago Press, 1978), 176, and "Hospitality, Justice and Responsibility," in *Questioning Ethics*, ed. R. Kearney and Mark Dooley (New York: Routledge, 1998), 71. Here Derrida talks of the "profound lesson" he and Levinas received from Husserl: "In the fifth *Cartesian Meditation* Husserl insists that there is no pure intuition of the other *as such*; that is, I have no originary access to the alter ego as such. I should go . . . through analogy or appresentation. The fact that there is no phenomenology, or phenomenality, of the other or alter ego as such is something which I think is irrefutable. Of course, it is a break within phenomenology, with the principle of phenomenology, and it is in the space opened by this break within phenomenology that Husserl found his way . . . When I have to explain to students what Levinas has in mind when he speaks of the 'infinity of the other' . . . I refer to Husserl. The other is infinitely other because we never have any access to the other as such. This is why he/she is *the* other. This separation, this dissociation is not only a limit, but it is also the condition of the relation to the other, a non-relation as relation. When Levinas speaks of separation, the separation is the condition of the social bond. There is such a non-intuitive relation—I don't know who the other is, I cannot be on the other side"; 71.

37. Derrida, *Of Hospitality*, 69.

38. On this metaphor of the messiah and messianic other, see Derrida, *Specters of Marx* (New York: Routledge, 1994). Derrida is influenced here not only by Levinas's notion of the messianic in *Totality and Infinity* but also by Walter's Benjamin's notion of a "weak messianism" without sovereignty or power.

39. Derrida, "Violence et métaphysique: Essai sur la pensée d'Emmanuel Levinas," *L'écriture et la différence* (Paris: Seuil, 1967), 176: "*Qui plus que Husserl s'est obstinément attaché à monter que la vision était originelment et essentiellement inadéquation de l'intériorité and de l'extériorité? Que la perception de la chose transcendante et étendu était par essence et à jamais inachevée?*" Derrida adds that, ironically, no one showed this more emphatically than Levinas himself, who critiques his mentor, Husserl, for not seeing what in fact he had taught Levinas to see in the first place! In a later essay, "La philosophie et l'éveil," in *Entre Nous*, 93, Levinas attempts to revise his earlier critique of Husserl in light of Derrida's critique. See also Derrida on Levinas's reading of Husserl's Fifth Cartesian Investigation in "Hospitality, Justice and Responsibility," 81: "Levinas says at some point that when phenomenology addresses the question of the other it interrupts itself. What does that mean? Is it possible to interrupt yourself? That is what

undecidability means and that is what my relation to Husserl is founded on, self-interruption. Levinas meant by this that it is in order to describe the things in themselves that we have to abandon the principle of intuition; it is because the other is *the* other that I must describe my relation to him/her ethically and not in a purely phenomenological fashion. But I do this in the name of phenomenology; in order to be a phenomenologist to the end. That is what is meant by self-interruption, which is another name for *différance*. Just as there would be no responsibility or decision without some self-interruption, neither would there be hospitality; as master and host, the self, in welcoming the other, must interrupt or divide himself or herself. This division is the condition of hospitality."

40. Derrida, *Of Hospitality*, 77. See also 135–136.
41. Ibid., 77.
42. Ibid., 159.
43. Ibid., 151.
44. For Ricoeur's critique of Levinas for his idea that the Other "hostages" the subject, see Study 10 of OA, especially 338; for Ricoeur's critique of Derrida, see the conclusion to *Memory, History and Forgetting*, trans. Kathleen Blamey and David Pellauer (Chicago: University of Chicago Press, 2004). Here Ricoeur contrasts his notion of "difficult" pardon with Derrida's notion of "impossible" pardon, gift, and hospitality.
45. Ricoeur, OA, 331.
46. Derrida himself refers to the absolute other as "hyperbolical hospitality," *Of Hospitality*, 75.
47. Ricoeur, OA, 339.
48. Ricoeur, *On Translation*, trans. Eileen Brennan (New York: Routledge, 2006), 10, 29, 23–24.
49. OA, 338.
50. See Ricoeur on this *difficile/impossible* distinction and "the test of the foreign" in *On Translation*, 3.
51. See Derrida, *Of Hospitality*, p 15. See Ricoeur's critique of Levinas in Study 10 of OA, 336–340.
52. See the introduction to *On Translation*, xxii.
53. Ricoeur, *On Translation*, 9.
54. Ibid., 25. In this passage he also recalls Husserl's notion of the everyday other as *der Fremde*.
55. Ricoeur, *On Translation*, 28–29.
56. Ibid., 10.
57. Derrida also speaks positively of Babel in his "Des Tours de Babel," in *Acts of Religion*, ed. Gil Anidjar (New York: Routledge, 2002).
58. Ricoeur, *On Translation*, 13, 18.
59. Ricoeur, OA, 356.
60. Ricoeur, *On Translation*, 25.
61. Heidegger, *Hölderlin's Hymn "The Ister"* (Bloomington: Indiana University Press, 1996). Antigone represents the "potentiality for being in which the

being of humans is fulfilled: being unhomely in becoming homely . . . Let us give thought to what is named in the choral ode (of *Antigone*) as that which the unhomely one who merely ventures around amid beings without any way out is unable to master."

62. Merleau-Ponty does not spring from nowhere. He draws much from Max Scheler's account of sympathy and Edith Stein's (Husserl's assistant) work on empathy. He also clearly learns much from Husserl's analysis of body/flesh and Heidegger's description of Dasein's thrown and mooded being-in-the-world. Outside of the phenomenological tradition, Merleau-Ponty's philosophy of embodiment is also informed by thinkers such as Schelling, Nietzsche, Marx, and Freud. But all these thinkers failed, in Merleau-Ponty's view, to offer a proper description of the perceptual and affective life or what he eventually terms "flesh." Merleau-Ponty conspicuously took exception to Sartre's account of flesh, as seen by the Look of the Other, as a threat to one's unconditional freedom.

63. Comportment, writes Merleau-Ponty, is "no more composed of parts which can be distinguished in it than a melody (always transferable) is made of the particular notes which are its momentary expression." *Structure of Behavior*, trans. Alden Fischer (Pittsburgh: Duquesne University Press, 2006), 132.

64. Ibid., 9.

65. Ibid., 7.

66. Prescinding from Merleau-Ponty for a moment, we might ask if this is not a message bequeathed to us by some of the oldest myths and narratives—stories all too often forgotten in our Western metaphysical and dualist traditions. Is it any wonder, for example, that it is Odysseus's dog, Argus, who recognizes his master when he returns to Ithaca disguised as a stranger? And does it not equally follow that the only humans to display similar hermeneutic flair are the nursemaid who sees the scar on her master's body and the swineherd, Eumaeus, who welcomes the exile home from his travels: "Every stranger and beggar come from Zeus/and whatever scrap they get from the likes of us/they'll find it welcome" (303). We might also recall here how certain holy persons have welcomed animal others into their lives. This is true of many Eastern wisdom traditions, where monkeys, birds, cows, and tigers are considered sacred beings. But it is equally true of some rare figures within the Christian Western tradition, inspired by the Hebrew celebration of all sentient beings in the Song of Songs. One thinks of the child Christ sharing a stable with cows and sheep; of Saint Kevin inviting birds to perch on his outstretched arms as he prayed before the lake of Glendalough; of Saint Gallus hosting the wild bears of Constance in his hermitage; of Saint Jeremiah with his lion in the cave. Or we might think, finally, of Saint Francis of Assisi, who called animals and plants his "brothers and sisters," thus professing what Max Scheler terms a "heresy of the heart" against the cold scholasticism of Christendom. In his *Nature of Sympathy*, Scheler holds that Francis inaugurated a phenomenology of sacred nature that embraced the human, animal, and divine in a single *ordo amoris*. It was, he believed, a natural expression of the Eucharistic sanctification of bread and wine as body and blood: Word as

flesh and flesh as word. Because of his hallowing of even the "lowest orders of nature," many of Francis's contemporaries thought him mad. For here, writes Scheler, was a "mystic who dared conjoin transcendence and immanence, the sacred and the secular, by calling all creatures his brothers, and by looking with the heart's keen insight into the inmost being of every creature, just as though he already entered into the freedom of glory of the children of God." In "The Sense of Unity in the Cosmos," *The Nature of Sympathy* (New York: Routledge and Kegan Paul, 1954), 88–89. For further analysis of a phenomenology of sacramental nature in Merleau-Ponty and Scheler, see Kearney *Anatheism* (New York: Columbia University Press, 2010), 99–100, 88–94.

67. Merleau-Ponty, *Phenomenology of Perception*, trans. Colin Smith (New York: Routledge, 1962), 352.

68. Merleau-Ponty, *Nature: Course Notes from the Collège de France* (Evanston, Ill.: Northwestern University Press), 218; hereafter cited as *Nature*.

69. Ibid., 210.

70. Ibid., 224.

71. Hannah Arendt, *The Human Condition* (Chicago: University of Chicago Press, 1958), 8.

72. Merleau-Ponty, *Visible and the Invisible*, trans. Alphonso Lingis (Evanston, Ill.: Northwestern University Press, 1968), 11.

73. Ibid.

74. We must acknowledge that since the pioneering work of Scheler, Merleau-Ponty, and Stein, other contemporary phenomenological accounts have supplemented disembodied epistemologies with similarly rich studies in embodiment and eros—e.g., Jean-Luc Marion, Bernhard Waldenfels, and Jean-Louis Chrétien. We offer our work here in this new tradition. See Didier Frank, *Chair et corps* (Paris: Editions de Minuit, 1981), and Michel Henry, *Phénoménologie matérielle* (Paris: Presses Universitaires de France, 1990). Ricoeur offers an overview of studies on "embodied givenness" on *Oneself as Another*, 323, 326 (notes), 330, and 333–334. Beyond the European and Continental tradition, we might also cite other contemporary investigations on embodiment and enacted cognition that have provoked excitement in the broader philosophical community—Sean Kelly, Evan Thompson, Shawn Gallaher, Andy Clark, and others.

75. On "incarnate" philosophy, see Anthony Steinbock's essay in this volume. For more on this turn in Merleau-Ponty, see Kearney in chapter 4 of *Anatheism*, "In the Flesh: Sacramental Imagination," and in Semonovitch and DeRoo, *Merleau-Ponty at the Limits of Art, Religion and Perception* (New York: Continuum, 2010).

76. OA, 317.

77. Bernhard Waldenfels offers his own supplementation of this history in *The Question of the Other* (Albany: State University of New York Press, 2007).

78. Merleau-Ponty, so prolific in his political writing and profound in his ontological work, failed to mediate between the two. Merleau-Ponty presents a politics and an ontology but no adequate ethics: no explicit description of the

subtle *phronesis* needed to translate between the real and ideal. Ricoeur's linguistic hospitality, like Derrida and Kristeva's paradigms, locates the enfleshed subject in a world overdetermined by geographic and political borders and edges.

79. These three terms correspond to the hermeneutic triad of prefiguration/configuration/refiguration in Kearney's *Poetique du possible* and Ricoeur's *Time and Narrative*, vol. 1, chap. 3, on "triple mimesis."

80. Kearney, *Poetics of Modernity*, xiii. Poetics here describes the sort of thinking "where significance is accorded a sense beyond the immediately graspable and calculable," Ibid. See also Kearney's *Poétique du possible* (Paris: Beauchesne, 1984) and *Poetics of Imagining* (New York: Fordham University Press, 1998).

81. Heidegger, "The Origin of the Work of Art," in *Poetry, Language, Thought* (New York: Harper & Row, 1971), 74.

82. Derrida, *Of Hospitality*, 2.

83. On one hand, the event at the threshold of experience is indeed one of *aesthesis:* of sensation and reception of the other who arrives. Aesthetics habitually refers to the study of the *reception* of the beautiful and sublime, the sensory and imaginary, the fictional and the artistic. Kant's *First Critique* postulates time and space as the structures of the transcendental *aesthetic* of all experience; the structures of intuition condition a fundamentally passive sensibility, distinguished from the activity of the constituting subject. The *Third Critique* describes the *aesthesis* of the beautiful, the formal uptake of the noumenal as phenomenal. The *Third Critique*'s distinction between the beautiful and the sublime is also relevant. If the sublime is the absolute Other who slips beneath the threshold—*sublimen*—of representation (concepts, categories, images), the beautiful would be equivalent to what we call the Foreigner, that is, the other as represented in the free play of our concepts and imagination. Where the sublime eludes and shatters our imagination, the beautiful encourages us to present otherness in conceptual keeping with nature. In between the two stands the Stranger. Astride the divide between beauty and the sublime, the Stranger keeps the door ajar.

84. On mimesis as originary ordering, see Ricoeur, *Time and Narrative*, trans. Kathleen McLaughlin and David Pellauer (Chicago: University of Chicago Press, 1984), vol. 1, where he distinguishes between $mimesis_1$, $mimesis_2$, and $mimesis_3$.

85. See Aristotle, *Poetics,* sections 20–22, on neologisms, diction, and metaphor.

86. Waldenfels, *The Question of the Other*, 34.

87. Heidegger, *On the Way to Language*, cited in Kearney, *Modern Movements*, 2nd ed. (Manchester: Manchester University Press, 1996), 41.

88. Derrida writes that one must "welcome the coming" of the other/guest in "Hostipitality," *Acts of Religion*, ed. Gil Andijar (London: Routledge, 2002), 361.

89. Merleau-Ponty, *Phenomenology of Perception*, 122. Levinas did develop a significant phenomenology of sensible welcome—a passivity before all passivity partially inspired by Husserl's account of passive synthesis—but he shows no real appreciation of the animal, ecological, or poetic dimensions of sensibility so

richly described in Merleau-Ponty. On these subjects, see the essays in this volume by Jeffrey Bloechl, David Wood, and Kelly Oliver.

90. See Emile Benveniste, *Indo-European Language and Society*, ed. L. R. Palmer and G. C. Lepschy, trans. Elizabeth Palmer (London: Faber & Faber, 1969), and Derrida, *Of Hospitality*.

91. For a more extended treatment of diacritical hermeneutics in relation to other related hermeneutic approaches—romantic, ontological, critical, and radical—see Kearney, "Introduction," *Strangers, Gods and Monsters*.

92. Kristeva envisions a cleansing by way of psychoanalysis of the political subject who comes to the recognition of the stranger in herself, and can thus participate in a cosmopolitan project. Kristeva advances a unique form of psychoanalytic phenomenology that addresses the illusions of the autonomous subject. She calls for a therapeutic undergoing that reveals a medley of unconscious differences—sexual, racial, somatic, oneiric—that condition consciousness.

93. Kristeva, *Strangers to Ourselves*, 192. She adds, significantly: "Therefore Freud does not talk about them (foreigners) . . . he sets the difference within us."

94. Ibid. See Kearney, *Strangers, Gods and Monsters*, 72–77, 244–247.

95. Ricoeur, OA, 355.

96. Arendt, *Human Condition*, 8.

97. "Myth of Sisyphus," *Basic Writings of Existentialism*, ed. Gordon Marino (New York: Modern Library, 2004), 150.

98. Ibid., 450.

99. He continues: "Springing from somewhere beyond our understanding, our curiosity as to the woman whom we love overleaps the bounds of that woman's character, which we might if we chose but probably will not choose to stop and examine." *Remembrance of Things Past: Within a Budding Grove*, trans. C. K. Moncrieff and Terence Kilmartin (New York: Random House, 1981), 956.

100. *Remembrance of Things Past*: Time Regained, x.

101. See Kearney, *Anatheism*, chaps. 1 and 2. In her doctoral dissertation *Thou Art: On the Representation of the Word and the Incarnation of the Human Subject*, Mary Anderson remarks, "By imaging an otherworldly beauty—both otherness and worldliness, alterity and mundanity—Gabriel presents an ambivalent image that signifies sensibility at a threshold, intra-subjective domains" (18).

102. On these and other such examples, see Kearney, *Strangers, Gods and Monsters*, chaps. 1–2, and On Stories (London: Routledge, 2002), chap. 9.

103. Both Caputo and Treanor mention such coincidences in their essays in this volume.

104. Proust, *Within a Budding Grove*, x.

105. Ricoeur might call this "linguistic hospitality." See *On Translation*, 10.

106. Merleau-Ponty himself recognizes the difficulty of translating and transitioning from literary and poetic thought to phenomenological thinking; he explains that one would have to "present infinite explanations and commentaries, clear up a thousand misunderstandings, and translate quite different systems of concepts into one another in order to establish an objective relationship between,

for example, Husserl's philosophy and Faulkner's words. And yet within us readers they are connected." *Signs*, 225. Moreover, it seems that we should take that connection within us readers as indication of a fascinating area of phenomenological investigation, *not* as a sign of a project doomed from the start.

107. Levinas makes this connection in *Time and the Other*, 108.

108. Merleau-Ponty "Eye and Mind," *Merleau-Ponty Aesthetics Reader*, ed. Galen Johnson (Evanston, Ill.: Northwestern University Press, 1993), 147.

109. Ricoeur, *On Translation*, 23–25. This is how Ricoeur proposes we found a "eucharistic hospitality" on linguistic hospitality: "Bringing the reader to the author, bringing the author to the reader, at the risk of serving and of betraying two masters: this is to practice what I like to call *linguistic hospitality*. It is this which serves as a model for other forms of hospitality that I think resemble it: confessions, religions, are they not like languages that are foreign to one another, with their lexicon, their grammar, their rhetoric, their stylistics which we must *learn* in order to make our way into them? And is Eucharistic hospitality not to be taken up with the same risks of translation-betrayal, but also with the same renunciation of the perfect translation?" (23–24).

1. Strangers at the Edge of Hospitality
Edward S. Casey

1. For a trenchant analysis of the role of borders in political life, and of the resulting "border work" called for, see Mary Watkins, "Psyches and Cities of Hospitality in an Era of Forced Migration: The Shadows of Slavery and Conquest on the 'Immigration' Debate," *Spring* 78 (2007): 1–25.

2. Regarding the decisive character of the glance in social situations, especially its darker sides, see E. S. Casey, *The World at a Glance* (Bloomington: Indiana University Press, 2007), chap. 5.

3. Jacques Derrida, *Of Hospitality*, trans. R. Bowlby (Stanford: Stanford University Press, 2000), 79, his italics. Derrida pitches this "reciprocal presupposition" (in Deleuze's term) as an "insoluble" and "non-dialectizable" "antinomy" of hospitality; see ibid., 77.

4. Ibid., 25, his italics. See Martin Heidegger on "making room" (*einräumen*) in *Being and Time*, trans. J. Macquarrie and E. Robinson (New York: Harper & Row, 1962), 146, where the context is the practical world of the ready-to-hand, far from the domain of hospitality.

5. I am here adapting J. J. Gibson's axiom for visual perception: "The surface is where the action is." Gibson, *The Ecological Approach to Visual Perception* (Hillsdale, N.J.: Erlbaum, 1986), 23.

6. Maurice Merleau-Ponty, *Phenomenology of Perception*, trans. C. Smith (New York: Routledge, 2002), 230: "The problem of the world and, to begin with, that of one's own body, consists in the fact that *it is all there (tout y demeure)*" (his italics).

7. This is the title of an essay by Jean-Luc Nancy. See Nancy, *Being Singular Plural*, trans. R. D. Richardson and Anne E. O'Byrne (Stanford: Stanford University Press, 2000), 159–176. I discuss the factor of surprise in *The World at a Glance*, 56–57, 125–130, 212–218, 243–244, 467–468.

2. Putting Hospitality in Its Place
Brian Treanor

1. Ed Casey, *Getting Back Into Place* (Bloomington: Indiana University Press, 1993; 2d ed., 2009). Through a stroke of good fortune, Casey, who is the preeminent philosopher of place in the contemporary continental dialogue, has also contributed to this volume. Although I was unable to be in Boston to hear Casey's contribution to the Guestbook Project at the conference, "Phenomenologies of Hospitality," I was able to listen to his paper on the conference website. I hope my own remarks will complement his reflections on the place-related aspects, gates, and edges of hospitality. For related accounts of the body or landscape see: Gaston Bachelard, *The Poetics of Space*, trans. Maria Jolas (Boston: Beacon Press, 1994); Maurice Merleau-Ponty, *The Phenomenology of Perception*, trans. Colin Smith (London: Routledge, 1995); Gabriel Marcel, *The Mystery of Being* (South Bend, Ind.: St. Augustine's Press, 2001).

2. Casey, *Getting Back Into Place*, esp. 9–10, 12.

3. Aristotle, *Physics*, 208b, 35–209a, 2 (cited in ibid., 13). Note, however, that on this list of material and mental objects and experienced or observed events, we do not have "anticipated" events or "hoped for" events, and so the *a venir* of deconstruction could still be said to be outside of place.

4. Casey, *Getting Back Into Place*, 18.

5. John D. Caputo, *The Weakness of God* (Bloomington: Indiana University Press, 2006), 57.

6. Ibid., 58.

7. Of course, such a claim presumes the primordiality of being. If, however, being is not primordial, if there is a "good beyond being" or a "God without being" then the fact that being is coextensive with place or implacement no longer assures the primordiality or co-primordiality of the latter.

8. Casey, *Getting Back Into Place*, 22–23.

9. Ibid., 23.

10. Ibid. Thoreau also argues that "where" we live suggests something about "who" we are, which is one of the central themes in the second chapter of *Walden*, "Where I Lived and What I Lived For." See Henry David Thoreau, *Walden* (Princeton: Princeton University Press, 2004).

11. Casey, *Getting Back Into Place*, 29–31.

12. Ibid., 28.

13. Ibid., 25.

14. Ibid., 25, 29.

15. For an excellent description of a place "built," literally and figuratively, for a specific person's body *and story*, see Michael Pollan, *A Place of My Own: The Architecture of Daydreams* (New York: Penguin, 2008).

16. See Casey, *Getting Back Into Place*, 26.

17. Ibid., 52. "Hereness," however, is more complex and multilocular than we suppose (ibid., 52–54).

18. Ibid., 48.

19. Ibid., 52.

20. Ibid., 34.

21. Ibid., ix. Pascal said, "The eternal silence . . . of infinite spaces terrifies me." These infinite spaces may well correspond to what, in Casey's terms, we might call "space without place."

22. Our experience of implacement and displacement has a profound effect on the way we view the world—socially, politically, economically, philosophically, and theologically. It may well be that the difference between experiencing being as a home or the comfort of a womb and experiencing it as the nocturnal menace of the *il y a* hinges the extent to which we feel implaced.

23. Casey, *Getting Back Into Place*, xv.

24. Though in emphasizing this existential displacement, we should not discount the liberating possibilities associated with such disorientation. As Henry David Thoreau noted, "not until we are lost, in other words, not till we have lost the world, do we begin to find ourselves, and realize where we are and the infinite extent of our relations" (Thoreau, *Walden*, 171). Note that, in this context, Thoreau suggests that finding oneself has to do with "where" one is rather than "who" one is.

25. Casey, *Getting Back Into Place*, 38, citing Cisco Lassiter, "Relocation and Illness: The Plight of the Navajo," in *Pathologies of the Modern Self: Postmodern Studies on Narcissism, Schizophrenia, and Depression*, ed. David Michael Levin (New York: New York University Press, 1987). Although Cisco's use of the term "modern," as well as its presence in the title of the collection, might suggest a focus on modernity, this term has different meanings for different people. The date of the essay (1987) as well as the use of "postmodern" in the subtitle, clearly indicate that the dislocation or displacement indicated is representative of our contemporary sociocultural environment, whether one calls it modern, postmodern, or post-postmodern.

26. Robert D. Putnam, *Bowling Alone: The Collapse and Revival of America Community* (New York: Simon & Schuster, 2001), 27.

27. Ibid., 183–284, especially 277–284.

28. One might justifiably object that Putnam's study is limited to the American experience, which is certainly true. However, most of the trends he identifies are becoming global phenomena and many communities that have, traditionally, been deeply grounded in place are now finding themselves struggling with problems associated with globalization, homogenization, and existential displacement.

29. Casey, *Getting Back Into Place*, 37.

30. Jacques Derrida, *Of Hospitality*, trans. Rachel Bowlby (Stanford: Stanford University Press, 2000), 75–77.

31. Immanuel Kant, *Perpetual Peace and Other Essays*, trans. Ted Humphrey (Indianapolis: Hackett, 1983), 118. See also Jacque Derrida, *On Cosmopolitanism and Forgiveness*, trans. Mark Dooley and Michael Hughes (London: Routledge, 2001), 20.

32. See, for example, the United Nations Convention Relating to the Status of Refugees (1951), the UN order Relating to the Status of Refugees' *Non-refoulement* (1951), and the UN Protocol Relating to the Status of Refugees 1967.

33. Derrida, *On Cosmopolitanism and Forgiveness*, 14.

34. Kant, *Perpetual Peace and Other Essays*, 118. Emphasis mine.

35. See Derrida, *On Cosmopolitanism and Forgiveness*, 12. Derrida uses the example of Algerian Muslims who were offered the "hospitality" of French citizenship on the (inhospitable) condition that they give up what they thought of as their culture (Derrida, *Of Hospitality*, 145).

36. Derrida, *On Cosmopolitanism and Forgiveness*, 5.

37. Derrida, *Of Hospitality*, 83.

38. Ibid., 77–79. "But even while keeping itself above the laws of hospitality, the unconditional law of hospitality needs the laws, it requires them. This demand is constitutive. It wouldn't be effectively unconditional, the law, if it didn't have to become effective, concrete, determined, if that were not its being as having-to-be" (79).

39. For some objections, see Richard Kearney, *Strangers, Gods, and Monsters* (London: Routledge, 2003).

40. Derrida, *Of Hospitality*, 79.

41. Jacques Derrida, *The Gift of Death*, trans. David Wills (Chicago: University of Chicago Press, 1995), 68. See also Emmanuel Levinas, *Totality and Infinity: An Essay on Exteriority*, trans. Alphonso Lingis, (Pittsburgh: Duquesne University Press, 1969).

42. Derrida, *On Cosmopolitanism and Forgiveness*, 19.

43. John D. Caputo, Mark Dooley, and Michael J. Scanlon, eds., *Questioning God* (Bloomington: Indiana University Press, 2001), 71.

44. *Taittiriya Upanishad*, I-xi-2–4.

45. The *Bhagavad Gita*, in *A Sourcebook in Indian Philosophy*, ed. Sarvepalli Radhakrishnan and Charles A. Moore (Princeton: Princeton University Press, 1957), 115.

46. As Aristotle says, "anyone can get angry—that is easy—or give or spend money; but to do this to the right person, to the right extent, at the right time, with the right motive, and in the right way, *that* is not for everyone, nor is it easy; wherefore goodness is both rare and laudable and noble." Aristotle, *Nicomachean Ethics*, 45. These various restrictions represent so many of the conditions with which Derrida is concerned.

47. See, for example, Gabriel Marcel, "On the Ontological Mystery" *The Philosophy of Existentialism*, trans. Manya Harari (New York: Carol, 1995).

48. See Chapter 1. Casey is quick to point out that we should not vilify gates simply because they offer a specific, and therefore limited, point of entry (i.e., a condition on the potential guest). Gates, by their very nature, *both* separate *and* bring together people.

49. Of course, there are innumerable examples of questions that *are* used to exclude, discriminate, or oppress. The point is merely that this is not always the

case. On the issue of discerning between various others, see Kearney, *Strangers, Gods, and Monsters*, 65–82, 108.

50. Derrida, *Of Hospitality*, 87. Emphasis mine.

51. See Derrida, *Of Hospitality*, 93–121, especially 111. Regarding this point, it would be interesting to consider what will become of this connection to place in an age of cremation, land use problems for graveyards, and so on.

52. Derrida, *Of Hospitality*, 89.

53. Ibid.

54. Ibid.

55. See Paul Ricoeur, *Time and Narrative*, vol. 1, trans. Kathleen McLaughlin and David Pellauer (Chicago: University of Chicago Press, 1990).

56. Richard Kearney, *On Stories* (London: Routledge, 2002), 29–30. As Kearney says, "nations are narratives" (79).

57. Paul Ricoeur, *Time and Narrative*, vol. 3, trans. Kathleen Blamey and David Pellauer (Chicago: University of Chicago Press, 1990), 246.

58. Ibid., emphasis mine.

59. Kearney, *On Stories*, 137.

60. Ibid., 92–96. Think, for example, of the changes wrought—regarding community *and* place—by the willingness of the people on the island of Ireland to reimagine themselves as "British, Irish, or both" (96).

61. See Derrida, *Of Hospitality*.

62. Of course, this can go too far (and so, again, brings us back to the idea of hospitality as a virtue, a mean between extremes). Taking advantage of a guest and using him or her for cooking duties, childcare, running errands, and the like would also fail with respect to hospitality.

63. Recalling Luke 9:58 and Exodus 2:22.

3. Things at the Edge of the World
David Wood

1. See Heidegger, *What Is a Thing?* (Chicago: Henry Regnery, 1968) and "The Origin of the Work of Art," in *Off the Beaten Track* (Cambridge: Cambridge University Press, 2002). See Hans Georg Gadamer, Truth and Method, trans. J. Weinsheimer and D. G. Marshall (New York: Crossroad, 1975).

2. The word "thing" is becoming something to be fought over. With an explicit negative reference to Heidegger, Bruno Latour appropriates it for political ends: "Long before designating an object thrown out of the political sphere and standing there objectively and independently, the Ding or Thing has for many centuries meant the issue that brings people together because it divides them." Bruno Latour, introduction to *Making Things Public: Atmospheres of Democracy*, ed. Bruno Latour and Peter Weibel (Cambridge, Mass.: MIT Press, 2005).

3. The extended book project *Things at the Edge of the World*, for which this essay serves as a trailer, outlines a truly fractal ontology.

4. An initial list of "things," which can be expanded very easily, included Mouth, Body, Animal, Tree, Sun, Painting, 9/11, God, Death, Woman, Book, and Earth.

5. And what is implied by the thought that the life made possible by the constancy of sun energy can now *think* this?

6. It should be clear that I have little in common with Bataille's "general economics," for which the sun's endless supply of energy provides an excess we need to spend. Eroticism does not need such a cosmological economics. And global warming has changed the name of the wider game.

7. In about five billion years, when the sun will "eat" the earth as it expands and dies.

8. See Aldo Leopold, *Sand County Almanac* (London: Oxford University Press, 1968).

9. "To whom does this terrace belong?/With its limestone crumbling into fine greyish dust,/Its bevy of bees, and its wind-beaten rickety sun-chairs./Not to me, but this lizard,/Older than I, or the cockroach." From "The Lizard," *Collected Poems of Theodore Roethke* (London: Faber and Faber, 1968).

10. "We reached the old wolf in time to watch the fierce green fire dying in her eyes. . . . There was something new to me in those eyes—something known only to her and the mountains. I was young then, and full of trigger-itch. I thought that because fewer wolves meant more deer that no wolves would mean hunter's paradise, but after seeing the green fire die, I sensed that neither the wolf nor the mountain agreed with such a view." Leopold, *Sand County Almanac*.

11. J. Von Uexkull, "A Stroll through the Worlds of Animals and Men," in *Instinctive Behavior*, ed. C. Schiller (New York: International Universities Press, 1957).

12. Martin Heidegger "What Is Metaphysics?" *Martin Heidegger: Basic Writings*, ed. David Ferrel Krell (New York: HarperCollins, 1993).

13. I will explain the infinite as the absence of measure in a phenomenon in which an absolute distinction and an absence of concrete measure are laminated together.

14. See her essay "Sexual Difference," in *The Irigaray Reader*, ed. Margaret Whitford (Cambridge: Basil Blackwell, 1991).

15. I explore this line of criticism in "Where Levinas Went Wrong: Some Questions for my Levinasian Friends" *The Step Back* (Albany: SUNY Press, 2005).

16. See Gadamer, *Truth and Method*, and "The Relevance of the Beautiful" in *The Relevance of the Beautiful and Other Essays*, trans. Nicholas Walker (New York: Cambridge University Press, 1986).

17. I explore these themes of existential temporal constitution with respect to Heidegger in "Reading Heidegger Responsibly: Glimpses of Being in Dasein's Development," in *Heidegger and Practical Philosophy*, ed. François Raffoul and David Pettigrew (Albany: State University of New York Press, 2002).

18. The Production Code, also known as the Hays Code, was the set of industry censorship guidelines, which governed the production of U.S. movies from 1930 to 1968.

19. Kelly Oliver, "Knock me up, knock me over" (lecture at Vanderbilt, April 2009).

20. Merleau-Ponty and I agree on the importance of a recurrent feature that is both structure and event, one whose boundaries are still to be negotiated. Sometimes, for example, it seems we are talking about a shortlist of privileged things that have an exemplary reversibility operator status. At other times, it seems that anything, suitably appreciated, can take on this role. (Compare Heidegger talking about great works of art.) What, then, is a thing? In another departure from Merleau-Ponty, my list of things radically exceeds the sensible. The inclusion of death makes this clear, where the double movement—both opening up (if you like) a world of meaning and facilitating a certain deconstruction of selfhood—is clearly in play.

21. The phrase comes from Winnicott, who studied with Klein. "The first ego organization comes from the experience of threats of annihilation which do not lead to annihilation and from which, repeatedly, there is recovery." Donald Winnicott, *Through Paediatrics to Psychoanalysis* (London: Hogarth, 1956).

22. Needless to say, agency is not dependent on (and may indeed preclude) an exaggerated sense of autonomy, and a "deconstruction" of the myth of the autonomous subject does not seek to abolish the agent-subject, but to make its constitutive relationality visible and productive. See, for instance, Judith Butler, *Bodies That Matter* (New York: Routledge, 1993).

23. See Nelson Goodman, *Ways of Worldmaking* (New York: Hackett, 1978).

24. The revelations of torture at Abu Ghraib prison left many people asking "Is that our America?"

25. Martin Heidegger, *Introduction to Metaphysics* (New Haven: Yale University Press, 2000), 123.

26. Ibid., 133.

27. This is an allusion to Simon Critchley's *Infinitely Demanding* (London: Verso, 2007).

4. Hospitality and the Trouble with God
John D. Caputo

1. See Steven Shakespeare, *Derrida and Theology* (London: T & T Clark, 2009), 212.

2. Jacques Derrida, "Hostipitality," in *Acts of Religion*, ed. Gil Anidjar (London: Routledge, 2002), 356–420.

3. Ibid., 360–362.

4. "Epoche and Faith: An Interview with Jacques Derrida" (with John D. Caputo, Yvonne Sherwood and Kevin Hart), in *Derrida and Religion: Other Testaments*, ed. Yvonne Sherwood and Kevin Hart (New York: Routledge, 2005), 28–31.

5. Hélène Cixous, *Le prénom de dieu* (Paris: Edition Bernard Grasset, 1967). See Hélène Cixous, "Promised Belief," in *Feminism, Sexuality and Religion*, ed. Linda Alcoff and John D. Caputo (Bloomington: Indiana University Press, 2011), 131.

6. Meister Eckhart, *Meister Eckhart: The Essential Sermons, Commentaries, Treatises and Defense*, trans. Edmund Colledge and Bernard McGinn (New York: Paulist Press, 1981), 200.

7. Ibid., 177.

8. Amy Hollywood, *The Soul As Virgin Wife: Mechthild of Magdeburg, Marguerite Porete, and Meister Eckhart* (Notre Dame, Ind.: University of Notre Dame Press, 2001).

9. Meister Eckhart, *Essential Sermons*, 180.

10. Michel Serres, *Angels: A Modern Myth*, trans. Francis Cowper (Paris: Flammarion, 1995), 129.

11. Jacques Derrida, *H. C. For Life, That Is to Say . . .*, trans. Laurent Melesi and Stefan Herbrechter (Stanford: Stanford University Press, 2006), 2–4.

12. Sharon Betcher, *Spirit and the Politics of Disablement* (Minneapolis: Fortress Press, 2007); Nancy Eiesland, *The Disabled God: Toward a Liberatory Theology of Disability* (Nashville: Abingdon Press, 1994); Jacques Derrida, *Rogues*, trans. Pascale-Anne Brault and Michael Haas (Stanford: Stanford University Press, 2005), 114; Derrida, "Epoche and Faith," 42–43; Marcella Althaus-Reid, *Indecent Theology* (London: Routledge, 2000).

13. Catherine Keller, *The Face of the Deep* (London: Routledge, 2003).

5. The Hospitality of Listening: A Note on Sacramental Strangeness
Karmen MacKendrick

1. Jean-Luc Nancy, *Listening*, trans. Charlotte Mandel (New York: Fordham University Press, 2007), 9.

2. Joseph Martos, *Doors to the Sacred: A Historical Introduction to Sacraments in the Catholic Church* (New York: Image Books, 1982), 41.

3. Ibid.

4. See Augustine, *City of God*. trans. Henry Bettenson (New York: Penguin Books, 2003), 5; see also his discussions of the good of marriage.

5. Augustine's "Tractates on the Gospel of John," Jn. 15:1–3, 80.3, gives "*verbum visibile*" and also links sacramental meaning to faith. Trans. John Gibb, from *Nicene and Post-Nicene Fathers*, vol. 7, ed. Philip Schaff (Buffalo, N.Y.: Christian Literature Publishing Co., 1888).

6. A notion that, in a 2009 survey, remained "very important" to 64 percent of American Catholics, "somewhat important" to another 23 percent. See http://www.catholicnews.com/data/stories/cns/0901682.htm.

7. Augustine even suggests that it is the community that determines whether a rite counts properly as sacrament (good) or magic (bad). R. A. Markus, *Signs and Meanings: World and Text in Ancient Christianity* (Liverpool: Liverpool University Press, 1996), 142. Cf. John M. Rist: "Thus verbal signs are of circumscribed usefulness and will clearly be effective only in a community . . . which

recognizes the relevant 'conventions' of communications." *Augustine: Ancient Thought Baptized* (Cambridge: Cambridge University Press, 1996), 34.

8. Louis Mackey, *Peregrinations of the Word* (Ann Arbor: University of Michigan Press, 1997), 74; see also 11.

9. I do not mean to imply that fidelity, particularly the fidelity of desire and concomitant attention central to my discussion here, is any more exhaustive of "faith" that the more closed-off propositional version would be. I do mean, or hope, that a reminder of this more open and responsive version of faith might function in usefully corrective tension with the disturbingly dominant dogmatism.

10. Jean-Luc Nancy, *Dis-Enclosure: The Deconstruction of Christianity*, trans. Bettina Bergo, Gabriel Malenfant, and Michael B. Smith (New York: Fordham University Press, 2008), 73.

11. So too, I cannot resist noting, does a *Reason Online* article on cloning Neanderthals: "Assume that scientists are able to produce healthy Neanderthal clones. What rights would they have? One way to approach the question is to ask if Neanderthals would be able to make and keep moral commitments. One significant clue that they might have this ability is the fact their genomes have the same version of the FOXP2 gene that we do. Our variant of that gene is necessary for articulate speech. The human (both modern and Neanderthal) FOXP2 gene differs from that found in chimps and most other primates by two changes in its genetic sequence. The fact that Neanderthals carried the same version means that it is possible that they could talk and might have been able to make and keep promises. If Neanderthals had this ability it strongly suggests that they would merit the same moral consideration that we give to our fellow human beings." Ronald Bailey, "Neanderthal Rights: The Morality of Resurrecting Our Closest Evolutionary Cousins," *Reason Online*, February 17, 2009, http://www.reason.com/news/show/131717.html.

12. Friedrich Nietzsche, *Zur Genealogie der Moral* (Leipzig: Philipp Reclam, 1998), essay 2, sec. 1: "*Ein Tier heranzüchten, das versprechen darf—ist das nicht gerade jene paradoxe Aufgabe selbst, welche sich die Natur in Hinsicht auf den Menschen gestellt hat?*" The ambiguity occurs in *versprechen darf*—may make promises, implying at once ability and permissibility.

13. Nietzsche, "On the Genealogy of Morals," trans. Walter Kaufmann, in *On the Genealogy of Morals and Ecce Homo* (New York: Vintage Books, 1967), 58.

14. Chapters 3 and 4, *Fragmentation and Memory* (New York: Fordham University Press, 2008).

15. This it has in common with the messianic promise in the thought of Derrida and Blanchot, which of course is likewise closely correlated, especially for the former, with questions of hospitality. My interests here, though obviously related, might be distinguished from these as less messianic and more incarnational.

16. Consider, as an example of the world without enticement, Augustine's vivid descriptions of his city after the death of his friend in the fourth book of

the *Confessions*, trans. Henry Chadwick (New York: Oxford University Press, 1991). My attention was drawn to the contrast between the empty world in the absence of love and the overfull world in the presence of beauty by Sarah Vitale during a seminar on the *Confessions* at Villanova University in 2009.

17. Georges Bataille, *Inner Experience*, trans. Leslie A. Boldt (Albany: State University of New York Press, 1988), 38.

18. As is probably obvious, I have particularly in mind Plotinus, Ennead 1.6. In *Plotinus: The Enneads*, trans. Stephen MacKenna (Burdett, N.Y.: Larson, 2004), 64–72.

19. *Confessions*10.6.9; cf. *Expositions on the Psalms* 148.7–10, trans. J. E. Tweed, from Schaff, *Nicene and Post-Nicene Fathers*, vol. 8.

20. Jean-Louis Chrétien, "The Offering of the World," in *The Ark of Speech*, trans. Andrew Brown (New York: Routledge, 2004), 139.

21. Stendhal, *Love*, trans. Gilbert and Suzanne Sale (New York: Penguin Books, 1975), 58, 181. See also Jean-Louis Chrétien, *The Call and the Response*, trans. Anne A. Davenport (New York: Fordham University Press, 2004), 3: "The Platonic tradition, from antiquity to the Renaissance, has thought beauty to be, in its very manifestation, a call, a vocation and provocation. Nor is calling superadded to beauty, as though accidental: things and forms do not beckon us because they are beautiful. . . . Rather, we call them beautiful precisely because they call us and recall us. Moreover, as soon as we are able to call them beautiful we must do so, in order to answer them."

22. Chrétien, "Does Beauty Say Adieu?" in *The Ark of Speech*, 79–80.

23. "*Da stieg en Baum. O reine Übersteigung!/O Orpheus singt! O hoher Baum im Ohr!/Und alles schwieg. Doch selbst in der Verschweigung/ ging neuer Anfang, Wink und Wandlung vor.*" In the M. D. Herter Norton translation, "There rose a tree, O pure transcendency!/O Orpheus singing! O tall tree in the ear!/And all was silent. Yet even in the silence/ new beginning, beckoning, change went on." Rainer Maria Rilke, *Sonnets to Orpheus* (New York: Norton, 1942), 16–17. Cf. Sonnet 2, 12, "*Jeder glückliche Rau mist Kind oder Enkel von Trennung,/den sie staunend durchgehn.*" "Each happy space they wander wondering through/is child or grandchild of parting." Ibid., 92–93.

24. I have recently argued that the revelation of God may be the, or an, intent of the repeated prayers of the *Confessions*. Conclusion, *Seducing Augustine*, with Virginia Burrus and Mark Jordan (New York: Fordham University Press, 2010).

25. There is even some indication in the *Confessions* that provoking this urge to join-in may be a, if not the, proper function of prayer. Yet this response is never quite adequate. See Chrétien: "The joy with which beauty strikes us delivers us to word and song, to thanks and praise, but how could the response to it not fall short of it? . . . To begin with, the way that the response falls short constitutes neither a contingent deficit nor a regrettable imperfection in the response that we give to manifestation of the beautiful that occurs in the form of a request. It is the very event of a wound by which our existence is altered and opened, and becomes itself the site of the manifestation of what it responds to.

There is true force only in weakness, a weakness that is opened up by what comes toward us. . . . The wound can bless and . . . benediction can wound." "Retrospection," in *The Unforgettable and the Unhoped For*, trans. Jeffrey Bloechl (New York: Fordham University Press, 2002), 122.

26. See the Ninth Duino Elegy: "*Sind wir vielleicht* hier, *um zu sagen: Haus,/ Brücke, Brunnen, Tor, Krug, Obstbaum, Fenster—/höchstens: Säule, Turm* . . ." "Perhaps we are *here* in order to say: house, bridge, fountain, gate, pitcher, fruit-tree, window—/at most: column, tower." Rainer Maria Rilke, in *The Selected Poetry of Rainer Maria Rilke*, trans. Stephen Mitchell (New York: Vintage Books, 1989), 199–201.

27. Rilke famously declares that "beauty is nothing but the beginning of terror" in the first of the *Duino Elegies*. Ibid., 151.

28. Chrétien, "Does Beauty Say Adieu?" 78. Perhaps this demand echoes the "alterity or unconditional alienation" that Nancy sees Christianity as demanding in the world. *Dis-Enclosure*, 10.

29. Ibid., 78–79.

30. Rilke, *Sonnets to Orpheus*, Sonnet 1,8: "*Nur im Raum der Rühmung darf die Klage/gehn . . .*" "Only in the realm of praising may Lament/go," 30–31.

31. Chrétien, "Retrospection," 127.

32. Friedrich Nietzsche, *The Gay Science*, trans. Walter Kaufmann (New York: Vintage Books, 1974), sec. 334.

33. Nancy, *Listening*, 7.

34. Cf. Nancy, *Dis-Enclosure*, 101–102: "Faith never consists—and this, no doubt, in any religious form—in making oneself believe something in the way that one might convince oneself that tomorrow one will be happy. Faith can only consist, by definition, in addressing what comes to pass, and it annihilates every belief, every economy, and any salvation. As the mystics know, without attaching any exaltation to this, faith consists in addressing or in being addressed to the other of the world, which is not 'an other world' except in the sense of being other than the world, the one that each time comes to an end without remission."

35. The use of Cusanus's terminology in this context I take from Chrétien, "The Unheard-of," in *The Ark of Speech*, 12.

36. Nancy, *Listening*, 1–2.

37. To suggest that we not be thus hermetic is not to argue that any rite should be open at any moment to anyone who comes; that ritual might require some form of knowledgeable acquaintance, some demonstrated fidelity, can be a matter of respect for disciplined attention and not simply of hostile exclusion.

38. Chrétien, *The Unforgettable and the Unhoped For*, 73.

6. Incarnate Experience
Anthony J. Steinbock

1. See Anthony J. Steinbock, *Phenomenology and Mysticism: The Verticality of Religious Experience* (Bloomington: Indiana University Press, 2007).

2. See Natalie Depraz's recent work *Le corps glorieux: Phenomenologie pratique de la* Philocalie *des Pères du desert et de Pères de l'Eglise*, which also treats the

phenomenon of the erotic. See also Amy Hollywood, *Sensible Ecstasy: Mysticism, Sexual Difference, and the Demands of History* (Chicago: University of Chicago Press, 2001); see Karmen MacKendrick, *Counterpleasures* (Albany: SUNY Press, 1999). See also Jeffery J. Kripal, *Roads of Excess, Palaces of Wisdom: Eroticism and Reflexivity in the Study of Mysticism* (Chicago: University of Chicago Press, 2001).

3. See Max Scheler, "Das Ressentiment im Aufbau der Moralen," in *Gesammelte Werke*, ed. Maria Scheler (Bern: Francke, 1955), 3:33–147. See also Margaret R. Miles, *Fullness of Life: Historical Foundations for a New Asceticism* (Philadelphia: Westminster Press, 1981).

4. Max Scheler, *Vom Ewigen im Menschen*, in *Gesammelte Werke*, 5:260.

5. By presentation, I mean a type of givenness that is peculiar to sensible and intellectual objects such that they are more or less dependent upon my power to usher things into appearance within a context of significance. Presentation is best known under the "subject: object" rubric and typical of perceptual experience. See my *Phenomenology and Mysticism*, especially the introduction.

6. See Anthony J. Steinbock, "Facticity and Insight as Problems of the Lifeworld: On Individuation," *Continental Philosophy Review* 37, no. 2 (2004): 241–261.

7. We might think here of the relation between tradition and reception in the German expression *Überlieferung* or the Hebrew term *kabbalah*.

8. Steinbock, *Phenomenology and Mysticism*.

9. *Collected Works of St. Teresa of Avila*, trans. Kieran Kavanaugh, O.C.D., and Otilio Rodriguez, O.C.D. (Washington, D.C.: ICS Publications, 1976), 1:19.10; hereafter, *Collected Works*. Because there are two different editions of the English collected works with different page numbers, I cite the chapter or section number, then the paragraph number.

10. See also ibid., 1:1, 25.2–25.5.

11. She continues: "Oh, God help me; and how He strengthens faith and increases love!" ibid., 1:25.18. Also: "While in this great affliction then (although at that time I had not begun to have any vision), these words alone were enough to take it away and bring me complete quiet: 'Do not fear, daughter; for I am, and I will not abandon you; do not fear.' It seems to me that from the way I felt many hours would have been necessary and no one would have been able to persuade me to be a peace." Ibid.

12. See also: "The Lord said to me: 'Don't be sad, for I shall give you a living book.' I was unable to understand why this was said to me, since I had not yet experienced any visions" Ibid., 1: 26.5.

13. Dov Baer Schneersohn, *Kuntres ha-hitpa 'alut* (Warsaw, 1876). Dobh Baer of Lubavitch, *Tract on Ecstasy*, trans. Louis Jacobs (London: Vallentine, Mitchell, 1963), 146; hereafter cited as *Tract*. When citing this work, I use the transcription provided by Jacobs, "Dobh Baer." In the text, however, I use the current form, "Dov Baer."

14. See Dobh Baer, *Tract*, 96. The term is transliterated and pronounced as *mitzraim/metzarim*.

15. Ibid., 118.

16. Rūzbihān Baqlī, *Unveiling of Secrets: Diary of a Sufi Master*, trans. Carl W. Ernst (Chapel Hill, N.C.: Parvardigar Press, 1997), §167; hereafter, *Unveiling*. References to *Unveiling of Secrets* are cited in the text itself according to the section headings supplied by Ernst. See Carl W. Ernst, *Rūzbihān Baqlī: Mysticism and the Rhetoric of Sainthood in Persian Sufism* (Richmond, UK: Curzon Press, 1996), 33.

17. Interestingly, he relates God eating, consuming, ingesting the prophets, messengers, saints, etc. (§57). "I said, 'God, you transcend eating and drinking. When I cried from regret, the angels drank my tears. What will they do with my weeping from longing and intimacy in witnessing? He (glory be to him) said, 'That is my wine'" (§146).

18. By "prayer," Saint Teresa means the experienced presence of the Holy (as in the "prayer of quiet" or the "prayer of interior delight," or the "prayer of union").

19. See Steinbock, *Phenomenology and Mysticism*, Chapter 2.

20. Saint Teresa writes: "Everything I see with my bodily eyes seems to be a dream and a mockery. What I have already seen with the eyes of my soul is what I desire; and since it is seen as something far away, this life is a death. In sum, the favor the Lord grants to whomever He gives visions like these is extraordinary." *Collected Works* 1:38.7.

In the Jewish tradition, similarly, hearing (*shimacha*) in Kabbalist teachings refers most profoundly to Understanding (*binah*). To say, "Oh Lord, I have learned of Your renown" (*Adonai shema'ati shimacha*), as the prophet Habakkuk writes (3:2), means literally, "Oh Lord, I have heard Your Hearing" or again, "Oh Lord, I have understood Your Understanding." According to Dov Baer, there are different ways of hearing. Some hear with great profundity, some hear and are moved to ecstasy quickly, but only superficially, etc. Dobh Baer, *Tract*, 147.

21. See, for example, "The Senses as Instruments of Communication," in *Color: Communication in Architectural Space*, ed. Gerhard Meerwein, Bettina Rodeck, and Frank H. Mahnke (Basel: Birkhäuser, 2007).

22. For a more detailed treatment of this problematic upon which this analysis draws, see *Phenomenology and Mysticism*, chapters 2 and 5.

23. Confirmation of experiences for Baqlī came in many forms: conformity to scripture, corroboration by a master or teacher, the joy expressed by all things (see *Unveiling*, §§ 44, 49, 114, 116). But by far the most predominant manner of confirmation arose in the form of intersubjective confirmations by saints, prophets, and the Prophet, either by Rūzbihān's observing the latter or by them having direct interactions with him. Often coming from the orientation of holiness (expressed as from the direction of Medina), they console him, bless him, long for him, welcome him; he is given among the chosen ones, and God even intervenes at times on his behalf so that others will respect him. See for example *Unveiling*, §§41, 44, 54, 68, 75, 83, 84, 103, 127, 136, 162, 171. See *Phenomenology and Mysticism*, Chapters 4 and 5.

24. See Sigmund Freud, *Three Case Histories*, ed. Philip Rieff (New York: Collier Books, 1963), esp. 103 ff.

25. See Daniel Paul Schreber, *Memoirs of My Nervous Illness*, trans. Ida Macalpine et al. (New York: New York Review of Books, 2000).

26. On the discernment of spirits, see Ignatius of Loyola, *The Spiritual Exercises and Selected Works*, ed. George E. Ganss, S.J., et al. (Mahwah, N.J.: Paulist Press, 1991), 113–214.

27. See Freud, *Three Case Histories*, esp. 133 ff.

28. Ibid., 117, 114.

29. See Anthony J. Steinbock *Home and Beyond: Generative Phenomenology After Husserl* (Evanston, Ill.: Northwestern University Press, 1995), esp. Section 3.

30. See the concern Talmudic rabbis express when relating the fates of four great Jewish sages who embarked on a mystical ascent to God. Rabbi Ben Azai, who so longed for God, immediately looked and died in his prime; Ben Abuyah, who remained intellectually confused, saw two gods instead of the One God and became an apostate; Ben Zoma, who had not reconciled ordinary life with his mystical experiences, gazed and went insane. Only Rabbi Akiba, who was perfectly balanced in the order of his heart and mind, entered *pardeis*, left the garden an enlightened saint, and later died a martyr at the hands of the Romans at the age of ninety. See Talmud, *Chagigah*, 14b.

7. The Time of Hospitality—Again
Kalpana Rahita Seshadri

1. Toward the end of *Aporias*, having engaged in a limpid close reading of Heidegger's notion of death as *Dasein*'s most proper possibility—an impossibility, thereby bringing every indivisible border between cultures, disciplines and concepts into crisis, Derrida says: "we will not deploy this aporetic 'logic' much longer. The principle of all the consequences that one can draw from it is fearsome [appears formidable]" (77). Derrida's phrase is *"paraît redoubtable."* Jacques Derrida, *Apories: Mourir—s'attendre aux "limites de la vérité"* (Paris: Editions Galilée, 1996), originally published in *Le passage des frontiers: Autour du travail de Jacques Derrida* (Paris: Editions Galilée, 1993). Translated as *Aporias* by Thomas Dutoit (Stanford: Stanford University Press, 1993). Page numbers are those of the 1996 French edition followed by the English translation, here 135, 77.

2. *Of Hospitality: Anne Dufourmantelle Invites Jacques Derrida to Respond*, trans. Rachel Bowlby (Stanford: Stanford University Press, 2000), 23. Originally published in 1997, the two lectures are based on a series of seminars led by Derrida in 1996.

3. Ibid, 25.

4. In *Adieu à Emmanuel Levinas* (trans. Pascale-Anne Brault and Michael Naas [Stanford: Stanford University Press, 1999]), Derrida says: "How is one to interpret this hospitality *in the name* of Levinas? . . . I will be guided by a question

that I will in the end leave in suspense. . . . It would concern, on first view, the relationships between an *ethics* of hospitality (an ethics *as* hospitality) and a *law* or a *politics* of hospitality, for example, in the tradition of what Kant calls the conditions of universal hospitality in *cosmopolitical law*: 'with a view to perpetual peace'" (19–20).

5. Derrida, *Of Hospitality*, 25.
6. Ibid., 75.
7. Ibid.
8. Derrida, *Aporias*, 30, 11.
9. Ibid., 31, 12.
10. Derrida, *Of Hospitality*, 77.
11. Ibid.
12. "Hostipitalty," trans. Barry Stocker with Forbes Morlock, *Angelaki: Journal of the Theoretical Humanities* 5, no. 3 (December 2000): 3–18.
13. Ibid., 12.
14. Derrida, *Of Hospitality*, 41.
15. Ibid., 135.
16. Ibid., 15.
17. Derrida, "Hostipitalty," 6.
18. All three biographies are available in James Robinson Smith's 1901 translation *The Earliest Lives of Dante* (New York: Henry Holt, 1901).
19. Villani in ibid., 99–100.
20. Derrida, "Hostipitalty," 6.
21. Ibid., 14.
22. The context of this remark, also richly pertinent to the concept of visitation, addresses the difference within languages. Just above the passage quoted, Derrida writes: "Babelization does not therefore wait for the multiplicity of languages. The identity of a language can only affirm itself as identity to itself by opening itself to the hospitality of a difference from itself or of a difference with itself. Condition of the self, such a difference *from* and *with* itself would then be its very thing . . . the stranger at home, the invited or the one who is called" Ibid., 28, 10.
23. Derrida, *Aporias*, 28–29, 10. For an elaboration of this theme of receiving, it is necessary to turn to Derrida's essay "*Khora*" first published in 1987, trans. Ian McLeod, included in *On the Name*, ed. Thomas Dutoit (Stanford: Stanford University Press, 1995). "It is difficult indeed, but perhaps we have not yet thought through what is meant by *to receive*, the receiving of the receptacle, what is said by *dekhomai, dekhomenon*. Perhaps it is from khora that we are beginning to learn it—to receive it, to receive from it what its name calls up. To receive it, if not to comprehend it, to conceive it" (95–96).
24. Ibid., 68, 34.
25. Ibid., 66–68, 33–34, emphasis added.
26. Derrida, "Hostipitalty," 6.
27. Ibid., 14.

28. Ibid.
29. Derrida, *Aporias*, 18, 3.
30. Ibid., 37, 16.
31. Ibid., 36, 15.
32. Ibid., 50, 23.
33. Ibid., 51, 23.
34. Derrida had made a previous reference to the river Styx without actually naming it. See ibid., 22, 6.
35. Derrida cites the following from Heidegger's *On the Way to Language*: "Mortals are they who can experience death as death [*den Tod als Tod erfahren können*]. Animals cannot do this. [*Das Tier vermag dies nicht.*] But animals cannot speak either. The essential relation between death and language flashes up before us, but remains still unthought [*ist aber noch ungedacht*]." Ibid., 69–70, 35. He also alludes in passing to Heidegger's 1929–30 course *The Fundamental Concepts of Metaphysics: World, Finitude, Solitude*, trans. William McNeill and Nicholas Walker (Bloomington: Indiana University Press, 1995), where the formulation of the "animal's poverty in world" is elaborated. See *Aporias*, 136, 78. Derrida's 1997 colloquium, recorded as "I don't know why we are doing this," takes up this text in detail. See chapter 4 of *The Animal That Therefore I Am*, trans. David Willis (New York: Fordham University Press, 2008). Another text where this course is taken up is the recently published second volume of his seminar on The Beast and the Sovereign: *Seminare: La bête et le souverain Vol II (2002–2003)* (Paris: Editions Galilée, 2010). See also Giorgio Agamben's *Language and Death: The Place of Negativity*, trans. Karen Pinkus and Michael Hardt (Minneapolis: University of Minnesota Press, 1991), and *The Open: Between Man and Animal*, trans. Kevin Attell (Stanford: Stanford University Press, 2003).
36. Derrida, *Aporias*, 84, 44.
37. Ibid., 110, 60.
38. "[E]verything is, to a certain extent tied to this corollary . . ." Ibid., 112, 61.
39. Ibid., 110, 60.
40. Ibid., 111, 61.
41. Ibid.
42. "I am here now reaching the end. If possible" Ibid., 113, 62.
43. Ibid., 115–116, 64.
44. Ibid., 117, 65.
45. "*Et cette référence est plus hétérologique que jamais, d'autres diraient aussi plus près que jamais des limites de la vérité, quand le s'attendre l'un l'autre a rapport à la mort, aux frontièrs de la mort, là où l'on s'attend l'un l'autre en sachant a priori, de façon absolument indéniable que, la vie étant toujours trop courte, l'un y attend l'autre, car l'un et l'autre n'y arrivent jamais ensemble, à ce rendez-vous; la mort est au fond le nom de la simultanéité impossible et d'une impossibilité que nous savons simultanément, à laquelle nous nous attendons pourtant ensemble, en même temps, ama comme on dit en grec: en même temps simultanément nous nous attendons à cette anachronie et à ce contretemps.*" Ibid., 117–118, 65.

46. Ibid., 121, 68.

47. Ibid.

48. I am quoting for the sake of simplicity from the Macquarrie and Robinson translation of *Being and Time*, 294.

49. Derrida chooses not to refer here to the theory of potentiality as always already constituted by impotentiality that Heidegger expounds in his 1931 seminar *Aristotle's Metaphysics θ 1–3: On the Essence and Actuality of Force*, original publication 1981, trans. Walter Brogan and Peter Warnek (Bloomington: Indiana University Press), 1995. See also Walter Brogan's *Heidegger and Aristotle: The Twofoldeness of Being* (Albany: SUNY Press, 2005). For a discussion of the problem of translating the Greek terms *dunamis* and *energeia* by "potentiality" and "actuality," see also William J. Richardson, *Heidegger Through Phenomenology to Thought*, 4th ed. (New York: Fordham University Press, 2003), 318.

50. Derrida, *Aporias*, 121–122, 68. Note that it is Derrida's decision here to not acknowledge the relative familiarity of this proposition. Instead he says that the idea of "the most proper possibility as the possibility of an impossibility" defies common sense and is a logical contradiction. Truth now, he says, "is no longer measured in terms of the logical form of judgment" (124, 70).

51. The crux of Derrida's reading proceeds thus: "In the following sentence the figure of unveiling, that is, the *truth* of this syntax, makes the impossible be, in the genitive form, the complement of the nun or the aporetic supplement of the possible (possibility *of* the impossible), but also the manifestation of the possible *as* impossible, the "as" (*als*) becoming the enigmatic figure of this monstrous coupling: 'The more unveiledly this possibility gets understood [*Je unverhüllter diese Moglichkeit verstanden wird*], the more purely does the understanding penetrate into it [advances into, *dringt vor*] *as the possibility of the impossibility of any existence at all* [underlined by Heidegger: *als die der Unmöglichkeit der Existenz überhaupt*].' The *als* means that the possibility is both unveiled and penetrated *as* impossibility. It is not only the paradoxical possibility of a possibility of impossibility: it is possibility *as impossibility*." Ibid., 124–125, 70.

52. Ibid., 125–126, 71.

8. The Null Basis-Being of a Nullity, Or Between Two Nothings: Heidegger's Uncanniness
Simon Critchley

1. Martin Heidegger, *Being and Time*, trans. J. Macquarrie and E. Robinson (Oxford: Blackwell, 1962). References are to the pagination of the German original, *Sein und Zeit*, given in the margins of the English translation.

2. Ibid., 269/314.

3. Ibid, 271. Here the call is a little like Socrates's *daimon*, which calls him back at times in the Platonic dialogues.

4. Ibid, 273.

5. Ibid, 271.

6. Ibid, 275.
7. Ibid, 281.
8. Ibid, 276–277.
9. Lacan, *The Ethics of Psychoanalysis*, trans. D. Porter (New York: Norton, 1992), 270–287.
10. Ibid, 277.
11. Ibid., 277–278.
12. Ibid., 280.
13. Simon Critchley, "Universal Shylockery: Money and Morality in *The Merchant of Venice*," *Diacritics* 34, no.1 (Spring 2004): 3–17.
14. Heidegger, *Being and Time*, 289.
15. Ibid., 284.
16. Ibid., 323.
17. Ibid., 285.
18. Ibid., 286–287.
19. Heidegger, *Introduction to Metaphysics*, trans. R. Mannheim (New Haven: Yale University Press, 1959), 121/158.
20. Heidegger, *Being and Time*, 287.
21. Ibid., 289.
22. Samuel Beckett, *Molloy* (New York: Grove Press, 2006), 79.

9. Heidegger and the Strangeness of Being
William J. Richardson

1. See Martin Heidegger, preface to W. Richardson, *Heidegger: Through Phenomenology to Thought*, 4th ed. (New York: Fordham University Press, 2003).
2. Martin Heidegger, *Being and Time*, translated by J. Macquarrie and E. Robinson (London: SCM, 1962), 59/35.
3. Ibid., 330/284.
4. Ibid., 237/192.
5. Ibid., 330/284.
6. Ibid., 330/284.
7. Ibid., 332–333/286–287.
8. Ibid., 32/12.
9. Martin Heidegger, *Elucidations of Hölderlin's Poetry*, trans. K. Hoeller (Amherst, N.Y.: Humanity Books, 2000): "Homecoming/To Kindred Ones," 23–49. "Remembrance," 101–173.
10. Sophocles, *Antigone*, trans. H. Lloyd-Jones (Cambridge, Mass.: Harvard University Press, 1994); Martin Heidegger, *Hölderlin's Hymn "The Ister"* (Bloomington: Indiana University Press, 1984).
11. Sophocles, cited in Heidegger, *Hölderlin's Hymn*, 58–59.
12. Ibid., 103.
13. Ibid., 64.
14. Ibid., 103.
15. Ibid.

16. Ibid., 112–113.
17. Ibid., 115.
18. Ibid., 117.
19. Ibid.
20. Sophocles, *Antigone*, lines 1–6.
21. Sophocles, *Antigone*, cited in Heidegger, *Hölderlin's Hymn*, 116.
22. Ibid., 117.
23. Heidegger, *Being and Time*, 311/266.
24. Heidegger, *Hölderlin's Hymn*, 121.

10. Progress in Spirit: Freud and Kristeva on the Uncanny
Vanessa Rumble

1. Julia Kristeva, *Strangers to Ourselves*, trans. Leon S. Roudiez (New York: Columbia University Press, 1991), 169. *Étrangers á nous-mêmes* was first published in 1989 in Paris (Fayard).
2. Ibid., 192.
3. See Charles Shepherdson's lucid questioning of Kristeva's historical treatment of narcissism in "Telling Tales of Love: Philosophy, Literature and Psychoanalysis," *Diacritics* 30, no. 1 (2000): 89–105. Shepherdson highlights the oddity of Kristeva's juxtaposition of (1) a historical narrative that attempts to locate narcissism in the linear progression of time and (2) the psychoanalytic circling of an (uncanny) "event" that cannot be dated, since it gives rise to the subject.
4. *Strangers*, 191. Interestingly, Kristeva closes with the seemingly gratuitous—and incorrect—observation: "There is no mention of foreigners in the *Unheimliche*." In fact, Freud's "The Uncanny" (1919) is rife with references to foreign places, foreign women, and foreign tongues. See Robin Lydenberg's rich reading of the text in her "Freud's Uncanny Narratives," *PMLA* 112m no. 4 (1997): 1072–1086.
5. *Strangers*, 192.
6. Ibid., 3.
7. Sigmund Freud, *Introductory Lectures on Psychoanalysis*, ed. and trans. James Strachey, in *The Standard Edition of the Complete Psychological Works of Sigmund Freud* (London: Hogarth Press, 1963), 15:145–147. Henceforth all citations of Freud's writings in English are from this edition will be cited by title and volume number in the *SE*.
8. See Nietzsche on the consequences of abandoning belief in the privileged status accorded humanity: "all power structures of the old society have been exploded—all of them are based on lies: there will be wars the like of which have never yet been seen on earth." Friedrich Nietzsche, *Ecce Homo*, in *Basic Writings of Nietzsche*, trans. Walter Kaufmann (New York: Random House, 2000), 783.
9. In "L'étranger," Roland Barthes's review of Kristeva's *Semiotike. Recherches pour une sémanalyse*, in *La quinzaine littéraire* 94 (1–15 May 1970), 1–15.
10. Rudi Visker, "The Strange(r) Within Me," *Ethical Perspectives: Journal of the European Ethics Network* 12, no. 4 (2005): 428.

11. Richard Kearney sees a disturbing likeness between Kristeva's notion of abjection, which can be said to underlie this "cosmopolitan" vision, Lacan/ Žižek's Monstrous Real, and Lyotard's reading of the aesthetic sublime. Kearney groups these notions under the rubric "postmodern sublime" and cautions against the "failure to distinguish adequately between different *kinds* of otherness." If the embrace of the "other within" is understood to call for the wholesale demolition of the distinction between self and Other, what basis remains for judgment? In Kristeva's problematizing of the categories of self and other, of native and stranger, Kearney sees the risk of despair and paralysis, the failure of ethics to guide action. Richard Kearney, *Strangers, Gods, and Monsters* (New York: Routledge, 2003), 108n.

12. See Suzanne Clark and Kathleen Hulle, "Cultural Strangeness and the Subject in Crisis," in *Julia Kristeva Interviews*, ed. Ross Mitchell Guberman (New York: Columbia University Press, 1999), 41.

13. Freud, "The Uncanny," *SE* 17:217–256.

14. In spite of Freud's explicit dismissal of the question of the meaning of human existence ("the idea of life having a purpose stands or falls with the religious system"), the entirety of *Civilization and Its Discontents* is concerned with understanding the genesis of the moral law in the individual and in society, as well as the advantages and disadvantages of these strictures. The question of purpose, of the "use and abuse," of the whole apparatus of social regulation is never far removed from these reflections. Freud, *Civilization and Its Discontents*, *SE* 21:75.

15. Freud, *Totem and Taboo*, *SE* 13:88.

16. Freud, *Moses and Monotheism*, *SE* 23:50.

17. Ibid., 114.

18. Ibid.: "the pre-eminence given to intellectual labours [by the Jews] . . . has helped to check the brutality and the tendency to violence which are apt to appear where the development of muscular strength is the popular ideal." With the first draft of the work written in 1934, the year after Hitler's *Machtergreifung* and the year prior to the adoption of the Nuremberg laws, the gist is plain. Michael F. Mach addressed Freud's numerous subterranean references to the Nazi politics of force in "Freud's *Moses and Monotheism* in its Historical Setting," Boston College lecture, February 16, 2010.

19. Kristeva likewise engages in an analysis of anti-Semitism: Her *Powers of Horror* is in large part devoted to an analysis of anti-Semitism. Her analysis echoes Freud's suggestions in *Moses and Monotheism*, though no citation of the work is made. See Kristeva, *Powers of Horror: An Essay on Abjection*, trans. Leon S. Roudiez (Columbia: Columbia University Press, 1882), chap. 9, and Diane Jonte-Pace *in Speaking the Unspeakable: Religion, Misogyny, and the Uncanny Mother in Freud's Cultural Texts* (Berkeley: University of California Press, 2001) 109.

20. Freud views the "spirit world" as either (1) remnants of early stages of development, in which the ego itself remains nascent, its outlines shifting, or (2)

projections of unwanted affects, a psychic maneuver resulting from the belief of children and neurotics in the omnipotence of their (hostile) wishes and the threat which they in consequence pose to others and themselves. Freud, "The Uncanny," 236–237.

21. This occurs most famously in the opening chapter of *Civilization and Its Discontents*, where the mother/infant bond, under the heading of the "oceanic feeling," is weighed as a source of religious feeling, only to be summarily brushed aside: "I cannot think of any need in childhood as strong as the need for a father's protection. Thus the part played by the oceanic feeling, which might seek something like the restoration of limitless narcissism, is ousted from a place in the foreground." Freud, *Civilization and Its Discontents*, 72.

22. Freud, *Group Psychology and the Analysis of the Ego*, SE 18:130.

23. Jean Laplanche, "Time and the Other," trans. Luke Thurston, in *Essays on Otherness*, ed. John Fletcher (London: Routledge, 1999), 247.

24. Freud's concern with the Oedipal complex is generally viewed as "the" obstacle to his appreciation of the role of primary narcissism in later object relations. I argue Freud's evolving interpretation of Oedipal dynamics, particularly in the wake of *Beyond the Pleasure Principle*, integrates these early relations within the Oedipal.

25. Freud, *Beyond the Pleasure Principle*, SE 18: chap. 6, esp. 52–53, and *Civilization and Its Discontents*, 118–119.

26. Freud remarks in a letter to Lou Andreas-Salome that formulating his theory of a death drive forced him to "read all kinds of things relevant to it, e.g., Schopenhauer, for the first time." *Sigmund Freud and Lou Andreas-Salomé: Letters*, ed. Ernst Pfeiffer (New York: Harcourt Brace Jovanovich, 1972), 99. Christopher Young and Andrew Brook argue for an early and pervasive, if indirect, familiarity of Freud with Schopenhauer's work in "Schopenhauer and Freud," *International Journal of Psychoanalysis* 75 (1994): 110–118. In the young Nietzsche's *Birth of Tragedy*, Schopenhauer's categories reappear, of course, as the Dionysian urge to fuse with others in defiance of the serene Apollonian embrace of the principle of individuation. Nietzsche soon came to regret his reliance, in the *Birth of Tragedy*, on the metaphysical duality of appearance and reality posited by Kant. The Dionysian was credited with noumenal reality, that is, with ultimate truth, in contrast to the ephemeral fantasy of the Apollonian. Nietzsche, *Birth of Tragedy*, ed. Raymond Guess and Ronald Speirs (Cambridge: Cambridge University Press, 1999).

27. Freud, *Beyond the Pleasure Principle*, 39.

28. Freud, *Civilization and Its Discontents*, 122.

29. Ibid., 65.

30. "At the height of being in love, the boundary between ego and object threatens to melt away. Against all the evidence of his senses, a man who is in love declares that 'I' and 'you' are one, and is prepared to behave as if it were a fact." Ibid., 66.

31. Jean Laplanche argues that the elements brought together by Freud under the heading of the death drive require not only analysis and clarification, but first

and foremost interpretation. Laplanche sees the theory of the death drive itself as a sort of compulsion or *Zwang* in Freud's thought, one analogous to "the oracular message irrevocably determining the destiny of Oedipus." See *Life and Death in Psychoanalysis*, trans. Jeffrey Mehlman (Baltimore: Johns Hopkins University Press, 1976), 110.

32. Freud, *Beyond the Pleasure Principle*, 54.

33. Freud, *Civilization and Its Discontents*, 119–121.

34. "If only we could succeed in relating these two polarities to each other and in deriving one from the other!" Freud, *Beyond the Pleasure Principle*, 53.

35. Freud, *Group Psychology*, 105.

36. Ibid. See Bennett Simon's and Rachel B. Blass's helpful discussion in "The Development and Vicissitudes of Freud's Ideas on the Oedipal Complex," in *The Cambridge Companion to Freud*, ed. Jerome Neu (Cambridge: Cambridge University Press, 1991), 161–174.

37. Ibid.

38. Ewa Ziarek, "The Uncanny Style of Kristeva's Critique of Nationalism," *Postmodern Culture* 5, no. 2 (1995).

39. Freud, *Civilization and Its Discontents*, 70.

40. Lacan's eventual recognition that the instauration of the symbolic order always leaves an uncanny remainder is anticipated in the prominent role accorded identification in Freud's reading of individual and group psychology. The "law of the father" defines this space of fruitful conflict; it does not resolve it.

41. "I had not only completed the draft of 'Beyond the Pleasure Principle' . . . but I also took up the little thing about the 'uncanny' again, and, with a simple-minded idea [*Einfall*], I attempted a [psychoanalytical] foundation for group psychology." *The Correspondence of Sigmund Freud and Sándor Ferenczi, vol. 2: 1914–1919*, trans. Peter T. Hoffer, ed. Ernst Falzeder and Eva Brabant (Cambridge, Mass.: Harvard University Press, 1999), letter 813.

42. This is similar to the twin dangers of tyranny and barbarism depicted by Schiller in his *Letters on the Aesthetic Education of Man*.

43. See Freud's distinction between "retrospective" screen memories and those that have "pushed forward" in "Screen Memories," *SE* 3:320. See also Laplanche's remarks on *Nachträglichkeit* in Cathy Caruth, "An Interview with Jean Laplanche," in *Postmodern Culture* 11, no. 2 (2001): §7–23.

44. Charles Shepherdson, *Lacan and the Limits of Language* (New York: Fordham University Press, 2008), 108. Shepherdson's reference is to Maurice Blanchot, *The Writing of the Disaster*, trans. Ann Smock (Lincoln: University of Nebraska Press, 1986), 1.

45. Freud, *Introductory Lectures on Psychoanalysis*, 108.

46. Freud, *Group Psychology*, 130, emphasis mine.

47. Ibid., 131.

48. Ibid., 113–114. See Shepherdson's reading of this phenomenon in "The Place of Memory in Psychoanalysis," in *Lacan and The Limits of Language*, 170.

49. In *Totem and Taboo*, the riddle concerns the mysterious conjunction of the two pillars of totemism: (1) the prohibition of incest and the associated regulation of sexual relations among tribes and subtribes, and (2) the prohibition against the killing or eating of the totem animal. The riddle remains unresolved throughout the greater part of the text, guides the interpretation of the extant secondary literature, and introduces a suspense in the reader which sets the stage for the dramatic introduction of the Oedipal complex.

50. Ibid., 132.

51. See Richard Bernstein's helpful discussion of and contribution to this debate in *Freud and The Legacy of Moses* (Cambridge: Cambridge University Press, 1998), 46–52, 104–109.

52. Ibid., 138.

53. Ibid., 132. Particularly in works preceding *The Ego and the Id* (1923), Freud tends to view the loving feelings toward the father as playing a role in "the repression of oedipal wishes, but not as oedipal per se." See Bennett Simon and Rachel B. Blass, "The Development and Vicissitudes of Freud's Ideas on the Oedipal Complex," in *The Cambridge Companion to Freud*, ed. Jerome Neu (Cambridge: Cambridge University Press, 1991), 161. As was seen in our reading of *Group Psychology*, the integration of this primal identification within the Oedipal structure shifted both its temporal frame and the depth of its anthropological significance.

54. Ibid., 105.

55. Note the difference between Freud's account here and the one offered by Nietzsche in Part 1, §11 of the *On the Genealogy of Morality*, trans. Carol Diethe (Cambridge: Cambridge University Press, 2006), where morality is said to arise from internalized aggression.

56. Freud's protest against the practicability (and prudence) of the exalted ideal of loving unknown "neighbors"—and enemies—as one's "own" comes to mind, as well as his scathing assessment of the historical record: Christianity's valorization of universal brotherhood extends all too often (in practice) no further than to the members of its own coterie, while Christendom's vigorous scapegoating of Jews gives the lie to its minimization of evil.

57. Freud, *Civilization and Its Discontents*, 68.

58. Ibid.

59. Freud, "The Uncanny," 236.

60. There, the uncanny is said to reflect the return of the infant's/child's belief in omnipotence of thought and the corresponding suspension of the "sharply demarcated ego-feeling" described above. Though Freud does not emphasize the role of the infant's first caregiver(s) in sustaining this early belief in omnipotence, object relations theorists, and most particularly Winnicott, will do so.

61. Similarly, Romain Rolland's advocacy of socialism as providing the conditions for peace is not shared by Freud.

62. Freud, *Civilization and Its Discontents*, 72.

63. This claim occurs in the midst of Freud's speculations concerning the source of the religious impulse. Freud specifically rejects the notion that religious

feeling has its origin in the longing for "restoration of a limitless narcissism," opting instead for the view that it is first and foremost longing for a specifically paternal protection against the power of fate. Freud nonetheless feels compelled to grant in the next breath that the desire for a return to "the oceanic feeling" may have become "connected with religion later on" (*Civilization and Its Discontents*, 72). His attempt to locate a principal source of religious feeling in maternal or paternal longing is puzzling given his recognition (seven years earlier, in *Group Psychology*) that the infant's earliest needs could not involve awareness of sexual differentiation. *Group Psychology*, 106.

64. Freud, *Civilization and Its Discontents*, 103–104.

65. See Sara Beardsworth's illuminating analysis of ethics, trauma, and futurity in *Moses and Monotheism* and Kristeva's *Strangers to Ourselves*. We return later to her rigorous questioning of what if any "ethics of psychoanalysis" is proffered in these two works: "The example of Freud's Moses—the (intolerable) tones of a foreign God opening up the Hebraic tradition through their impact on Moses's followers, and the consequences of that impact—displays both real otherness and a certain future in the phenomenon of the return of the repressed." *Julia Kristeva: Psychoanalysis and Modernity* (Albany: State University of New York Press, 2004), 200.

66. Freud, *Moses and Monotheism*, 24.

67. Ibid., 22.

68. Ibid., 41.

69. Ibid., 129.

70. Ibid., 51. Freud adds, enigmatically, "It is honour enough to the Jewish people that they could preserve such a tradition and produce men who gave it a voice—even though the initiative to it came from outside, from a great foreigner."

71. The nature of the "progress" that Freud attributes to the Jewish people seems an "ocean" away from the ethics that Kristeva will associate with psychoanalysis. The Freudian equation of progress/spirit with intellectuality and instinctual renunciation is in stark opposition to Kristeva's concern with an ethics of psychoanalysis rooted in the experience of the uncanny and its connection to early maternal relations. The similarity between the two can be glimpsed, however, in the emergence of certain recurrent themes in *Moses and Monotheism* that nonetheless are not accounted for within Freud's own narrative. I have in mind here Freud's presentation of his technique of dream analysis in his *Introductory Lectures on Psychoanalysis*—a technique that can of course be applied to Freud's own work. The first dictum is to bracket the explicit "plot" of the dream, its overt narrative, and then to attend, piece by piece, to the isolated images and events. Freud, *Introductory Lectures on Psychoanalysis*, SE 15:181.

72. Freud claims that monotheism returns in an increasingly "purified" form in the course of history. Note Freud's inversion of Nazi propaganda: Freud's purification involves a reappropriation of the Mosaic monotheism which founded Jewish history and for which the latter has served as a conduit. Hitler's version of *Judenrein* was different.

73. The nature of this reciprocity may be usefully likened to the relation of Lacan's law-bound symbolic domain and the realm of the real. See Charles Shepherdson, "The Intimate Alterity of the Real," in *Lacan and the Limits of Language* (New York: Fordham University Press, 2008), 1–49. In his working through of Lévi-Strauss's and Derrida's thinking on the incest taboo, Shepherdson remarks, "the scandalous or paradoxical character of the incest prohibition is not an ambiguity to be eliminated, but must rather be taken as the actual positive content of the concept itself; it suggests that, properly speaking, the incest taboo must be situated prior to the division between nature and culture, . . . 'as the condition of their possibility.'" Ibid., 19. Shepherdson's citation is of Derrida's "Structure, Sign, and Play in the Discourse of Human Sciences," in *Writing and Difference*, trans. Alan Bass (Chicago: University of Chicago Press, 1978), 283.

74. "Freud . . . argues that the murder of the primal father is the formative event not only for religion, but for the origin of society and ethics. It is at once disturbing and humbling to realize that this act of violence is a condition for the very genesis of religion and ethics." Bernstein, *Freud and the Legacy of Moses*, 100–101.

75. *Sigmund Freud and Andreas-Salome: Letters*, 204–207. Quoted by Richard Bernstein in *Freud and the Legacy of Moses*, 119–120.

76. "Freud, in the passages we have cited, is no longer the disinterested psychoanalyst seeking to understand the origin and nature of Jewish monotheism, but speaking in his own voice as a passionate "godless *Jew*," taking pride in the spiritual and intellectual power of his *own* tradition." Bernstein, *Freud and the Legacy of Moses*, 35.

77. I am indebted to Sara Beardsworth for her cogent discussion of the shared "vision and project" of these works, as well as to her critical assessment of Kristeva's ethics in *Strangers*. See her *Julia Kristeva: Psychoanalysis and Modernity*, 55–111, 169–206.

78. Kristeva, *Tales of Love*, trans. Leon S. Roudiez (New York: Columbia University Press, 1987) 21. Kristeva's reading of "On Narcissism" is confirmed by a remarkable passage in Freud's *Group Psychology and the Analysis of the Ego* where his attempt to distinguish between identification and "extreme developments of being in love" is repeatedly confounded. Freud, *Group Psychology*, 113–114.

79. Freud, "On Narcissism: An Introduction," 34.

80. *Tales of Love*, 22.

81. Ibid., 24.

82. In Kant's *Critique of Judgment*, the concept of "rational ideas" of God, freedom. and immortality, which can never be adequately represented by sensibility, is complemented by the oft-neglected notion of aesthetic ideas, in which the imagination presents a superabundance of sense which no concept of understanding can capture. It is the feeling associated with such an idea, Kant claims, which "connects language, which otherwise would be mere letters, with spirit." Immanuel Kant, *The Critique of Judgment*, trans. Werner S. Pluhar (Indianapolis: Hackett, 1987) 185.

83. In accordance with Freud's analysis in *Group Psychology*, 108.
84. Kristeva, *Tales of Love*, 28.
85. Ibid., 25–26.
86. Ibid., 28.
87. Beardsworth, *Julia Kristeva*, 203.

11. The Uncanny Strangeness of Maternal Election: Levinas and Kristeva on Parental Passion
Kelly Oliver

1. Sigmund Freud, "The Uncanny," trans. James Strachey, *The Standard Edition of the Complete Psychological Works of Sigmund Freud* (London: Hogarth Press, 1919), 13:224. Hereafter abbreviated as *SE*.

2. Ibid., 244–245, 247–249.

3. See Sigmund Freud, *Totem and Taboo*, trans. James Strachey (New York: Norton, 1913); see Kelly Oliver, *Animal Lessons: How They Teach Us to Be Human* (New York: Columbia University Press, 2009), 247–276.

4. See *SE*, 13:243.

5. See *SE*, 13:245.

6. Emmanuel Levinas, *Totality and Infinity*, trans. Alphonso Lingis (Pittsburgh: Duquesne University Press, 1969), 254.

7. Ibid., 266.
8. Ibid., 267.
9. Ibid.
10. Ibid., 268.
11. Ibid., 272.
12. Ibid., 269.
13. Ibid., 271.
14. Ibid., 269.
15. Ibid., 278.
16. Ibid., 273.

17. Kelly Oliver, "Fatherhood and the Promise of Ethics," *Diacritics: A Review of Contemporary Criticism* 27, no. 1 (1997): 45–58.

18. See Julia Kristeva, *Hatred and Forgiveness: Powers and Limits of Psychoanalysis III*, trans. Janine Herman (New York: Columbia University Press, 2011). Pagination was not available at the time of publication of the present book.

19. Julia Kristeva, *This Incredible Need to Believe*, trans. Beverley Bie Brahic (New York: Columbia University Press, 2009), 61. See Julia Kristeva, "A Father Is Being Beaten to Death," paper presented in 2006.

20. Kristeva, *Hatred and Forgiveness*.
21. Ibid.
22. Ibid.
23. For a discussion of Kristeva on animals, see Oliver, *Animal Lessons*.
24. Julia Kristeva, *Powers of Horror*, trans. Leon Roudiez (New York: Columbia University Press, 1982).

25. Julia Kristeva, *The Sense and Non-Sense of Revolt*, trans. Jeanine Herman (New York: Columbia University Press, 2000).

26. Kristeva, *This Incredible Need to Believe* and "A Father is Being Beaten to Death."

27. Kristeva, *Hatred and Forgiveness*.

28. Ibid.

29. Ibid.

30. Kristeva, *The Portable Kristeva*, ed. Kelly Oliver (New York: Columbia University Press, 2002), 10.

31. Kristeva, *Hatred and Forgiveness*. Subsequent quotations are from this book.

12. Being, the Other, the Stranger
Jean Greisch

1. See J. Derrida, *De la grammatologie* (Paris: Minuit, 1967), 145–202, and *Marges de la philosophie* (Paris: Minuit, 1972), i–xxv.

2. See C. Lévi-Strauss, *Structural Anthropology* (New York: Doubleday, 1967), 2:328–332. This concept of ethnocentrism should be compared with Roger Bastide's research on acculturation; see R. Bastide, *Le prochain et le lointain* (Paris: Cujas, 1970); see also C. Geertz, "The Impact of the Concept of Culture on the Concept of Man," in *The Interpretation of Cultures* (New York: Basic Books, 1973), 33–54.

3. Geertz, "Impact," 15.

4. Ibid., 26, quoting M. Merleau-Ponty, *Signes* (Paris: Plon, 1960), 138.

5. Lévi Strauss, *Structural Anthropology*, 2:33–43.

6. Quoted, ibid., 34.

7. Quoted, ibid., 35.

8. Ibid.

9. Ibid., 36.

10. Ibid., 328.

11. Ibid.

12. F. Nietzsche, *Also Sprach Zarathustra* (Stuttgart: Reclam, 1964), 111.

13. E. Levinas, *De Dieu qui vient à l'idée* (Paris: Vrin, 1982), 173.

14. Ibid., 178.

15. The true revolution in Levinas's thought is this reversal of the value of the proximity-intimacy from *for* the other into persecution *by* the other: "in proximity the absolutely other, the stranger whom I have 'neither conceived nor given birth to,' I already have on my arms, already bear, according to the Biblical formula, 'in my breast as the nurse bears the nurseling' (Numbers 11, 12). He has no other place, is not autochthonous, is uprooted, without a country, not an inhabitant, exposed to the cold and the heat of the seasons. To be reduced to having recourse to me is the homelessness or strangeness of the neighbor. It is incumbent on me." *Autrement qu'être ou au-delà de l'essence* (The Hague: Nijhoff, 1972), 115–116.

16. *Ethique et Infini* (Paris: Fayard, 1982), 90–91.

17. "The epiphany that is produced as a face is not constituted as are all other beings, precisely because it 'reveals' infinity. Signification is infinity, that is, the Other." *Totality and Infinity: An Essay on Exteriority*, trans. Alphonso Lingis (Pittsburgh: Duquesne University Press, 1969), 207. For a possible "aesthetic" verification of this "ethical" analysis, see G. Deleuze, *Cinéma 1. L'image-mouvement* (Paris: Minuit, 1983), 125–144.

18. *De Dieu qui vient à l'idée*, 258–265.

19. Ibid., 261.

20. Ibid., 31.

21. Ibid., 32.

22. Ibid., 188.

23. See St. Breton, "L'un et l'etre. Réflexions sur la différence méontologique," *Revue philosophique de Louvain* 83 (1985): 5–23.

24. See M. Theunissen, *Der Andere, Studien zur Sozialontologie der Gegenwart*, 2nd ed. (Berlin: De Gruyter, 1977), 413–438. The same author forcefully underscores that all Heideggerian analysis of being-with-the-other presupposes the findings of Husserlian research on the status of intersubjectivity. Ibid., 157–186.

25. See A. Schütz and Th. Luckmann, *Strukturen der Lebenswelt* (Frankfurt: Suhrkamp, 1979), 1:87–124.

26. M. Heidegger, *Sein und Zeit* (Tübingen: Niemeyer, 1967), 16: "*Dasein* is ontically 'closest' to itself and ontologically farthest; but pre-ontologically it is surely not a stranger."

27. See S. Freud, *Das Unheimliche* (1919), in *Gesammelte Werke*, 12:229–268.

28. Heidegger, *Sein und Zeit*, 43–44: "But what is closer to me than myself? . . . I at least have difficulty at this point, and I find my own self hard to grasp: I have become for myself a soil which is cause of difficulty and much sweat."

29. Ibid., 183.

30. Ibid., 188.

31. Ibid.

32. Ibid., 189.

33. For a detailed analysis of this "hestiological" economy, I refer to chapter IV of my work *La parole heureuse: Martin Heidegger entre les choses et les mots* (Paris: Beauchesne, 1987), and my essay: "Am 'Herdfeuer des Seyns': die 'Geistesgegenwart' und ihre Voraussetzungen," in *Die Gegenwart des Gegenwärtigen. Festschrift für P. Gerd Haeffner SJ zum 65. Geburtstag*, ed. Margarethe Drewsen and Mario Fischer (Freiburg: K. Alber, 2006), 110–127.

34. M. Heidegger, *Hölderlins Hymne "Der Ister"* (Frankfurt: Klostermann, 1984), 182: "The Ister *is* that river in which already at the source the stranger is a guest and present, in whose flow the dialogue of one's own and the stranger constantly speaks." ["*Der Ister ist jener Strom, bei dem schon an der Quelle das Fremde zu Gast und gegenwärtig ist, in dessen Strömen die Zwiesprache des Eigenen und Fremden ständig spricht.*"]

35. Ibid., 60.
36. Ibid., 118.
37. On this topic see my essay, "'Who Stands Fast?' Do Philosophers Make Good Resistants?" in *Bonhoeffer and Continental Thought*, ed. B. Gregor and J. Zimmermann (Bloomington: Indiana University Press, 2009), 84–101.
38. "*Der Strom ist die Ortschaft der Wanderschaft. Der Strom ist die Wanderschaft der Ortschaft.*" Heidegger, *Hölderlins Hymne*, 39, 52.
39. See J. F. Mattei, "Le chiasme heideggérien ou la mise-à-l'écart de la philosophie," in *La métaphysique à la limite*, ed. D. Janicaud and F. Mattei (Paris: Presses Universitaires de France, 1983), 49–162.
40. M. Heidegger, *Aus der Erfahrung des Denkens*, 2nd ed. (Pfullingen: Neske, 1965), 23. "Letter to Richardson," in W. Richardson, *Heidegger: Through Phenomenology to Thought* (The Hague: Nijhoff, 1963), vii–xxiii.
41. "*Der Strom bringt . . . den Menschen ins Eigene und behält ihn im Eigenen.*" Heidegger, *Hölderlins Hymne*, 23.
42. Ibid., 51.
43. "Logos is the ambiguousness of being and entities: the primordial amphibology." *Autrement qu'être*, 54.
44. M. Heidegger, *Was heisst Denken?* (Tübingen: Niemeyer, 1971), 1–8.
45. Heidegger, *Hölderlins Hymne*, 60–61.
46. Ibid., 71 and 83–91.
47. Ibid., 84.
48. For the use and measurement of the category of stranger relative to the hermeneutical problem of historical understanding, I refer to the judicious remarks of P. Ricoeur in *Temps et Récit III* (Paris: Seuil, 1985), 203–227.
49. For a more detailed analysis of the Heideggerian conception of translation, I refer to my study "Faire entendre l'Origine en son pur surgissement: Hölderlin et Heidegger," in *Hölderlin, vu de France* (Tübingen: Gunter Narr, 1987), 113–128.
50. Heidegger, *Hölderlins Hymne*, 80.
51. Ibid., 133.
52. "*Das Dichten ist ein sagendes Finden des Seins.*" Ibid., 149.
53. Ibid., 140.
54. Ibid., 156.
55. Ibid., 173.
56. See E. Levinas, "L'être et l'autre," in *Sens et existence: Hommage à Paul Ricoeur* (Paris: Seuil, 1975), 28.
57. "Art creates self-distance . . . perhaps poetry, like art, advances with a self-forgetting I toward the uncanny and alien, and then sets itself—but where? but at what place? but with what? but as what?—free again?" [*Kunst schafft Ich-Ferne . . . vielleicht geht die Dichtung, wie die Kunst, mit einem selbstvergessenen Ich zu jenem Unheimlichen und Fremden, und setzt sich—doch wo? doch an welchem Ort? doch womit? doch als was?—wieder frei?*] P. Celan, *Gesammelte Werke* (Frankfurt: Suhrkamp, 2000), 3:193.

58. Ibid., 195.
59. Ibid.
60. Ibid., 190.
61. Ibid., 197.
62. Ibid., 195.
63. *"Wirklichkeit ist nicht, Wirklichkeit will gesucht und gewonnen sein."* Heidegger, *Hölderlins Hymne*, 168.
64. Ibid., 149.
65. P. Celan, *Speech-Grille and Selected Poems*, trans. J. Neugroschel (New York: E. P. Dutton, 1971), 209.

13. Words of Welcome: Hospitality in the Philosophy of Emmanuel Levinas
Jeffrey Bloechl

1. E. Levinas, *Totality and Infinity: An Essay on Exteriority*, trans. A. Lingis (Pittsburgh: Duquesne University Press, 1998), 172. Throughout this essay, I will uniformly employ "Other" for instances of a singular personal alterity. This calls for occasional modification of translations.

2. Ibid., 155. Note that Woman is represented here by the impersonal *autre*, albeit as capitalized.

3. Ibid.

4. Ibid., 24–25, note.

5. See, e.g., E. Levinas, *Otherwise Than Being, or Beyond Essence*, trans. A. Lingis (Pittsburgh: Duquesne University Press, 1998), 84. I note in passing that the term "obsession" is originally religious and not psychological, and that good theology would surely side with Levinas's stated intention (83) to conceptualize a relation with otherness that refuses recuperation into any dialectic.

6. Ibid., 61.

7. The argument is made most forcefully, and perhaps at the intended pinnacle of phenomenology, against Merleau-Ponty. See E. Levinas, "Meaning and Sense," in *Basic Philosophical Writings*, ed. A. Peperzak et al. (Bloomington: Indiana University Press, 1996), especially 48f.

8. In *Totality and Infinity* (72–101), justice is proposed as a name for the sociality that would not be reducible to either politics or ontology. There is justice where and insofar as one recognizes that the Other is one's master, and at the same time that there are other Others likewise calling for help. *Otherwise Than Being or Beyond Essence* is admirably succinct, but also more radical: justice is moved in "forgetting oneself" (202).

9. Ibid., 113.

10. Ibid., 59.

11. Simone de Beauvoir offers this shortsighted but influential characterization in her introduction to *The Second Sex* (New York: Vintage, 1989), xxii n. 3.

12. These terms must not be introduced without bearing in mind that Levinas resists every philosophical anthropology that would be settled on essence or identity. *Totality and Infinity*, and indeed all of Levinas's work, belongs to the inheritance of a late modern revolt against humanism—but without ever its sense of

the importance of ethics, even as other posthumanists left it aside for many decades.

13. What may pass as concise development can be found in J. Lacan, "Le symbolique, l'imaginaire, et le reel," *Bulletin de l'Association freudienne* 1 (1982): 4–13.

14. Neither Close nor Strange: Levinas, Hospitality, and Genocide
William H. Smith

1. Emanuel Levinas, *Totality and Infinity*, trans. Alphonso Lingis (Pittsburgh: Duquesne University Press, 1969), 39; hereafter cited as TI.
2. Ibid.
3. Ibid., 43.
4. Ibid., 215.
5. Ibid., 198.
6. Ibid., 199.
7. Ibid., 198.
8. Ibid.
9. Ibid., 51.
10. Ibid., 198–199.
11. Levinas anticipates this distinction between the neighbor as close (one who is proximal) and the stranger as guest (one who is disengaged). Levinas writes, for instance: "A relation with the Transcendent free from all captivation by the Transcendent is a social relation. It is here that the Transcendent, infinitely other, solicits us and appeals to us. The proximity of the Other, the proximity of the neighbor, is in being an ineluctable moment of the revelation of an absolute presence (that is, disengaged from every relation), which expresses itself. His very epiphany consists in soliciting us by his destitution in the face of the Stranger, the widow, and the orphan." TI 78.
12. For this characterization of the face, see E. Levinas and R. Kearney, "Dialogue with Emmanuel Levinas," *Face to Face with Levinas*, ed. R. Cohen (Albany: SUNY Press, 1986), esp. 29–30.
13. TI, 75.
14. Ibid., 51.
15. Ibid., 39.
16. Ibid., 201.
17. Ibid.
18. Ibid., 199.
19. Ibid., 75.
20. Ibid., 76.
21. The phrasing here comes from Levinas himself; see ibid.
22. Ibid., 251.
23. See ibid., 80, 297, 49–52, 210–212.
24. Ibid., 78.
25. Ibid., 79.

26. Ibid., 245.
27. Ibid., 244.
28. Ibid., 178.
29. Ibid., 27.
30. Ibid., 299.
31. Ibid., 156.
32. Ibid., 172.
33. Ibid., 173.
34. Ibid., 305.
35. Ibid., 76.
36. Ibid., 77.
37. Ibid., 172–173.
38. Ibid., 77.
39. Susan Sontag, preface to Jean Hatzfeld, *Machete Season: The Killers in Rwanda Speak* (New York: Picador, 2005), vii.
40. Hatzfeld, *Machete Season*, 20.
41. Ibid., 91–92.
42. Ibid., 235.
43. Ibid., 27.
44. TI, 21.
45. Ibid., 22.
46. Ibid., 21.
47. It is at this point that we might wish to supplement Levinas's phenomenology of the stranger with another phenomenological account of intersubjectivity. Although I am not in a position to defend the claim here, it may be that a full phenomenological account of genocide will require a social ontology such as that of Merleau-Ponty, Schutz, or more controversially, Heidegger. In the case of Heidegger, we might refer especially to his notions of *das Man* and fallenness, which seems useful in explicating the testimonials above and those that follow. However, given the complexity of reading Levinas and Heidegger together—which is controversial for both philosophical and biographical reasons—such a move must be attempted elsewhere.
48. Hatzfeld, *Machete Season*, 47.
49. Ibid., 24.
50. Ibid., 71.
51. Ibid., 48–49.
52. TI, 66.
53. Hatzfeld, *Machete Season*, 21–22.
54. Ibid., 47.
55. I have in mind here the crisis in the Darfur region of Sudan. One can find this claim made not only by human rights groups like Human Rights Watch or Amnesty International, but also by former President Bush: "President's Statement on Violence in Darfur, Sudan," Office of the Press Secretary, September 9,

2004. In 2007, conservative statistics estimated that 200,000 were dead, 2.5 million forced from their homes due to violence. More recent numbers suggest that as many as 300,000 were killed in the violence from 2003 to 2005.

56. TI, 51.

57. Ibid., 306.

15. Between Mourning and Magnetism: Derrida and Waldenfels on the Art of Hospitality
Christopher Yates

1. Plutarch, *Plutarch's Lives*, ed. A. H. Clough (New York: A. L. Burt, 1932), 1:157.

2. Victor Hugo, *Les Misérables*, trans. Lee Fahnestock and Norman MacAfee (New York: New American Library, 1987), 176.

3. Richard Kearney, *Strangers, Gods and Monsters* (New York: Routledge, 2003), 3. For an insightful and creative treatment of the question of interreligious hospitality, see also Richard Kearney, *Anatheism: Returning to God After God* (New York: Columbia University Press), 2010.

4. Homer, *The Odyssey*, trans. Robert Fagles (New York: Penguin Books, 1997); see 220, 310, 313.

5. Bishop Bienvenu's hospitality also bears witness to the New Testament conception of refuge. Saint Paul, for examples, writes to the Ephesians: "So then you are no longer strangers and sojourners, but you are fellow citizens with the saints and members of the household of God, built upon the foundation of the apostles and prophets, Christ Jesus himself being the chief cornerstone, in whom the whole structure is joined together and grows into a holy temple in the Lord; in whom you also are built into it for a dwelling place for God in the Spirit" (Ephesians 2:18–22). Later in the novel, when Valjean and his adopted daughter, Cosette, hide in a convent garden, Hugo sharpens the thematic discord between the religious refuge and the positive law. He says of Valjean: "And then he reflected that two houses of God had received him in succession at the two critical moments of his life, the first when every door was closed and human society rejected him; the second, when human society was once more howling on his track, and prison once more gaped for him; and that, had it not been for the first, he would have fallen back into crime, and had it not been for the second, into punishment" (573).

6. Jacques Derrida, *Of Hospitality*, trans. Rachel Bowlby (Stanford: Stanford University Press, 2000), 155. Several further narratives of hosts and guests are telling. Homer's *Odyssey*, for example, traces the adventures of Odysseus, whom fate has rendered a wandering stranger and guest of many, to return from Troy and reclaim his home in Ithaca from unwelcome squatters. In *1 Kings*, Adonijah and Joab seek refuge in Solomon's Israel by laying hold of the horns of the altar. In the fourth century, Constantine sanctions church sanctuaries as sites of asylum and renders himself a guest to the theological council at Nicea. Fyodor Dostoevsky's *The Brothers Karamazov* (1881) provides the image of one Father Zossima,

who, upon welcoming a visitor to his hermitage, says, "I beg you not to disturb yourself. I particularly beg you to be my guest." Fyodor Dostoyevsky, *The Brothers Karamazov*, trans. Constance Garnett., ed. Manuel Komroff (New York: Penguin, 1980), 52. In Albert Camus's *The Fall* (1957), protagonist Jean Baptiste Clamence selects as his sanctuary an Amsterdam bar and confesses his life to an unnamed stranger. See Albert Camus, *The Fall*, trans. Justin O'Brien (New York: Vintage International, 1984). In his film *The Virgin Spring* (1960), Ingmar Bergman depicts the colossal tragedy of a Christian father who, having welcomed two goatherds as guests in his home, soon discovers that they have raped and killed his daughter.

7. See Emmanuel Levinas, *Totality and Infinity: An Essay on Exteriority*, trans. Alphonso Lingis (Pittsburgh: Duquesne University Press, 1969) and Jean-Paul Sartre, *Being and Nothingness: An Essay on Phenomenological Ontology*, trans. Hazel E. Barnes (New York: Philosophical Library, 1956).

8. Bernhard Waldenfels, "Strangeness, Hospitality, and Enmity," trans. Mark Gedney, in *Philosophy and the Return of Violence: Studies from This Widening Gyre* (London: Continuum, 2011), ed. Nathan Eckstrand and Christopher Yates.

9. Paul Valéry, *Cahiers* (Paris: Gallimard, 1973–74), 2:499. The Hölderlin reference appears at *Question of the Other* 25 and is from the unfinished poem, "Conciliator, You That No Longer Believed In . . ." The Valéry quote appears at 50.

10. Waldenfels, "Strangeness, Hospitality, and Enmity." And yet, as is often noted, the root of the term already tells us as much; the Latinate forms, *hospes* and *hospitis*, after all, can denote host, guest, or stranger, and *hostis* can suggest stranger as friend or foe. Indeed, the linguistic and etymological background to the thematic terrain of hospitality is one of the principal ways in which scholars of the matter endeavor to show how its existential or phenomenological occurrence is already freighted with a provocative hermeneutic weight. Hospitality is a drama between host and guest that may be parsed according to the roles of stranger, friend, foreigner, Other, citizen, alien, enemy, and self. Derrida, for example, opens his discussion by excavating the meaning of the "foreigner" (*Xenos*) in Plato's *Sophist*, then follows the usage of the term by Socrates in the *Apology*, and finally compares it with the more narrow French usage of *étranger* (Derrida, *Of Hospitality*, 7, 15–19, 43–49). Waldenfels demonstrates the status of the "alien" as a "peculiar phenomenon" by unpacking the depth of meaning beneath the German *fremd*, the self-referential *ichfremd* ("alien to me"), and the uneasy dichotomy between Latinate *idem* ("Same") and *aliud* ("Other") (*The Question of the Other* [Hong Kong: The Chinese University Press, 2007], 5–6, 24, 7). Other approaches are also telling: Julia Kristeva delineates the historical origins of the legal status of the "foreigner" in terms of *jus soli* and *jus sanguinis* (law of soil, blood), and navigates the strangeness of/in the self by following Freud's interest in the "uncanny" disclosure of unconscious dynamics—the play of the German *unheimlich* on the adjective *Heimlich* (Julia Kristeva, *Strangers to*

Ourselves [New York: Columbia University Press, 1991], 95, 182–183). In Paul Ricoeur's specific treatment of "translation as a wager," he premises a call for "*linguistic hospitality*" on the difficult yet fortunate experience of an *épreuve* ("test") that has "the double sense of 'ordeal' [*peine endurée*] and 'probation'." Paul Ricoeur, *On Translation*, trans. Eileen Brennan, (London and New York: Routledge, 2006), 10, 3.

11. Waldenfels, *The Question of the Other*. Waldenfels says of Husserl, Henri Bergson, and William James, for example, "they all understood [the transition between nineteenth and twentieth century thought] as a search for a non-empiricist philosophy of experience. Such a philosophy implies a strong concept of experience i.e. a sort of experience which does not supply us with pure data but which organizes, structures and forms itself without being governed by fixed laws" (38).

12. By "constitution" I mean, as Dan Zahavi interprets it, the "process that permits that which is constituted to appear, unfold, articulate, and show itself as what it is." Dan Zahavi, *Husserl's Phenomenology* (Stanford: Stanford University Press, 2003), 72. Waldenfels explains the pertinence and meaning of "intentionality" as follows: "What does it mean to claim that something is intended? To put it in simple terms, it means that something is given, apprehended, understood or interpreted *as something*, i.e., endowed with a certain sense. In this respect, together with hermeneutics and analytical philosophy, phenomenology belongs to a larger family which may be termed the philosophy of sense. Traditional distinctions such as outer vs. inner world, physical vs. mental entities, real conditions vs. ideal rules are overcome by this tiny word, *as, als, comme* . . . which functions as a sort of joint, connecting the disconnected." Waldenfels, *Question of the Other*, 72.

13. Ibid., 3. Waldenfels describes the manifestation of this same habit in the "normalcy" undergirding our current state of affairs: "Hospitality has to be considered as a *para-institution*. It never stands on its own foundation but is grafted, rather onto normal places: a family's house, an ethnic community, the public places of a city, or the open territory of a country." "Strangeness, Hospitality, and Enmity," 94.

14. Waldenfels, *Question of the Other*, 3; Waldenfels, "Strangeness, Hospitality, and Enmity," 94.

15. Waldenfels, *Question of the Other*, 23, 51, 81.

16. Ibid., 14.

17. Waldenfels, "Strangeness, Hospitality, and Enmity," 89–90.

18. Waldenfels, *Question of the Other*, 4.

19. Derrida, *Of Hospitality*, 3.

20. Plato, "Apology," in *Five Dialogues*, trans. G. M. A. Grube (Indianapolis: Hackett, 2002), 23.

21. Space does not permit a full treatment of the theme of *language* in hospitality, though Waldenfels and Derrida have much to offer on the topic. Suffice it to say that the Athenian assembly's presumed attitude toward Socrates's speech

fits well with what Plutarch (writing on the life of *Lycurgus*) says of the banishment of strangers from Lacedaemon if they failed to uphold the state: "With strange people, strange words must be admitted; these novelties produce novelties in thought; and on these follow views and feelings whose discordant character destroys the harmony of the state" (111). Compare Hugo's fascinating discussion of the argot of Paris (980–993); of this "language of combat" (982), he observes, for example: "When we listen, on the side of honest people, at the door of society, we overhear the dialogue of those who are *outside*" (984, my emphasis).

22. Derrida, *Of Hospitality*, 15.
23. Ibid., 15.
24. Ibid., 25–29.
25. Ibid., 25.
26. Waldenfels, *Question of the Other*, 13.
27. Ibid., 14, 17–18.
28. Ibid., 81, 22.
29. Ibid., 38.
30. Ibid.
31. Waldenfels, "Strangeness, Hospitality, and Enmity," 95.
32. Waldenfels, *Question of the Other*, 39, 40, 42.
33. Ibid., 51.
34. Derrida, *Of Hospitality*, 35.
35. Ibid., 43, 51.
36. Ibid., 77.
37. Waldenfels, *Question of the Other*, 74.
38. Ibid, 35. Elsewhere Waldenfels speaks of our "fractured mode of belonging": "The guest dwells as the stranger on the threshold, neither truly inside nor truly outside." "Strangeness, Hospitality, and Enmity," 94.
39. Kristeva describes the psychological bearing of such a moment: "Strange indeed is the encounter with the other—whom we perceive by means of sight, hearing, smell, but do not 'frame' within our consciousness. The other leaves us separate, incoherent; even more so, he can make us feel that we are not in touch with our own feelings, that we reject them or, on the contrary, that we refuse to judge them—we feel 'stupid,' we have 'been had' . . . Confronting the foreigner whom I reject and with whom at the same time I identify, I lose my boundaries, I no longer have a container, the memory of experiences which I had been abandoned overwhelm me, I lose my composure." *Strangers to Ourselves*, 187.
40. Derrida, *Of Hospitality*, 135.
41. Waldenfels, *Question of the Other*, 44.
42. Ibid., 74.
43. Ibid.
44. Ibid., 82.
45. Homer, *Odyssey*, 175.
46. Waldenfels, *Question of the Other*, 75.
47. Ibid., 83.

48. Ibid., 85.

49. Maurice Merleau-Ponty, *The Visible and the Invisible*, trans. Alphonso Lingis (Evanston, Ill.: Northwestern University Press, 1968), 254; cited in Waldenfels, *Question of the Other*, 9.

50. Derrida, *Of Hospitality*, 77.

51. See Kristeva, *Strangers to Ourselves*, 96–97.

52. See Derrida, *Of Hospitality*, 53–54, 73.

53. Homer, *Odyssey*, 303.

54. Waldenfels, "Strangeness, Hospitality, and Enmity," 91.

55. Waldenfels, *Question of the Other*, 6.

56. Ibid., 8–9.

57. Ibid., 34, 49.

58. Ibid., 42.

59. Waldenfels, "Strangeness, Hospitality, and Enmity," 90.

60. Ibid. The magnetism can be clarified by considering two passages from two different texts in which Waldenfels describes it. First, there is the spectral way in which the threshold is a mediating sense: "The between can be understood as mediating, as Logos—the law or right that regulates the exchange between substantial beings without itself arising from this exchange." Second, there is the impossible way in which the threshold hosts a traversal of self and other without reconciling them: "The between which connects us with each other and simultaneously separates us from each other can be radically conceived only in terms of a *self-doubling in the other*, i.e., as a lived impossibility, impossible measure on the possibilities which are available for me, for you and for us altogether. I *am* where you cannot be, and you *are* where I cannot be" (*Question of the Other*, 49).

61. Waldenfels, *Question of the Other*, 50. Kristeva makes a point similar to Waldenfels's notion of "doubling": "By recognizing *our* uncanny strangeness we shall neither suffer from it nor enjoy it from the outside. The foreigner is within me, hence we are all foreigners." But where Waldenfels's focus concerns the horizon of "sense" generation, Kristeva presses the matter of doubling toward a political ethics that "would involve a cosmopolitanism of a new sort that, cutting across governments, economies, and markets, might work for a mankind whose solidarity is founded on the consciousness of the unconscious—desiring, destructive, fearful, empty, impossible" (*Strangers to Ourselves*, 192). Such a vision is an ambitious application of the complexity now disclosed in ipseity, but one wonders whether a cosmopolitanism anchored in unconscious points of intersubjective reference is a plausible translation of the "between."

62. See Waldenfels, *Question of the Other*, 34, 65.

63. David Brainerd, *The Life and Diary of David Brainerd*, ed. Jonathan Edwards and Philip E. Howard Jr. (Chicago: Moody Press, 1949), 236–237.

64. Ibid., 237–238.

65. Brainerd's situation is a close embodiment of the interreligious empathy Simone Weil describes when noting how "the study of different religions does not lead to a real knowledge of them unless we transport ourselves for a time by

faith to the very center of whichever one we are studying." And yet, in Brainerd's case, such empathy and such faith came as an unexpected event. See S. Weil, *Waiting for God*, trans. Emma Craufurd (New York: Perennial-HarperCollins, 2001), 118–119.

66. Waldenfels, *Question of the Other*, 22.
67. Ibid., 72.
68. The first quotation is from *Totality and Infinity*, 299. The second is from *Autrement qu'être ou au-delà de l'essence* (The Hague: Martinus Nijoff, 1974), 142. Derrida cites both phrases in *On Hospitality*, 109.
69. Ibid., 111.
70. Ibid., 117.
71. Ibid., 77.
72. See also Kearney's discussion of Derrida's treatment of desire, messianicity, and absolute hospitality in *Anatheism* (esp. 62–65).

16. The Stranger in the Polis: Hospitality in Greek Myth
John Panteleimon Manoussakis

1. Cited by Jacques Derrida, *Of Hospitality*, trans. Rachel Bowlby (Stanford: Stanford University Press, 2000), 135.

2. The story of the anonymous stranger who arrives at the gates of the city only to be confronted with the enigmas of the queen or princess; the story of his desire for that woman even at the risk of death; and, finally, his triumph over her enigmas has been told in different variations throughout human history. Here I would only like to call the reader's attention to the rendering of that story by Puccini in his last opera, *Turandot*. Calaf, the anonymous stranger who remains so to the end of the opera, arrives at the gates of Peking and subsequently falls in love with the city's princess, Turandot, who promises to offer herself as a wife to that stranger who would succeed in solving her three enigmas. The admission to the city and to one's own desire passes through the recognition of the lost father (*"Padre! Mio Padre!"*). That the object of the stranger's desire might not exist at all is said here explicitly (*"Turandot non esiste!"*). Different as they might be, not only in terms of their genre (although Greek tragedy is closer than any other artistic form to our opera, and I remind the reader that Sophocles's Sphinx *sings* her enigma very much like Puccini's heroine), the two stories converge at the question of the stranger's name and the *nomos, la legge* of hospitality. The figure of the stranger, the foreigner, is not only without a name but also unknowable (*"il nome dell'Ignoto"*).

3. "The guilty one is Thebes," writes Derrida. "It is Thebes which, without knowing it, unconscious Thebes, the city-unconscious, the unconscious at the heart of the town, the *polis*, the political unconscious . . . which bears responsibility for the crime." *Of Hospitality*, 39.

4. For the symbolic role of the Serpent in Genesis, see Paul Ricoeur, *The Symbolism of Evil*, trans. Emerson Buchanan (Boston: Beacon Press, 1967). As Ricoeur notes "we seek to exculpate ourselves and make ourselves appear innocent by accusing an Other," in this case the serpent, which would then "be a part

of ourselves which we do not recognize; he would be the seduction of ourselves by ourselves" (256).

5. "Suburban bliss has as its condition the terror that it shuts out." J. P. Lawrence, "Schelling's Metaphysics of Evil," in *The New Schelling*, ed. Judith Norman and Alistair Welchman (New York: Continuum, 2004), 170.

6. "This character," writes Jan Patocka in reference to Oedipus, "is even more negative, for within it, thought its fate is to be shown, what is the fundamental threat to humanity to be found within us." *Plato and Europe* (Stanford: Stanford University Press, 2002), 56.

7. The latter Oedipus is real (as opposed to the imaginary Oedipus of the first part of the drama) insofar as he can feel pain, both emotional and physical. Thus, he assumes depth as a character.

8. In his brief reading of the Oedipus story, Jan Patocka sees an element of hubris in Oedipus's failure to recognize that the clarity of knowledge does not belong to man. So he writes: "Clarity is the domain of the gods. Man has blindly wandered into it, and man blindly wanders within it. Blindly wander those who had human sympathy for Oedipus, and blindly wanders within it Oedipus himself. He blindly wanders not only in the moment he commits those horrible deeds, first of all the murder of his father and then the marriage with his mother, but also at the moment he apparently is completely victorious, when he frees Thebes from the kingdom of the Sphinx—and he frees it with the aid of knowledge, with the aid of enlightenment which he has, which the gods have inspired in him, which is not his." *Plato and Europe*, 56.

9. See Lawrence, "Schelling's Metaphysics of Evil," 169, and P. Florensky's "supralogical ground" of reason in *The Pillar and Ground of Truth* (Princeton: Princeton University Press, 1997), 48.

10. "Prometheus and Oedipus on the one hand, Job on the other, recognized the cosmic dimensions of brute chaos." Ricoeur, *The Symbolism of Evil*, 258. The Oedipus referred to here by Ricoeur is, of course, the blinded hero at the end of *Oedipus Rex*.

11. G. K. Chesterton, *The Flying Inn* (Minneola: Dover Publications, 2001), 192.

12. Derrida, *Of Hospitality*, 43.

13. See *Oxford Classical Dictionary*, 3rd ed. (1996), under the entry "friendship, ritualized"). As the author of the entry explains, "ritualized friends were, by virtue of their prescribed duties, veritable co-parents. A *xenos* or *hospes* was supposed to show a measure of protective concern for his partner's son, to help him in any emergency, and to save his life." Also of interest to our story is *xenia*'s "assumption of perpetuity. . . . The bond did not expire with the death of the parents themselves, but outlived them, passing on in the male line to their descendants." This last point is very important with regard to the relationship between Theseus and Oedipus who are such descendants of *xenia*.

14. Pindar tells the story in his *First Olympian Ode*.

15. A full account of the Theseus story is to be found in Plutarch's *Lives*.

Contributors

Jeffrey Bloechl, Associate Professor of Philosophy at Boston College, is the editor of the annual book series *Levinas Studies: An Annual Review*. He has published and lectured widely on themes and questions in contemporary European philosophy, philosophy of religion, and psychoanalysis. His current research is divided between book-length projects in phenomenological theology and the later Freud's interpretation of religion and ethics.

John D. Caputo is Thomas J. Watson Professor of Religion and Humanities and Professor of Philosophy at Syracuse University. His latest books are *Philosophy and Theology* (Abingdon, 2006); *The Weakness of God: A Theology of the Event* (Indiana, 2006), winner of the 2007 AAR Book Award, "Constructive-Reflective Studies"; *What Would Jesus Deconstruct?* (Baker, 2007); and *After the Death of God* (with Gianni Vattimo; ed. Jeffrey Robbins) (Columbia, 2007). He has recently co-edited with Linda Alcoff *St. Paul Among the Philosophers* (Indiana, 2009) and *Feminism, Sexuality, and the Return of Religion* (Indiana, 2011). He is editor of the Fordham University Press book series "Perspectives in Continental Philosophy" and Chairman of the Board of Editors of *Journal of Cultural and Religious Theory*.

Edward S. Casey is Distinguished Professor of Philosophy at SUNY, Stony Brook, and is the immediate past president of the American Philosophical Association, Eastern Division. Among his published books are

Imagining, Second Edition (Indiana, 2000); *Remembering, Second Edition* (Indiana, 2000); *Representing Place* (Minnesota, 2002); *Earth-Mapping* (Minnesota, 2005); *The Fate of Place* (California, 2006); *The World at a Glance* (Indiana, 2007); and *Getting Back into Place, Second Edition* (Indiana, 2009). He describes himself as an unrepentant peri-phenomenologist. His essay in this volume reflects a concern with edges that will find full expression in a forthcoming book, *The World on Edge.*

Simon Critchley is Chair of Philosophy at the New School for Social Research in New York and part-time Professor of Philosophy at the University of Tilburg in the Netherlands. He is the author and editor of many books, including *Infinitely Demanding: Ethics of Commitment, Politics of Resistance* (Verso, 2007); *On Heidegger's Being and Time* (Routledge, 2008); and *The Book of Dead Philosophers* (Vintage, 2009). *The Faith of the Faithless* is forthcoming.

Jean Greisch, the former Dean of the Faculty of Philosophy of the Institut Catholique in Paris and a member of the Institut International de Philosophie, is currently teaching as the Romano Guardini Chair at the Humboldt-Universität zu Berlin in Germany. His numerous publications include *Entendre d'une autre oreille. Les enjeux philosophiques de l'herméneutique biblique* (Ed. Bayard, 2006), *Qui sommes-nous? Chemins phénoménologiques vers l'homme* (Peeters, 2009), and *Fehlbarkeit und Fähigkeit. Paul Ricoeurs philosophische Anthropologie* (LIT, 2009).

Richard Kearney holds the Charles B. Seelig Chair in Philosophy at Boston College and is visiting professor at University College Dublin. He is the author of two novels and a volume of poetry. His recent publications include *The God Who May Be* (Indiana, 2001); *Strangers, Gods, and Monsters* (Routledge, 2002); *Navigations: Collected Irish Essays, 1976–2006* (Syracuse, 2006); and *Anatheism: Returning to God after God* (Columbia, 2009).

Karmen MacKendrick is Joseph C. Georg Professor in the Philosophy Department at Le Moyne College. Her most recent books include *Fragmentation and Memory* (Fordham, 2008) and (as co-author) *Seducing Augustine: Bodies, Desires, Confessions* (Fordham, 2010).

John Panteleimon Manoussakis is Edward Bennett Williams Fellow Assistant Professor at the College of the Holy Cross. He is the author of

Theos Philosophoumenos (Ellinika Grammata, 2004) and *God After Metaphysics: A Theological Aesthetic* (Indiana, 2007). He has published several articles and edited a number of volumes on a variety of topics from Heidegger and phenomenology to Dionysius and medieval philosophy.

Kelly Oliver, W. Alton Jones Professor of Philosophy at Vanderbilt University, is the author of more than fifty articles and fifteen books. Her most recent books include *The Colonization of Psychic Space: A Psychoanalytic Social Theory of Oppression* (Minnesota, 2004); *Women as Weapons of War: Iraq, Sex, and the Media* (Columbia, 2007); and *Animal Lessons: How They Teach Us to Be Human* (Columbia, 2009).

William J. Richardson, is the author of *Heidegger: Through Phenomenology to Thought* (Preface by Martin Heidegger), Fourth Edition (Fordham, 2003) and co-author (with John P. Muller) of *Lacan and Language: A Reader's Guide to the Ecrits* (International Universities Press, 1994) and *The Purloined Poe: Lacan, Derrida, and Psychoanalytic Reading* (Johns Hopkins, 1988). A graduate of the William Alanson White Institute (1974), he has written widely in the fields of philosophy and psychoanalysis and at present is preparing a study on the ethics of psychoanalysis. He is Professor of Philosophy Emeritus at Boston College and maintains a private practice of psychoanalysis in Newton, Massachusetts.

Vanessa Rumble is Associate Professor of Philosophy at Boston College and has served as president of the Søren Kierkegaard Society. She works on German Romanticism and psychoanalysis and participates in the translation and editing of the new English-language critical edition of *Søren Kierkegaard's Journals and Notebooks*.

Kascha Semonovitch is a lecturer in Philosophy at Seattle University and the co-editor of *Merleau-Ponty at the Limits of Art, Perception, and Religion* (Continuum, 2010). Her philosophy essays and poems have appeared in numerous journals, most recently *Literary Imagination* and *The Southern Review*.

Kalpana Rahita Seshadri is Associate Professor of English at Boston College. Her primary research is in the area of race theory. She is the author of *HumAnimal: Between Law and Language* (forthcoming) and *Desiring Whiteness: A Lacanian Analysis of Race* (Routledge, 2000) and co-editor of *The Pre-Occupation of Post-Colonial Studies* (Duke, 2000).

William H. Smith is a Core Lecturer in the Department of Philosophy at Seattle University. He publishes in the areas of phenomenology, existentialism, and moral theory and is the author of *The Phenomenology of Moral Normativity* (Routledge, 2011).

Anthony J. Steinbock is Professor of Philosophy and directs the Phenomenology Research Center at Southern Illinois University, Carbondale. His most recent books include *Home and Beyond: Generative Phenomenology after Husserl* (Northwestern, 1995) and *Phenomenology and Mysticism: The Verticality of Religious Experience* (Indiana, 2007).

Brian Treanor is Associate Professor of Philosophy and Director of Environmental Studies at Loyola Marymount University in Los Angeles. He is the author of *Aspects of Alterity: Levinas, Marcel, and the Contemporary Debate* (Fordham, 2006) and co-editor of *A Passion for the Possible: Thinking with Paul Ricoeur* (Fordham, 2010). His current work takes place at the intersection of hermeneutics, virtue ethics, and environmental ethics. He also teaches and publishes in the areas of continental philosophy and theology.

David Wood is W. Alton Jones Professor of Philosophy at Vanderbilt University. His books include *Philosophy at the Limit* (Unwin Hyman, 1990); *The Deconstruction of Time* (Northwestern, 2001); *Thinking after Heidegger* (Blackwell/Polity, 2002); *The Step Back: Ethics and Politics After Deconstruction* (SUNY, 2005); *Time after Time* (Indiana, 2007); and the forthcoming (with Richard Kearney) *Things at the End of the World*. He teaches continental and environmental philosophy, and he is an earth artist.

Christopher Yates received an M.A. in Philosophy from the University of Memphis and a Ph.D. in Philosophy from Boston College. His areas of study include phenomenology, aesthetics, and ethics. His articles have appeared in publications such as *Philosophy and Social Criticism*, *Foucault Studies*, and *Religion and the Arts*.

Index of Names

Alighieri, Dante, 33, 130–31, 308*n*18
Andréas-Salomé, Lou, 191, 315*n*26
Aquinas, Thomas, 101
Arendt, Hannah, 16, 64, 291*n*71, 293*n*96
Aristotle, 18, 29, 292*n*85, 295*n*3, 297*n*46
Augustine, Saint, of Hippo, 33, 46, 85, 96–101, 104, 223, 301*n*4, 301*n*5, 301*n*7

Bachelard, Gaston, 6, 295*n*1
Bal Shem Tov, 118
Baqlī, Rūzbihān, 33, 112, 114–20, 305*n*23
Barthes, Roland, 170, 312*n*9
Bataille, Georges, 67, 101, 299*n*6
Beckett, Samuel, 23, 151, 153–54, 311*n*22
Benveniste, Emile, 128, 293*n*90
Betcher, Sharon, 96, 301*n*12
Boccaccio, Giovanni, 130
Bonhoeffer, Dietrich, 95
Brainerd, David, 36, 270–72, 330*n*63
Bruni, Leonardo, 130

Camus, Albert, 23, 275, 327*n*6
Celan, Paul, 35, 229–31, 322*n*57, 323*n*65
Chesterton, G. K., 282, 332*n*11

Chrétien, Jean-Louis, 32–33, 101–4, 107, 291*n*74, 303*nn*20–22, 303*n*25, 303*n*38, 304*n*28
Cixous, Hélène, 87, 93

Dante: *see* Alighieri
De Beauvoir, Simone, 10, 19, 206, 239, 288*n*35, 323*n*11
Deleuze, Gilles, 88, 89, 294*n*3, 321*n*17
Derrida, Jacques, 6, 7, 11–14, 17–19, 31–33, 35–36, 43–46, 49–50, 57–63, 71–72, 77, 84–87, 93, 95, 126–29, 131–40, 154, 169, 221, 240, 258–74, 282–83, 286*n*7, 287*nn*32–33, 288–89, 292–93, 294*n*3, 296–98, 300*n*2, 301*n*11, 302*n*15, 307–10, 318*n*73, 320*n*1, 326, 328–32
Dov Baer, Rabbi, 33, 112–15, 117, 119, 305*n*13, 306*n*20

Eckhart, Meister, 33, 87–92, 301*n*6
Edwards, Jonathan, 270, 330*n*63

Freud, Sigmund, 4, 21, 34, 122–23, 138, 147, 168–98, 203–8, 223–24, 285*n*1,

337

290n62, 293n93, 307n24, 307n27,
  312–19, 321n27, 327n10

Gadamer, Hans Georg, 68, 74, 261,
  298n1, 299n16
Goethe, Johann Wolfgang, 173

Hegel, G. W. F., 6–7, 11, 67, 150, 173,
  198
Heidegger, Martin, 4, 6, 7, 10, 15, 17–21,
  27, 32, 34–35, 68, 70–72, 76–77, 85,
  91, 93, 128, 137–40, 145–67, 169,
  216, 219–30, 234, 242, 248, 261, 285,
  286n6, 287n29, 287n34, 289n61,
  290n62, 292n81, 294n4, 298nn1–2,
  299n12, 299n17, 300n20, 300n25,
  307n1, 309n35, 310–11, 321–22,
  325n47
Herder, Gottfried, 173
Hölderlin, Friedrich, 19, 35, 160, 166,
  225–31, 260, 289n61, 311n9, 322n49
Hollywood, Amy, 88, 301n8, 305n2
Hugo, Victor, 24, 258, 263, 326n2,
  326n5, 329n21
Husserl, Edmund, 7–17, 45–46, 198, 200,
  222, 235–36, 242, 261, 265, 286–90,
  292n89, 294n106, 321n24, 328n11

Jung, Carl, 174, 176

Kant, Immanuel, 11, 44, 47–48, 58, 150,
  193, 256, 292n83, 296n31, 297n34,
  308n4, 314n26, 318n82
Keller, Catherine, 96, 301n13
Klein, Melanie, 74, 300n21
Kristeva, Julia, 4, 7, 14, 21, 34–35,
  168–95, 197–98, 203–11, 223, 268,
  285n1, 286n4, 292n78, 293, 312–13,
  317, 318n77–78, 319–20, 327n10,
  329n39, 330n51, 330n61

Lacan, Jacques, 146, 148, 174–75, 177,
  180, 193, 240, 285n1, 311n9, 313n11,
  318n73, 324n13
Lawrence, D. H., 33, 67, 70, 133–36
Lévi-Strauss, Claude, 217–18, 318n73,
  320n2, 320n5
Leopold, Aldo, 70, 299n8, 299n10

Levinas, Emmanuel, 6, 7, 9–14, 17, 19,
  28, 35–36, 46, 67, 71–73, 76–78, 91,
  103, 126, 138, 169, 196–202, 208–10,
  219–30, 232–57
Löwith, Karl, 223

Mackey, Louis, 33, 99, 302n8
Marcel, Gabriel, 62, 295n1, 297n47
Marion, Jean-Luc, 91, 291n74
Martineau, Emmanuel, 225
Marx, Karl, 290n62

Nancy, Jean-Luc, 32–33, 46, 98–99, 104,
  107, 294n7, 301n1, 302n10, 304
Nietzsche, Friedrich, 67, 6, 100, 104,
  148–52, 169, 218, 290n62,
  302nn12–13, 304n32, 312n8, 314n26,
  316n55, 320n12

Pascal, Blaise, 229, 296n21
Pindar, 226, 332n14
Plato, 5, 7, 67, 71, 76, 164, 263, 286n7,
  310n3, 327n10, 328n20
Plutarch, 258, 326n1, 329n21, 332n15
Proust, Marcel, 23–25, 29, 65
Putnam, Robert, 56, 296n26, 296n28

Ricoeur, Paul, 7–8, 13–21, 28, 64–65,
  200, 286–87, 289, 291n74, 292–94,
  298n55, 298n57, 322n48, 328n10,
  331n4, 332n10
Rilke, Rainer Maria, 67, 71, 102–3,
  303n23, 304
Roethke, Theodore, 70, 299n9

Sartre, Jean-Paul, 10–11, 19, 23, 42, 67,
  70, 72, 200, 235, 260, 290n62, 327n7
Scheler, Max, 32, 111, 290n62, 290n66,
  291n74, 305nn3–4
Schelling, Friedrich, 19, 290n62, 332n5
Schopenhauer, Arthur, 175, 314n26
Schreber, Daniel Paul, 122–23, 307n25
Schütz, Alfred, 223, 325n47
Serres, Michel, 91, 301n10
Sharrad, Lewis, 46
Socrates, 263, 286n7, 310n3, 327n10,
  328n21

Sophocles, 5, 19, 34, 36, 77, 160–67, 227, 263–66, 275–83, 311*n*10, 312*nn*20–21, 331*n*2
Stein, Edith, 286*n*23, 290*n*62, 291*n*74
Stendhal, 102, 303*n*21,

Taylor, Charles, 216
Teresa of Avila, 33, 112, 119, 122

Uexkull, Jacob von, 71, 299*n*11

Valéry, Paul, 260, 327*n*9
Villani, Filippo, 130, 308*n*19

Waldenfels, Bernard, 16, 18, 36, 258–73
Watkins, Mary, 294*n*1
Weil, Simone, 32, 330*n*65
Winnicott, Donald, 194, 300*n*21, 316*n*60
Wittgenstein, Ludwig, 74, 215

Zahavi, Dan, 286*nn*17–18, 328*n*12

Perspectives in Continental Philosophy

John D. Caputo, series editor

John D. Caputo, ed., *Deconstruction in a Nutshell: A Conversation with Jacques Derrida*.
Michael Strawser, *Both/And: Reading Kierkegaard—From Irony to Edification*.
Michael D. Barber, *Ethical Hermeneutics: Rationality in Enrique Dussel's Philosophy of Liberation*.
James H. Olthuis, ed., *Knowing Other-wise: Philosophy at the Threshold of Spirituality*.
James Swindal, *Reflection Revisited: Jürgen Habermas's Discursive Theory of Truth*.
Richard Kearney, *Poetics of Imagining: Modern and Postmodern*. Second edition.
Thomas W. Busch, *Circulating Being: From Embodiment to Incorporation—Essays on Late Existentialism*.
Edith Wyschogrod, *Emmanuel Levinas: The Problem of Ethical Metaphysics*. Second edition.
Francis J. Ambrosio, ed., *The Question of Christian Philosophy Today*.
Jeffrey Bloechl, ed., *The Face of the Other and the Trace of God: Essays on the Philosophy of Emmanuel Levinas*.
Ilse N. Bulhof and Laurens ten Kate, eds., *Flight of the Gods: Philosophical Perspectives on Negative Theology*.
Trish Glazebrook, *Heidegger's Philosophy of Science*.
Kevin Hart, *The Trespass of the Sign: Deconstruction, Theology, and Philosophy*.
Mark C. Taylor, *Journeys to Selfhood: Hegel and Kierkegaard*. Second edition.
Dominique Janicaud, Jean-François Courtine, Jean-Louis Chrétien, Michel Henry, Jean-Luc Marion, and Paul Ricœur, *Phenomenology and the "Theological Turn": The French Debate*.

Karl Jaspers, *The Question of German Guilt*. Introduction by Joseph W. Koterski, S.J.

Jean-Luc Marion, *The Idol and Distance: Five Studies*. Translated with an introduction by Thomas A. Carlson.

Jeffrey Dudiak, *The Intrigue of Ethics: A Reading of the Idea of Discourse in the Thought of Emmanuel Levinas*.

Robyn Horner, *Rethinking God as Gift: Marion, Derrida, and the Limits of Phenomenology*.

Mark Dooley, *The Politics of Exodus: Søren Keirkegaard's Ethics of Responsibility*.

Merold Westphal, *Overcoming Onto-Theology: Toward a Postmodern Christian Faith*.

Edith Wyschogrod, Jean-Joseph Goux, and Eric Boynton, eds., *The Enigma of Gift and Sacrifice*.

Stanislas Breton, *The Word and the Cross*. Translated with an introduction by Jacquelyn Porter.

Jean-Luc Marion, *Prolegomena to Charity*. Translated by Stephen E. Lewis.

Peter H. Spader, *Scheler's Ethical Personalism: Its Logic, Development, and Promise*.

Jean-Louis Chrétien, *The Unforgettable and the Unhoped For*. Translated by Jeffrey Bloechl.

Don Cupitt, *Is Nothing Sacred? The Non-Realist Philosophy of Religion: Selected Essays*.

Jean-Luc Marion, *In Excess: Studies of Saturated Phenomena*. Translated by Robyn Horner and Vincent Berraud.

Phillip Goodchild, *Rethinking Philosophy of Religion: Approaches from Continental Philosophy*.

William J. Richardson, S.J., *Heidegger: Through Phenomenology to Thought*.

Jeffrey Andrew Barash, *Martin Heidegger and the Problem of Historical Meaning*.

Jean-Louis Chrétien, *Hand to Hand: Listening to the Work of Art*. Translated by Stephen E. Lewis.

Jean-Louis Chrétien, *The Call and the Response*. Translated with an introduction by Anne Davenport.

D. C. Schindler, *Han Urs von Balthasar and the Dramatic Structure of Truth: A Philosophical Investigation*.

Julian Wolfreys, ed., *Thinking Difference: Critics in Conversation*.

Allen Scult, *Being Jewish/Reading Heidegger: An Ontological Encounter*.

Richard Kearney, *Debates in Continental Philosophy: Conversations with Contemporary Thinkers*.

Jennifer Anna Gosetti-Ferencei, *Heidegger, Hölderlin, and the Subject of Poetic Language: Towards a New Poetics of Dasein*.

Jolita Pons, *Stealing a Gift: Kirkegaard's Pseudonyms and the Bible*.

Jean-Yves Lacoste, *Experience and the Absolute: Disputed Questions on the Humanity of Man*. Translated by Mark Raftery-Skehan.

Charles P. Bigger, *Between* Chora *and the Good: Metaphor's Metaphysical Neighborhood*.

Dominique Janicaud, *Phenomenology "Wide Open": After the French Debate.* Translated by Charles N. Cabral.

Ian Leask and Eoin Cassidy, eds., *Givenness and God: Questions of Jean-Luc Marion.*

Jacques Derrida, *Sovereignties in Question: The Poetics of Paul Celan.* Edited by Thomas Dutoit and Outi Pasanen.

William Desmond, *Is There a Sabbath for Thought? Between Religion and Philosophy.*

Bruce Ellis Benson and Norman Wirzba, eds., *The Phenomoenology of Prayer.*

S. Clark Buckner and Matthew Statler, eds., *Styles of Piety: Practicing Philosophy after the Death of God.*

Kevin Hart and Barbara Wall, eds., *The Experience of God: A Postmodern Response.*

John Panteleimon Manoussakis, *After God: Richard Kearney and the Religious Turn in Continental Philosophy.*

John Martis, *Philippe Lacoue-Labarthe: Representation and the Loss of the Subject.*

Jean-Luc Nancy, *The Ground of the Image.*

Edith Wyschogrod, *Crossover Queries: Dwelling with Negatives, Embodying Philosophy's Others.*

Gerald Bruns, *On the Anarchy of Poetry and Philosophy: A Guide for the Unruly.*

Brian Treanor, *Aspects of Alterity: Levinas, Marcel, and the Contemporary Debate.*

Simon Morgan Wortham, *Counter-Institutions: Jacques Derrida and the Question of the University.*

Leonard Lawlor, *The Implications of Immanence: Toward a New Concept of Life.*

Clayton Crockett, *Interstices of the Sublime: Theology and Psychoanalytic Theory.*

Bettina Bergo, Joseph Cohen, and Raphael Zagury-Orly, eds., *Judeities: Questions for Jacques Derrida.* Translated by Bettina Bergo and Michael B. Smith.

Jean-Luc Marion, *On the Ego and on God: Further Cartesian Questions.* Translated by Christina M. Gschwandtner.

Jean-Luc Nancy, *Philosophical Chronicles.* Translated by Franson Manjali.

Jean-Luc Nancy, *Dis-Enclosure: The Deconstruction of Christianity.* Translated by Bettina Bergo, Gabriel Malenfant, and Michael B. Smith.

Andrea Hurst, *Derrida Vis-à-vis Lacan: Interweaving Deconstruction and Psychoanalysis.*

Jean-Luc Nancy, *Noli me tangere: On the Raising of the Body.* Translated by Sarah Clift, Pascale-Anne Brault, and Michael Naas.

Jacques Derrida, *The Animal That Therefore I Am.* Edited by Marie-Louise Mallet, translated by David Wills.

Jean-Luc Marion, *The Visible and the Revealed.* Translated by Christina M. Gschwandtner and others.

Michel Henry, *Material Phenomenology.* Translated by Scott Davidson.

Jean-Luc Nancy, *Corpus.* Translated by Richard A. Rand.

Joshua Kates, *Fielding Derrida.*

Michael Naas, *Derrida From Now On.*

Shannon Sullivan and Dennis J. Schmidt, eds., *Difficulties of Ethical Life.*

Catherine Malabou, *What Should We Do with Our Brain?* Translated by Sebastian Rand, Introduction by Marc Jeannerod.

Claude Romano, *Event and World*. Translated by Shane Mackinlay.

Vanessa Lemm, *Nietzsche's Animal Philosophy: Culture, Politics, and the Animality of the Human Being*.

B. Keith Putt, ed., *Gazing Through a Prism Darkly: Reflections on Merold Westphal's Hermeneutical Epistemology*.

Eric Boynton and Martin Kavka, eds., *Saintly Influence: Edith Wyschogrod and the Possibilities of Philosophy of Religion*.

Shane Mackinlay, *Interpreting Excess: Jean-Luc Marion, Saturated Phenomena, and Hermeneutics*.

Kevin Hart and Michael A. Signer, eds., *The Exorbitant: Emmanuel Levinas Between Jews and Christians*.

Bruce Ellis Benson and Norman Wirzba, eds., *Words of Life: New Theological Turns in French Phenomenology*.

William Robert, *Trials: Of Antigone and Jesus*.

Brian Treanor and Henry Isaac Venema, eds., *A Passion for the Possible: Thinking with Paul Ricoeur*.

Kas Saghafi, *Apparitions—Of Derrida's Other*.

Nick Mansfield, *The God Who Deconstructs Himself: Sovereignty and Subjectivity Between Freud, Bataille, and Derrida*.

Don Ihde, *Heidegger's Technologies: Postphenomenological Perspectives*.

Françoise Dastur, *Questioning Phenomenology*. Translated by Robert Vallier.

www.ingramcontent.com/pod-product-compliance
Lightning Source LLC
Chambersburg PA
CBHW031231290426
44109CB00012B/248